LF

Twentieth-Century Short Story Explication New Series

Volume I 1989–1990

With Checklists of Books and Journals Used

Warren S. Walker
Horn Professor Emeritus of English
Texas Tech University

The Shoe String Press, 1993

First published 1993 by The Shoe String Press, Inc.
Hamden, Connecticut 06514

The paper in this book meets the guidelines for
permanence and durability of the Committee on
Production Guidelines for Book Longevity of the
Council on Library Resources. ANSI Z39.48-1984 ∞
Library of Congress Cataloging-in-Publication Data

Walker, Warren S.
Twentieth-century short story explication : new series;
with checklists of books and journals used/
Warren S. Walker.
p. cm.
Includes bibliographical references and index.
Summary: Contains nearly 6000 entries that provide
a bibliography of interpretations for short stories
published between 1989 and 1990.
1. Short stories—Indexes. [1. Short stories—Indexes.]
I. Title
Z5917.S5W35 1993 [PN3373] 92-22790
016.8093'1—dc20 ISBN 0-208-02340-2 (v. 1)

Contents

Preface

The original series of *Twentieth-Century Short Story Explication* was concluded in 1992 with the publication of *An Index to the Third Edition and Its Five Supplements, 1961–1991*. The present work initiates a New Series which is a continuation, not a replacement, that will bring the entire series into the next century. Any entry in this volume preceded by a plus sign (+) is a reprinting of an earlier study which can be located in the original series by consulting the *Index*. All other entries are new and appear here for the first time.

More than 5,650 entries are included in this volume which carries the coverage of the *Third Edition* forward through December 31, 1990. Of the 815 short story authors cited, 343 are new, bringing to a total of 2,647 the number of authors represented in this entire reference work. Many of the newcomers are among the 133 Hispanic writers of short fiction. That most of these are New World Hispanics should come as no surprise, for the mid-century "boom" in Latin American literature continues to reverberate strongly. What may well be unexpected is the smaller but increased number of Chinese writers (73) whose stories have received critical attention in this volume.

Twentieth-Century Short Story Explication is a bibliography of interpretations that have appeared since 1900 of short stories published since 1800. The term *short story* here has the same meaning it carries in the Wilson Company's *Short Story Index:* "A brief narrative of not more than 150 average-sized pages." By *explication* I suggest simply interpretation or explanation of the meaning of the story, including observations on theme, symbol, and sometimes structure. This excludes from the bibliography what are essentially studies of source, biographical data, and background materials. Occasionally there are explicatory passages cited in works otherwise devoted to these external considerations. All page numbers refer strictly to interpretive passages, not to the longer works in which they occur.

Whatever the original language of the stories themselves, the explications here are limited to those published in the major languages of Western Europe. Although these parameters may seem unduly restrictive, the fact of the matter is that they encompass the vast majority of critical studies of the genre. The growing numbers of competent Indian writers, for example, are far more frequently discussed in English than they are in Hindi, Bengali, or Tamil. Similarly, despite the emphasis on indigenous languages among African states that were formerly colonies, their literary journals are usually printed in French or English.

The profusion of interpretations generated in the "knowledge explosion" of recent decades made it impossible to provide full publication data within each entry included. Consequently a system of coding was required, and we have developed an abbreviated format which has proven satisfactory to most users of *Twentieth-Century Short Story Explication*. Each book is cited by author or editor and a short title; the full title and publication details are provided in "A Checklist of Books Used"—and 536 were used in the compilation of this volume. For an article in a journal or an essay in a critical collection, the full publication information is provided in the text the first time the study is cited. In subsequent entries, only the critic's or scholar's name and a short title are used as long as these entries appear under the name of the same short story author; if an article or essay explicates stories of two or more authors, a complete initial entry is made for each author. As in previous volumes, we have again included "A Checklist of Journals Used"—and this time 321 were used. This latter checklist should be especially helpful to students who may not be familiar with titles of professional journals, much less the abbreviations for such titles.

Although most of the entries in this volume were published during 1989 and 1990, there are some exceptions to this generalization. (1) A few are earlier interpretations that were either unavailable or overlooked previously. (2) A few are new reprintings of earlier studies, and these are (as already mentioned) preceded by a plus sign (+).

In the preparation of this book I have been indebted to the editors and contributors of such journals as *PMLA*, *Modern Fiction Studies*, *Studies in Short Fiction*, and *Journal of Modern Literature*. I wish to extend thanks to the Interlibrary Loan Department of the Texas Tech University Library, especially to its Director, Amy Chang, and her very competent assistants Carol Roberts and Delia Arteaga. As usual, I am most grateful for the invaluable assistance and constant encouragement of my wife, Barbara K. Walker.

WARREN S. WALKER
TEXAS TECH UNIVERSITY

YAHYA TAHER ABDULLAH

"Granddad Hasan"
Harlow, Barbara. "*Mismar Goha*: The Arab Challenge to Cultural Dependency," *So Atlantic Q*, 87 (1988), 122.

"The Lofty One"
Harlow, Barbara. ". . . Cultural Dependency," 121.

"The Tattoo"
Harlow, Barbara. ". . . Cultural Dependency," 121.

ABE KŌBŌ

"The Caecum"
Matthew, Robert. *Japanese Science Fiction* . . . , 185–186.

"The Wall: The Crime of Mr. S. Karuma"
Matthew, Robert. *Japanese Science Fiction* . . . , 185.

FEDOR ABRAMOV

"The Final Stage"
Starikova, Elizaveta. "The Sociological Aspects of Contemporary 'Village Prose,' " *Soviet Stud Lit*, 26, i (1989–1990), 57–58.

"Mamonikha"
Shneidman, N. N. *Soviet Literature* . . . , 99–100.

SHOLEM YANKEV ABRAMOVITSH [pseudonym MENDELE MOCHER SFORIM]

"Shem and Japhet on the Train"
Alter, Robert, Ed. *Modern Hebrew Literature*, 15–18.
Roskies, David G. "Protest and Parody in Czarist Russia," in Roskies, David G., Ed. *The Literature of Destruction* . . . , 117.

JOSÉ V. ABREU

"Guasina"
Ramos, Elías A. *El cuento venezolano* . . . , 89–90.

"Seguridad Nacional"
Ramos, Elías A. *El cuento venezolano* . . . , 87–89.

CHINUA ACHEBE

"Akueke"
Innes, C. L. *Chinua Achebe*, 127–128.

"Chike's School Days"
Innes, C. L. *Chinua Achebe*, 121–123.

"Civil Peace"
Innes, C. L. *Chinua Achebe*, 126–127.

"Dead Man's Path"
Innes, C. L. *Chinua Achebe*, 11–12.

"Girls at War"
Innes, C. L. *Chinua Achebe*, 130–133.

"In a Village Church"
Innes, C. L. *Chinua Achebe*, 10.

"The Madman"
Innes, C. L. *Chinua Achebe*, 123–124.

"Marriage Is a Private Affair"
Innes, C. L. *Chinua Achebe*, 10–11.

"The Sacrificial Egg"
Innes, C. L. *Chinua Achebe*, 123–124.

"Uncle Ben's Choice"
Innes, C. L. *Chinua Achebe*, 124–125.

"Vengeful Creditor"
Innes, C. L. *Chinua Achebe*, 128–130.

"The Voter"
Innes, C. L. *Chinua Achebe*, 125.

ALICE ADAMS

"Beautiful Girl"
Upton, Lee. "Changing the Past: Alice Adams' Revisionary Nostalgia," *Stud Short Fiction*, 26 (1989), 34–35.

"Berkeley House"
Upton, Lee. "Changing the Past . . . ," 38–39.

"Home Is Where"
Upton, Lee. "Changing the Past . . . ," 35–36.

"Lost Luggage"
Waxman, Barbara F. *From the Hearth* . . . , 82–88.

"Molly's Dog"
Upton, Lee. "Changing the Past . . . ," 37–38.

"My First and Only House"
Upton, Lee. "Changing the Past . . . ," 39–40.

"Return Trip"
Upton, Lee. "Changing the Past . . . ," 36–37.

"To See You Again"
Waxman, Barbara F. *From the Hearth* . . . , 88–94.

"A Wonderful Woman"
Waxman, Barbara F. *From the Hearth* . . . , 76–82.

WARREN ADLER

"The Angel of Mercy"
Yahnke, Robert E., and Richard M. Eastman. *Aging in Literature* . . . , 30.

SHMUEL [SHAY] YOSEF AGNON [SHMUEL YOSEF CZACZKES]

"Agunot"
Aberbach, David. *Surviving Trauma* . . . , 32–34.
Alter, Robert, Ed. *Modern Hebrew Literature*, 179–182.

"Another Prayer Shawl" [same as "Another Talit"]
Holtz, Avraham. "The Allusive and Elusive Text of S. Y. Agnon, and the English Reader: On 'Talit Aheret,' " in Yudkin, Leon I., Ed. *Agnon: Text and Context* . . . , 267–274.

"At the Outset of the Day"
Alter, Robert, Ed. *Modern Hebrew Literature*, 215–217.

"The Candles"
Aberbach, David. "Agnon and Psychoanalysis: An Eclectic Gestalt Approach," in Yudkin, Leon I., Ed. *Agnon: Text and Context* . . . , 50–52.

"Edo and Enam"
Aberbach, David. "Agnon and Psychoanalysis . . . ," 37–39.

"The Fable of the Goat"
Aphek, Edna. "The Realization of Aspects of Redemption and Messianism as a Semiotic System in a Literary Text," *Linguistics & Lit*, 2 (1983–1984), 110–134.

"Forevermore"
Alter, Robert. "The Genius of S. Y. Agnon," *Commentary*, 32 (1961), 111; rpt. in his *After the Tradition* . . . , 145–146.
———, Ed. *Modern Hebrew Literature*, 227–230.
Sokoloff, Naomi. "Elements of Plot in Agnon's 'Ad Olam,' " in Yudkin, Leon I., Ed. *Agnon: Text and Context* . . . , 199–231.

"Friendship"
Aberbach, David. "Agnon and Psychoanalysis . . . ," 52–55.

"Hitherto"
Kurzweil, Baruch. "Religion in Agnon's Works," *Ariel I*, 17 (1966–1967), 14–16.

"The Kerchief"
Alter, Robert. "The Genius . . . ," 111–112; rpt. in his *After the Tradition* . . . , 146–147.

"Knots upon Knots"
Aberbach, David. "Agnon and Psychoanalysis . . . ," 55–56.

"The Lady and the Peddler"
Alter, Robert, Ed. *Modern Hebrew Literature*, 197–200.

"The Letter"
Kurzweil, Baruch. "Religion . . . ," 17–22.

"Metamorphosis"
Frieden, Ken. "Intertextual and Interlinguistic Approaches to Agnon's Writing," in Yudkin, Leon I., Ed. *Agnon: Text and Context* . . . , 71–72.

"Nights"
Alter, Robert. "The Genius . . . ," 112; rpt. in his *After the Tradition* . . . , 147.

"The Orchestra"
Alter, Robert. "The Genius . . . ," 111; rpt. in his *After the Tradition* . . . , 144.

"The Sign"
Roskies, David G. "Broken Tablets," in Roskies, David G., Ed. *The Literature of Destruction* . . . , 568–569.

"A Simple Tale"
Aberbach, David. "Agnon and Psychoanalysis . . . ," 45–46.
Yehoshua, A. B. "Plot and Denouement in *Sippur Pashut*," in Yudkin, Leon I., Ed. *Agnon: Text and Context* . . . , 142–161.

"Le Veit Abba"
Frieden, Ken. "Intertextual and Interlinguistic Approaches . . . ," 72–73.

"The Well of Miriam"
Aberbach, David. *Surviving Trauma* . . . , 35.

"A Whole Loaf"
Aberbach, David. "Agnon and Psychoanalysis . . . ," 52.

"Yedidut"
Coffin, Edna A. "Do Words Conceal or Reveal? Verbal Expressions, Thought Process, and Written Symbols in 'Yedidut,' " in Yudkin, Leon I., Ed. *Agnon: Text and Context* . . . , 235–266.

AI MING-CHIH

"The Wife"
Hsia, C. T. "Residual Femininity: Women in Chinese Communist Fiction," in Birch, Cyril, Ed. *Chinese Communist Literature*, 168.

AI WU [TANG DAOGENG]

"I Curse That Smile of Yours"
Lundberg, Lennart. "Ai Wu," in Slupski, Zbigniew, Ed. *A Selective Guide* . . . , II, 25–26.

"In the Mountain Gorge"
Anderson, Marston. *The Limits* . . . , 195–196.

"A Lesson in Life"
Anderson, Marston. *The Limits* . . . , 194–195.

"The New Home"
Hsia, C. T. "Residual Femininity: Women in Chinese Communist Fiction," in Birch, Cyril, Ed. *Chinese Communist Literature*, 167–168.

"On the Island"
Anderson, Marston. *The Limits* . . . , 196.

"Rain"
Hsia, C. T. "Residual Femininity . . . ," 167.

"Return at Night"
Hsia, C. T. "Residual Femininity . . . ," 165–167.

"Roaring Xujiatun"
Sorokin, V. F. "Ai Wu," in Slupski, Zbigniew, Ed. *A Selective Guide* . . . , II, 27–28.

ILSE AICHINGER

"Bound Man"
Olshan, Marc A. "Freedom vs. Meaning: Aichinger's 'Bound Man' and the Old Order Amish," in Enninger, Werner, Joachim Raith, and Karl-Heinz Wandt, Eds. *Internal and External Perspectives* . . . , 170–185.

"Eliza Eliza"
Pickar, Gertrud B. " 'Kalte Grotesken': Walser, Aichinger, and Dürrenmatt and the Kafka Legacy," in Haymes, Edward R., Ed. *Crossings-Kreuzungen* . . . , 123–124.

"Mein Vater aus Stroh"
Pickar, Gertrud B. " 'Kalte Grotesken' . . . ," 124.

"Das Plakat"
Pickar, Gertrud B. " 'Kalte Grotesken' . . . ," 123.

AMA ATA AIDOO

"Everything Counts"
Brown, Lloyd W. "Ama Ata Aidoo: The Art of the Short Story," in Priebe, Richard K., Ed. *Ghanaian Literatures*, 213–214.

"A Gift from Somewhere"
Brown, Lloyd W. "Ama Ata Aidoo . . . ," 208–210.

"In the Cutting of a Drink"
Brown, Lloyd W. "Ama Ata Aidoo . . . ," 205–208.

"No Sweetness Here"
Brown, Lloyd W. "Ama Ata Aidoo . . . ," 212–213.

"Something to Talk About on the Way to the Funeral"
Brown, Lloyd W. "Ama Ata Aidoo . . . ," 210–212.

CONRAD AIKEN

"Mr. Arcularis"
Carlile, Robert E. "A Musico-Literary Artisan," in Spivey, Ted R., and Arthur Waterman, Eds. *Conrad Aiken . . .*, 183–185.
Wheeler, James. "The Dreamworlds of Conrad Aiken," in Spivey, Ted R., and Arthur Waterman, Eds. *Conrad Aiken . . .*, 157–159.

"Silent Snow, Secret Snow"
Swan, Jesse G. "At the Edge of the Sound and Silence: Conrad Aiken's 'Senlin: A Biography' and 'Silent Snow, Secret Snow,' " *Southern Lit J*, 22, i (1989), 41–49.

AKUTAGAWA RYŪNOSUKE

"Kappa"
Matthew, Robert. *Japanese Science Fiction . . .*, 186–187.

LOUISA MAY ALCOTT

"My Brothers"
Diffley, Kathleen. "Where My Heart Is Turning Ever: Civil War Stories and National Stability from Fort Sumter to the Centennial," *Am Lit Hist*, 2 (1990), 649–653.

"Transcendental Wild Oats"
Pfaelzer, Jean. "The Sentimental Promise and the Utopian Myth: Rebecca Harding Davis's 'The Harmonists' and Louisa May Alcott's 'Transcendental Wild Oats,' " *Am Transcendental Q*, 3, N.S. (1989), 91–98.

IGNACIO ALDECOA

"A ti no te enterramos"
Jordan, Barry. *Writing and Politics . . .*, 71–72.

"Muy de mañana"
Jordan, Barry. *Writing and Politics . . .*, 72.

SHOLEM ALEICHEM [SHOLOM RABINOWITZ]

"On Account of a Hat"
Sherman, Joseph. " 'God and the Tsar': Ironic Ambiguity and Restorative Laughter in Gogol's 'Overcoat' and Sholem Aleykhem's 'On Account of a Hat,' " in Monday, Henrietta, Ed. *The Waking Sphinx* . . . , 59–82.

NELSON ALGREN

"Design for Departure"
Drew, Bettina. *Nelson Algren* . . . , 149–151.

DAVID ALIZO

"El arco iris"
Ramos, Elías A. *El cuento venezolano* . . . , 39–40.

"Los convidados"
Ramos, Elías A. *El cuento venezolano* . . . , 135.

"La declaración de Ercilio Telardo"
Ramos, Elías A. *El cuento venezolano* . . . , 135–136.

"Griterío"
Ramos, Elías A. *El cuento venezolano* . . . , 40–41.

"Ohmico"
Ramos, Elías A. *El cuento venezolano* . . . , 131.

"La señora Numa"
Ramos, Elías A. *El cuento venezolano* . . . , 31–32.

WOODY ALLEN

"The Kugelmass Episode"
McCann, Graham. *Woody Allen* . . . , 59–60.

"The Lunatic's Tale"
McCann, Graham. *Woody Allen* . . . , 122.

"Remembering Needleman"
McCann, Graham. *Woody Allen* . . . , 155.

"Retribution"
McCann, Graham. *Woody Allen* . . . , 122–123.

"The Whore of Mensa"
McCann, Graham. *Woody Allen* . . . , 89–92.

ISABEL ALLENDE

"The Judge's Wife"
Roberts, Edgar V., and Henry E. Jacobs. *Instructor's Manual* . . . , 2nd ed., 70–71.

VIRGILIO ALMENAR

"El héroe"
Ramos, Elías A. *El cuento venezolano* . . . , 105–106.

YEHUDA AMICHAI [AMIHAI]

"The Class Reunion"
Abramson, Glenda. *The Writing* . . . , 181–182.

"Inverted Love"
Abramson, Glenda. *The Writing* . . . , 189–191.

"My Father's Death"
Abramson, Glenda. *The Writing* . . . , 182–185.

"Nina from Ashkelon"
Abramson, Glenda. *The Writing* . . . , 191–192.

"The Poetry Recital"
Abramson, Glenda. *The Writing* . . . , 192–193.

"The Snow"
Abramson, Glenda. *The Writing* . . . , 179–181.

"The Times My Father Died"
Alter, Robert, Ed. *Modern Hebrew Literature*, 313–315.

"The World in a Room"
Abramson, Glenda. *The Writing* . . . , 186–188.

KINGSLEY AMIS

"All the Blood Within Me"
McDermott, John. *Kingsley Amis* . . . , 185–186.

"Court of Inquiry"
McDermott, John. *Kingsley Amis* . . . , 183–184.

"Darkwater Hall"
Brandford, Richard. *Kingsley Amis*, 70–71.

"I Spy Strangers"
McDermott, John. *Kingsley Amis* . . . , 184–185.

"My Enemy's Enemy"
McDermott, John. *Kingsley Amis* . . . , 183.

"To See the Sun"
Brandford, Richard. *Kingsley Amis*, 71–72.

"Who or What Is It?"
McDermott, John. *Kingsley Amis* . . . , 187.

SHERWOOD ANDERSON

"Adventure"
White, Ray L. *"Winesburg, Ohio"* . . . , 69–73.

"An Awakening"
White, Ray L. *"Winesburg, Ohio"* . . . , 47–48.

"The Book of the Grotesque"
White, Ray L. *"Winesburg, Ohio"* . . . , 21–24.

"Death"
Dunne, Robert. "Beyond Grotesqueness in *Winesburg, Ohio*," *Midwest Q*, 31 (1990), 187–188.
White, Ray L. *"Winesburg, Ohio"* . . . , 63–64.

"Departure"
White, Ray L. *"Winesburg, Ohio"* . . . , 49–50.

"Drink"
White, Ray L. *"Winesburg, Ohio"* . . . , 84–86.

"Godliness"
Dewey, Joseph. "No God in the Sky and No God in Myself: 'Godliness' and Anderson's *Winesburg*," *Mod Fiction Stud*, 35 (1989), 251–259.
Tebbetts, Terrell L. "Incarnation and Romanticism in *Winesburg, Ohio*," *Pubs Arkansas Philol Assoc*, 15, i (1989), 135–136.
White, Ray L. *"Winesburg, Ohio"* . . . , 65–69.

"Hands"
Brown, Lynda. "Anderson's Wing Biddlebaum and Freeman's Louisa Ellis," *Stud Short Fiction*, 27 (1990), 413–414.
Morgan, Gwendolyn. "Anderson's 'Hands,' " *Explicator*, 48, i (1989), 46–47.
Tebbetts, Terrell L. "Incarnation . . . ," 132–133.
White, Ray L. *"Winesburg, Ohio"* . . . , 56–58.

"Loneliness"
Bredahl, A. Carl. *New Ground* . . . , 64–66.
White, Ray L. *"Winesburg, Ohio"* . . . , 79–81.

"A Man of Ideas"
Bidney, Martin. "Refashioning Coleridge's Supernatural Trilogy: Sherwood Anderson's 'A Man of Ideas' and 'Respectability,' " *Stud Short Fiction*, 27 (1990), 222–228.
White, Ray L. *"Winesburg, Ohio"* . . . , 39–40.

"The Man Who Became a Woman"
Chi, Weij-jan. "The Power of the Imagination in 'The Man Who Became a Woman,' " *Fu Jen Stud*, 21 (1988), 61–72.

"Mother"
Colquitt, Clare. "Motherlove in Two Narratives of Community: *Winesburg, Ohio* and *The Country of Pointed Firs*," in Crowley, John W., Ed. *New Essays* . . . , 89–93.
Dunne, Robert. "Beyond Grotesqueness . . . ," 186–187.
White, Ray L. *"Winesburg, Ohio"* . . . , 61–63.

"Nobody Knows"
White, Ray L. *"Winesburg, Ohio"* . . . , 45–46.

"Paper Pills"
White, Ray L. *"Winesburg, Ohio"* . . . , 58–61.

"The Philosopher"
White, Ray L. *"Winesburg, Ohio"* . . . , 64–65.

"Queer"
White, Ray L. *"Winesburg, Ohio"* . . . , 81–84.
Yingling, Thomas. "*Winesburg, Ohio* and the End of Collective Experience," in Crowley, John W., Ed. *New Essays* . . . , 111–114.

"Respectability"
Bidney, Martin. "Refashioning Coleridge's Supernatural Trilogy . . . ," 228–234.
Tebbetts, Terrell L. "Incarnation . . . ," 133–134.
White, Ray L. *"Winesburg, Ohio"* . . . , 73–75.

"Sophistication"
Dunne, Robert. "Beyond Grotesqueness . . . ," 189–190.
White, Ray L. *"Winesburg, Ohio"* . . . , 48–49.
Yingling, Thomas. ". . . End of Collective Experience," 99–101.

"The Strength of God"
Tebbetts, Terrell L. "Incarnation . . . ," 134–135.
White, Ray L. *"Winesburg, Ohio"* . . . , 88–93.

"Tandy"
White, Ray L. *"Winesburg, Ohio"* . . . , 41–42.

"The Teacher"
Bredahl, A. Carl. *New Ground* . . . , 64.
White, Ray L. *"Winesburg, Ohio"* . . . , 91–93.

"The Thinker"
Tebbetts, Terrell L. "Incarnation . . . ," 137.
White, Ray L. *"Winesburg, Ohio"* . . . , 75–78.

"The Untold Lie"
Tebbetts, Terrell L. "Incarnation . . . ," 136–137.
White, Ray L. *"Winesburg, Ohio"* . . . , 86–88.

ENRIQUE ANDERSON IMBERT

"The General Makes a Fine Corpse"
Simpson, Amelia S. *Detective Fiction* . . . , 131–134.

LEONID ANDREYEV

"The Abyss"
Woodward, James B. *Leonid Andreyev* . . . , 68–73.

"At the Window"
Woodward, James B. *Leonid Andreyev* . . . , 46–50.

"The Curse of the Beast"
Woodward, James B. *Leonid Andreyev* . . . , 187–188.

"Darkness"
Woodward, James B. *Leonid Andreyev* . . . , 177–185.

"The Governor"
Hutchings, Stephen. "Discourse, Story and the Fantastic in the Short Stories of Leonid Andreyev," *Essays Poetics*, 13, ii (1988), 13–16.
———. *A Semiotic Analysis* . . . , 135–138.
Woodward, James B. *Leonid Andreyev* . . . , 110–116.

"The Grand Slam"
Woodward, James B. *Leonid Andreyev* . . . , 48–50.

"In the Fog"
Woodward, James B. *Leonid Andreyev* . . . , 70–75.

"Judas Iscariot"
Hutchings, Stephen. "Discourse, Story . . . ," 3–6.
———. *A Semiotic Analysis* . . . , 68–71.

"Laughter"
Woodward, James B. *Leonid Andreyev* . . . , 60–62.

"Lazarus"
Woodward, James B. *Leonid Andreyev* . . . , 147–151.

"The Lie"
Hutchings, Stephen. "Discourse, Story . . . ," 16–17.
Woodward, James B. *Leonid Andreyev* . . . , 61–63.

"The Life of Vasiliy Fiveisky"
Hutchings, Stephen. "Discourse, Story . . . ," 18–20.
Woodward, James B. *Leonid Andreyev* . . . , 87–97.

"My Memoirs" [same as "My Notes"]
Hutchings, Stephen. "Discourse, Story . . . ," 6–8.
Woodward, James B. *Leonid Andreyev* . . . , 196–201.

"The Red Laugh"
Hutchings, Stephen. "Discourse, Story . . . ," 16.
———. *A Semiotic Analysis* . . . , 139–140.
Woodward, James B. *Leonid Andreyev* . . . , 98–107.

"The Seven Who Were Hanged"
Woodward, James B. *Leonid Andreyev* . . . , 190–199.
"Silence"
Hutchings, Stephen. *A Semiotic Analysis* . . . , 63.
"Thought"
Hutchings, Stephen. "Discourse, Story . . . ," 10–11.
———. *A Semiotic Analysis* . . . , 182–183.
Woodward, James B. *Leonid Andreyev* . . . , 77–87.

IVO ANDRIĆ

"Bar 'Titanic' "
Mukerji, Vanita S. *Ivo Andrić* . . . , 123–130.

JERZY ANDRZEJEWSKI

"The Passion Week"
Krzyznowski, Jerzy R. "Jerzy Andrzejewski's 'The Passion Week': A Holocaust Story," in Clayton, J. Douglas, and Gunter Schaarschmidt, Eds. *Poetica Slavica* . . . , 97–104.

MICHAEL ANTHONY

"The Distant One"
Binder, Wolfgang. " 'This Quality of Fact in Fiction'—Mayaro and Childhood Experience in Michael Anthony's Short Stories," in Stummer, Peter O., Ed. *The Story Must Be Told* . . . , 72–73.
"Drunkard of the River"
Binder, Wolfgang. " 'This Quality . . . ,' " 72.
"The Girl and the River"
Binder, Wolfgang. " 'This Quality . . . ,' " 71–72.
"The Holiday by the Sea"
Binder, Wolfgang. " 'This Quality . . . ,' " 71.
"The Valley of Cocoa"
Binder, Wolfgang. " 'This Quality . . . ,' " 70–71.

LAURA ANTILLANO

"La cola"
Ramos, Elías A. *El cuento venezolano* . . . , 33–34.

MAX APPLE

"My Real Estate"
Klinkowitz, Jerome. "Ritual: Max Apple's History in Our Times," in D'haen, Theo, and Hans Bertens, Eds. *History and Post-war Writing*, 191–192.

"Noon"
Klinkowitz, Jerome. "Ritual . . . ," 191–192.

"The Oranging of America"
Klinkowitz, Jerome. "Ritual . . . ," 200–201.

"Walt and Will"
Klinkowitz, Jerome. "Ritual . . . ," 196–197.

JUOZAS APUTIS

"Autumn Grass"
Silbajoris, Rimvydas. "Socialist Realism and Fantastic Reality in Recent Soviet Lithuanian Prose," in Mandelker, Amy, and Robert Reeder, Eds. *The Supernatural* . . . , 311–314.

"Silent, They Drove Fast"
Silbajoris, Rimvydas. "Socialist Realism . . . ," 310.

"Wild Boars Run on the Horizon"
Silbajoris, Rimvydas. "Socialist Realism . . . ," 309.

LOUIS ARAGON

"Chance Meeting"
Atack, Margaret. *Literature and the French Resistance* . . . , 115–117.

"Les Jeunes Gens"
Atack, Margaret. *Literature and the French Resistance* . . . , 117–119.

ORLANDO ARAÚJO

"Manos 0010"
Ramos, Elías A. *El cuento venezolano* . . . , 104–105.

KATHLEEN M. ARCHIBALD

"Clipped Wings"
Sanders, Reinhard W. *The Trinidad Awakening* . . . , 67–69.

MANUEL E. ARGUILLA

"Ato"
Tiempo, Edilberto K. "The Fiction of Manuel E. Arguilla," *Lit Apprentice*, 15, xviii (1952), 119–120.

"Caps and Lower Case"
Grow, L. M. "The External World of Manuel E. Arguilla: Landscape and Orientation," *Pilipinas*, 11 (Fall, 1988), 64.

"Felisa"
Grow, L. M. "The External World . . . ," 66–67.

"Midsummer"
Tiempo, Edilberto K. "The Fiction . . . ," 120.

"Morning in Nagrebcan"
Tiempo, Edilberto K. "The Fiction . . . ," 119.

"Rice"
Grow, L. M. "The External World . . . ," 64–65.

ROBERTO ARLT

"The Little Hunchback"
Drucaroff Aguiar, Elsa. "Femina infame," *Nuevo Texto Crítico*, 2, iv (1989), 103–113.

"El traje del fantasma"
Lindstrom, Naomi. *Literary Expressionism in Argentina* . . . , 42–43.

ALFREDO ARMAS ALONZO

"La espalda de la muerte"
Ramos, Elías A. *El cuento venezolano* . . . , 66.

"La hora que no llegó"
Ramos, Elías A. *El cuento venezolano* . . . , 65–66.

"La hora y punto"
Ramos, Elías A. *El cuento venezolano* . . . , 66–67.

"La liviana ceniza"
Ramos, Elías A. *El cuento venezolano* . . . , 45.

"La mano sobre la tierra"
Ramos, Elías A. *El cuento venezolano* . . . , 45–46.

INÉS ARREDONDO

"Canción de cuna"
Arenas, Rogelio. "Los cuentos de Inés Arredondo en la *Revista Mexicana de Literatura*," in López González, Aralia, Amelia Malagamba, and Elena Urrutia, Eds. *Mujer y literatura* . . . , 67–68.

"La casa de los espejos"
Arenas, Rogelio. "Los cuentos de Inés Arredondo . . . ," 65–66.

"La señal"
Arenas, Rogelio. "Los cuentos de Inés Arredondo . . . ," 64–65.

"La Sunamita"
Arenas, Rogelio. "Los cuentos de Inés Arredondo . . . ," 66–67.

JUAN JOSÉ ARREOLA

"Autrui"
Acker, Bertie. *El cuento mexicano contemporaneo . . .*, 72–74.

"La Canción de Personelle"
Valencia, Juan O. "La estructura del *Confabulario*," in Bleznick, Donald, Ed. *Variaciones interpretativas . . .*, 106–107.

"A Compact with the Devil"
Valencia, Juan O. "La estructura . . .," 106–107.

"The Disciple"
Acker, Bertie. *El cuento mexicano contemporaneo . . .*, 102–103.

"El faro"
Acker, Bertie. *El cuento mexicano contemporaneo . . .*, 86.

"Gravitación"
Acker, Bertie. *El cuento mexicano contemporaneo . . .*, 88–89.

"Monólogo del insumiso"
Acker, Bertie. *El cuento mexicano contemporaneo . . .*, 100–102.

"Pablo"
Acker, Bertie. *El cuento mexicano contemporaneo . . .*, 67–71.

"Private Life"
Acker, Bertie. *El cuento mexicano contemporaneo . . .*, 86–87.

"The Silence of God"
Acker, Bertie. *El cuento mexicano contemporaneo . . .*, 66–67.
Valencia, Juan O. "La estructura . . .," 107–108.

"The Switchman"
Acker, Bertie. *El cuento mexicano contemporaneo . . .*, 71–72, 108–109.
Knapp, Bettina L. *Machine, Metaphor . . .*, 98–111.
Valencia, Juan O. "La estructura . . .," 102–104.

"You and I"
Acker, Bertie. *El cuento mexicano contemporaneo . . .*, 88.

ISAAC ASIMOV

"The Big and the Little"
Panshin, Alexel, and Cory Panshin. *The World Beyond . . .*, 633–637.

"Catch That Rabbit"
Cowan, S. A. "Five-Finger Exercise: Asimov's Clues to the Plot Solution of 'Catch That Rabbit,' " *Sci-Fiction Stud*, 16, i (1989), 90–93.

"Dead Hand"
Panshin, Alexel, and Cory Panshin. *The World Beyond . . .*, 637–638.

"Nightfall"
Huntington, John. *Rationalizing Genius . . .*, 145–151.

"Stowaway"
Panshin, Alexel, and Cory Panshin. *The World Beyond* . . . , 309–310.

VIKTOR ASTAFEV

"The Blind Fisherman"
Shneidman, N. N. *Soviet Literature* . . . , 109–110.

MARGARET ATWOOD

"Bluebeard's Egg"
Godard, Barbara. "Palimpsest: Margaret Atwood's 'Bluebeard's Egg,' " *Recherches Anglaises et Nord-Américaines*, 20 (1987), 71–75.
"Giving Birth"
Korte, Barbara. "In Sorrow Thou Shalt Bring Forth Children—On Childbirth in Literature," *Orbis Litterarum*, 45 (1990), 44.
"Polarities"
Palmer, Paulina. *Contemporary Women's Fiction* . . . , 26–28.
"The Sin Eater"
Burdette, Martha. "Sin Eating and Sin Making: The Power and Limits of Language," in Detweiler, Robert, and Willard G. Doty, Eds. *The Daemonic Imagination* . . . , 159–167.
DeContini, Barbara. "Narrative Hunger," in Detweiler, Robert, and Willard G. Doty, Eds. *The Daemonic Imagination* . . . , 111–122.
McVann, Mark. "Destroying Death: Jesus in *Mark* and Joseph in 'The Sin Eater,' " in Detweiler, Robert, and Willard G. Doty, Eds. *The Daemonic Imagination* . . . , 129–135.
Morey, Ann-Janice. "The Old In/Out," in Detweiler, Robert, and Willard G. Doty, Eds. *The Daemonic Imagination* . . . , 175–179.
"Sunrise"
Rooke, Constance. *Fear of the Open Heart* . . . , 165–167.

LOUIS AUCHINCLOSS

"Suttee"
Yahnke, Robert E., and Richard M. Eastman. *Aging in Literature* . . . , 31–32.

JOSÉ AUGUSTÍN

"Cuál es la onda"
Dávila Gutiérrez, Joel. "Tres cuentos mexicanos, tres," in Pavón, Alfredo, Ed. *Paquette: Cuento* . . . , 152–153.

MARY AUSTIN

"The Walking Woman"
Jaycox, Faith. "Regeneration Through Liberation: Mary Austin's 'The Walking Woman' and Western Narrative Formula," *Legacy*, 66, i (1989), 5–12.

FRANCISCO AYALA

"El abrazo"
Martínez, Antonio. "Dialectica del poder y la libertad en *Los usurpadores* y *La cabeza del cordero* de Francisco Ayala," *Diálogos Hispánicos*, 9 (1990), 17.
Orringer, Nelson R. "Historicity and Historiography in Francisco Ayala's *Los usurpadores*," *Letras Peninsulares*, 3, i (1990), 133–135.

"The Ace of Clubs"
Irizarry, Estelle. *Francisco Ayala*, 88–90.

"The Ailing King"
Irizarry, Estelle. *Francisco Ayala*, 44–45.

"The Bell of Huesca"
Irizarry, Estelle. *Francisco Ayala*, 45–46.
Orringer, Nelson R. "Historicity . . . ," 123–124.

"The Bewitched"
Irizarry, Estelle. *Francisco Ayala*, 48–49.
Martínez, Antonio. "Dialectica del poder . . . ," 16.
Orringer, Nelson R. "Historicity . . . ," 125–128.

"The Boxer and an Angel"
Irizarry, Estelle. *Francisco Ayala*, 31–33.

"The Captain's Beard"
Irizarry, Estelle. *Francisco Ayala*, 70–71.

"Day of Mourning"
Irizarry, Estelle. *Francisco Ayala*, 132–133.

"Dialogue of Love"
Irizarry, Estelle. *Francisco Ayala*, 128–131.

"Dialogue of the Dead"
Irizarry, Estelle. *Francisco Ayala*, 53–54.

"Erika Facing Winter"
Irizarry, Estelle. *Francisco Ayala*, 35–37.

"A Fish"
Irizarry, Estelle. *Francisco Ayala*, 92–93.

"Fragrance of Jasmines"
Irizarry, Estelle. *Francisco Ayala*, 134–135.

"Happy Days"
Irizarry, Estelle. *Francisco Ayala*, 131–138.

"Hunter at Dawn"
Irizarry, Estelle. *Francisco Ayala*, 30–31.

"The Impostors"
Irizarry, Estelle. *Francisco Ayala*, 46–48.
Martínez, Antonio. "Dialectica del poder . . . ," 16.

"Incident"
Irizarry, Estelle. *Francisco Ayala*, 140–141.

"The Inquisitor"
Irizarry, Estelle. *Francisco Ayala*, 50–52.
Martínez, Antonio. "Dialectica del poder . . . ," 16–17.
Orringer, Nelson R. "Historicity . . . ," 128–131.

"The Lamb's Head"
Espina, Eduardo. "Francisco Ayala y la narración como estructura temporal," *Círculo*, 18 (1989), 217–222.
Irizarry, Estelle. *Francisco Ayala*, 61–63.
Martínez, Antonio. "Dialectica del poder . . . ," 20.
Skyrme, Raymond. "Substance and Shadow: The Anatomy of Self-Reflection in 'La cabeza del cordero,' " *Hispanic J*, 10, ii (1989), 95–112.

"The Last Supper"
Irizarry, Estelle. *Francisco Ayala*, 73–74.

"Let's Have Fun"
Irizarry, Estelle. *Francisco Ayala*, 130–131.

"Meeting"
Irizarry, Estelle. *Francisco Ayala*, 71–72.

"The Message"
Irizarry, Estelle. *Francisco Ayala*, 57–58.

"Monkey Story"
Irizarry, Estelle. *Francisco Ayala*, 67–70.

"The 'New Art' Chalet"
Irizarry, Estelle. *Francisco Ayala*, 139–140.

"No World Really Is Clean"
Irizarry, Estelle. *Francisco Ayala*, 144–145.

"One's Life for Reputation"
Irizarry, Estelle. *Francisco Ayala*, 63–64.

"Polar Star"
Irizarry, Estelle. *Francisco Ayala*, 33–34.

"Rape in California"
Irizarry, Estelle. *Francisco Ayala*, 91–92.

"El regreso"
Martínez, Antonio. "Dialectica del poder . . . ," 19–20.

"A Resounding Wedding"
Irizarry, Estelle. *Francisco Ayala*, 90–91.

"St. John the Divine"
Irizarry, Estelle. *Francisco Ayala*, 41–44.
Orringer, Nelson R. "Historicity . . . ," 131–133.

"A Story by Maupassant"
Irizarry, Estelle. *Francisco Ayala*, 74–76.

"The Tagus"
Irizarry, Estelle. *Francisco Ayala*, 58–59.

"The Unknown Colleague"
Irizarry, Estelle. *Francisco Ayala*, 76–77.

"Your Absence"
Irizarry, Estelle. *Francisco Ayala*, 137–138.

ISAAC BABEL

"First Love"
Armstrong, Judith M. "Babel's 'First Love,' " *Essays Poetics*, 14, i (1989), 99–106.

"Guy de Maupassant"
Rougle, Charles. "Art and the Artist in Babel's 'Guy de Maupassant,' " *Russian R*, 48 (1989), 171–180.

"The Story of a Horse"
Kornblatt, Judith D. "Legacy or Travesty: The Mystic Cossack Heroes of Gogol and Babel," *Selected Proceedings of the Kentucky Foreign Language Conference, Slavic Section*, 6, i (1989–1990), 11–13.

"The Story of My Dovecote"
Greenstein, Michael. "Jewish Pegasus," *Jewish Book Forum*, 45 (1990), 46–47.

MURRAY BAIL

"The Drover's Wife"
Arens, Werner. "The Ironical Fate of 'The Drover's Wife': Four Versions from Henry Lawson (1892) to Barbara Jefferis (1980)," in Stummer, Peter O., Ed. *The Story Must Be Told . . .*, 124–126.
Jose, Nicholas. "Possibilities of Love in Recent Australian Stories," in Stummer, Peter O., Ed. *The Story Must Be Told . . .*, 137–138.

JAMES BALDWIN

"Sonny's Blues"
Cox, Clyde. "A Lasting Legacy: Brotherly Love and the Language of Jazz in 'Sonny's Blues,' " *Mid-America R*, 10, ii (1990), 127–135.

JOSÉ BALZA

"Bella a las once"
Ramos, Elías A. *El cuento venezolano* . . . , 107–110.

"Itinerario"
Ramos, Elías A. *El cuento venezolano* . . . , 37–38.

"Minaces"
Ramos, Elías A. *El cuento venezolano* . . . , 38–39.

HONORÉ BALZAC

"Facino Cane"
Beizer, Janet L. *Family Plots* . . . , 23–26.
Rashkin, Esther. "Phantom Legacies: Balzac's 'Facino Cane,' " *Romanic R*, 80 (1989), 529–540.

"The Girl with the Golden Eyes"
Beizer, Janet L. *Family Plots* . . . , 64–67.
Tremblay, Victor-Laurent. "Démasquer 'La Fille aux yeux d'or,' " *Nineteenth-Century French Stud*, 19 (1990), 72–82.
Vanoncini, André. "Les 'Trompettes de 1789' et 'L'Abattement de 1814': Moments de tableau parisien dans 'La Fille aux yeux d'or,' " *L'Année Balzacienne*, 11 (1990), 231–232.

"Gobseck"
Testa, Carlo. "At the Expense of Life: Death by Desire in Balzac, Bataille, and Goethe's *Faust*," *Comparatist*, 14 (May, 1990), 57–58.

"Louis Lambert"
Beizer, Janet L. *Family Plots* . . . , 143–144.

"The Message"
Chambers, Ross. "Reading and the Voice of Death: Balzac's 'Le Message,' " *Nineteenth-Century French Stud*, 18 (1990), 408–423.

"A Passion in the Desert"
Beizer, Janet L. *Family Plots* . . . , 48–49.
Kelly, Dorothy. *Fictional Genders* . . . , 94–106.

"The Unknown Masterpiece"
Kelly, Dorothy. *Fictional Genders* . . . , 169–179.

"El Verdugo"
Beizer, Janet L. *Family Plots* . . . , 13–17.

TONI CADE BAMBARA

"Basement"
Vertreace, Martha M. "The Dance of Character and Community," in Pearlman, Mickey, Ed. *American Women* . . . , 163.

"Gorilla, My Love"
Vertreace, Martha M. "The Dance . . . ," 157–159.

"Happy Birthday"
Vertreace, Martha M. "The Dance . . . ," 157.

"The Johnson Girls"
Vertreace, Martha M. "The Dance . . . ," 164–165.

"The Lesson"
Cartwright, Jerome. "Bambara's 'The Lesson,' " *Explicator*, 47, iii (1989), 61–63.
Vertreace, Martha M. "The Dance . . . ," 159.

"Maggie of the Green Bottle"
Vertreace, Martha M. "The Dance . . . ," 161–162.

"My Man Bovanne"
Vertreace, Martha M. "The Dance . . . ," 159–160.

"The Organizer's Wife"
Vertreace, Martha M. "The Dance . . . ," 163–164.

"Raymond's Run"
Palmer, Paulina. *Contemporary Women's Fiction* . . . , 23–24.
Roberts, Edgar V., and Henry E. Jacobs. *Instructor's Manual* . . . , 2nd ed., 71–72.
Vertreace, Martha M. "The Dance . . . ," 160–161.

"Talking Bout Sonny"
Palmer, Paulina. *Contemporary Women's Fiction* . . . , 87–88.

HERMAN BANG

"Irene Holm"
Eddy, Beverley D. "Herman Bang's 'Irene Holm' as a Study of Life and Art," *Scandinavica*, 28, i (1989), 17–27.

JOHN BANVILLE

"Nightwind"
Imhof, Rüdiger. *John Banville* . . . , 22–24.

"The Possessed"
Imhof, Rüdiger. *John Banville* . . . , 24–35.

ASHER BARASH

"At Heaven's Gate"
Alter, Robert, Ed. *Modern Hebrew Literature*, 161–164.

JULES-AMÉDÉE BARBEY d'AUREVILLY

"At a Dinner Party of Atheists"
Bernheimer, Charles. *Figures of Ill Repute* . . . , 81–88.

"A Woman's Vengeance"
Bernheimer, Charles. *Figures of Ill Repute* . . . , 75–81.

ARTURO BAREA

"Coñac"
Percival, Anthony. "The Spanish Civil War Story: From Neo-Realism to Postmodernism," in Bevan, David, Ed. *Literature and War*, 91–92.

"Servicio de noche"
Percival, Anthony. "The Spanish Civil War Story . . . ," 88–89.

ROBERT BARR

"The Doom of London"
Bradshaw, James S. "The Science Fiction of Robert Barr," *Sci-Fiction Stud*, 16 (July, 1989), 202–203.

"Within an Ace of the End of the World"
Bradshaw, James S. ". . . Robert Barr," 203–204.

JOHN BARTH

"Anonymiad"
Olster, Stacey. *Reminiscence* . . . , 130–131.

"Bellerophoniad"
Fogel, Stan, and Gordon Slethaug. *Understanding John Barth*, 144–147.

"Dunyazadiad"
Fogel, Stan, and Gordon Slethaug. *Understanding John Barth*, 140–141.
Schulz, Max F. *The Muses* . . . , 30–32.

"Life-Story"
Fogel, Stan, and Gordon Slethaug. *Understanding John Barth*, 123–124.

"Lost in the Funhouse"
Boehm, Beth A. "Educating Readers: Creating New Expectations in *Lost in the Funhouse*," in Phelan, James, Ed. *Reading Narrative* . . . , 105–107.

"Menelaiad"
Boehm, Beth A. "Educating Readers . . . ," 109–113.
Fogel, Stan, and Gordon Slethaug. *Understanding John Barth*, 124–125.

"Night-Sea Journey" [same as "Petition"]
Boehm, Beth A. "Educating Readers . . . ," 104–105.

"Perseid"

Fogel, Stan, and Gordon Slethaug. *Understanding John Barth*, 141–144.

Olster, Stacey. *Reminiscence* . . . , 127–128.

Poznar, Susan. "Barth's Compulsion to Repeat: Its Hazards and Its Possibilities," *R Contemp Fiction*, 10, ii (1990), 64–67.

Schulz, Max F. *The Muses* . . . , 27–28.

"Title"

Boehm, Beth A. "Educating Readers . . . ," 107–108.

DONALD BARTHELME

"The Abduction from the Seraglio"

Trachtenberg, Stanley. *Understanding Donald Barthelme*, 148–149.

"Affection"

Trachtenberg, Stanley. *Understanding Donald Barthelme*, 156–159.

"The Agreement"

Trachtenberg, Stanley. *Understanding Donald Barthelme*, 128.

"Alice"

Olsen, Lance. *Circus of the Mind* . . . , 108.

"And Then"

Trachtenberg, Stanley. *Understanding Donald Barthelme*, 131–132.

"At the End of the Mechanical Age"

Trachtenberg, Stanley. *Understanding Donald Barthelme*, 129–131.

"At the Tolstoy Museum"

Trachtenberg, Stanley. *Understanding Donald Barthelme*, 76–78.

"The Balloon"

Saltzman, Arthur M. *Design of Darkness* . . . , 4–5.

Trachtenberg, Stanley. *Understanding Donald Barthelme*, 61–64.

"Basil from Her Garden"

Trachtenberg, Stanley. *Understanding Donald Barthelme*, 214–220.

"The Big Broadcast of 1938"

Trachtenberg, Stanley. *Understanding Donald Barthelme*, 49–51.

"Bishop"

Trachtenberg, Stanley. *Understanding Donald Barthelme*, 33–34.

"Bone Bubbles"

Saltzman, Arthur M. *Design of Darkness* . . . , 103–104.

"Captain Blood"

Trachtenberg, Stanley. *Understanding Donald Barthelme*, 154–155.

"The Captured Woman"

Trachtenberg, Stanley. *Understanding Donald Barthelme*, 126–127.

"The Catechist"

Trachtenberg, Stanley. *Understanding Donald Barthelme*, 118–119.

"City Life"

Trachtenberg, Stanley. *Understanding Donald Barthelme*, 94–101.

"Cortes and Montezuma"
Trachtenberg, Stanley. *Understanding Donald Barthelme*, 145–148.

"Critique de la Vie Quotidienne"
Trachtenberg, Stanley. *Understanding Donald Barthelme*, 107–108.

"Daumier"
Trachtenberg, Stanley. *Understanding Donald Barthelme*, 119–124.

"The Death of Edward Lear"
Trachtenberg, Stanley. *Understanding Donald Barthelme*, 144–145.

"The Dolt"
Trachtenberg, Stanley. *Understanding Donald Barthelme*, 66–67.

"Edward and Pia"
Trachtenberg, Stanley. *Understanding Donald Barthelme*, 69–70.

"Engineer-Private Paul Klee Misplaces an Aircraft Between Milbertshofen and Cambrai, March 1916"
Trachtenberg, Stanley. *Understanding Donald Barthelme*, 116–118.

"The Explanation"
Trachtenberg, Stanley. *Understanding Donald Barthelme*, 87–91.

"The Falling Dog"
Trachtenberg, Stanley. *Understanding Donald Barthelme*, 78–79.

"A Few Moments of Sleeping and Waking"
Trachtenberg, Stanley. *Understanding Donald Barthelme*, 69–71.

"For I'm the Boy Whose Only Joy Is Loving You"
Trachtenberg, Stanley. *Understanding Donald Barthelme*, 48–49.

"The Glass Mountain"
Olsen, Lance. *Circus of the Mind* . . . , 107–108.
Trachtenberg, Stanley. *Understanding Donald Barthelme*, 79–82.

"Great Days"
Trachtenberg, Stanley. *Understanding Donald Barthelme*, 138–139.

"The Great Hug"
Trachtenberg, Stanley. *Understanding Donald Barthelme*, 132–133.

"Hiding Man"
Trachtenberg, Stanley. *Understanding Donald Barthelme*, 46–47.

"I Bought a Little City"
Trachtenberg, Stanley. *Understanding Donald Barthelme*, 127–128.

"The Indian Uprising"
Trachtenberg, Stanley. *Understanding Donald Barthelme*, 57–61.

"January"
Trachtenberg, Stanley. *Understanding Donald Barthelme*, 240–242.

"Jaws"
Trachtenberg, Stanley. *Understanding Donald Barthelme*, 247–248.

"Kierkegaarde Unfair to Schlegel"
Trachtenberg, Stanley. *Understanding Donald Barthelme*, 91–94.

"The King of Jazz"
Trachtenberg, Stanley. *Understanding Donald Barthelme*, 142–144.

"The Leap"
Trachtenberg, Stanley. *Understanding Donald Barthelme*, 139–142.

"Lightning"
Trachtenberg, Stanley. *Understanding Donald Barthelme*, 155–156.

"Me and Miss Mandible"
Trachtenberg, Stanley. *Understanding Donald Barthelme*, 51–53.

"Momma Don't 'Low"
Trachtenberg, Stanley. *Understanding Donald Barthelme*, 133–134.

"Morning"
Trachtenberg, Stanley. *Understanding Donald Barthelme*, 136–137.

"The New Music"
Trachtenberg, Stanley. *Understanding Donald Barthelme*, 134–136.

"On the Steps of the Conservatory"
Trachtenberg, Stanley. *Understanding Donald Barthelme*, 137–138.

"Our Work and Why We Do It"
Trachtenberg, Stanley. *Understanding Donald Barthelme*, 124–126.

"Overnight to Many Distant Cities"
Trachtenberg, Stanley. *Understanding Donald Barthelme*, 161–162.

"Paraguay"
Trachtenberg, Stanley. *Understanding Donald Barthelme*, 84–87.

"The Party"
Trachtenberg, Stanley. *Understanding Donald Barthelme*, 108–110.

"Phantom of the Opera's Friend"
Trachtenberg, Stanley. *Understanding Donald Barthelme*, 82–84.

"A Picture History of the War"
Trachtenberg, Stanley. *Understanding Donald Barthelme*, 67–69.

"Robert Kennedy Saved from Drowning"
Trachtenberg, Stanley. *Understanding Donald Barthelme*, 64–66.

"The Sandman"
Campbell, Ewing. "Dark Matter: Barthelme's Fantastic, Freudian Subtext in 'The Sandman,' " *Stud Short Fiction*, 27 (1990), 517–524.
Trachtenberg, Stanley. *Understanding Donald Barthelme*, 113.

"The Sea of Hesitation"
Trachtenberg, Stanley. *Understanding Donald Barthelme*, 159–161.

"See the Moon"
Trachtenberg, Stanley. *Understanding Donald Barthelme*, 71–75.

"A Shower of Gold"
Olsen, Lance. *Circus of the Mind . . .*, 109–110.
Trachtenberg, Stanley. *Understanding Donald Barthelme*, 54–57.

"The Temptation of St. Anthony"
Trachtenberg, Stanley. *Understanding Donald Barthelme*, 110–112.

"Terminus"
Trachtenberg, Stanley. *Understanding Donald Barthelme*, 161.

"Tickets"
Trachtenberg, Stanley. *Understanding Donald Barthelme*, 242–243.

"Up, Aloft in the Air"
Trachtenberg, Stanley. *Understanding Donald Barthelme*, 49–50.

"The Viennese Opera Ball"
Trachtenberg, Stanley. *Understanding Donald Barthelme*, 53–54.

"Visitors"
Trachtenberg, Stanley. *Understanding Donald Barthelme*, 153–154.

"What to Do Next"
Trachtenberg, Stanley. *Understanding Donald Barthelme*, 128–129.

H. E. BATES

"Where the Cloud Breaks"
Yahnke, Robert E., and Richard M. Eastman. *Aging in Literature . . .*, 32–33.

HARRY BATES and DESMOND WINTER HALL

"Hawk Carse"
Panshin, Alexel, and Cory Panshin. *The World Beyond . . .*, 231.

RICHARD BAUSCH

"Wise Men at Their End"
Yahnke, Robert E., and Richard M. Eastman. *Aging in Literature . . .*, 33–34.

BARBARA BAYNTON

"Billy Skywonkie"
Colmer, John. "Multiple Perspectives in Barbara Baynton's Short Stories," in Stummer, Peter O., Ed. *The Story Must Be Told . . .*, 112.

"Bush Church"
Colmer, John. "Multiple Perspectives . . .," 113–115.

"The Chosen Vessel"
Colmer, John. "Multiple Perspectives . . .," 108–111.

"Scrammy 'And"
Colmer, John. "Multiple Perspectives . . .," 111–112.

"Squeaker's Mate"
Colmer, John. "Multiple Perspectives . . .," 117–118.

GEORGII BAZHENOV

"Dasha"
Shneidman, N. N. *Soviet Literature* . . . , 54–55.

ANN BEATTIE

"Shifting"
DeZure, Deborah. "Images of Void in Beattie's 'Shifting,' " *Stud Short Fiction*, 26 (1989), 11–15.

SIMONE DE BEAUVOIR

"The Age of Discretion"
Patterson, Yolanda. *Simone de Beauvoir* . . . , 235–243.

"Monologue"
Patterson, Yolanda. *Simone de Beauvoir* . . . , 243–249.

"A Very Easy Death"
Kadish, Doris Y. "Simone de Beauvoir's 'Une Mort très douce': Existential and Feminist Perspectives," *French R*, 62 (1989), 631–639.
Patterson, Yolanda. *Simone de Beauvoir* . . . , 195–218.

"The Woman Destroyed"
Moi, Toril. *Feminist Theory* . . . , 61–93.

SAMUEL BECKETT

"All Strange Away"
Albright, Daniel. "Beckett's Recent Activities: The Liveliness of Dead Imagination," in Dick, Susan, Declan Kiberd, Dougald McMillan, and Joseph Ronsley, Eds. *Essays for Richard Ellmann* . . . , 377–378.

"As the Story Was Told"
Murphy, P. J. *Reconstructing Beckett* . . . , 141–142.

"Assumption"
Murphy, P. J. *Reconstructing Beckett* . . . , 7–9.
Phillips, K. J. *Dying Gods* . . . , 60–61.

"The Calmative"
Murphy, P. J. *Reconstructing Beckett* . . . , 23–25.

"Dream of Fair to Middling Women"
Murphy, P. J. *Reconstructing Beckett* . . . , 13–15.

"Imagination Dead Imagine"
Astro, Alan. *Understanding Samuel Beckett*, 188–190.
Catanzaro, Mary F. "The Space of the Couple in Beckett's 'Imagination Dead Imagine,' " in Bauer, Roger, and Douwe

Fokkema, Eds. *Proceedings of the XIIth Congress . . .* , III, 206–211.

"Sounds"
Murphy, P. J. *Reconstructing Beckett . . .* , 137–141.

"Still"
Murphy, P. J. *Reconstructing Beckett . . .* , 135–137.

LILIIA BELIAEVA

"Seven Years Wasted"
Shneidman, N. N. *Soviet Literature . . .* , 185–187.

EDWARD BELLAMY

"Lost"
Gabler-Hover, Janet. "Man's Fragile Tenure: Discontinuous Time and the Ethos of Temporality in Edward Bellamy's Short Fiction," *Texas Stud Lit & Lang*, 32 (1990), 313–320.

"The Old Folks Party"
Gabler-Hover, Janet. "Man's Fragile Tenure . . . ," 304–312.

"A Summer Evening's Dream"
Gabler-Hover, Janet. "Man's Fragile Tenure . . . ," 320–325.

"To Whom This May Come"
Scheick, William J. "The Letter Killeth: Edward Bellamy's 'To Whom This May Come,' " *Am Transcendental Q*, 3, i (1989), 55–67.

SAUL BELLOW

"A Father-to-Be"
Kiernan, Robert F. *Saul Bellow*, 128–131.

"The Gonzaga Manuscript"
Kiernan, Robert F. *Saul Bellow*, 124–128.

"Him with His Foot in His Mouth"
Kiernan, Robert F. *Saul Bellow*, 190–195.

"Leaving the Yellow House"
Dillard, Annie. *Living by Fiction*, 157–158.
Kiernan, Robert F. *Saul Bellow*, 113–116.

"Looking for Mr. Green"
Kiernan, Robert F. *Saul Bellow*, 121–124.

"Mosby's Memoirs"
Kiernan, Robert F. *Saul Bellow*, 132–135.

"The Old System"
Johnson, Gregory. "Jewish Assimilation and Codes of Manners in Saul Bellow's 'The Old System,' " *Stud Am Jewish Lit*, 9, i (1990), 48–60.
Kiernan, Robert F. *Saul Bellow*, 116–121.

"Seize the Day"
Bach, Gerhard. "An Open Channel to the Soul: German Thought on Saul Bellow's Planet," in Freese, Peter, Ed. *Germany and German Thought* . . . , 250–251.
Bouson, J. Brooks. *The Empathic Reader* . . . , 64–81.
Glenday, Michael K. "Some Versions of Real: The Novellas of Saul Bellow," in Lee, A. Robert, Ed. *The Modern American Novella*, 164–171.
Ikeda, Chōko. "Human Relations in Saul Bellow's 'Seize the Day,' " *Kyushu Am Lit*, 30 (December, 1989), 21–26.
Kiernan, Robert F. *Saul Bellow*, 57–75.

"A Sermon by Dr. Pep"
Phillips, K. J. *Dying Gods* . . . , 93–96.

"A Silver Dish"
Friedrich, Marianne. "Bellow's Renaissance Courtier: Woody Selbst in 'A Silver Dish,' " *Saul Bellow J*, 9, i (1990), 21–35.
Kiernan, Robert F. *Saul Bellow*, 205–210.
Knight, Karl F. "The Rhetoric of Bellow's Woody Selbst: Religion and Irony," *Saul Bellow J*, 8, i (1989), 35–43.

"What Kind of a Day Did You Have?"
Friedrich, Marianne M. "Artistic Representation in Bellow's 'What Kind of a Day Did You Have?' " *Saul Bellow J*, 8, i (1989), 51–67.
Glenday, Michael K. "Some Versions of Real . . . ," 171–176.

"Zetland: By a Character Witness"
Kiernan, Robert F. *Saul Bellow*, 201–205.

VASILII BELOV

"That's How Things Are"
Starikova, Elizaveta. "The Sociological Aspects of Contemporary 'Village Prose,' " *Soviet Stud Lit*, 26, i (1989–1990), 60–63.

JUAN BENET

"Duelo"
Diaz, Epicteto. " 'Duelo' y 'Viator': Ironía y parodia en los relatos de Juan Benet," *Anales de la literatura Española*, 15, i–iii (1990), 13–27.

"Viator"
Diaz, Epicteto. " 'Duelo' y 'Viator' . . . ," 13–27.

STEPHEN VINCENT BENÉT

"By the Waters of Babylon"
Banãles, Victoria. "Diversidad y congruencia: Los ríos de Rulfo, Benét, Guimarães Rosa y Hesse," *Romance Lang Annual*, 1 (1989), 374–375.

GOTTFRIED BENN

"Gehirne"
Hohendahl, Peter U. "The Loss of Reality: Gottfried Benn's Early Prose," in Huyssen, Andreas, and David Bathrick, Eds. *Modernity and the Text* . . . , 84–86.

"Die Insel"
Hohendahl, Peter U. "The Loss of Reality . . . ," 86–87.

HEMDA BEN-YEHUDAH

"The Farm of the Sons of Rechab"
Ramras-Rauch, Gila. *The Arab* . . . , 10–11.

THOMAS BERNHARD

"Viktor Halbnarr"
Gelus, Marjorie. "Thomas Bernhard's 'Viktor Halbnarr': *Faust* in Contemporary Idiom," *Archiv*, 225 (1988), 269–284.

GINA BERRIAULT

"The Diary of K. W."
Yahnke, Robert E., and Richard M. Eastman. *Aging in Literature* . . . , 206.

ALFRED BESTER

"Fondly Fahrenheit"
Huntington, John. *Rationalizing Genius* . . . , 173–178.
Roberts, Thomas J. *An Aesthetics* . . . , 158–159.

BI YE [HUANG CHAOYANG]

"Fruits of Slavery"
Kinnemark-Lander, Britta. "Bi Ye," in Slupski, Zbigniew, Ed. *A Selective Guide* . . . , II, 36–37.

H. N. BIALIK

"The Short Friday"
Alter, Robert, Ed. *Modern Hebrew Literature*, 105–108.

AMBROSE BIERCE

"The Boarded Window"
Joshi, S. T. *The Weird Tale*, 148–149.

"Chickamauga"
Joshi, S. T. *The Weird Tale*, 155–156.

"The Coup de Grâce"
Joshi, S. T. *The Weird Tale*, 158–159.

"The Death of Halpin Frayser"
Joshi, S. T. *The Weird Tale*, 161–162.

"The Eyes of the Panther"
Joshi, S. T. *The Weird Tale*, 149–150.

"Jupiter Doke, Brigadier-General"
Couser, G. Thomas. "Writing the Civil War: Ambrose Bierce's 'Jupiter Doke, Brigadier-General,' " *Stud Am Fiction*, 18 (1990), 87–98.

"The Moonlit Road"
Joshi, S. T. *The Weird Tale*, 162–163.

"Moxon's Master"
Joshi, S. T. *The Weird Tale*, 151–155.

"An Occurrence at Owl Creek Bridge"
Conlogue, William. "Bierce's 'An Occurrence at Owl Creek Bridge,' " *Explicator*, 48, i (1989), 37–38.
Joshi, S. T. *The Weird Tale*, 163–164.

"One of the Missing"
Joshi, S. T. *The Weird Tale*, 159–160.

"One Summer Night"
Joshi, S. T. *The Weird Tale*, 165–166.

SABINE CORINNA BILLE

"The Savage Maiden"
Huber-Staffelbach, Margrit. " 'La Demoiselle sauvage'—Eros als Schicksal bei Corinna Bille," *Französich Heute*, 20, iii (1990), 245–253.

SANDRA BIRDSELL

"Rock Garden"
Bastein, Friedel H. "Sandra Birdsell, *Night Travellers*: A Contemporary Canadian Short Story Cycle," in Stummer, Peter O., Ed. *The Story Must Be Told . . .*, 103–104.

JOHN PEALE BISHOP

"Resurrection"
Tulloss, Thomas. *"Et Ego in Arcadia*: Death in 'Resurrection,' John Peale Bishop's World War One Fiction," *Focus on Robert Graves*, 1, vii (1988), 18–23.

JEROME BIXBY

"It's a *Good* Life"
Huntington, John. *Rationalizing Genius* . . . , 130–133.

ALGERNON BLACKWOOD

"The Damned"
Joshi, S. T. *The Weird Tale*, 101–102.

"A Descent into Egypt"
Joshi, S. T. *The Weird Tale*, 103–104.

"Everywhere and Otherwise"
Joshi, S. T. *The Weird Tale*, 129–130.

"The Listener"
Burleson, Donald R. "Algernon Blackwood's 'The Listener': A Hearing," *Stud Weird Fiction*, 5 (Spring, 1989), 15–19.

"The Man Who Found Out"
Joshi, S. T. *The Weird Tale*, 128–129.

"The Man Who Lived Backwards"
Joshi, S. T. *The Weird Tale*, 107–108.

"May Day Eve"
Joshi, S. T. *The Weird Tale*, 106–107.

"The Nemesis of Fire"
Joshi, S. T. *The Weird Tale*, 114–115.

"The Prayer"
Joshi, S. T. *The Weird Tale*, 118–119.

"A Psychical Invasion"
Joshi, S. T. *The Weird Tale*, 96–97.

"The Regeneration of Lord Ernie"
Joshi, S. T. *The Weird Tale*, 102–103.

"Secret Worship"
Joshi, S. T. *The Weird Tale*, 115–116.

"The Temptation of the Clay"
Joshi, S. T. *The Weird Tale*, 108–109.

"The Touch of Pan"
Joshi, S. T. *The Weird Tale*, 117–118.

"The Wendigo"
Joshi, S. T. *The Weird Tale*, 119–120.

"The Willows"

Dziemianowicz, Stefan. " 'The Green Meadow' and 'The Willows': Lovecraft, Blackwood, and a Peculiar Coincidence," *Lovecraft Stud*, 19–20 (Fall, 1989), 33–39.

Joshi, S. T. *The Weird Tale*, 114–115.

EDUARDO BLANCO

"Claudia"

Ratcliff, Dillwyn F. *Venezuelan Prose Fiction*, 42–43.

JAMES BLISH

"Surface Tension"

Huntington, John. *Rationalizing Genius . . .*, 40–42.

CAROL BLY

"Gunnar's Sword"

Yahnke, Robert E., and Richard M. Eastman. *Aging in Literature . . .*, 35–36.

JORGE LUIS BORGES

"Abenjacán the Bojarí, Dead in His Labyrinth" [same as "Ibn-Hakkan al-Bokarí . . ."]

Gómez Mango, Edmundo. "Duelo, oxímoron y objetos mágicos en la narrativa de Borges," *Río de la Plata*, 2 (1986), 84–85.

"The Aleph"

Gómez Mango, Edmundo. "Duelo, oxímoron . . .," 85–86.

Monterroso, Augusto. "El Aleph de Ercilla," *Nuevo Texto Critico*, 1 (1988), 229–232.

"Brodie's Report" [same as "Dr. Brodie's Report"]

Cordero, Sergio. "Filosofía y lingüística en los cuentos fantásticos de Jorge Luis Borges," *La Palabra*, 74 (April–June, 1990), 193–194.

"The Circular Ruins"

Dillard, Annie. *Living by Fiction*, 115–116.

Penuel, Arnold M. "Paradox and Parable: The Theme of Creativity in Borges' 'The Circular Ruins,' " *Latin Am Lit R*, 17 (July–December, 1989), 52–61.

Smulian, Dan. "Jorge Luis Borges, Author of *Alice Through the Looking Glass*," *Romance Q*, 36, i (1989), 79–85.

"The Congress"

Feldman, Sharon. "Reading, Writing, and Revelation in Borges' 'El congreso,' " *Dactylus*, 9 (1988–1989), 56–61.

"Death and the Compass"
Orban, Clara. "How Borges and Robbe-Grillet Use Geometry," *Aleph*, [n.v.], (1988), 3–15.
Sanz Morales, Manuel. "Hermes, Jano y un error de Borges en 'La muerte y la brújula,' " *Epos*, 6 (1990), 561–564.
Simpson, Amelia S. *Detective Fiction* . . . , 141–142.
Sussman, Henry. *Afterimages of Modernity* . . . , 158–160.

"Emma Zunz"
Armisén, Antonio. " 'Emma Zunz': Sobre la lectura, los modelos y los limites del relato," in Fonquerne, Yves-René, and Aurora Egido, Eds. *Formas breves* . . . , 297–308.
Brodzki, Bella. " 'She was unable not to think': Borges' 'Emma Zunz' and the Female Subject," *Mod Lang Notes*, 100 (1985), 330–347; rpt. Bloom, Harold, Ed. *Modern Latin American Fiction*, 49–57.
Moon, Harold K. "Wordsworth the Guide: Borges's 'Emma Zunz' and Similitude in Dissimilitude," *Hispanófila*, 32, ii (1989), 65–71.

"Funes the Memorious"
Alvarez, Nicolás E. "Borges: Autor implícito, narrador, protagonista y lector en 'Funes el memorioso,' " *Círculo*, 19 (1990), 147–152.

"The Garden of Forking Paths"
Balderston, Daniel. "Historical Situations in Borges," *Mod Lang Notes*, 105 (1990), 333–343.
Capobianco, Michael F. "Quantum Theory, Spacetime, and Borges' Bifurcations," *Ometeca*, 1, i (1989), 27–38.

"The God's Script" [same as "The Writing of the Lord"]
Detweiler, Robert. *Breaking the Fall* . . . , 122–128.
Giskin, Howard. "The Mystical Experience in Borges: A Problem of Perception," *Hispanófila*, 98 (January, 1990), 75–77.

"The Gospel According to Mark"
Haberly, David T. "The Argentine Gospels of Borges," *Bull Hispanic Stud*, 66, i (1989), 47–54.

"Guayaquil"
Sherman, Alvin F. "Confrontation and the Force of Will in Borges's 'Guayaquil,' " in Paolini, Gilbert, Ed. *La Chispa '89* . . . , 297–303.

"The House of Asterión"
Shaw, Donald L. "A propósito de 'La Casa de Asterión' de Borges," in Neumeister, Sebastián, Ed. *Actas del IX Congreso* . . . , II, 721–724.

"The Improbable Impostor Tom Castro"
Alonso Aldama, Juan A., Marian García Collado, and José María Nadal. "Análisis semiótico de 'El impostor inverosímil Tom Castro,' " in Menchacatorre, Félix, Ed. *Ensayos de literatura europea* . . . , 23–29.

"Pierre Menard, Author of *Quixote*"
Balderston, Daniel. "Historical Situations . . . ," 343–346.
Grandis, Rita de. " 'Pierre Menard, autor del *Quijote*': A Phenomenological Approach," *Revista Canadiense*, 13, i (1988), 11–27.

"The South"
Shaw, Donald L. "Jorge Luis Borges: *Ficciones*," in Swanson, Philip, Ed. *Landmarks* . . . , 41–42.
Wight, Doris T. "Fantastic Labyrinths in Fictions by Borges, Cortázar, and Robbe-Grillet," *Comparatist*, 13 (May, 1989), 28–29.

"Theme of the Traitor and the Hero"
Matteo, Sante. "History as a Web of Fiction: Plato, Borges, and Bertolucci," *Weber Stud*, 6, i (1989), 12–29.

"Three Versions of Judas"
Méndez-Ramírez, Hugo. "La estrategia narrativa y la unidad estructural en 'Tres versiones de Judas' de Jorge Luis Borges," *Revista Interamericana*, 40, ii (1990), 207–211.

"Tlön, Uqbar, Orbis Tertius"
Cordero, Sergio. "Filosofía y lingüística . . . ," 191–192.
Dillard, Annie. *Living by Fiction*, 59–60.
Irby, James E. "Borges and the Idea of Utopia," in Dunham, Lowell, and Ivar Ivask, Eds. *The Cardinal Points* . . . , 35–45; Spanish ed., 77–89.
Lunsford, Kern L. "Jorge Luis Borges's 'Tlön, Uqbar, Orbis Tertius': Epistemology and History; Language and Literary Creation," *Cincinnati Romance R*, 8 (1989), 101–109.
Sussman, Henry. *Afterimages of Modernity* . . . , 143–157.

"The Two Kings and the Two Labyrinths"
Holloway, James E. "Borges' Subversive Parable, 'Los dos reyes y los dos laberintos,' " *Stud Short Fiction*, 26 (1989), 335–338.

"Utopia of a Tired Man"
Cordero, Sergio. "Filosofía y lingüística . . . ," 190–191.

"The Zahir"
Gómez Mango, Edmundo. "Duelo, oxímoron . . . ," 78–84.

M. C. BOTHA

"Frans Malan"
Trump, Martin. "Afrikaner Literature and the South African Liberation Struggle," *J Commonwealth Lit*, 25, i (1990), 63.

"The Price You Have to Pay"
Trump, Martin "Afrikaner Literature . . . ," 66–67.

"The Short Life of an Average Man"
Trump, Martin. "Afrikaner Literature . . . ," 63–64.

"Untitled 3"
Trump, Martin. "Afrikaner Literature . . . ," 65.

ANTHONY BOUCHER

"The Quest for Saint Aquin"
Huntington, John. *Rationalizing Genius* . . . , 170–173.

ELIZABETH BOWEN

"The Cat Jumps"
Morris, J. A. "Elizabeth Bowen's Stories of Suspense," in Bloom, Clive, Ed. *Twentieth-Century Suspense* . . . , 122–124.
"The Demon Lover"
Morris, J. A. ". . . Stories of Suspense," 117–119.
"Human Habitation"
Hildebidle, John. *Five Irish Writers* . . . , 88–91.
"Ivy Gripped the Steps"
Morris, J. A. ". . . Stories of Suspense," 126–127.
"Look at All Those Roses"
Hildebidle, John. *Five Irish Writers* . . . , 110–113.
Morris, J. A. ". . . Stories of Suspense," 119–121.
"A Love Story: 1939"
Hildebidle, John. *Five Irish Writers* . . . , 98–100.
"Mysterious Kôr"
Morris, J. A. ". . . Stories of Suspense," 124–126.
Showalter, Elaine. *Sexual Anarchy* . . . , 88–89.
"Pink May"
Morris, J. A. ". . . Stories of Suspense," 127–128.
"Summer Night"
Hildebidle, John. *Five Irish Writers* . . . , 102–104.

KAY BOYLE

"Cabaret"
Meyer, Martin. "Kay Boyle's Postwar Germany," in Freese, Peter, Ed. *Germany and German Thought* . . . , 213–214.

T. CORAGHESSAN BOYLE

"Hard Sell"
Pope, Dan. "A Different Kind of Post-Modernism," *Gettysburg R*, 3 (1990), 664–665.
"Modern Love"
Pope, Dan. "A Different Kind of Post-Modernism," 664.

"Peace of Mind"
Pope, Dan. "A Different Kind of Post-Modernism," 665.

"Sorry Fugu"
Pope, Dan. "A Different Kind of Post-Modernism," 664.

RAY BRADBURY

"Mars Is Heaven"
Huntington, John. *Rationalizing Genius* . . . , 89–93.

"The Sound of Thunder"
Huntington, John. *Rationalizing Genius* . . . , 158–159.

YOSEF HAIM BRENNER

"Between Water and Water"
Ramras-Rauch, Gila. *The Arab* . . . , 38–39.

"Nerves"
Ramras-Rauch, Gila. *The Arab* . . . , 36–37.
Wallenrod, Reuben. . . . *Modern Israel*, 28–31.

"The Way Out"
Alter, Robert, Ed. *Modern Hebrew Literature*, 141–144.

BREYTEN BREYTENBACH

"The Double Dying of an Ordinary Criminal"
Trump, Martin. "Afrikaner Literature and the South African Liberation Struggle," *J Commonwealth Lit*, 25, i (1990), 61–62.

GREGORIO BRILLANTES

"Excerpts from the Autobiography of the Middle-aged Ghostwriter with Insomnia"
Dimalanta, Ophelia A. "City Fiction: Manila, a Way of Life and Art," in Villacorta, Wilfrido V., Isagani R. Cruz, and Ma. Lourdes Brillantes, Eds. *Manila* . . . , 280.

"Janis Joplin, the Revolution, and the Melancholy Widow of Gabriela Silang Street"
Dimalanta, Ophelia A. "City Fiction . . . ," 279–280.

"The Living and the Dead"
Bernad, Miguel A. *Bamboo and the Greenwood Tree* . . . , 72–74.

"Wind Over the Earth"
Bernad, Miguel A. *Bamboo and the Greenwood Tree* . . . , 71–72.

"The Year"
Bernad, Miguel A. *Bamboo and the Greenwood Tree* . . . , 74–75.

LUIS BRITTO GARCÍA

"Bomba"
Ramos, Elías A. *El cuento venezolano* . . . , 106.

"El brazo de la justicia-El"
Ramos, Elías A. *El cuento venezolano* . . . , 73–74.

"El brazo de la justicia-Ella"
Ramos, Elías A. *El cuento venezolano* . . . , 71–72.

"Dios"
Ramos, Elías A. *El cuento venezolano* . . . , 28–30.

"Grupo"
Ramos, Elías A. *El cuento venezolano* . . . , 107.

"La Venta"
Ramos, Elías A. *El cuento venezolano* . . . , 71–72.

CHARLOTTE BRONTË

"Albion and Marina"
Taylor, Irene. *Holy Ghosts* . . . , 112–115.

"Captain Henry Hastings"
Taylor, Irene. *Holy Ghosts* . . . , 144–146.

"Caroline Vernon"
Taylor, Irene. *Holy Ghosts* . . . , 148–149.

FREDRIC BROWN

"Arena"
Huntington, John. *Rationalizing Genius* . . . , 112–116.

"Paradox Lost"
Panshin, Alexel, and Cory Panshin. *The World Beyond* . . . , 610–612.

MIKHAIL BULGAKOV

"The Adventures of Chichikov in the Soviet Union"
Milne, Lesley. *Mikhail Bulgakov* . . . , 56–58.
Natov, Nadine. "The Supernatural in Bulgakov and Gogol," in Mandelker, Amy, and Robert Reeder, Eds. *The Supernatural* . . . , 248–250.
Wright, A. Colin. *Mikhail Bulgakov* . . . , 40–41.

"Baptism by Rotation"
Milne, Lesley. *Mikhail Bulgakov* . . . , 132–135.

"A Chinese Story"
Milne, Lesley. *Mikhail Bulgakov* . . . , 55–56.
Wright, A. Colin. *Mikhail Bulgakov* . . . , 57–59.

"Diaboliad"
Milne, Lesley. *Mikhail Bulgakov* . . . , 41–45.
Wright, A. Colin. *Mikhail Bulgakov* . . . , 50–54.

"The Embroidered Towel"
Milne, Lesley. *Mikhail Bulgakov* . . . , 129–133.

"Fatal Eggs" [originally "The Ray of Life"]
Milne, Lesley. *Mikhail Bulgakov* . . . , 45–51.
Wright, A. Colin. *Mikhail Bulgakov* . . . , 54–57.

"The Fire of the Khans"
Milne, Lesley. *Mikhail Bulgakov* . . . , 53–55.

"Heart of a Dog" [originally "A Dog's Happiness"]
Wright, A. Colin. *Mikhail Bulgakov* . . . , 59–63.

"Morphine"
Milne, Lesley. *Mikhail Bulgakov* . . . , 137–138.

"No. 13, The Elpit-Rabcommun Building"
Milne, Lesley. *Mikhail Bulgakov* . . . , 51–53.

"The Red Crown"
Milne, Lesley. *Mikhail Bulgakov* . . . , 13–15, 143–145.

"The Speckled Rash"
Milne, Lesley. *Mikhail Bulgakov* . . . , 136–138.

"The Vanishing Eye"
Milne, Lesley. *Mikhail Bulgakov* . . . , 138–140.

CARLOS BULOSAN

"As Long as the Grass Shall Grow"
De Rivera, Lina B. Diaz. "The Female Principle and Woman Reading in a Carlos Bulosan Story," *Diliman R*, 37, iii (1989), 11–14.

EDWARD GEORGE BULWER-LYTTON

"Arasmanes the Seeker"
Roberts, Marie. *Gothic Immortality* . . . , 168–169.

"The Tale of Kosem Kesamim"
Roberts, Marie. *Gothic Immortality* . . . , 166–167.

EDGAR RICE BURROUGHS

"Under the Moons of Mars"
Wolfe, Gary K. "Frontiers in Space," in Mogen, David, Mark Busby, and Paul Bryant, Eds. *The Frontier Experience* . . . , 252–253.

VASILY BYKOV

"The Quarry"
Shneidman, N. N. *Soviet Literature* . . . , 135–137.

"The Token"
Shneidman, N. N. *Soviet Literature* . . . , 132–134.

JAMES BRANCH CABELL

"The Music from Behind the Moon"
Riemer, James D. *From Satire to Subversion* . . . , 46–49.

"The Way of Ecben"
Riemer, James D. *From Satire to Subversion* . . . , 49–51.

"The White Robe"
Riemer, James D. *From Satire to Subversion* . . . , 51–53.

GEORGE WASHINGTON CABLE

" 'Tite Poulette"
Elfenbein, Anna S. *Women on the Color Line* . . . , 35–46.

JULIO CALCAÑO

"El rei de Tebas"
Ratcliff, Dillwyn F. *Venezuelan Prose Fiction*, 31.

ITALO CALVINO

"The Adventure of a Bather"
Ricci, Franco. *Difficult Games* . . . , 69–70.

"The Adventure of a Clerk"
Ricci, Franco. *Difficult Games* . . . , 69–72.

"The Adventure of a Driver" [originally "The Night Driver"]
Ricci, Franco. *Difficult Games* . . . , 84–87.

"The Adventure of a Poet"
Ricci, Franco. *Difficult Games* . . . , 79–82.

"The Adventure of a Reader"
Ricci, Franco. *Difficult Games* . . . , 76–79.

"The Adventure of a Soldier"
Di Bucci Felicetti, Simona. "Il 'mistero bucco' di Italo Calvino," in Di Fazio, Margherita, Ed. *Narrare* . . . , 205–214.

"The Argentine Ant"
Ricci, Franco. *Difficult Games* . . . , 91–96.

"The Baron in the Tree"
Cannon, JoAnn. *Postmodern Italian Fiction . . .*, 34–39.

"Fear on the Footpath"
Re, Lucia. . . . *Fables of Estrangement*, 159–163.

"Il guidatore notturno"
Porush, David. "Cybernetic Fiction and Postmodern Science," *New Lit Hist*, 20 (1989), 373–396.

"Last Comes the Crow"
Re, Lucia. . . . *Fables of Estrangement*, 163–169.

"The Master's Eye"
Ricci, Franco. *Difficult Games . . .*, 58–60.

"Meiosis"
Fenwick, Julie. "Sex, Language, and Narrative: Continuity and Discontinuity in Italo Calvino's 'Meiosis,' " *Stud Short Fiction*, 27 (1990), 203–209.

"Moon and Gnac"
Ricci, Franco. *Difficult Games . . .*, 40–42.

"The Name, the Nose"
De Vivo, Albert. " 'Sotto il sole giaguaro' di Italo Calvino," *Cristallo*, 31, iii (1989), 75–90.

"A Plunge into Real Estate"
Ricci, Franco. *Difficult Games . . .*, 96–102.

"Reading a Wave"
Devivo, Albert. "Calvino's Palomar and Deconstruction: Similarities and Differences," *Italian Q*, 30 (Winter–Spring, 1989), 81–91.

"Smog"
Ricci, Franco. *Difficult Games . . .*, 102–107.

JOHN W. CAMPBELL

"Forgetfulness"
Panshin, Alexel, and Cory Panshin. *The World Beyond . . .*, 422–423.

"Twilight"
Huntington, John. *Rationalizing Genius . . .*, 159–164.

"When the Atoms Failed"
Bartter, Martha A. *The Way to Ground Zero . . .*, 60–61.

ALBERT CAMUS

"The Adulterous Woman"
Amoia, Alba. *Albert Camus*, 125–126.
Barbeito, Patricia. "Perception and Ideology: Camus as Colonizer in 'The Adulterous Woman,' " *Celfan R*, 7, iii (1988), 34–38.
Ellison, David R. *Understanding Albert Camus*, 177–183.

"The Fall"
Amoia, Alba. *Albert Camus*, 59–67.
Dembo, L. S. *Detotalized Totalities* . . . , 139–144.
Ellison, David R. *Understanding Albert Camus*, 141–164.
Thody, Philip. *Albert Camus*, 75–96.

"The Growing Stone"
Amoia, Alba. *Albert Camus*, 129–130.
Ellison, David R. *Understanding Albert Camus*, 204–212.

"The Guest"
Altes, Elizabeth K. "Normes et valeurs dans le récit," *Revue des Sciences Humaines*, 72, i (1986), 35–47.
Black, Moishe. "Camus's 'L'Hôte' as a Ritual of Hospitality," *Nottingham French Stud*, 28, i (1989), 39–52.
Cervo, Nathan. "Camus's 'L'Hôte,' " *Explicator*, 48 (1990), 222–224.
Ellison, David R. *Understanding Albert Camus*, 194–199.

"Jonas, or The Artist at Work"
Amoia, Alba. *Albert Camus*, 128–129.
Ellison, David R. *Understanding Albert Camus*, 199–204.

"The Renegade"
Amoia, Alba. *Albert Camus*, 126–127.
Ellison, David R. *Understanding Albert Camus*, 183–190.
Lynch, Martha. "Le *Je* utopique dans 'Le Renégat,' " *La Revue des Lettres Modernes*, 904–910 (1989), 129–139.
Stephenson, Katherine. "Camus's 'Le Renégat': The Interior Monologue as Psycho-Babble," in Deely, John, and Jonathan Evans, Eds. *Semiotics 1986*, 108–114.

"The Silent Men"
Amoia, Alba. *Albert Camus*, 127–128.
Ellison, David R. *Understanding Albert Camus*, 190–194.

"The Stranger"
Amoia, Alba. *Albert Camus*, 39–47.
Dembo, L. S. *Detotalized Totalities* . . . , 123–124.
Ellison, David R. *Understanding Albert Camus*, 49–67.
Longstaffe, Moya. "A Happy Life and a Happy Death: The Quest of Camus' 'Étranger,' " *French R*, 64, i (1990), 54–68.
McCann, J. "The Verdict of Meursault," *Nottingham French Stud*, 29, i (1990), 51–63.
Nelson, Roy J. *Causality and Narrative* . . . , 157–172.
Showalter, English. . . . *Humanity and the Absurd*, 21–115.
Thody, Philip. *Albert Camus*, 14–44.

TRUMAN CAPOTE

"One Christmas"
Moates, Marianne M. *A Bridge of Childhood* . . . , 98–99.

EMILIO CARBALLIDO

"Danza antigua"
Troiano, James J. "Illusory Worlds in Three Stories by Emilio Carballido," *Hispanic J*, 10, ii (1989), 67–72.

"La desterrada"
Troiano, James J. "Illusory Worlds . . . ," 72–78.

"Los huéspedes"
Troiano, James J. "Illusory Worlds . . . ," 63–67.

ORSON SCOTT CARD

"America"
Collings, Michael R. *In the Image of God* . . . , 62–66.

"Ender's Game"
Collings, Michael R. *In the Image of God* . . . , 90–91, 143–144.

"Kingsmeat"
Collings, Michael R. *In the Image of God* . . . , 75–79, 81–83.

"The Porcelain Salamander"
Collings, Michael R. *In the Image of God* . . . , 80–81.

"Salvage"
Collings, Michael R. *In the Image of God* . . . , 60–62.

"Worthing Farm"
Collings, Michael R. *In the Image of God* . . . , 148–149.

GUSTAVO CARERRA

"Los brazos del cielo"
Ramos, Elías A. *El cuento venezolano* . . . , 97.

"Pobre de solemnidad"
Ramos, Elías A. *El cuento venezolano* . . . , 56–58.

"La Ventana"
Ramos, Elías A. *El cuento venezolano* . . . , 49–50.

PETER CAREY

"He Found Her in Late Summer"
Jose, Nicholas. "Possibilities of Love in Recent Australian Stories," in Stummer, Peter O., Ed. *The Story Must Be Told* . . . , 138–139.

WILLIAM CARLETON

"Phelim O'Toole's Courtship"
Mercier, Vivian. "English Readers: Three Historical 'Moments,' " in Komesu, Okifumi, and Masaru Sekine, Eds. *Irish Writers* . . . , 29–32.

EDWARD CARPENTER

"Narayan"
Bakshi, Parminder K. "Homosexuality and Orientalism: Edward Carpenter's Journey to the East," in Brown, Tony, Ed. . . . *Late Victorian Realism*, 168–169.

ALEJO CARPENTIER

"Histoire de Lunes"
Padura Fuentes, Leonardo. "La magia del ciclo: Notas para un cuento olvidado, 'Una historia de lunes,' " *La Palabra y Hombre*, 73 (1990), 267–271.

"Like the Night"
Espinosa Rodríguez, Eduardo L. "La modelación artística en 'Semejante a la noche,' " *Universidad*, 230 (1987), 81–92.
Richard, Renaud. "La hora de nadie: Significado del reloj temático-estructural de 'Semejante a la noche,' " *Iris*, 2 (1989), 175–185.

"Manhunt"
Adelstein, Miriam. " 'El acoso': A View of the Dynamic Components of the Protagonist's Psyche," *Crítica Hispánica*, 12, i–ii (1990), 141–147.
Boldy, Steven. "Making Sense in Carpentier's 'El acoso,' " *Mod Lang R*, 85, iii (1990), 612–622.

ERNEST A. CARR

"Black Mother"
Sander, Reinhard W. *The Trinidad Awakening* . . . , 52–53.

JOHN DICKSON CARR

"The Ends of Justice"
Joshi, S. T. *John Dickson Carr* . . . , 85–86.

ESTO CARRERA

"Líder en tres tiempos"
Ramos, Elías A. *El cuento venezolano* . . . , 71.

ANGELA CARTER

"Black Venus"
Hutcheon, Linda. . . . *Postmodernism*, 145–149.

"The Loves of Lady Purple"
Hutcheon, Linda. . . . *Postmodernism*, 32–33.

RAYMOND CARVER

"The Bath"

Gearhart, Michael W. "Breaking the Ties That Bind: Inarticulation in the Fiction of Raymond Carver," *Stud Short Fiction*, 26 (1989), 439–446.

"Boxes"

Verley, Claudine. "The Window and the Eye in Raymond Carver's 'Boxes,' " *J Short Story Engl*, 15 (Autumn, 1990), 95–106.

"Cathedral"

Brown, Arthur. "Raymond Carver and Postmodern Humanism," *Critique S*, 31 (1990), 133–136.

"I Could See the Smallest Things"

Fontana, Ernest. "Insomnia in Raymond Carver's Fiction," *Stud Short Fiction*, 26 (1989), 448–449.

"Menudo"

Fontana, Ernest. "Insomnia . . . ," 449–450.

"The Pheasant"

Brown, Arthur. "Raymond Carver . . . ," 127–128.

"Preservation"

Henning, Barbara. "Minimalism and the American Dream: 'Shiloh' by Bobbie Ann Mason and 'Preservation' by Raymond Carver," *Mod Fiction Stud*, 35 (1989), 689–698.

"Put Yourself in My Shoes"

Brown, Arthur. "Raymond Carver . . . ," 129–132.

"A Small, Good Thing"

Gearhart, Michael W. "Breaking the Ties . . . ," 439–446.

"So Much Water So Close to Home"

Clarke, Graham. "Inventing the Glimpse: Raymond Carver and the Syntax of Science," in Clarke, Graham, Ed. *The New American Writing* . . . , 112–113.

"The Student's Wife"

Fontana, Ernest. "Insomnia . . . ," 447–448.

"What We Talk About When We Talk About Love"

Carlin, Warren. "Just Talking: Raymond Carver's Symposium," *Cross Currents*, 38, i (1988), 87–92.

"Where I'm Calling From"

Skenazy, Paul. "Life in Limbo: Ray Carver's Fiction," *Enclitic*, 11, i (1988), 77–83.

Verley, Claudine. "Narration and Interiority in Raymond Carver's 'Where I'm Calling From,' " *J Short Story Engl*, 13 (August, 1989), 91–102.

"Whoever Was Using This Bed"

Fontana, Ernest. "Insomnia . . . ," 450–451.

ROSARIO CASTELLANOS

"Aceite guapo"
Furnival, Chloe. "Confronting Myths of Oppression: The Short Stories of Rosario Castellanos," in Bassnett, Susan, Ed. *Knives and Angels* . . . , 55–56.

"The Caprice Waltz"
González, Alfonso. "La soledad y los patrones del dominio en la cuentística de Rosario Castellanos," in Ahern, Maureen, and Mary S. Vásquez, Eds. *Homenaje a Rosario Castellanos*, 111–112.

"The Cooking Lesson"
Furnival, Chloe. "Confronting Myths . . . ," 62–64.

"The Death of the Tiger"
Furnival, Chloe. "Confronting Myths . . . ," 54–55.

"Family Album"
Furnival, Chloe. "Confronting Myths . . . ," 64–66.

"Guests in August"
Furnival, Chloe. "Confronting Myths . . . ," 60–61.
González, Alfonso. "La soledad y los patrones . . . ," 110–111.

"Modesta Gómez"
Furnival, Chloe. "Confronting Myths . . . ," 57–58.
Sarfati-Arnaud, Monique. "Los 'buenos' y los 'malos' en 'Modesta Gómez': Lectura ideológica de un cuento de Rosario Castellanos," in Neumeister, Sebastián, Ed. *Actas del IX Congreso* . . . , II, 703–709.

"Sunday"
González, Alfonso. "La soledad y los patrones . . . ," 112–113.

"Teodoro Méndez's Luck"
Furnival, Chloe. "Confronting Myths . . . ," 56.

"The Truce"
Furnival, Chloe. "Confronting Myths . . . ," 56–57.

"The Widower Román"
González, Alfonso. "La soledad y los patrones . . . ," 109–110.

WILLA CATHER

"Before Breakfast"
Thurin, Erik I. *The Humanization* . . . , 357–358, 359–362.

"The Best Years"
Burgess, Cheryll. "Willa Cather's Homecomings: A Meeting of Selves," in Murphy, John J., Linda H. Adams, and Paul Rawlins, Eds. *Willa Cather* . . . , 53–54.
Donovan, Josephine. *After the Fall* . . . , 126–127.

"The Bohemian Girl"
Lee, Hermione. *Willa Cather* . . . , 101–103.
Levy, Helen F. "Mothers and Daughters in 'The Bohemian Girl' and

The Song of the Lark," in Murphy, John J., Linda H. Adams, and Paul Rawlins, Eds. *Willa Cather* . . . , 163–167.
Thacker, Robert. *The Great Prairie Fact* . . . , 149–151.
Thurin, Erik I. *The Humanization* . . . , 154–157.

"A Chance Meeting"
Lee, Hermione. *Willa Cather* . . . , 349–354.

"Coming, Aphrodite!"
Lee, Hermione. *Willa Cather* . . . , 161–164.
Thurin, Erik I. *The Humanization* . . . , 221–228.

"Count of Crow's Nest"
Thurin, Erik I. *The Humanization* . . . , 98–100.

"A Death in the Desert"
Lee, Hermione. *Willa Cather* . . . , 76–77.
Thurin, Erik I. *The Humanization* . . . , 126–128.

"The Diamond Mine"
Ryder, Mary R. "Loosing the Tie That Binds: Sisterhood in Cather," in Murphy, John J., Linda H. Adams, and Paul Rawlins, Eds. *Willa Cather* . . . , 43–44.

"Double Birthday"
Lee, Hermione. *Willa Cather* . . . , 57–58.

"Eleanor's House"
Thurin, Erik I. *The Humanization* . . . , 147–149.

"The Enchanted Bluff"
Donovan, Josephine. *After the Fall* . . . , 100–101.
Lee, Hermione. *Willa Cather* . . . , 97–101.

"Eric Hermannson's Soul"
Donovan, Josephine. *After the Fall* . . . , 95–96.
Thurin, Erik I. *The Humanization* . . . , 106–109.

"Flavia and Her Artists"
Harris, Jeane. "A Code of Her Own: Attitudes Toward Women in Willa Cather's Short Fiction," *Mod Fiction Stud*, 36 (1990), 86–88.
Thurin, Erik I. *The Humanization* . . . , 124–126.

"The Garden Lodge"
Thurin, Erik I. *The Humanization* . . . , 132–134.

"Jack-a-Boy"
Thurin, Erik I. *The Humanization* . . . , 109–113.

"The Joy of Nelly Deane"
Donovan, Josephine. *After the Fall* . . . , 101–102.
Hall, Joan W. "Nordic Mythology in Willa Cather's 'The Joy of Nelly Deane,' " *Stud Short Fiction*, 26 (1989), 339–341.
Thurin, Erik I. *The Humanization* . . . , 152–154.

"The Namesake"
Thurin, Erik I. *The Humanization* . . . , 141–144.

"Neighbour Rosicky"
Lee, Hermione. *Willa Cather . . .*, 315–318.
Ostwalt, Conrad E. *After Eden . . .*, 70–71.
Rosowski, Susan J. "Willa Cather's Chosen Family: Fictional Formations and Transformations," in Murphy, John J., Linda H. Adams, and Paul Rawlins, Eds. *Willa Cather . . .*, 76–77.
Skaggs, Merrill M. "Cather's Complex Tale of a Simple Man, 'Neighbour Rosicky,' " in Murphy, John J., Linda H. Adams, and Paul Rawlins, Eds. *Willa Cather . . .*, 79–83.
Thurin, Erik I. *The Humanization . . .*, 321–322.

"Old Mrs. Harris"
Baker, Bruce P. " 'Old Mrs. Harris' and the Intergenerational Family," in Murphy, John J., Linda H. Adams, and Paul Rawlins, Eds. *Willa Cather . . .*, 33–40.
Donovan, Josephine. *After the Fall . . .*, 123.
Lee, Hermione. *Willa Cather . . .*, 318–326.
Ramonda, Karen S. "Three in One Woman in 'Old Mrs. Harris,' " in Murphy, John J., Linda H. Adams, and Paul Rawlins, Eds. *Willa Cather . . .*, 175–180.
Thurin, Erik I. *The Humanization . . .*, 322–324.
Woodress, James. "A Dutiful Daughter: Willa Cather and Her Parents," in Murphy, John J., Linda H. Adams, and Paul Rawlins, Eds. *Willa Cather . . .*, 26–27.

"On the Divide"
Ostwalt, Conrad E. *After Eden . . .*, 68–69.
Thacker, Robert. *The Great Prairie Fact . . .*, 147–148.

"On the Gull's Road"
Donovan, Josephine. *After the Fall . . .*, 88–89.
Thurin, Erik I. *The Humanization . . .*, 149–152.

"Paul's Case"
Briggs, Cynthia K. "Insulated Isolation: Willa Cather's Room with a View," in Rosowski, Susan J., Ed. *Cather Studies*, 161–164.
Kvasnicka, Mellanee. "Fragmented Families, Fragmented Lives in 'Paul's Case,' *My Antonia*, and *A Lost Lady*," in Murphy, John J., Linda H. Adams, and Paul Rawlins, Eds. *Willa Cather . . .*, 103–108.
Summers, Claude J. " 'A Losing Game in the End': Aestheticism and Homosexuality in Cather's 'Paul's Case,' " *Mod Fiction Stud*, 36 (1990), 103–119; rpt. in his *Gay Fictions . . .*, 62–77.
Thurin, Erik I. *The Humanization . . .*, 134–137.
Wasserman, Loretta. "Is Cather's Paul a Case?" *Mod Fiction Stud*, 36 (1990), 121–129.

"Peter"
Thacker, Robert. *The Great Prairie Fact . . .*, 148–149.

"The Portrait of Phaedra"
Thurin, Erik I. *The Humanization . . .*, 128–130.

"The Professor's Commencement"
Thurin, Erik I. *The Humanization . . .*, 113–115.

"Profile"
Madigan, Mark J. "Willa Cather and Dorothy Canfield Fisher," in Rosowski, Susan J., Ed. *Cather Studies*, 119–122.
Thurin, Erik I. *The Humanization* . . . , 144–146.

"A Resurrection"
Thurin, Erik I. *The Humanization* . . . , 100–102.

"The Sculptor's Funeral"
Lee, Hermione. *Willa Cather* . . . , 75–76.
Wasserman, Loretta. "Going Home: 'The Sculptor's Funeral,' 'The Namesake,' and 'The Two Friends,' " in Murphy, John J., Linda H. Adams, and Paul Rawlins, Eds. *Willa Cather* . . . , 58–59.

"A Son of the Celestial"
Thurin, Erik I. *The Humanization* . . . , 96.

"The Tale of the White Pyramid"
Thurin, Erik I. *The Humanization* . . . , 95.

"Tommy the Unsentimental"
Harris, Jeane. "A Code of Her Own . . . ," 85–86.

"The Treasure of Far Island"
Burgess, Cheryll. "Willa Cather's Homecomings . . . ," 51–52.
Donovan, Josephine. *After the Fall* . . . , 96–98.
Thurin, Erik I. *The Humanization* . . . , 115–118.

"Two Friends"
Lee, Hermione. *Willa Cather* . . . , 311–315.
Thurin, Erik I. *The Humanization* . . . , 324–329.
Wasserman, Loretta. "Going Home . . . ," 59–62.

"Uncle Valentine"
Miller, Robert K. "What Margie Knew," in Murphy, John J., Linda H. Adams, and Paul Rawlins, Eds. *Willa Cather* . . . , 133–137.

"A Wagner Matinée"
Thurin, Erik I. *The Humanization* . . . , 131–132.

"The Way of the World"
Donovan, Josephine. *After the Fall* . . . , 94–95.
Harris, Jeane. "A Code of Her Own . . . ," 83–85.
Thurin, Erik I. *The Humanization* . . . , 97–98.

"The Willing Muse"
Thurin, Erik I. *The Humanization* . . . , 146–147.

ROSA CHACEL

"En la ciudad de las grandes pruebas"
Myers, Eunice D. "Folklore and Classical Animal Imagery in Two Short Stories of Rosa Chacel," *Letras Peninsulares*, 3, i (1990), 71–73.

"Suma"
Rodriguez, Mercedes M. de. "Chacel's Journey into the Fantastic," *Letras Peninsulares*, 3, i (1990), 78–81.

"La ùltima batalla"
Myers, Eunice D. "Folklore . . . ," 67–70.

EILEEN CHANG [ZHANG AILING]

"The Golden Cangue"
Miller, Lucien, and Hui-chan Chang. "Fiction and Autobiography: Spatial Form in 'The Golden Cangue' and *The Woman Warrior*," in Duke, Michael S., Ed. *Modern Chinese Women Writers . . .*, 25–43.

CHANG HSIN-HSIN [same as ZHANG XINXIN]

"The Dream of Our Generation"
Bucher, Ida. "Zwischen Traum und Realität: Zhang Xinxins Erzählung 'Der Traum unserer Generation,' " *Horen*, 34, iv (1989), 69–74.

"On a Plain"
Goatkoei, Lang-Tan. "Die Ebenen der Liebe: Formen des Widerspruchs in Zhang Xinxins Erzählung 'Auf einer Ebene,' " *Horen*, 34, iv (1989), 84–94.

CHAO SHU-LI

"Blackie Gets Married"
Birch, Cyril. "Chao Shu-li: Creative Writing in a Communist State," *New Mexico Q*, 25 (1955), 187–191.

"The Heirloom"
Hsia, C. T. "Residual Femininity: Women in Chinese Communist Fiction," in Birch, Cyril, Ed. *Chinese Communist Literature*, 160.

FRANÇOIS-RENÉ DE CHATEAUBRIAND

"Atala"
Baran, James. "Chateaubriand's 'Atala': A Lacanian *Atelier*," *Cincinnati Romance R*, 7 (1988), 51–63.
Segal, Naomi. *Narcissus and Echo . . .*, 54–58.

"René"
Segal, Naomi. *Narcissus and Echo . . .*, 58–68.

R. CHEE [ARCHIE WELLER]

"Stolen Car"
Bosse-Bearlin, Jenny. "Black-White Relations in the Contemporary Black and White Short Story in Australia," in Stummer, Peter O., Ed. *The Story Must Be Told . . .*, 164–165.

JOHN CHEEVER

"The Brigadier and the Golf Widow"
O'Hara, James E. *John Cheever* . . . , 62–64.

"The Common Day"
O'Hara, James E. *John Cheever* . . . , 139–140.

"The Country Husband"
Hipkiss, Robert A. " 'The Country Husband'—A Model Cheever Achievement," *Stud Short Fiction*, 27 (1990), 577–585.
O'Hara, James E. *John Cheever* . . . , 42–46.

"The Day the Pig Fell in the Well"
Morace, Robert A. "From Parallels to Paradise: The Lyrical Structure of Cheever's Fiction," in O'Hara, James E. *John Cheever* . . . , 140–143; rpt., expanded, *Twentieth Century Lit*, 35 (1989), 507–510.

"An Educated American Woman"
O'Hara, James E. *John Cheever* . . . , 65–67.

"The Enormous Radio"
O'Hara, James E. *John Cheever* . . . , 18–21.

"Expelled"
O'Hara, James E. *John Cheever* . . . , 4–5.

"Fall River"
O'Hara, James E. *John Cheever* . . . , 5–6.

"The Five-Forty-Eight"
Fogelman, Bruce. "A Key Pattern of Images in John Cheever's Short Fiction," *Stud Short Fiction*, 26 (1989), 471.

"Goodbye, My Brother"
Fogelman, Bruce. "A Key Pattern . . . ," 470–471.
O'Hara, James E. *John Cheever* . . . , 29–34.

"The Housebreaker of Shady Hill"
O'Hara, James E. *John Cheever* . . . , 46–49.

"In Passing"
O'Hara, James E. *John Cheever* . . . , 7–10.

"Independence Day at St. Botolph's"
O'Hara, James E. *John Cheever* . . . , 37–41.

"The Island"
O'Hara, James E. *John Cheever* . . . , 81–83.

"The Jewels of the Cabots"
O'Hara, James E. *John Cheever* . . . , 76–79.

"The Lowboy"
O'Hara, James E. *John Cheever* . . . , 52–55.

"Manila"
O'Hara, James E. *John Cheever* . . . , 16–18.

"A Miscellany of Characters That Will Not Appear" [originally "Some People, Places, and Things That Will Not Appear in My Next Novel"]
O'Hara, James E. *John Cheever* . . . , 57–63.

"O Youth and Beauty"
O'Hara, James E. *John Cheever* . . . , 34–37.

"Roseheath"
O'Hara, James E. *John Cheever* . . . , 21–23.

"The Season of Divorce"
O'Hara, James E. *John Cheever* . . . , 136–137.
Roberts, Edgar V., and Henry E. Jacobs. *Instructor's Manual* . . . , 2nd ed., 72–73.

"The Shape of a Night"
O'Hara, James E. *John Cheever* . . . , 13–14.

"Summer Theatre"
Fogelman, Bruce. "A Key Pattern . . . ," 463–465.

"The Swimmer"
Allen, William R. "Allusions to *The Great Gatsby* in Cheever's 'The Swimmer,' " *Stud Short Fiction*, 26 (1989), 289–293.
Blythe, Hal, and Charlie Sweet. "An Historical Allusion in Cheever's 'The Swimmer,' " *Stud Short Fiction*, 26 (1989), 557–559.
———. "Man-made vs. Natural Cycles: What Really Happens in 'The Swimmer,' " *Stud Short Fiction*, 27 (1990), 415–418.
Fogelman, Bruce. "A Key Pattern . . . ," 465–468.
O'Hara, James E. *John Cheever* . . . , 67–70.

"Torch Song"
O'Hara, James E. *John Cheever* . . . , 23–25.

"The Trouble of Marcie Flint"
O'Hara, James E. *John Cheever* . . . , 49–52.

"The World of Apples"
Fogelman, Bruce. "A Key Pattern . . . ," 468–470.
O'Hara, James E. *John Cheever* . . . , 72–75.

ANTON CHEKHOV

"About Love"
Freedman, John. "Narrative Technique and the Art of Story-telling in Anton Chekhov's 'Little Trilogy,' " *So Atlantic R*, 53, i (1988), 9–14; rpt. Eekman, Thomas A., Ed. *Critical Essays* . . . , 109–115.
Lindheimer, Ralph. "Chekhov's Trilogy: Variations on a Figure," in Belknap, Robert L., Ed. *Russianness* . . . , 74–93.

"At Christmas"
Waszink, Paul M. "Double Connotation in Čechov's 'At Christmas,' " *Russian, Croatian*, 28, ii (August 15, 1990), 245–276.

"The Black Monk"
Chances, Ellen B. *Conformity's Children* . . . , 143–144.
Conrad, Joseph L. "Vestiges of Romantic Gardens and Folklore Devils in Chekhov's 'Verochka,' 'The Kiss,' and 'The Black Monk,' " in Eekman, Thomas A., Ed. *Critical Essays* . . . , 84–89.

"A Dreary Story" [same as "A Boring Story," "A Dull Story," or "A Tedious Tale"]
Connolly, Julian. "The Nineteenth Century: Between Realism and Modernism, 1880–95," in Moser, Charles H., Ed. . . . *Russian Literature*, 365–366.
Engelberg, Edward. *Elegiac Fictions* . . . , 87–93.

"Gooseberries"
Freedman, John. "Narrative Technique . . . ," 7–9; rpt. Eekman, Thomas A., Ed. *Critical Essays* . . . , 107–109.
Lindheim, Ralph. "Chekhov's Trilogy . . . ," 74–93.

"Gusev"
Connolly, Julian. "The Nineteenth Century . . . ," 367–368.

"The Kiss"
Conrad, Joseph L. "Vestiges of Romantic Gardens . . . ," 81–84.

"The Lady with the Dog" [same as "The Lady with the Lapdog," "The Lady with the Pet Dog," "The Lady with the Small Dog"]
Creasman, Boyd. "Gurov's Flights of Emotion in Chekhov's 'The Lady with the Dog,' " *Stud Short Fiction*, 27 (1990), 257–260.
+Roberts, Edgar V., and Henry E. Jacobs. *Instructor's Manual* . . . , 2nd ed., 73–74.
+Smith, Virginia L. " 'The Lady with the Dog,' " in Eekman, Thomas A., Ed. *Critical Essays* . . . , 118–123.

"The Man in the Case" [same as "The Man in the Shell"]
Freedman, John. "Narrative Technique . . . ," 2–7; rpt. Eekman, Thomas A., Ed. *Critical Essays* . . . , 104–107.
Lindheim, Ralph. "Chekhov's Trilogy . . . ," 74–93.

"The Name Day" [same as "The Name-Day Party"]
Heldt, Barbara. "Men Who Give Birth: A Feminist Perspective on Russian Literature," in Kelly, Catriona, Michael Makin, and Donald Shepherd, Eds. *Discontinuous Discourses* . . . , 163.

"Verochka"
Conrad, Joseph L. "Vestiges of Romantic Gardens . . . ," 79–81.

"Ward No. 6"
Chances, Ellen B. *Conformity's Children* . . . , 144–145.
Connolly, Julian. "The Nineteenth Century . . . ," 368–369.
Stone, John. "The Wisdom of Pain: A Responsive Reading," *Lit & Medicine*, 9 (1990), 142–149.
Wolff, Sally. "The Wisdom of Pain in Chekhov's 'Ward Number Six,' " *Lit & Medicine*, 9 (1990), 134–141.

"A Woman's Kingdom"
+Jackson, Robert L. "Chekhov's 'A Woman's Kingdom': A Drama of Character and Fate," in Eekman, Thomas A., Ed. *Critical Essays* . . . , 91–102.

CHEN BAICHEN [CHEN ZENGHONG]

"A Lonely Room"
Eide, Elisabeth. "Chen Baichen," in Slupski, Zbigniew, Ed. *A Selective Guide* . . . , II, 45–46.

"Silence"
Eide, Elisabeth. "Chen Baichen," 43–45.

WILLI CHEN

"Caesar"
Harney, Steve. "Willi Chen and Carnival Nationalism in Trinidad," *J Commonwealth Lit*, 25, i (1990), 125.

"King of the Carnival"
Harney, Steve. "Willi Chen . . . ," 124.

"Lalloo's Wrath"
Harney, Steve. "Willi Chen . . . ," 126–127.

"No Pork, Cheese"
Harney, Steve. "Willi Chen . . . ," 127–128.

"Trotters"
Harney, Steve. "Willi Chen . . . ," 128–129.

GEORGE TOMKYNS CHESNEY

"The Battle of Dorking"
Panshin, Alexel, and Cory Panshin. *The World Beyond* . . . , 71–73.
Pierce, John J. *Foundations of Science Fiction* . . . , 51–52.

CHARLES W. CHESNUTT

"Cicely's Dream"
Fienberg, Lorne. "Charles W. Chesnutt's *The Wife of His Youth*: The Unveiling of the Black Storyteller," *Am Transcendental Q*, 4, N.S. (1990), 229–231.

"The Goophered Grapevine"
Filetti, Jean S. "Chesnutt's 'The Goophered Grapevine,' " *Explicator*, 48 (1990), 201–203.

"A Matter of Principle"
Fienberg, Lorne. ". . . Black Storyteller," 226–228.

"The Passing of Grandison"
Fienberg, Lorne. ". . . Black Storyteller," 231–233.

"The Sheriff's Children"
Hathaway, Heather. " 'Maybe Freedom Lies in Hating': Miscegenation and the Oedipal Conflict," in Yaeger, Patricia, and Beth Kowaleski-Wallace, Eds. *Refiguring the Father* . . . , 153–167.

"The Web of Circumstance"
Fienberg, Lorne. ". . . Black Storyteller," 233–236.

"The Wife of His Youth"
Fienberg, Lorne. ". . . Black Storyteller," 223–225.

GILBERT KEITH CHESTERTON

"The Innocence of Father Brown"
Knedlik, Janet B. "Derrida Meets Father Brown: Chestertonian 'Deconstruction' and That Harlequin 'Joy,' " in Macdonald, Michael H., and Andrew A. Tadie, Eds. *G. K. Chesterton* . . . , 273–289.

LOUISE E. CHOLLET

"Tom Lodowne"
Diffley, Kathleen. "Where My Heart Is Turning Ever: Civil War Stories and National Stability from Fort Sumter to the Centennial," *Am Lit Hist*, 2 (1990), 638–639.

KATE CHOPIN

"After the Winter"
Papke, Mary E. *Verging on the Abyss* . . . , 52–53.

"At Chénière Caminada"
Taylor, Helen. *Gender, Race, and Region* . . . , 174–175.

"At the 'Cadian Ball"
Elfenbein, Anna S. *Women on the Color Line* . . . , 135–139.

"Athénaïse"
Papke, Mary E. *Verging on the Abyss* . . . , 64–65.
Taylor, Helen. *Gender, Race, and Region* . . . , 180–182.

"Azélie"
Papke, Mary E. *Verging on the Abyss* . . . , 60–62.

"La Bella Zoraïde"
Elfenbein, Anna S. *Women on the Color Line* . . . , 131–134.

"Beyond the Bayou"
Papke, Mary E. *Verging on the Abyss* . . . , 52–53.

"Désirée's Baby"
Elfenbein, Anna S. *Women on the Color Line* . . . , 126–131.
Papke, Mary E. *Verging on the Abyss* . . . , 53–56.
Péel, Ellen. "Semiotic Subversion in 'Désirée's Baby,' " *Am Lit*, 62 (1990), 223–237.

"An Egyptian Cigarette"
Papke, Mary E. *Verging on the Abyss* . . . , 68–69.

"Her Letters"
Papke, Mary E. *Verging on the Abyss* . . . , 66–67.

"In Sabine"
Elfenbein, Anna S. *Women on the Color Line* . . . , 118–119.

"A Life Fable"
Papke, Mary E. *Verging on the Abyss* . . . , 34–36.

"Ma'ame Pélagie"
Papke, Mary E. *Verging on the Abyss* . . . , 56–59.

"A No-Account Creole"
Papke, Mary E. *Verging on the Abyss* . . . , 36–38.
Taylor, Helen. *Gender, Race, and Region* . . . , 179–180.

"Ozème's Holiday"
Elfenbein, Anna S. *Women on the Color Line* . . . , 120–121.

"A Pair of Silk Stockings"
Papke, Mary E. *Verging on the Abyss* . . . , 65–66.

"A Point at Issue"
Papke, Mary E. *Verging on the Abyss* . . . , 40–42.

"A Shameful Affair"
Elfenbein, Anna S. *Women on the Color Line* . . . , 124–125.

"The Storm"
Elfenbein, Anna S. *Women on the Color Line* . . . , 139–142.
Papke, Mary E. *Verging on the Abyss* . . . , 175–176.

"The Story of an Hour"
Papke, Mary E. *Verging on the Abyss* . . . , 62–64.

"Wise as a God"
Papke, Mary E. *Verging on the Abyss* . . . , 38–39.

CHOU LI-PO

"Guest from Peking"
Shih, C. W. "Co-operatives and Communes in Chinese Communist Fiction," in Birch, Cyril, Ed. *Chinese Communist Literature*, 201–202.

EUGENE CLANCY

"The Cleansing Tears"
Fanning, Charles. *The Irish Voice* . . . , 252–254.

CLARÍN [LEOPOLDO ALAS]

"Adios, Cordera!"
Oliver, Walter. "Clarín's 'Adios, Cordera!' as a Critical Assessment of Provincial Life and Politics," *Romance Notes*, 28, i (1987), 77–83.

"Cuervo"
González Herrán, José M. "The Structure and Meaning of 'Cuervo,' " trans. Kathleen M. March, in Valis, Noël, Ed. *"Malevolent Insemination"* . . . , 167–182.

"Las dos cajas"
Rivkin, Laura. "Clarín's Musical Ideal," in Valis, Noël, Ed. *"Malevolent Insemination"* . . . , 205–220.

"Pipá"
Rogers, Douglass M. "Language, Image, and the Thought Process in Clarín's 'Pipá,' " in Valis, Noël, Ed. *"Malevolent Insemination"* . . . , 193–204.

ARTHUR C. CLARKE

"The Nine Billion Names of God"
Huntington, John. *Rationalizing Genius* . . . , 151–153.

KATE M. CLEARY

"The Stepmother"
Fanning, Charles. *The Irish Voice* . . . , 180–181.

LUCY CLIFFORD

"The New Mother"
Schell, Heather. "Clifford's 'The New Mother' and the Menace of the Lower Classes," *Turn-of-the-Century Women*, 5, i–ii (1990), 43–47.

SIDONIE-GABRIELLE COLETTE

"Chéri"
King, Adele. *French Women Novelists* . . . , 78–79.

"The Last of Chéri"
King, Adele. *French Women Novelists* . . . , 75–78.

PEDRO-EMILIO COLL

"Borracho criollo"
Ratcliff, Dillwyn F. *Venezuelan Prose Fiction*, 198.

"Cuento del Espíritu Santo"
Ratcliff, Dillwyn F. *Venezuelan Prose Fiction*, 199–200.

"Cuento del Hijo"
Ratcliff, Dillwyn F. *Venezuelan Prose Fiction*, 200–201.

"Cuento del Padre"
Ratcliff, Dillwyn F. *Venezuelan Prose Fiction*, 198.

"Opoponax"
Ratcliff, Dillwyn F. *Venezuelan Prose Fiction*, 197–198.

RICHARD CONNELL

"The Most Dangerous Game"
Carroll, Noël. *The Philosophy of Horror*, 138.

JOSEPH CONRAD

"Amy Foster"
Krajka, Wieslaw. "The Dialogue of Cultures in Joseph Conrad's 'Amy Foster,' " *New Comparison*, 9 (1990), 149–157.

"The Black Mate"
Wollaeger, Mark A. *Joseph Conrad . . .*, 37–38.

"The End of the Tether"
Hampson, Robert. "Frazer, Conrad and the 'Truth of Primitive Passion,' " in Fraser, Robert, Ed. *Sir James Frazer . . .*, 182–183.
La Bossière, Camille R. *The Victorian "Fol Sage" . . .*, 94–97.
Rising, Catharine. *Darkness at Heart . . .*, 83–88.

"Falk"
Hampson, Robert. "Frazer, Conrad . . .," 172–173.

"Gaspar Ruiz"
Martin, W. R. "Faulkner's Pantaloon and Conrad's Gaspar Ruiz," *Conradiana*, 21 (1989), 47–51.

"Heart of Darkness"
Benson, Donald R. "Ether, Atmosphere, and the Solidarity of Men and Nature in 'Heart of Darkness,' " in Slade, Joseph W., and Judith Y. Lee, Eds. *Beyond the Two Cultures . . .*, 161–173.
Bouson, J. Brooks. *The Empathic Reader . . .*, 92–104.
Brague, Rémi. "Joseph Conrad et la dialectiquedes des Lumières: Le Mal dans 'Coeur des tenèbres,' " *Études Philosophiques*, 1 (January–March, 1990), 21–36.
Brown, Dennis. *The Modernist Self . . .*, 22–29.
Dobrinsky, Joseph. *The Artist . . .*, 1–27.
Fothergill, Anthony. *Heart of Darkness*, 102–108.
Fox, Claire. "Writing Africa with Another Alphabet: Conrad and Abish," *Conradiana*, 22 (1990), 111–118.
Goonetilleke, D. C. R. A. *Joseph Conrad . . .*, 62–93.
Hampson, Robert. "Frazer, Conrad . . .," 177–181.

Hansen, Frantz L. "Conrads clairobscur," *Kultur og Klasse*, 17, iii (1990), 48–74.
Hawthorn, Jeremy. *Joseph Conrad* . . . , 171–202.
+Karl, Frederick R. "Introduction to the *Danse Macabre*: Conrad's " 'Heart of Darkness,' " in Murfin, Ross C., Ed. *Joseph Conrad—"Heart of Darkness"* . . . , 123–136.
London, Bette. "Reading Race and Gender in Conrad's Dark Continent," *Criticism*, 31 (1989), 235–252.
Lynn, David H. *The Hero's Tale* . . . , 12–27.
Mandel, Miriam B. "Significant Patterns of Color and Animal Imagery in Conrad's 'Heart of Darkness,' " *Neophilologus*, 73 (1989), 305–319.
+Miller, J. Hillis. " 'Heart of Darkness' Revisited," in Murfin, Ross C., Ed. *Joseph Conrad—"Heart of Darkness"* . . . , 209–224.
Pecora, Vincent P. *Self and Form* . . . , 149–175.
Peters, Bradley T. "The Significance of Dream Consciousness in 'Heart of Darkness' and *Palace of the Peacocks*," *Conradiana*, 22 (1990), 127–141.
Rising, Catharine. *Darkness at Heart* . . . , 40–50.
Rosmarin, Adena. "Darkening the Reader: Reader-Response Criticism and " 'Heart of Darkness,' " in Murfin, Ross C., Ed. *Joseph Conrad—"Heart of Darkness"* . . . , 148–169.
Scheick, William J. *Fictional Structure and Ethics* . . . , 114–128.
Sedlak, Valerie F. " 'A World of Their Own': Narrative Distortions and Fictive Exemplifications, in the Portrayal of Women in 'Heart of Darkness,' " *Coll Lang Assoc J*, 32 (1989), 443–465.
Shetty, Sandhya. " 'Heart of Darkness': Out of Africa Some New Thing Rarely Comes," *J Mod Lit*, 15 (1989), 461–474.
Smith, Johanna M. " 'Too Beautiful Altogether': Patriarchal Ideology in 'Heart of Darkness,' " in Murfin, Ross C., Ed. *Joseph Conrad—"Heart of Darkness"* . . . , 179–195.
Thomas, Brook. "Preserving and Keeping Order by Killing Time in 'Heart of Darkness,' " in Murfin, Ross C., Ed. *Joseph Conrad—"Heart of Darkness"* . . . , 237–255.
Todorov, Tzvetan. "Knowledge in the Void: 'Heart of Darkness,' " trans. Walter C. Putnam, *Conradiana*, 21 (1989), 161–172.
Wollaeger, Mark A. *Joseph Conrad* . . . , 61–67.
Woodring, Carl. *Nature into Art* . . . , 209–212.
Young, Gloria. "Kurtz as Narcissistic Megalomaniac in Joseph Conrad's 'Heart of Darkness,' " in Kakouriotis, A., and R. Parkin-Gounelas, Eds. *Working Papers* . . . , 256–263.

"The Idiots"
Rising, Catharine. *Darkness at Heart* . . . , 37–39.

"Karain"
Wollaeger, Mark A. *Joseph Conrad* . . . , 42–51.

"The Lagoon"
Richardson, Donna. "Art of Darkness: Imagery in Conrad's 'The Lagoon,' " *Stud Short Fiction*, 27 (1990), 247–255.
Wollaeger, Mark A. *Joseph Conrad* . . . , 39–41.

"An Outpost of Progress"
Bock, Martin. *Crossing the Shadow-Line* . . . , 91–93.
Hawthorn, Jeremy. *Joseph Conrad* . . . , 11–17, 159–170.
Rising, Catharine. *Darkness at Heart* . . . , 39–40.
Wollaeger, Mark A. *Joseph Conrad* . . . , 24–26.

"Prince Roman"
Wollaeger, Mark A. *Joseph Conrad* . . . , 6–7.

"The Return"
Wollaeger, Mark A. *Joseph Conrad* . . . , 51–54.

"The Secret Sharer"
Bouson, J. Brooks. *The Empathic Reader* . . . , 82–92.
Dawson, Anthony B. "In the Pink: Self and Empire in 'The Secret Sharer,' " *Conradiana*, 22 (1990), 185–196.
Dobrinsky, Joseph. *The Artist* . . . , 63–76.
Goonetilleke, D. C. R. A. *Joseph Conrad* . . . , 112–117.
Hansford, James. "Closing, Enclosure and Passage in 'The Secret Sharer,' " *Conradian*, 15, i (1990), 30–55.
Rising, Catharine. *Darkness at Heart* . . . , 118–121.
Santana, Pedro. " 'The Secret Sharer': Una narración triumfal y melancólica," in *Actas de las I jornadas de lengua* . . . , 75–82.
White, James F. "The Third Theme in 'The Secret Sharer,' " *Conradiana*, 21 (1989), 37–46.
Woodring, Carl. *Nature into Art* . . . , 212–214.

"The Shadow Line"
Bock, Martin. *Crossing the Shadow-Line* . . . , 104–106.
Goonetilleke, D. C. R. A. *Joseph Conrad* . . . , 117–122.
Rising, Catharine. *Darkness at Heart* . . . , 148–155.

"A Smile of Fortune"
Erdinast-Vulcan, Daphna. " 'A Smile of Fortune' and the Romantic Paradox," *Conradian*, 15, i (1990), 1–11.

"The Tale"
Hawthorn, Jeremy. *Joseph Conrad* . . . , 261–268.

"Typhoon"
Bock, Martin. *Crossing the Shadow-Line* . . . , 97–99.
Chon, Soo-Young. " 'Typhoon': Silver Dollars and Stars," *Conradiana*, 22 (1990), 25–43.
Goonetilleke, D. C. R. A. *Joseph Conrad* . . . , 105–112.
Hawthorn, Jeremy. *Joseph Conrad* . . . , 221–235.
Rising, Catharine. *Darkness at Heart* . . . , 79–83.
Wollaeger, Mark A. *Joseph Conrad* . . . , 123–124.

"Youth"
Lynn, David H. *The Hero's Tale* . . . , 8–12.
Rising, Catharine. *Darkness at Heart* . . . , 76–79.
+Roberts, Edgar V., and Henry E. Jacobs. *Instructor's Manual* . . . , 2nd ed., 74–76.

BENJAMIN CONSTANT

"Adolphe"
Segal, Naomi. *Narcissus and Echo* . . . , 68–84.
Wégimont, Marie A. "Constant's 'Adolphe,' " *Explicator*, 48 (1990), 182–183.

BETTY COON

"Diary"
Yahnke, Robert E., and Richard M. Eastman. *Aging in Literature* . . . , 38–39.

ROBERT COOVER

"Aesop's Forest"
Chenetier, Marc. "Ideas of Order at Delphi," in Ziegler, Heide, Ed. *Facing Texts* . . . , 84–108.

"Charlie in the House of Rue"
Puche, Thomas. "The Cackle of Fiction: 'Charlie in the House of Rue' and the Question of Comic Form," *Delta*, 28 (June, 1989), 83–95.

"Klee Dead"
Saltzman, Arthur M. *Design of Darkness* . . . , 14–16.

"The Leper's Helix"
Taft-Kaufman, Jill. "Creating the Process of Creating in Robert Coover's 'The Leper's Helix,' " *Lit Performance*, 8, ii (1988), 66–75.

"The Magic Poker"
Stengel, Wayne B. "Robert Coover's 'Writing Degree Zero': 'The Magic Poker,' " *Arizona Q*, 45, i (1989), 101–110.

"Panel Game"
Saltzman, Arthur M. *Design of Darkness* . . . , 13–14.

JULIO CORTÁZAR

"After Breakfast"
Kason, Nancy M. "El juego y la ambigüedad en 'Después del almuerzo,' " in Fernández Jiménez, Juan, José J. Labrador Herraiz, and L. Teresa Valdivieso, Eds. *Estudios en homenaje* . . . , 341–346.

"Apocalypse at Solentiname"
Muñoz, Willy O. "Julio Cortázar: Vertices de una figura comprometida," *Revista Iberoamericana*, 56 (1990), 547–550.
Zamora, Lois P. *Writing the Apocalypse* . . . , 86–88.

"Axolotl"

Ortega, Bertín. "Cortázar: 'Axolotl' y la cinta de Moebius," *Nuevo Texto Crítico*, 2 (1989), 135–140.

"La Banda"

Morello-Frosch, Marta. "La Banda de los Otros: política fantástica en un cuento de Julio Cortázar," in Lerner, Lia S., and Isaís Lerner, Eds. *Homenaje a Ana María Barrenchea*, 497–502.

"Blow-Up" [originally "Las babas del diable"]

Muñoz, Willy O. "Julio Cortázar . . . ," 540–547.

"The Condemned Door"

Stavans, Ilán. "Cortázar: 'La puerta condenana' y los fantasmas," *Plural*, 204 (September, 1988), 86–90.

"Continuity of Parks"

Lagmanovich, David. "Estrategias del cuento breve en Cortázar: Un paseo por 'Continuidad de los parques,' " *Explicación de Textos Literarios*, 17, i (1989), 177–187.

"Diario para un cuento"

Cunha-Giabbai, Gloria da. "Cortázar y su diario de amor, de locura y de muerte," in Fernández Jiménez, Juan, José J. Labrador Herraiz, and L. Teresa Valdivieso, Eds. *Estudios en homenaje . . .* , 123–130.

"End of the Game"

Cavallari, Hector Mario. "Julio Cortázar: Todos los juegos el juego," *Explicación de Textos Literarios*, 17, i (1989), 111–120.

"The Gates of Heaven"

Lange-Churion, Pedro. "Lo fantástico en 'Las puertas del cielo' de Julio Cortázar: Literatura de evasión semantica," *Cincinnati Romance R*, 9 (1990), 111–121.

"The Isle at Noon"

González-Cruz, Luis F. "Disruptive Tensions: Ego and Shadow in Julio Cortázar's Narrative," *Hispanic J*, 2, i (1990), 149–151.

"Letters from Mama"

Pucciarelli de Colantonio, Graciela. "Los símbolos de la culpa en 'Cartas de Mamá,' " *Letras*, 19–20 (May, 1988—August, 1989), 79–90.

"The Night Face Up"

Wight, Doris T. "Fantastic Labyrinths in Fictions by Borges, Cortázar, and Robbe-Grillet," *Comparatist*, 13 (May, 1989), 29–30.

"The Pursuer"

Jiménez, Antonio. "El sensualismo y 'la otra realidad' en 'El perseguidor' de Cortázar," *Mester*, 19, i (1990), 49–54.

Lazarte Dishman, Amalia. "Otro enfoque a 'El perseguidor' de Julio Cortázar," *Alba de América*, 8, xiv–xv (1990), 187–202.

Zamora, Lois P. *Writing the Apocalypse . . .* , 78–82.

"Recortes de prensa"
Gertel, Zunilda. "Lecciones de mirar y ver: Texto e ideología en la narrativa de Cortázar," *Revista de Occidente*, 102 (November, 1989), 75–86.

"Return Trip Tango"
Yovanovich, Gordana. "Character Development and the Short Story: Julio Cortázar's 'Return Trip Tango,' " *Stud Short Fiction*, 27 (1990), 545–552.

"Reunion"
Zamora, Lois P. *Writing the Apocalypse* . . . , 85–86.

"Second Time Around"
Zamora, Lois P. *Writing the Apocalypse* . . . , 88–89.

"Torito"
Alegría, Fernando. "El 'Torito': Pasión y descanso," *Explicación de Textos Literarios*, 17, i (1989), 412–422.

"We Love Glenda So Much"
Paulino, Maria das Graças Rodriguez. "A Perfeição Mortal," *Cadernos de Lingüística*, 7 (December, 1985), 125–132.
Zamora, Lois P. *Writing the Apocalypse* . . . , 89–93.

BERNARDO COUTO CASTILLO

"Asesino?"
Pavón, Alfredo. "De la violencia en los modernistas," in Pavón, Alfredo, Ed. *Paquette: Cuento* . . . , 81–82.

"Blanco y rojo"
Pavón, Alfredo. "De la violencia . . . ," 83–84.

"Lo inevitable"
Pavón, Alfredo. "De la violencia . . . ," 79–80.

"Una obsesión"
Pavón, Alfredo. "De la violencia . . . ," 78–79.

STEPHEN CRANE

"And If He Wills, We Must Die"
Wolford, Chester L. *Stephen Crane* . . . , 78.

"The Blue Hotel"
Church, Joseph. "The Determined Stranger in Stephen Crane's 'Blue Hotel,' " *Stud Hum*, 16, ii (1989), 99–110.
Gross, David S. "The Western Stories of Stephen Crane," *J Am Culture*, 11, iv (1988), 19–20.
Halliburton, David. *The Color of the Sky* . . . , 206–226.
Petite, Joseph. "Expressionism and Stephen Crane's 'The Blue Hotel,' " *J Evolutionary Psych*, 10 (1989), 322–327.
Wolford, Chester L. *Stephen Crane* . . . , 30–34.

ARTURO CROCE

"El cerro iluminado"
Ramos, Elías A. *El cuento venezolano* . . . , 24–25.

"Un simple fantasma"
Ramos, Elías A. *El cuento venezolano* . . . , 27–28.

"La tierra de todos"
Ramos, Elías A. *El cuento venezolano* . . . , 26–27.

RONALD ANTHONY CROSS

"The Heavenly Blue Answer"
Franklin, H. Bruce. "The Vietnam War as American Science Fiction and Fantasy," *Sci-Fiction Stud*, 17 (1990), 350.

ANDRES CRISTOBAL CRUZ

"White Wall"
Dimalanta, Ophelia A. "City Fiction: Manila, a Way of Life and Art," in Villacorta, Wilfrido V., Isagani R. Cruz, and Ma. Lourdes Brillantes, Eds. *Manila* . . . , 283–284.

SUSAN DAITCH

"The Colorist"
Siegle, Robert. *Suburban Ambush* . . . , 357–358.

LÉON-GONTRAN DAMAS

"On a Tune for a Guitar"
+Jones, Bridget. "Léon Damas as Storyteller: 'Sur un air de guitare,' " in Warner, Keith Q., Ed. *Critical Perspectives* . . . , 161–166.

RUBÉN DARÍO

"La canción del oro"
Szmetan, Ricardo. "El escritor frente a la sociedad en algunos cuentos de Rubén Darío," *Revista Iberoamericana*, 55 (1989), 423.

"The Nymph"
Brownlow, Jeanne P. "La ironía estética de Darío: Humor y discrepancia en los cuentos de *Azul*," *Revista Iberoamericana*, 55 (1989), 388–389.
Franco, Adolfo M. "Transmutación de Rubén Darío en el cuento 'La ninfa,' " in Paolini, Gilbert, Ed. *La Chispa '89* . . . , 119–128.

"El pájaro azul"
Szmetan, Ricardo. "El escritor . . . ," 421–422.

"The Palace of the Sun"
Brownlow, Jeanne P. "La ironía estética . . . ," 380.

"El Rey Burgués"
Szmetan, Ricardo. "El escritor . . . ," 420–421.

"El sátiro sordo"
Szmetan, Ricardo. "El escritor . . . ," 421.

"El velo de la reina Mab"
Szmetan, Ricardo. "El escritor . . . ," 422.

ALPHONSE DAUDET

"La Chèvre de M. Seguin"
Reid, Ian. "Destabilizing Frames for Story," in Lohafer, Susan, and Jo Ellyn Clarey, Eds. *Short Story Theory* . . . , 299–310.

"La Légende de l'homme à la cervelle d'or"
Grant, Lois. "Une Analyse textuelle de 'La Légende de l'homme à la cervelle d'or' d'Alphonse Daudet," *Francofonia*, 9 (Spring, 1989), 17–36.

GUY DAVENPORT

"The Antiquities of Elis"
Olsen, Lance. *Circus of the Mind* . . . , 52–53.

"Apples and Pearls"
Arias-Misson, Alain. "Erotic Ear, Amoral Eye," *Chicago R*, 35, iii (1986), 68–70.

"Au Tombeau de Charles Fournier"
Olsen, Lance. *Circus of the Mind* . . . , 48–50.

"C. Musonius Rufus"
Olsen, Lance. *Circus of the Mind* . . . , 44–45.

"A Field of Snow on a Slope of the Rosenberg"
Olsen, Lance. *Circus of the Mind* . . . , 53–54.

"Fifty-Seven Views of Fujiyama"
Arias-Misson, Alain. "Erotic Ear . . . ," 67–68.

"The Haile Selassie Funeral Train"
Olsen, Lance. *Circus of the Mind* . . . , 50–51.

"Ithaka"
Olsen, Lance. *Circus of the Mind* . . . , 51–52.

"John Charles Tapner"
Olsen, Lance. *Circus of the Mind* . . . , 47–48.

"The Jules Verne Steam Balloon"
Schöpp, Joseph C. " 'Perfect Landscape with Pastoral Figures': Guy Davenport's Danish Eclogue a la Fourier," in Ziegler, Heide, Ed. *Facing Texts* . . . , 128–139.

"The Richard Nixon Freischutz Rag"
Olsen, Lance. *Circus of the Mind* . . . , 42–44.

"The Wooden Dove of Archytas"
Olsen, Lance. *Circus of the Mind* . . . , 46–47.

AMPARO DÁVILA

"Detrás de la reja"
Frouman-Smith, Erica. "Patterns of Female Entrapment and Escape in Three Short Stories by Amparo Dávila," *Chasqui*, 18, ii (1989), 52–54.
———. "Descent into Madness: Women in Short Stories of Amparo Dávila," *Discurso literario*, 7, i (1989), 201–211.

"El huésped"
Frouman-Smith, Erica. "Patterns . . . ," 51–52.

"La señorita Julia"
Frouman-Smith, Erica. "Descent into Madness . . . ," 203–206.

"El última verano"
Frouman-Smith, Erica. "Patterns . . . ," 54.

MATILDE DAVÍN

"El girar de un girasol"
Ramos, Elías A. *El cuento venezolano* . . . , 124.

JACK DAVIS

"Pay Back"
Bosse-Bearlin, Jenny. "Black-White Relations in the Contemporary Black and White Short Story in Australia," in Stummer, Peter O., Ed. *The Story Must Be Told* . . . , 166.

LYDIA DAVIS

"The Letter"
Perloff, Marjorie. "Fiction as Language Game: The Hermeneutic Parables of Lydia Davis and Maxine Chernoff," in Friedman, Ellen G., and Miriam Fuchs, Eds. *Breaking the Sequence* . . . , 208–211.

"Once a Very Stupid Man"
Perloff, Marjorie. "Fiction as Language Game . . . ," 211–212.

"Story"
Perloff, Marjorie. "Fiction as Language Game . . . ," 206–208.

REBECCA HARDING DAVIS

"The Harmonists"
Pfaelzer, Jean. "The Sentimental Promise and the Utopian Myth: Rebecca Harding Davis's 'The Harmonists' and Louisa May Alcott's 'Transcendental Wild Oats,' " *Am Transcendental Q*, 3, N.S. (1989), 87–91.

"Life in the Iron Mills"
Harris, Sharon M. "Rebecca Harding Davis: From Romanticism to Realism," *Am Lit Realism*, 21 (1989), 4–20.

DAZAI OSAMU

"Chance"
Wolfe, Alan. *Suicidal Narrative* . . . , 207–209.

"The Courtesy Call"
Wolfe, Alan. *Suicidal Narrative* . . . , 188–192.

RALPH DE BOISSIÈRE

"Miss Winter"
Sander, Reinhard W. *The Trinidad Awakening* . . . , 117–118.

"The Old Year Passes"
Sander, Reinhard W. *The Trinidad Awakening* . . . , 54–55.

"The Woman on the Pavement"
Sander, Reinhard W. *The Trinidad Awakening* . . . , 117–118.

L. SPRAGUE DeCAMP

"Living Fossil"
Panshin, Alexel, and Cory Panshin. *The World Beyond* . . . , 291–292.

MICHAEL J. DEEBLE

"Yacua: A West Indian Romance"
Sander, Reinhard W. *The Trinidad Awakening* . . . , 53–54.

CONSTANCE DEJONG

"I.T.I.L.O.E."
Siegle, Robert. *Suburban Ambush* . . . , 151.

"Twice Told Tales"
Siegle, Robert. *Suburban Ambush* . . . , 134–135.

POLI DÉLANO

"La misma esquina del mundo"
Castillo de Berchenko, Adriana. "La llaga del exilio en un relato de Poli Délano," *Ventanal*, 9 (1985), 13–26.

HÉCTOR DE LIMA

"Discothèque"
Ramos, Elías A. *El cuento venezolano* . . . , 41–42.

"Pasa raya y suma"
Ramos, Elías A. *El cuento venezolano* . . . , 136.

LESTER DEL REY

"Helen O'Loy"
Huntington, John. *Rationalizing Genius* . . . , 95–100.

"Kindness"
Panshin, Alexel, and Cory Panshin. *The World Beyond* . . . , 615–617.

RICK DE MARINIS

"Pagans"
Pope, Dan. "A Different Kind of Post-Modernism," *Gettysburg R*, 3 (1990), 662–663.

SHASHI DESHPANDE

"The Intrusion"
Riemenschneider, Dieter. "Indian Women Writing in English: The Short Story," in Stummer, Peter O., Ed. *The Story Must Be Told* . . . , 173.

ABRAHAM DE VRIES

"The Mice"
Trump, Martin. "Afrikaner Literature and the South African Liberation Struggle," *J Commonwealth Lit*, 25, i (1990), 55–56.

CARLOS DÍAZ DUFOO

"Una duda"
Pavón, Alfredo. "De la violencia en los modernistas," in Pavón, Alfredo, Ed. *Paquette: Cuento* . . . , 69–70.

"Por qué la mató"
Pavón, Alfredo. "De la violencia . . . ," 66–69.
"Un problema fin de siglo"
Pavón, Alfredo. "De la violencia . . . ," 71–73.

RAMÓN DÍAZ SÁNCHEZ

"El caminante"
Ramos, Elías A. *El cuento venezolano* . . . , 63–64.
"La virgen no tiene cara"
Ramos, Elías A. *El cuento venezolano* . . . , 62–63.

GUSTAVO DÍAZ SOLÍS

"Arco secreto"
Ramos, Elías A. *El cuento venezolano* . . . , 132–133.

CHARLES DICKENS

"The Child's Story"
Newcomb, Mildred. *The Imagined World* . . . , 89–91.
"A Christmas Tree"
Newcomb, Mildred. *The Imagined World* . . . , 91–97.
"The Haunted House"
Newcomb, Mildred. *The Imagined World* . . . , 169–170.
"Mugby Junction"
Newcomb, Mildred. *The Imagined World* . . . , 74–76.
"The Signalman"
Day, Gary. "Figuring Out the Signalman: Dickens and the Ghost Story," in Bloom, Clive, Brian Docherty, Jane Gibb, and Keith Shand, Eds. *Nineteenth-Century Suspense* . . . , 26–45.
Greenman, David J. "Dickens's Ultimate Achievement in the Ghost Story: 'To Be Taken with a Grain of Salt' and 'The Signalman,' " *Dickensian*, 85, i (1989), 43–47.
"To Be Taken with a Grain of Salt"
Greenman, David J. "Dickens's Ultimate Achievement . . . ," 41–43.

ISAK DINESEN [BARONESS KAREN BLIXEN]

"Babette's Feast"
Bassoff, Bruce. "Babette Can Cook: Life and Art in Three Stories by Isak Dinesen," *Stud Short Fiction*, 27 (1990), 386–389.
"The Cardinal's First Tale"
Aiken, Susan H. *Isak Dinesen* . . . , 11–25.

"The Deluge at Norderney"
Aiken, Susan H. *Isak Dinesen . . .*, 84–111.

"The Diver"
Bassoff, Bruce. "Babette Can Cook . . .," 385.

"The Dreamers"
Aiken, Susan H. "Isak Dinesen and the Poetics of Displacement," in Broe, Mary L., and Angela Ingram, Eds. *Women's Writing in Exile*, 116–131.
———. *Isak Dinesen . . .*, 50–62.

"The Immortal Story"
Aiken, Susan H. *Isak Dinesen . . .*, 62–63.

"The Invincible Slave Owners"
Yacobi, Tamar. "Dimensions of Space: Isak Dinesen," in Bauer, Roger, and Douwe Fokkema, Eds. *Proceedings of the XIIth Congress . . .*, III, 83–84.

"The Monkey"
Aiken, Susan H. *Isak Dinesen . . .*, 133–153.

"The Old Chevalier"
Aiken, Susan H. *Isak Dinesen . . .*, 112–132.

"The Poet"
Aiken, Susan H. *Isak Dinesen . . .*, 187–192.

"The Ring"
Bassoff, Bruce. "Babette Can Cook . . .," 385–386.

"The Roads Round Pisa"
Aiken, Susan H. *Isak Dinesen . . .*, 154–175.
Gallagher, Susan V., and Roger Lundin. *Literature Through the Eyes of Faith*, 96–97.

"Sorrow-Acre"
Aiken, Susan H. *Isak Dinesen . . .*, 251–253.
Larsen, Svend E. "Spaces in Isak Dinesen: 'Sorrow-Acre,' " in Bauer, Roger, and Douwe Fokkema, Eds. *Proceedings of the XIIth Congress . . .*, III, 86–91.

"The Supper at Elsinore"
Aiken, Susan H. *Isak Dinesen . . .*, 176–185.

"The Young Man with a Carnation"
Yacobi, Tamar. "Dimensions of Space . . .," 79–80.

DING LING [TING LING]

"Adolph the Poet"
Chang Jun-mei. *Ting Ling . . .*, 67.

"The Affair in East Village"
Barlow, Tani E. " 'Thoughts on March 8' and the Literary Expression of Ding Ling's Feminism," in *La Littérature chinoise . . .*, 135.

"The Diary of Miss Sophie"
Feuerwerker, Yi-tsi Mei. "Ding Ling," in Slupski, Zbigniew, Ed. *A Selective Guide* . . . , II, 47–48.

"Enlisted"
Chang Jun-mei. *Ting Ling* . . . , 79.

"In the Hospital"
Barlow, Tani E. " 'Thoughts on March 8' . . . ," 141–142.
Chang Jun-mei. *Ting Ling* . . . , 81–84.

"Meng Ko"
Chang Jun-mei. *Ting Ling* . . . , 25–28.

"New Faith"
Barlow, Tani E. " 'Thoughts on March 8' . . . ," 135.

"Night"
Chang Jun-mei. *Ting Ling* . . . , 80–81.
Kubin, Wolfgang. "Ding Ling's Yan'an Short Story 'The Night' (1940)," in *La Littérature chinoise* . . . , 147–153.

"The Unfired Bullet"
Harnisch, Thomas. "Ding Ling," in Slupski, Zbigniew, Ed. *A Selective Guide* . . . , II, 51.

"Water"
Anderson, Marston. *The Limits* . . . , 184–187.

"When I Was in Xia Village"
Barlow, Tani E. " 'Thoughts on March 8' . . . ," 136.
Chang Jun-mei. *Ting Ling* . . . , 79–80.
Harnisch, Thomas. "Ding Ling," 54–55.

ALFRED DÖBLIN

"Die Ermurdung einer Butterblume"
Huguet, Louis. "Alfred Döblin: Etudiant a Fribourg-en-Brisgau (1904–1905): Un Episode de sa vie sentimentale ou comment lire la nouvelle *L'Assassinat d'une renconcule*," *Recherches Germaniques*, 16 (1986), 119–146.

RICHARD DOKEY

"The Autumn of Henry Simpson"
Yahnke, Robert E., and Richard M. Eastman. *Aging in Literature* . . . , 39.

"The Teacher"
Yahnke, Robert E., and Richard M. Eastman. *Aging in Literature* . . . , 39–40.

STEPHEN R. DONALDSON

"The First Chronicles of Thomas Covenant"
Senior, W. A. "The Significance of Names: Mythopoesis in 'The First Chronicles of Thomas Covenant,' " *Extrapolation*, 31 (1990), 258–269.

FYODOR DOSTOEVSKY

"The Double"
Breger, Louis. *Dostoevsky* . . . , 119–126.
Gasperette, David. " 'The Double': Dostoevskij's Self-Effacing Narrative," *Slavic & East European J*, 33 (1989), 217–234.
Rosenthal, Richard J. "Dostoevsky's Experiment with Projective Mechanisms and the Theft of Identity in 'The Double,' " in Rancour-Laferriere, Daniel, Ed. *Russian Literature* . . . , 59–88.

"The Eternal Husband"
Breger, Louis. *Dostoevsky* . . . , 79–80.

"The Grand Inquisitor"
Lynch, Michael F. *Creative Revolt* . . . , 152–153.
Swediuk-Cheyne, Helen. "Dostoevsky's Grand Inquisitor and Schiller's Marquis Posa: Philanthropists or Tyrants?" *Germano-Slavica*, 6 (1990), 299–309.

"A Nasty Tale" [same as "A Disgraceful Affair"]
Breger, Louis. *Dostoevsky* . . . , 164–165.

"Notes from Underground"
Bouson, J. Brooks. *The Empathic Reader* . . . , 33–50.
Breger, Louis. *Dostoevsky* . . . , 181–183.
Chances, Ellen B. *Conformity's Children* . . . , 96–98.
Dumoulié, Camille. "La Littérature dans le souterrain," in Bauer, Roger, and Douwe Fokkema, Eds. *Proceedings of the XIIth Congress* . . . , III, 269–274.
Gunn, Judith. *Dostoevsky* . . . , 89–91.
McElroy, Bernard. . . . *Modern Grotesque*, 22–29.
Murav, Harriet. "Dora and the Underground Man," in Rancour-Laferriere, Daniel, Ed. *Russian Literature* . . . , 417–430.

"The Peasant Marey"
Breger, Louis. *Dostoevsky* . . . , 148–150.
Rice, James L. "Psychoanalysis of 'Peasant Marej': Some Residual Problems," in Rancour-Laferriere, Daniel, Ed. *Russian Literature* . . . , 245–261.

ELLEN DOUGLAS

"On the Lake"
Broughton, Panthea R., and Susan M. Williams. "Ellen Douglas," in Inge, Tonette B., Ed. *Southern Women Writers* . . . , 54–55.

FREDERICK DOUGLASS

"The Heroic Slave"
Yarborough, Richard. "Race, Violence, and Manhood: The Masculine Ideal in Frederick Douglass's 'The Heroic Slave,' " in Sundquist, Eric J., Ed. *Frederick Douglass* . . . , 168–188.

ARTHUR CONAN DOYLE

"The Adventure of Charles Augustus Milverton"
Morris, Virginia B. *Double Jeopardy* . . . , 144–146.

"The Adventure of the Copper Beeches"
Wein, Richard A. "The Real Mystery of 'The Copper Beeches,' " *Baker Street J*, 39, iv (1989), 219–222.

"The Adventure of the Dancing Men"
Pearce, Barbara. "Holmes Connects with an Infamous Chicagoan," *Baker Street J*, 39, iv (1989), 223–225.

"The Adventure of the Empty House"
Caplan, Richard M. "Why Coal-Tar Derivatives at Montpellier?" *Baker Street J*, 39, i (1989), 29–33.
Farrell, Thomas J. "Deconstructing Moriarty: False Armageddon at the Reichenbach," in Walker, Ronald G., and June M. Frazer, Eds. *The Cunning Craft* . . . , 61–64.

"The Adventure of the Speckled Band"
Pratte, Pierce. "The Uncelebrated Accomplice of the Speckled Band," *Baker Street J*, 40, iii (1990), 144–148.
Hennessy, Rosemary, and Rajeswari Mohan. "The Construction of Woman in Three Popular Texts of Empire: Towards a Critique of Materialist Feminism," *Textual Practice*, 3 (1989), 329–337.

"The Case of the Lady Sannox"
Showalter, Elaine. *Sexual Anarchy* . . . , 134, 136–137.

"The Final Problem"
Farrell, Thomas J. "Deconstructing Moriarty . . . ," 55–61.

"The Musgrave Ritual"
Trodd, Anthea. *Domestic Crimes* . . . , 46–47.

"The Problem at Thor Bridge"
Maginn, Diane. "Suicide Disguised as Murder: A Munchausen-Related Event at Thor Bridge," *Baker Street J*, 39, i (1989), 13–15.

"Silver Blaze"
Bengtsson, Hans-Uno. " 'And the Calculation Is a Simple One,' " *Baker Street J*, 39, iv (1989), 232–236.

LEON DRISKELL

"Dun-Roving"
Arnold, Edwin T. "Falling Apart and Staying Together: Bobbie Ann Mason and Leon Driskell Explore the State of the Modern Family," *Appalachian J*, 12, ii (1985), 140.

"A Miss Is as Good as a Mile"
Arnold, Edwin T. "Falling Apart . . . ," 140–141.

"That'll Be the Day"
Arnold, Edwin T. "Falling Apart . . . ," 140.

ANNETTE VON DROSTE-HÜLSHOFF

"Die Judenbuche"
Guthrie, John. *Annette von Droste-Hülshoff* . . . , 78–83.

DUANMU HONGLIANG [CAO JINGPING]

"Fengling Ferry"
Ashley, Derek. "Duanmu Hongliang," in Slupski, Zbigniew, Ed. *A Selective Guide* . . . , II, 61.

"Hatred"
Ashley, Derek. "Duanmu Hongliang," 60.

"Little Qing"
Ashley, Derek. "Duanmu Hongliang," 62.

"Snail Valley"
Ashley, Derek. "Duanmu Hongliang," 61–62.

"Under the Yoke"
Ashley, Derek. "Duanmu Hongliang," 62.

ALICE DUNBAR-NELSON

"The Pearl in the Oyster"
Hull, Gloria T. "Shaping Contradictions: Alice Dunbar-Nelson and the Black Creole Experience," *New Orleans R*, 15, i (1988), 35–36.

"The Stones of the Village"
Hull, Gloria T. "Shaping Contradictions . . . ," 36–37.

LORD DUNSANY [EDWARD JOHN MORETON DRAX PLUNKETT]

"Bethmoora"
Joshi, S. T. *The Weird Tale*, 52–53.

"Darwin Superseded"
Joshi, S. T. *The Weird Tale*, 77–78.

"The Ghost in the Corridor"
Joshi, S. T. *The Weird Tale*, 83–84.

"The Hashish Man"
Joshi, S. T. *The Weird Tale*, 52–53.

"Jetsam"
Joshi, S. T. *The Weird Tale*, 49–50.

"The Raft-Builders"
Joshi, S. T. *The Weird Tale*, 76–77.

"The Sorrow of Search"
Joshi, S. T. *The Weird Tale*, 50–51.

MARGUERITE DURAS [MARGUERITE DONADIEU]

"Moderato cantabile"
Hill, Leslie. "Marguerite Duras: Sexual Difference and Tales of Apocalypse," *Mod Lang R*, 84 (1989), 605–614.

FRIEDRICH DÜRRENMATT

"Abu Chanifa and Anan ben David"
Whitton, Kenneth S. *Dürrenmatt* . . . , 80–82.

"Christmas"
Pickar, Gertrud B. " 'Kalte Grotesken': Walser, Aichinger, and Dürrenmatt and the Kafka Legacy," in Haymes, Edward R., Ed. *Crossings-Kreuzungen* . . . , 125.
Whitton, Kenneth S. *Dürrenmatt* . . . , 8–9.

"Dark of the Moon"
Whitton, Kenneth S. *Dürrenmatt* . . . , 88–89.

"The Director of the Theatre"
Whitton, Kenneth S. *Dürrenmatt* . . . , 14–15.

"The Dog"
Whitton, Kenneth S. *Dürrenmatt* . . . , 22–23.

"The Dying of Pythias"
Whitton, Kenneth S. *Dürrenmatt* . . . , 84–85.

"From the Papers of a Caretaker"
Whitton, Kenneth S. *Dürrenmatt* . . . , 20–21.

"Mister X Takes a Holiday"
Whitton, Kenneth S. *Dürrenmatt* . . . , 55–56.

"The Old Man"
Whitton, Kenneth S. *Dürrenmatt* . . . , 12.

"Picture of Sisyphus"
Whitton, Kenneth S. *Dürrenmatt* . . . , 13–14.

"Pilatus"
Whitton, Kenneth S. *Dürrenmatt* . . . , 17–18.

"The Rebel"
Whitton, Kenneth S. *Dürrenmatt* . . . , 90–91.

"Smithy"
Whitton, Kenneth S. *Dürrenmatt* . . . , 82–84.

"The Son"
Whitton, Kenneth S. *Dürrenmatt* . . . , 11.

"Staying in a Small Town"
Whitton, Kenneth S. *Dürrenmatt* . . . , 55.

"The Torturer"
Pickar, Gertrud B. " 'Kalte Grotesken' . . . ," 125–126.
Whitton, Kenneth S. *Dürrenmatt* . . . , 9–11.

"The Town"
Whitton, Kenneth S. *Dürrenmatt* . . . , 19–20.

"The Trap"
Whitton, Kenneth S. *Dürrenmatt* . . . , 15–17.

"The Tunnel"
Whitton, Kenneth S. *Dürrenmatt* . . . , 23–25.

"The Winter War in Tibet"
Whitton, Kenneth S. *Dürrenmatt* . . . , 86–88.

JORGE EDWARDS

"La experienca"
Cortinez, Carlos. "El estallido del debil, en 'La experienca' de Jorge Edwards," *Revista Chilena Literatura*, 35 (1990), 135–140.

GEORGE EGERTON

"A Cross-Line"
Showalter, Elaine. *Sexual Anarchy* . . . , 156–157.

"An Empty Frame"
Showalter, Elaine. *Sexual Anarchy* . . . , 65–66.

ALBERT EHRENSTEIN

"Dezembergang"
White, Alfred D. "Albert Ehrenstein's Short Stories: Are They Autobiographical?" *Germ Life & Letters*, 42 (1989), 372.

"Mitgefühl"
White, Alfred D. "Albert Ehrenstein's Short Stories . . . ," 371–372.

"Tai-gin"
White, Alfred D. "Albert Ehrenstein's Short Stories . . . ," 372–373.

"Tututsch"
White, Alfred D. "Albert Ehrenstein's Short Stories . . . ," 369–371.

"241"
White, Alfred D. "Albert Ehrenstein's Short Stories . . . ," 371.

"Wodianer"
White, Alfred D. "Albert Ehrenstein's Short Stories . . . ," 374.

JOSEPH VON EICHENDORFF

"The Marble Statue"
Beller, Manfred. "Narziss und Venus: Klassische Mythologie und romanische Allegorie in Eichendorffs Novelle 'Das Marmorbild,' " *Euphorion*, 62 (1968), 117–142.
McGlathery, James M. "Magic and Desire in Eichendorff's 'Das Marmorbild,' " *Germ Life & Letters*, 42 (1989), 257–268.
Pikulik, Lothar. "Die Mythisierung des Geschlechtstiebes in Eichendorffs 'Das Marmorbild,' " *Euphorion*, 71 (1977), 128–140.
Radner, Lawrence. "Eichendorff's 'Marmorbild': 'Götterdämerung' and Deception," *Monatshefte*, 52 (1960), 183–188.

GEORGE ELIOT [MARY ANN EVANS]

"Amos Barton" [same as "The Sad Fortunes of Amos Barton"]
Jumeau, Alain. "Images de la femme dans les *Scenes of Clerical Life* de George Eliot," *Cahiers Victoriens & Edouardiens*, 31 (April, 1990), 54–55.
Norton, Alexandra M. "The Seeds of Fiction: George Eliot's *Scenes of Clerical Life*," *J Narrative Technique*, 19 (1989), 217–220.

"Janet's Repentance"
Jumeau, Alain. "Images de la femme . . . ," 57–59.
Morris, Virginia B. *Double Jeopardy* . . . , 74–75.
Norton, Alexandra M. "The Seeds of Fiction . . . ," 225–231.

"Mr. Gilfil's Love Story"
Jumeau, Alain. "Images de la femme . . . ," 55–57.
Morris, Virginia B. *Double Jeopardy* . . . , 72–74.
Norton, Alexandra M. "The Seeds of Fiction . . . ," 220–225.

STANLEY ELKIN

"Among the Witnesses"
Dougherty, David C. *Stanley Elkin*, 133.

"The Bailbondsman"
Dougherty, David C. *Stanley Elkin*, 114–117.
LeClair, Thomas. "The Obsessional Fiction of Stanley Elkin," *Contemp Lit*, 16 (1975), 161–162.
Wilde, Alan. *Horizons of Assent* . . . , 129–132.

"The Condominium"
Danon-Boileau, Laurent. "Declinasion du non," *Delta*, 20 (February, 1985), 111–125.
Dougherty, David C. *Stanley Elkin*, 120–121.

"The Conventional Wisdom"
Dougherty, David C. *Stanley Elkin*, 123–125.

"Criers and Kibitzers, Kibitzers and Criers"
Dougherty, David C. *Stanley Elkin*, 129–130.

"I Look Out for Ed Wolfe"
Dougherty, David C. *Stanley Elkin*, 130–132.

"In the Alley"
Dougherty, David C. *Stanley Elkin*, 132–133.

"The Making of Ashenden"
Dougherty, David C. *Stanley Elkin*, 117–120.
Edinger, Harry G. "Bears in Three Contemporary Fictions," *Humanities Assoc R*, 28 (1976), 142–144.

"A Poetics for Bullies"
Dougherty, David C. *Stanley Elkin*, 133–135.

RALPH ELLISON

"King of the Bingo Game"
List, Robert N. "An Object-Relations Approach to Ellison's 'King of the Bingo Game,' " *Researcher*, 13, iii (1990), 15–32.

EVGENII EVTUSHENKO

"Ardabiola"
Shneidman, N. N. *Soviet Literature* . . . , 160–161.

BEVERLEY FARMER

"Café Veneto"
Jacobs, Lyn. "The Fiction of Beverley Farmer," *Australian Lit Stud*, 14 (1990), 332.

"Fire and Flood"
Jacobs, Lyn. "The Fiction . . . ," 333.

"Home Times"
Jacobs, Lyn. "The Fiction . . . ," 330–331.

"Ismini"
Jacobs, Lyn. "The Fiction . . . ," 327–328.

"Milk"
Jacobs, Lyn. "The Fiction . . . ," 326.

"Our Lady of the Beehives"
Jacobs, Lyn. "The Fiction . . . ," 329–330.

"Place of Birth"
Jacobs, Lyn. "The Fiction . . . ," 328–329.

PHILIP JOSÉ FARMER

"Sail On! Sail On!"
Roberts, Thomas J. *An Aesthetics* . . . , 182–185.

WILLIAM FAULKNER

"Artist at Home"

Hamblin, Robert W. "Carcassonne in Mississippi: Geography of the Imagination," in Fowler, Doreen, and Ann J. Abadie, Eds. *Faulkner and the Craft* . . . , 159–160.

Ross, Stephen M. *Fiction's Inexhaustible Voice* . . . , 238–242.

"Barn Burning"

Cackett, Kathy. " 'Barn Burning': Debating the American Adam," *Notes Mississippi Writers*, 21, i (1989), 1–17.

Hall, Joan W. "Faulkner's Barn Burners: Ab Snopes and the Duke of Marlborough," *Notes Mississippi Writers*, 21, ii (1989), 65–68.

Moreland, Richard C. "Compulsive and Revisionary Repetition: Faulkner's 'Barn Burning' and the Craft of Writing Difference," in Fowler, Doreen, and Ann J. Abadie, Eds. *Faulkner and the Craft* . . . , 59–67.

Ross, Stephen M. *Fiction's Inexhaustible Voice* . . . , 13–15.

Zender, Karl F. "Character and Symbol in 'Barn Burning,' " *Coll Lit*, 16, i (1989), 48–59.

"The Bear"

Bassett, John E. *Visions and Revisions* . . . , 160–164.

Devlin, Albert J. "History, Sexuality, and Wilderness in the McCaslin Family Chronicle," in Kinney, Arthur F., Ed. . . . *The McCaslin Family*, 191–197.

Faris, Wendy B. "Marking Space, Charting Time: Text and Territory in Faulkner's 'The Bear' and Carpentier's *Los pasos perdidos*," in Pérez Firmat, Gustavo, Ed. . . . *Common Literature?*, 243–265.

Hoffman, Daniel. *Faulkner's Country Matters* . . . , 128–132.

Ross, Stephen M. *Fiction's Inexhaustible Voice* . . . , 158–166.

Sachs, Viola. *The Myth of America* . . . , 125–142.

Sullivan, Walter. *"In Praise of Bloody Sports"* . . . , 112–113.

Timms, David. "Contrasts in Form: Hemingway's 'The Old Man and the Sea' and Faulkner's 'The Bear,' " in Lee, A. Robert, Ed. *The Modern American Novella*, 97–112.

Turner, Frederick. *Spirit of Place* . . . , 221–230.

Wolfe, Gary K. "Frontiers in Space," in Mogen, David, Mark Busby, and Paul Bryant, Eds. *The Frontier Experience* . . . , 259–261.

Zuckert, Catherine H. *Natural Right* . . . , 210–218.

"A Bear Hunt"

Ross, Stephen M. *Fiction's Inexhaustible Voice* . . . , 75–76.

"Beyond"

Gidley, Mick. "Beyond 'Beyond': Aspects of Faulkner's Representation of Death," in Hönnighausen, Lothar, Ed. *Faulkner's Discourse* . . . , 223-233.

"Black Music"

Hamblin, Robert W. "Carcassonne in Mississippi . . . ," 162–163.

"Carcassonne"
Hamblin, Robert W. "Carcassonne in Mississippi . . . ," 151–153.
Ross, Stephen M. *Fiction's Inexhaustible Voice* . . . , 135–147.
———. " 'Lying Beneath Speech': Preliminary Notes on the Representation of Thought in 'Carcassonne,' " in Hönnighausen, Lothar, Ed. *Faulkner's Discourse* . . . , 159–169.

"A Courtship"
Gidley, Mick. "Sam Fathers' Fathers: Indians and the Idea of Inheritance," in Kinney, Arthur F., Ed. . . . *The McCaslin Family*, 127–128.

"Death Drag"
Lind, Ilse D. "The Language of Stereotype in 'Death Drag,' " in Hönnighausen, Lothar, Ed. *Faulkner's Discourse* . . . , 127–131.

"Delta Autumn"
Hoffman, Daniel. *Faulkner's Country Matters* . . . ," 169–171.

"Dry September"
Rogalus, Paul. "Faulkner's 'Dry September,' " *Explicator*, 48 (1990), 211–212.
Volpe, Edmond. " 'Dry September': Metaphor for Despair," *Coll Lit*, 16, i (1989), 60–65.

"Elly"
Ross, Stephen M. *Fiction's Inexhaustible Voice* . . . , 143–144.

"An Error in Chemistry"
Irwin, John T. "*Knight's Gambit*: Poe, Faulkner, and the Tradition of the Detective Story," *Arizona Q*, 46, iv (1990), 95–104.

"The Fire and the Hearth"
Bassett, John E. *Visions and Revisions* . . . , 151–156.
Hoffman, Daniel. *Faulkner's Country Matters* . . . , 128–132.
Zuckert, Catherine H. *Natural Right* . . . , 202–206.

"Go Down, Moses"
Bassett, John E. *Visions and Revisions* . . . , 148–149.

"A Justice"
Gidley, Mick. "Sam Fathers' Fathers . . . ," 123–124.
Matthews, John T. "Faulkner's Narrative Frames," in Fowler, Doreen, and Ann J. Abadie, Eds. *Faulkner and the Craft* . . . , 83–86.

"Knight's Gambit"
Irwin, John T. "*Knight's Gambit* . . . ," 104–115.

"The Leg"
Hamblin, Robert W. "Carcassonne in Mississippi . . . ," 163–164.

"Lion"
Matthews, John T. "Faulkner's Narrative Frames," 86–89.

"An Odor of Verbena"
Mann, Susan G. "Seasonal Imagery and the Pattern of Revenge in *The Unvanquished*," *Notes Mississippi Writers*, 21, ii (1989), 41–51.

"Old Man"
Bašić, Sonja. "Faulkner's Narrative: Between Involvement and Distancing," in Hönnighausen, Lothar, Ed. *Faulkner's Discourse* . . . , 144–146.
Brumm, Ursula. "Theme and Narrative Voice in Faulkner's 'Old Man,' " in Hönnighausen, Lothar, Ed. *Faulkner's Discourse* . . . , 242–253.

"The Old People"
Hoffman, Daniel. "The Last of the Chickasaws," *Shenandoah*, 39, i (1989), 51–59.
———. *Faulkner's Country Matters* . . . , 137–145.

"Pantaloon in Black"
Bassett, John E. *Visions and Revisions* . . . , 149–151.
Martin, W. R. "Faulkner's Pantaloon and Conrad's Gaspar Ruiz," *Conradiana*, 21 (1989), 47–51.
Ross, Stephen M. *Fiction's Inexhaustible Voice* . . . , 106–107.
Weinstein, Philip M. "Thinking I Was I Was Not Who Was Not Was Not Who: The Vertigo of Faulknerian Identity," in Fowler, Doreen, and Ann J. Abadie, Eds. *Faulkner and the Craft* . . . , 177–178.

"Raid"
Gibb, Robert. "Moving Fast Sideways: A Look at Form and Image in *The Unvanquished*," *Faulkner J*, 3, ii (1988), 40–47.

"Red Leaves"
Gidley, Mick. "Sam Fathers' Fathers . . . ," 122–123.

"A Rose for Emily"
Blythe, Hal. "Faulkner's 'A Rose for Emily,' " *Explicator*, 47, ii (1989), 49–50.
Burns, Margie. "A Good Rose Is Hard to Find: 'Southern Gothic' as Social Dislocation in Faulkner and O'Connor," *Works & Days*, 6, i–ii (1988), 185–201.
Jay, Gregory S. *America the Scrivener* . . . , 331–334.

"That Evening Sun"
Hurst, Mary J. *The Voice of the Child* . . . , 136–148.
Matthews, John T. "Faulkner's Narrative Frames," 76–78.

"Was"
Anderson, Carl L. "Faulkner's 'Was': 'A Deadlier Purpose Than Simple Pleasure,' " *Am Lit*, 61 (1989), 414–428.
Bassett, John E. *Visions and Revisions* . . . , 146–147.
Devlin, Albert J. "History, Sexuality . . . ," 189–191.
Hoffman, Daniel. *Faulkner's Country Matters* . . . , 107–127.
Zuckert, Catherine H. *Natural Right* . . . , 199–202.

MORDEKHAI ZE'EV FEIERBERG

"In the Evening"
Alter, Robert, Ed. *Modern Hebrew Literature*, 65–67.

FENG SHULAN [same as YUANJUN or YIAN or GAN NÜSHI]

"Burnt to Ashes"
Eide, Elisabeth. "Feng Shulan," in Slupski, Zbigniew, Ed. *A Selective Guide . . .*, II, 64–65.

"A Secret Grief"
Eide, Elisabeth. "Feng Shulan," 64.

"A Virtuous Lady"
Eide, Elisabeth. "Feng Shulan," 65.

FENG TS'UN

"Beautiful"
Hsia, C. T. "Residual Femininity: Women in Chinese Community Fiction," in Birch, Cyril, Ed. *Chinese Communist Literature*, 176–177.

SÁNCHEZ FERLOSIO

"Hermanos"
Jordan, Barry. *Writing and Politics . . .*, 71.

"Niño fuerte"
Jordan, Barry. *Writing and Politics . . .*, 70–71.

MACEDONIO FERNÁNDEZ

"El Zapallo que se hizo cosmos"
Askeland, Jon. "Fantasía, juego y metáforo: Un estudio comparativo de 'La lengua' y de 'El Zapallo que se hizo cosmos,' " *Río de la Plata*, 4–6 (1987), 237–244.

CRISTINA FERNÁNDEZ CUBAS

"Los altillos de Brumal"
Talbot, Lynn K. "Journey into the Fantastic: Cristina Fernández Cubas' 'Los altillos de Brumal,' " *Letras Femeninas*, 15, i–ii (1989), 37–47.

ALEJANDRO FERNÁNDEZ GARCÍA

"Las manos frágiles"
Ratcliff, Dillwyn F. *Venezuelan Prose Fiction*, 201–202.

"Perucho"
Ratcliff, Dillwyn F. *Venezuelan Prose Fiction*, 205–206.

"Tierra y alma"
Ratcliff, Dillwyn F. *Venezuelan Prose Fiction*, 205.
"La tragedia del oro"
Ratcliff, Dillwyn F. *Venezuelan Prose Fiction*, 202.

ROSARIO FERRÉ

"El collar de camándulas"
Acosta Cruz, María I. "Historia, ser e identidad femenina en 'El collar de camándulas' y 'Maldito amor' de Rosario Ferré," *Chasqui*, 19, ii (1990), 24–26.
"Maldito amor"
Acosta Cruz, María I. "Historia . . . ," 26–30.
"When Women Love Men"
Mullen, Edward. "Interpreting Puerto Rico's Cultural Myths: Rosario Ferré and Manuel Ramos Otero," *Americas R*, 17, iii (1989), 90–94.

M. F. K. FISHER

"Another Love Story"
Yahnke, Robert E., and Richard M. Eastman. *Aging in Literature* . . . , 40.
"Answer in the Affirmative"
Yahnke, Robert E., and Richard M. Eastman. *Aging in Literature* . . . , 40–41.
"The Reunion"
Yahnke, Robert E., and Richard M. Eastman. *Aging in Literature* . . . , 41.

F. SCOTT FITZGERALD

"Absolution"
Butterfield, Herbie. " 'All Very Rich and Sad': A Decade of Fitzgerald Short Stories," in Lee, A. Robert, Ed. *Scott Fitzgerald* . . . , 103–104.
Petry, Alice H. *Fitzgerald's Craft* . . . , 126–129.
"The Adjuster"
Petry, Alice H. *Fitzgerald's Craft* . . . , 112–116.
"The Baby Party"
Petry, Alice H. *Fitzgerald's Craft* . . . , 117–122.
"Babylon Revisited"
Butterfield, Herbie. " 'All Very Rich . . . ,' " 108–109.
Cowart, David. "Fitzgerald's 'Babylon Revisited,' " *Lost Generation J*, 8, i (1987), 16–19.

Turner, Joan. "Fitzgerald's 'Babylon Revisited,' " *Explicator*, 48 (1990), 282–283.

"Benediction"
Petry, Alice H. *Fitzgerald's Craft* . . . , 36–37.

"The Bridal Party"
Harding, Brian. "Made for—or against—the Trade: The Radicalism of Fitzgerald's *Saturday Evening Post* Stories," in Lee, A. Robert, Ed. *Scott Fitzgerald* . . . , 125–127.

"The Captured Shadow"
Petry, Alice H. *Fitzgerald's Craft* . . . , 159–160.

"The Curious Case of Benjamin Button"
Petry, Alice H. *Fitzgerald's Craft* . . . , 78–79.

"The Cut-Glass Bowl"
Petry, Alice H. *Fitzgerald's Craft* . . . , 49–51.

"Dalyrimple Goes Wrong"
Petry, Alice H. *Fitzgerald's Craft* . . . , 39–43.

"The Diamond as Big as the Ritz"
Butterfield, Herbie. " 'All Very Rich . . . ,' " 100–102.

"The Fiend"
Petry, Alice H. *Fitzgerald's Craft* . . . , 179–181.

"Forging Ahead"
Harding, Brian. "Made for . . . ," 124–125.

"The Freshest Boy"
Petry, Alice H. *Fitzgerald's Craft* . . . , 170–171.

"Head and Shoulders"
Petry, Alice H. *Fitzgerald's Craft* . . . , 48.

"The Ice Palace"
Butterfield, Herbie. " 'All Very Rich . . . ,' " 95–97.
Petry, Alice H. *Fitzgerald's Craft* . . . , 28–29.

"The Last of the Belles"
Butterfield, Herbie. " 'All Very Rich . . . ,' " 104–105.

"The Lees of Happiness"
Kelly, Lionel. "Hemingway and Fitzgerald: Two Short Stories," in Hanson, Clare, Ed. *Re-reading* . . . , 104–109.
Petry, Alice H. *Fitzgerald's Craft* . . . , 79–81.

"The Love Boat"
Harding, Brian. "Made for . . . ," 123–124.

"Majesty"
Petry, Alice H. *Fitzgerald's Craft* . . . , 184–186.

"May Day"
Butterfield, Herbie. " 'All Very Rich . . . ,' " 97–99.
Harding, Brian. "Made for . . . ," 118–120.
Petry, Alice H. *Fitzgerald's Craft* . . . , 66–69.

"O Russet Witch!"
Petry, Alice H. *Fitzgerald's Craft* . . . , 71–76.

GUSTAVE FLAUBERT

Roe, David. *Gustave Flaubert*, 90–94.

"A Simple Heart"
Bell, Michael. *The Sentiment of Reality* . . . , 166–167.
Hayman, David. "A De-Simplified Heart: Flaubert Through a Joycean Optic," in Nischik, Reingard M., and Barbara Korte, Eds. *Modes of Narrative* . . . , 46–55.
Humphries, Jefferson. "Flaubert's Parrot . . . ," 325–326.
Marsh, Leonard. "Félicité on the Road: A Synchronic Reading of 'Un coeur simple,' " *Romanic R*, 81 (1990), 56–65.

FORD MADDOX FORD

"Blood"
Dooley, Michael. "Readers and Writers: Ford's Narrative Technique in Stories from the Past: *Zeppelin Nights*," *J Short Story Engl*, 13 (Autumn, 1989), 50.

"No Heroes"
Dooley, Michael. "Readers and Writers . . . ," 41–44.

"St. George's Day"
Dooley, Michael. "Readers and Writers . . . ," 48–49.

"St. Mark's Day"
Dooley, Michael. "Readers and Writers . . . ," 45–47.

"Trafalgar"
Dooley, Michael. "Readers and Writers . . . ," 52–53.

E. M. FORSTER

"Albergo Empedocle"
Land, Stephen K. *Challenge and Conventionality* . . . , 19–25.

"Ansell"
Heldreth, Leonard G. "Fantasy as Criticism in Forster's Short Fiction," in Saciuk, Olena H., Ed. *The Shape of the Fantastic* . . . , 10.
Land, Stephen K. *Challenge and Conventionality* . . . , 15–19.

"Arthur Snatchfold"
Heldreth, Leonard G. "Fantasy as Criticism . . . ," 11–12.
Land, Stephen K. *Challenge and Conventionality* . . . , 223–225.
Summers, Claude J. *Gay Fictions* . . . , 105–107.

"The Celestial Omnibus"
Heldreth, Leonard G. "Fantasy as Criticism . . . ," 12–13.
Land, Stephen K. *Challenge and Conventionality* . . . , 110–113.

"The Curate's Friend"
Land, Stephen K. *Challenge and Conventionality* . . . , 107–110.
Summers, Claude J. *Gay Fictions* . . . , 81–83.

"Dr. Woolacott"
Land, Stephen K. *Challenge and Conventionality* . . . , 222–223.

"The Eternal Moment"
Land, Stephen K. *Challenge and Conventionality* . . . , 33–44.

"The Life to Come"
Land, Stephen K. *Challenge and Conventionality* . . . , 219–221.
Summers, Claude J. *Gay Fictions* . . . , 103–105.

"The Machine Stops"
Land, Stephen K. *Challenge and Conventionality* . . . , 137–139.

"The Other Boat"
Heldreth, Leonard G. "Fantasy as Criticism . . . ," 10–11.
Land, Stephen K. *Challenge and Conventionality* . . . , 226–228.

"Other Kingdom"
Heldreth, Leonard G. "Fantasy as Criticism . . . ," 17.
Land, Stephen K. *Challenge and Conventionality* . . . , 169–173.

"The Other Side of the Hedge"
Land, Stephen K. *Challenge and Conventionality* . . . , 25–27.

"The Point of It"
Heldreth, Leonard G. "Fantasy as Criticism . . . ," 15–16.
Land, Stephen K. *Challenge and Conventionality* . . . , 173–175.

"The Purple Envelope"
Land, Stephen K. *Challenge and Conventionality* . . . , 67–70.

"Ralph and Tony"
Rahman, Tariq. "The Use of the Double Plot in E. M. Forster's 'Ralph and Tony' and Other Stories," *Lit Endeavour*, 9, i–iv (1987–1988), 49–55.

"The Road from Colonus"
Doloff, Steven. "Forster's 'The Road from Colonus,' " *Explicator*, 48, i (1989), 20–21.
Heldreth, Leonard G. "Fantasy as Criticism . . . ," 14–15.
Land, Stephen K. *Challenge and Conventionality* . . . , 11–14.
Yahnke, Robert E., and Richard M. Eastman. *Aging in Literature* . . . , 41.

"The Rock"
Land, Stephen K. *Challenge and Conventionality* . . . , 103–106.

"The Story of a Panic"
Heldreth, Leonard G. "Fantasy as Criticism . . . ," 13–14.
Land, Stephen K. *Challenge and Conventionality* . . . , 2–11.

"The Story of the Siren"
Land, Stephen K. *Challenge and Conventionality* . . . , 27–31.

JOHN FOWLES

"The Ebony Tower"
Kersnowski, Frank. "John Fowles' 'The Ebony Tower': A Discourse with Critics," *J Short Story Engl*, 13 (Autumn, 1989), 57–65.

"The Enigma"
Broich, Ulrich. "John Fowles, 'The Enigma' and the Contemporary British Short Story," in Nischik, Reingard M., and Barbara Korte, Eds. *Modes of Narrative* . . . , 182–187.

JANET FRAME

"The Bath"
Yahnke, Robert E., and Richard M. Eastman. *Aging in Literature* . . . , 41–42.

ANATOLE FRANCE

"Amycus and Célestin"
Dargan, Edwin P. *Anatole France*, 463–464.

"Balthasar"
Dargan, Edwin P. *Anatole France*, 436–438.

"The Legend of St. Thaïs"
Dargan, Edwin P. *Anatole France*, 152–154.

"On the White Stone"
Nöckler, Horst-Werner. "Gesellschaftsutopie und Geschichtssich in 'Sur la pierre blanche' von Anatole France," *Wissenschaftliche Zeitschrift der Ernst Moritz Arndt-Universität Greifswald*, 38, ii–iii (1989), 67–73.

MARY E. WILKINS FREEMAN

"Amanda and Love"
Reichart, Mary R. " 'Friends of My Heart': Women as Friends and Rivals in the Short Stories of Mary Wilkins Freeman," *Am Lit Realism*, 22, ii (1990), 65–66.

"The Apple Tree"
Luscher, Robert M. "Seeing the Forest for the Trees: The 'Intimate Connection' of Mary Wilkins Freeman's *Six Trees*," *Am Transcendental Q*, 3 N.S. (1989), 376–378.

"The Balsam Fir"
Luscher, Robert M. "Seeing the Forest . . . ," 373–374.

"The Elm Tree"
Luscher, Robert M. "Seeing the Forest . . . ," 368–370.

"Evelina's Garden"
Donovan, Josephine. *After the Fall* . . . , 10–11.

"The Great Pine"
Luscher, Robert M. "Seeing the Forest . . . ," 371–373.

"The Lombardy Poplar"
Luscher, Robert M. "Seeing the Forest . . . ," 374–376.

"Louisa"
Cutter, Martha J. "Mary E. Wilkins Freeman's Two New England Nuns," *Colby Q*, 26 (1990), 213–217, 220–225.
Maik, Thomas A. "Dissent and Affirmation: Conflicting Voices of Female Roles in Selected Stories of Mary Wilkins Freeman," *Colby Q*, 26 (1990), 60–68.

"A Mistaken Charity"
Yahnke, Robert E., and Richard M. Eastman. *Aging in Literature* . . . , 42–43.

"A New England Nun"
Cutter, Martha J. ". . . Two New England Nuns," 213–220.

"Old Woman Magoun"
Donovan, Josephine. *After the Fall* . . . , 15–16.

"A Poetess"
Donovan, Josephine. *After the Fall* . . . , 17–19.

"The Revolt of Mother"
Church, Joseph. "Reconstructing Woman's Place in Freeman's 'The Revolt of Mother,' " *Colby Q*, 26 (1990), 195–200.

"Sister Liddy"
Reichart, Mary R. " 'Friends of My Heart' . . . ," 62–64.

"A Village Singer"
Reichart, Mary R. " 'Friends of My Heart' . . . ," 59.

"The White Birch"
Luscher, Robert M. "Seeing the Forest . . . ," 370–371.

"The Winning Lady"
Reichart, Mary R. " 'Friends of My Heart' . . . ," 58–59.

CARLOS FUENTES

"Aura"
Acker, Bertie. *El cuento mexicano contemporaneo* . . . , 149–157.

"Chac Mool"
Acker, Bertie. *El cuento mexicano contemporaneo* . . . , 118–119.
Ramírez Mattei, Aida Elsa. *La Narrativa* . . . , 7–8.
Tyler, Joseph. " 'Chac Mool': A Journey into the Fantastic," *Hispanic J*, 10 (1989), 177–183.

"The Cost of Life"
Acker, Bertie. *El cuento mexicano contemporaneo* . . . , 130.
Ramírez Mattei, Aida Elsa. *La Narrativa* . . . , 24–25.

"The Doll Queen"
Acker, Bertie. *El cuento mexicano contemporaneo* . . . , 142–143.
Ramírez Mattei, Aida Elsa. *La Narrativa* . . . , 20–21.

"Estos fueron los palacios"
Chanady, Amaryll. "La problematización del pasado en 'Estos fueron los palacios,' " in Hernández de López, Ana María, Ed. *La obra de Carlos Fuentes . . .*, 289–296.

"The Gods Speak" [same as "By the Mouth of the Gods"]
Ramírez Mattei, Aida Elsa. *La Narrativa . . .*, 13–16.

"In a Flemish Garden" [same as "Tlactocatzine, the One from the Flemish Garden"]
Acker, Bertie. *El cuento mexicano contemporaneo . . .*, 145–148.
Ramírez Mattei, Aida Elsa. *La Narrativa . . .*, 9–11.

"In Defense of Trigolibia"
Ramírez Mattei, Aida Elsa. *La Narrativa . . .*, 8–9.

"Litany of the Orchids"
Acker, Bertie. *El cuento mexicano contemporaneo . . .*, 122–123.
Ramírez Mattei, Aida Elsa. *La Narrativa . . .*, 11–12.

"The Man Who Invented Gunpowder"
Acker, Bertie. *El cuento mexicano contemporaneo . . .*, 124.

"Mother's Day"
Boling, Becky. "Parricide and Revolution: Fuentes's 'El día de las madres' and *Gringo Viejo*," *Hispano*, 95 (January, 1989), 75–77.

"The Old Morality"
Acker, Bertie. *El cuento mexicano contemporaneo . . .*, 130–132.
Benedetti, Mario. *Crítica cómplice*, 189–190.
Ramírez Mattei, Aida Elsa. *La Narrativa . . .*, 23–24.

"A Pure Soul"
Acker, Bertie. *El cuento mexicano contemporaneo . . .*, 132–133, 140–142.
Ramírez Mattei, Aida Elsa. *La Narrativa . . .*, 25–26.

"To the Sea Serpent"
Acker, Bertie. *El cuento mexicano contemporaneo . . .*, 133–135.
Ramírez Mattei, Aida Elsa. *La Narrativa . . .*, 26–28.

"El trigo errante"
Ramírez Mattei, Aida Elsa. *La Narrativa . . .*, 17–18.

"The Two Helens"
Acker, Bertie. *El cuento mexicano contemporaneo . . .*, 126–128.
Benedetti, Mario. *Crítica cómplice*, 189.
Ramírez Mattei, Aida Elsa. *La Narrativa . . .*, 19–20.

"What Fortune Brought"
Acker, Bertie. *El cuento mexicano contemporaneo . . .*, 128–130.
Ramírez Mattei, Aida Elsa. *La Narrativa . . .*, 21–23.

MARY GAITSKILL

"Romantic Weekend"
Feinstein, Wiley. "Twentieth-Century Feminist Responses to Boccaccio's Alibech Story," *Romance Lang Annual*, 1 (1989), 119.

MAVIS GALLANT

"Acceptance of Their Ways"
Grabes, Herbert. "Creating to Dissect: Strategies of Character Portrayal and Evaluation in Short Stories by Margaret Laurence, Alice Munro, and Mavis Gallant," in Nischik, Reingard M., and Barbara Korte, Eds. *Modes of Narrative* . . . , 124–126.

"An Autobiography"
Besner, Neil. "The Corruption of Memory: Mavis Gallant's 'An Autobiography,' " *Recherches Anglaises et Nord-Américaines*," 20 (1987), 35–40.

"Bernadette"
Keefer, Janice K. *Reading Mavis Gallant*, 44–45.

"Careless Talk"
Keefer, Janice K. *Reading Mavis Gallant*, 145–146.

"The Colonel's Child"
Keefer, Janice K. *Reading Mavis Gallant*, 189–190.

"The Doctor"
Keefer, Janice K. *Reading Mavis Gallant*, 103–105.

"The Flowers of Spring"
Keefer, Janice K. *Reading Mavis Gallant*, 73–74.

"A Flying Start"
Woolford, Daniel. "Mavis Gallant's *Overhead in a Balloon*: Politics and Religion, Language and Art," *Stud Canadian Lit*, 14, ii (1989), 43–44.

"The Four Seasons"
Keefer, Janice K. *Reading Mavis Gallant*, 183–184.

"From Cloud to Cloud"
Keefer, Janice K. *Reading Mavis Gallant*, 151–152.

"Going Ashore"
Keefer, Janice K. *Reading Mavis Gallant*, 111–113.

"Good Morning and Goodbye"
Keefer, Janice K. *Reading Mavis Gallant*, 111–113.

"Irina"
Keefer, Janice K. *Reading Mavis Gallant*, 147–148.
Rooke, Constance. *Fear of the Open Heart* . . . , 27–40.

"Lena"
Keefer, Janice K. *Reading Mavis Gallant*, 190–192.

"Luc and His Father"
Keefer, Janice K. *Reading Mavis Gallant*, 110–111.
Woolford, Daniel. ". . . Language and Art," 29–36.

"Malcolm and Bea"
Keefer, Janice K. *Reading Mavis Gallant*, 170–171.

"The Old Place"
Keefer, Janice K. *Reading Mavis Gallant*, 168–170.

"The Other Paris"
Keefer, Janice K. *Reading Mavis Gallant*, 139–141.

"Overhead in a Balloon"
Schaub, Danielle. "Narrative and Stylistic Devices in Mavis Gallant's 'Overhead in a Balloon,' " *J Short Story Engl*, 12 (Spring, 1989), 53–62.
Sturgess, Charlotte. "Narrative Strategies in 'Overhead in a Balloon,' " *J Short Story Engl*, 12 (Spring, 1989), 45–52.

"The Pegnitz Junction"
Keefer, Janice K. *Reading Mavis Gallant*, 171–177.

"The Rejection"
Keefer, Janice K. *Reading Mavis Gallant*, 113–115.

"The Remission"
Keefer, Janice K. *Reading Mavis Gallant*, 89–95.

"Rose"
Keefer, Janice K. *Reading Mavis Gallant*, 115–118.

"Saturday"
Keefer, Janice K. *Reading Mavis Gallant*, 48–50.

"Señor Pinedo"
Keefer, Janice K. *Reading Mavis Gallant*, 166–168.

"Speck's Idea"
Keefer, Janice K. *Reading Mavis Gallant*, 148–149.
Woolford, Daniel. " . . . Language and Art," 34–43.

"Statues Taken Down"
Keefer, Janice K. *Reading Mavis Gallant*, 146–147.

"Three Brick Walls"
Keefer, Janice K. *Reading Mavis Gallant*, 72–73.

"Voices Lost in Snow"
Keefer, Janice K. *Reading Mavis Gallant*, 76–77, 102–103.

RÓMULO GALLEGOS

"Los aventureros"
Ratcliff, Dillwyn F. *Venezuelan Prose Fiction*, 238–239.

"La ciudad muerta"
Weissberger, Barbara F. "Confinement and Escape in the Short Stories of Rómulo Gallegos," *Chasqui*, 18, i (1989), 28–29.

"El cuarto de enfrence"
Weissberger, Barbara F. "Confinement . . . ," 30–31.

"Estrellas sobre el barranco"
Ratcliff, Dillwyn F. *Venezuelan Prose Fiction*, 237–238.

"El milagro del año"
Ratcliff, Dillwyn F. *Venezuelan Prose Fiction*, 239–241.

"El paréntesis"
Weissberger, Barbara F. "Confinement . . . ," 31–32.

"El piano viejo"
Weissberger, Barbara F. "Confinement . . . ," 32–33.

"Una resolución enérgica"
Weissberger, Barbara F. "Confinement . . . ," 29–30.

JOHN GALSWORTHY

"The Japanese Quince"
Cervo, Nathan. "Galsworthy's 'The Japanese Quince,' " *Explicator*, 47, ii (1989), 38–42.

MAILA GANINA

"Golden Solitude"
Barker, Adele. "Women Without Men in the Writings of Soviet Women Writers," in Rancour-Laferriere, Daniel, Ed. *Russian Literature* . . . , 440–442.

"Listen to Your Hour"
Shneidman, N. N. *Soviet Literature* . . . , 182–183.

GAO XIAOSHENG

"Li Shunda Builds a House"
Lee, Yee. "A Reflection of Reality," in Lee, Yee, Ed. *The New Realism* . . . , 8–9.

GABRIEL GARCÍA MÁRQUEZ

"Artificial Roses"
Bell-Villada, Gene H. *García Márquez* . . . , 121–122.
Carrillo, Germán D. *La narrativa* . . . , 120–122.
McNerney, Kathleen. *Understanding* . . . , 114.
Mose, Kenrick. *Defamiliarization* . . . , 158–159.

"Baltazar's Wonderful Afternoon"
Bell-Villada, Gene H. *García Márquez* . . . , 123–124.
Carrillo, Germán D. *La narrativa* . . . , 115–116.

Linker, Susan M. "Myth and Legend in Two Prodigious Tales of García Márquez," *Hispanic J*, 9, i (1987), 90–95.
McNerney, Kathleen. *Understanding* . . . , 111–112.
Miller, Beth. "Alegoría y ideologia en 'La prodigiosa tarde de Baltazar': El artista del Tercer Mundo y su producto," *Revista de Crítica*, 11, xxiii (1986), 53–62.
Mora, Gabriela. " 'La prodigiosa tarde de Baltazar': Problemas del significado," *Inti*, 16–17 (1982–1983), 83–92.
Mose, Kenrick. *Defamiliarization* . . . , 152–155.

"Big Mama's Funeral"
Bell-Villada, Gene H. *García Márquez* . . . , 126–128.
Benson, John. "Literatura y periodismo de García Márquez: La Mamá Grande y la gran mamá," *Explicación de Textos Literarios*, 15, i (1986–1987), 21–31.
Carrillo, Germán D. *La narrativa* . . . , 122–123.
McNerney, Kathleen. *Understanding* . . . , 114–115.
Mose, Kenrick. *Defamiliarization* . . . , 167–177.
Perus, Françoise. "Algunas consideraciones histórico-teóricas para el estudio del cuento," *Plural*, 9 (June 16, 1987), 37–39.

"Bitterness for Three Sleepwalkers"
Mose, Kenrick. *Defamiliarization* . . . , 29–30.

"Blacamán the Good, Vendor of Miracles"
Bell-Villada, Gene H. *García Márquez* . . . , 135.
Carrillo, Germán D. *La narrativa* . . . , 140–159.
McNerney, Kathleen. *Understanding* . . . , 124–125.

"Chronicle of a Death Foretold"
Bell-Villada, Gene H. *García Márquez* . . . , 181–191.
McNerney, Kathleen. *Understanding* . . . , 137–144.
Zamora, Lois P. *Writing the Apocalypse* . . . , 42–43.

"Death Constant Beyond Love"
Bell-Villada, Gene H. *García Márquez* . . . , 137–138.
McNerney, Kathleen. *Understanding* . . . , 123–124.

"Dialogue with the Mirror"
Mose, Kenrick. *Defamiliarization* . . . , 28–29.

"Eva Is Inside Her Cat"
McNerney, Kathleen. *Understanding* . . . , 99–100.
Mose, Kenrick. *Defamiliarization* . . . , 24–26.

"Eyes of a Blue Dog"
Mose, Kenrick. *Defamiliarization* . . . , 30–32.

"The Handsomest Drowned Man in the World"
Aronne-Amestoy, Lida. "Fantasía y compromiso en un cuento de Gabriel García Márquez," *Symposium*, 38, iv (Winter, 1984–1985), 287–297.
Felten, Hans. " 'El ahogado más hermoso del mundo': Lectura plural de un texto de García Márquez," in Neumeister, Sebastián, Ed. *Actas del IX Congreso* . . . , II, 535–542.
McNerney, Kathleen. *Understanding* . . . , 121–122.

Speratti-Pinero, Emma S. "De las fuertes y su utilización en 'El ahogado más hermoso del mundo,' " in Lerner, Lia S., and Isaís Lerner, Eds. *Homenaje a Ana María Barrenchea*, 549–555.

"The Incredible and Sad Tale of Innocent Eréndira and Her Heartless Grandmother"

Aponte, Barbara B. "El rito de la iniciación en el cuento hispanoamericano," *Hispanic R*, 51, ii (1983), 129–146.
Bell-Villada, Gene H. *García Márquez* . . . , 177–181.
McNerney, Kathleen. *Understanding* . . . , 125–128.
Mills, Moylan C. "Magic Realism and García Márquez's 'Eréndira,' " *Lit/Film Q*, 17, ii (1989), 113–122.
Ortiz, Efren. " 'La cándida Eréndira': Una lectura mítica," *Texto Crítico*, 6 (1980), 248–254.
Reis, Roberto. "O fantástico do Poder e o Poder do Fantástico," *Ideologies and Literature*, 3, xiii (1980), 3–22.

"The Last Voyage of the Ghost Ship"

Bell-Villada, Gene H. *García Márquez* . . . , 141–145.
McNerney, Kathleen. *Understanding* . . . , 125.
Pineda Botero, Alvaro. "Agresión y poesía: A propósito de dos cuentos de García Márquez," *Univ Dayton R*, 18, i (1986), 62–65.

"Leaf Storm"

Bell-Villada, Gene H. *García Márquez* . . . , 141–145.
Benedetti, Mario. *Crítica cómplice*, 150–151.

"Monologue of Isabel Watching It Rain at Macombo"

Mose, Kenrick. *Defamiliarization* . . . , 39–43.

Montiel's Widow"

Bell-Villada, Gene H. *García Márquez* . . . , 124–125.
Carrillo, Germán D. *La narrativa* . . . , 116–118.
Linker, Susan M. "Myth and Legend . . . ," 95–97.
McNerney, Kathleen. *Understanding* . . . , 112–113.
Mose, Kenrick. *Defamiliarization* . . . , 155–158.

"Nabo, the Negro Who Made the Angels Wait"

Mose, Kenrick. *Defamiliarization* . . . , 37–38.

"The Night of Bitterness"

Mose, Kenrick. *Defamiliarization* . . . , 33–35.

"The Night of the Curlews"

McNerney, Kathleen. *Understanding* . . . , 45–46.

"One Day After Saturday"

Bell-Villada, Gene H. *García Márquez* . . . , 125.
Carrillo, Germán D. *La narrativa* . . . , 118–120.
McNerney, Kathleen. *Understanding* . . . , 113.
Mose, Kenrick. *Defamiliarization* . . . , 159–167.

"One of These Days"

Carrillo, Germán D. *La narrativa* . . . , 112–113.
McNerney, Kathleen. *Understanding* . . . , 110.
Mose, Kenrick. *Defamiliarization* . . . , 148–149.

"The Other Side of Death"
Mose, Kenrick. *Defamiliarization* . . . , 26–28.

"The Sea of Lost Time"
McNerney, Kathleen. *Understanding* . . . , 122–123.
Mose, Kenrick. *Defamiliarization* . . . , 177–183.

"Someone Has Been Disarranging These Roses"
Mose, Kenrick. *Defamiliarization* . . . , 35–37.

"Tale of a Castaway"
Müller-Bergh, Klaus. " 'Relato de un náufrage': Gabriel García Márquez's Tale of a Shipwreck and Survival at Sea," *Books Abroad*, 47 (1973), 460–466.

"There Are No Thieves in This Town"
Bell-Villada, Gene H. *García Márquez* . . . , 125–126.
Carrillo, Germán D. *La narrativa* . . . , 114.
McNerney, Kathleen. *Understanding* . . . , 110–111.
Mose, Kenrick. *Defamiliarization* . . . , 149–152.

"The Third Resignation"
Mose, Kenrick. *Defamiliarization* . . . , 22–24.

"Tuesday Siesta"
Bell-Villada, Gene H. *García Márquez* . . . , 121.
Carrillo, Germán D. *La narrativa* . . . , 111–112.
Castilla, Alberto. "Una primorosa miniatura narrativa: 'La siesta del martes,' " in Fernández Jiménez, Juan, José J. Labrador Herraiz, and L. Teresa Valdivieso, Eds. *Estudios en homenaje* . . . , 77–85.
McNerney, Kathleen. *Understanding* . . . , 109–110.
Mose, Kenrick. *Defamiliarization* . . . , 146–148.
Pineda Botero, Alvaro. "Agresión y poesía . . . , 59–61.

"A Very Old Man with Enormous Wings"
Bell-Villada, Gene H. *García Márquez* . . . , 136–137.
Roberts, Edgar V., and Henry E. Jacobs. *Instructor's Manual* . . . , 2nd ed., 76–77.

"The Woman Who Came at Six O'Clock"
Bell-Villada, Gene H. *García Márquez* . . . , 141.
Mose, Kenrick. *Defamiliarization* . . . , 32–33.

PARMÉNIDES GARCÍA SALDAÑA

"Goodbye, Belinda"
Dávila Gutiérrez, Joel. "Tres cuentos mexicanos, tres," in Pavón, Alfredo, Ed. *Paquette: Cuento* . . . , 153–154, 156.

HAMLIN GARLAND

"Among the Corn Rows"
Thacker, Robert. *The Great Prairie Fact* . . . , 133–134.

SALVADOR GARMENDIA

"El divino niño"
Ramos, Elías A. *El cuento venezolano* . . . , 30–31.

"En señor Duro"
Ramos, Elías A. *El cuento venezolano* . . . , 34–35.

"Estar solo"
Ramos, Elías A. *El cuento venezolano* . . . , 118–119.

"Estrictamente personal"
Ramos, Elías A. *El cuento venezolano* . . . , 130.

"Noche, 9:30"
Ramos, Elías A. *El cuento venezolano* . . . , 130–131.

"El occiso"
Ramos, Elías A. *El cuento venezolano* . . . , 119.

"1:30 P.M."
Ramos, Elías A. *El cuento venezolano* . . . , 36–37.

"El peatón melancólico"
Ramos, Elías A. *El cuento venezolano* . . . , 37.

"Tensión dinámica"
Ramos, Elías A. *El cuento venezolano* . . . , 125.

"Toc-Toc"
Ramos, Elías A. *El cuento venezolano* . . . , 35–36.

HELEN GARNER

"Other People's Children"
José, Nicholas. "Possibilities of Love in Recent Australian Stories," in Stummer, Peter O., Ed. *The Story Must Be Told* . . . , 142–143.

HUGH GARNER

"The Yellow Sweater"
Szanto, George. "Mediation by Place: Juan Rulfo's 'Macario' and Hugh Garner's 'The Yellow Sweater,' " in Bauer, Roger, et al. [10], Eds. *Proceedings of the XIIth Congress* . . . , II, 71–76.

GEORGE GARRETT

"The Old Army Game"
Madden, David. "Continually Astonished by Everything: The Army Stories of George Garrett," in Ruffin, Paul, and Stuart Wright, Eds. *To Come Up Grinning* . . . , 50–52.

"Unmapped Country"
Madden, David. "Continually Astonished . . . ," 52.

"The Wounded Soldier"
Madden, David. "Continually Astonished . . . ," 52–53.

ELENA GARRO

"Las cabezas bien pensantes"
Rojas-Trempe, Lady. "El estado en 'Las cabezas bien pensantes' de Elena Garro," *Revista Canadiense*, 14, iii (1990), 597–605.

"El Duende"
Larson, Catherine. "The Dynamics of Conflict in 'Qué hora es?' and 'El Duende,' " in Stoll, Anita K., Ed. *A Different Reality* . . . , 109–115.

"Perfecto Luna"
Duncan, Cynthia. "The Theme of the Avenging Dead in 'Perfecto Luna': A Magical Realist Approach," in Stoll, Anita K., Ed. *A Different Reality* . . . , 90–101.

"What Time Is It?"
Larson, Catherine. "The Dynamics of Conflict . . . ," 102–108.

VSEVOLOD GARSHIN

"Four Days"
Kramer, Karl D. "Impressionist Tendencies in the Work of Vsevolod Garshin," in Terras, Victor, Ed. *American Contributions to the Seventh International Congress* . . . , II, 344–345.

"From the Reminiscences of Private Ivanov"
Kramer, Karl D. "Impressionist Tendencies . . . ," 345–346.

"The Meeting"
Kramer, Karl D. "Impressionist Tendencies . . . ," 347–348.

"Nadezda Nikolaeva"
Kramer, Karl D. "Impressionist Tendencies . . . ," 349–353.

"An Occurrence"
Kramer, Karl D. "Impressionist Tendencies . . . ," 348–349.

"The Red Flower"
Kramer, Karl D. "Impressionist Tendencies . . . ," 342–343.

"That Which Never Was"
Kramer, Karl D. "Impressionist Tendencies . . . ," 346.

EDUARDO GASCA

"Un viejo soldado"
Ramos, Elías A. *El cuento venezolano* . . . , 103–104.

ELIZABETH CLEGHORN GASKELL

"Cousin Phillis"
Easson, Angus. "Introduction," *"Cousin Phillis" and Other Stories* [by Elizabeth Gaskell], xii–xiv.

"Curious, If True"
Easson, Angus. "Introduction," xii.

"A Dark Night's Work"
Trodd, Anthea. *Domestic Crimes . . .*, 59–61.

"The Doom of the Griffiths"
Wright, Edgar. "Introduction," *"My Lady Ludlow" and Other Stories* [by Elizabeth Gaskell], xv.

"Half a Life-Time Ago"
Easson, Angus. "Introduction," x–xi.

"Lizzie Leigh"
Thompson, Joanne. "Faith of Our Mothers: Elizabeth Gaskell's 'Lizzie Leigh,' " *Victorian Newsletter*, 78 (Fall, 1990), 22–26.

"Lois the Witch" [originally "The Crooked Branch"]
Easson, Angus. "Introduction," xi–xii.

"Mr. Harrison's Confession"
Wright, Edgar. "Introduction," xvii–xviii.

"My Lady Ludlow"
Wright, Edgar. "Introduction," x–xiv.

"The Old Nurse's Story"
Easson, Angus. "Introduction," x.
Martin, Carol A. "Gaskell's Ghosts: Truths in Disguise," *Stud Novel*, 21 (1989), 34–35.

"The Poor Clare"
Martin, Carol A. "Gaskell's Ghosts . . . ," 35–37.
Wright, Edgar. "Introduction," xv–xvii.

THÉOPHILE GAUTIER

"Arria Marcella"
Crichfield, Grant. "Fantasmagoria and Optics in Théophile Gautier's 'Arria Marcella,' " in Saciuk, Olena H., Ed. *The Shape of the Fantastic . . .*, 85–92.

"Celle-ci ou celle-là"
Majewski, Henry. *Paradigm & Parody . . .*, 124–129.

"Mademoiselle Dafné"
Eigeldinger, Marc. "L'Intertextualité dans 'Mademoiselle Dafné' de Gautier," *Rivista di Letterature*, 39, ii (1986), 143–156.
Schapira, Marie Claude. "L'Imaginaire des profondeurs dans 'Mademoiselle Dafné,' " *Bull de la Soc Théophile Gautier*, 10 (1988), 45–60.

"Onuphrius"
Majewski, Henry. *Paradigm & Parody* . . . , 129–133.

CHESTER S. GEIER

"Environment"
Panshin, Alexel, and Cory Panshin. *The World Beyond* . . . , 622–624.

ZULFIKAR GHOSE

"The Zoo People"
New, W. H. "Structures of Uncertainty: Reading Ghose's 'The Zoo People,' " *R Contemp Fiction*, 9, ii (1989), 192–197.

ANDRÉ GIDE

"Geneviève"
Apter, Emily S. *André Gide* . . . , 134–146.

"The Immoralist"
Apter, Emily S. *André Gide* . . . , 113–120.
Brosman, Catharine S. "Gide et le démon," *Claudel Stud*, 13, ii (1986), 46–56.
Cohn, Robert G. "Man and Woman in Gide's 'The Immoralist,' " *Romanic R*, 80 (1989), 419–433.
Lévy, Zvi H. "André Gide entre Oedipe et Thésée," *French Stud*, 44 (1990), 34–46.
MacKenzie, Louis A. "The Language of Excitation in Gide's 'L'Immoraliste,' " *Romance Q*, 37 (1990), 309–319.
Nelson, Roy J. *Causality and Narrative* . . . , 21–36.
O'Keefe, Charles. " 'La Courte Haleine' of Rousseau: Ironic Intertext of Gide's 'L'Immoraliste,' " *Comparatist*, 13 (May, 1989), 22–28.
Walker, David H. *André Gide*, 25–41.
Wight, Doris T. "Confessions in Gide's 'L'Immoraliste' and Yourcenar's *Coup de grâce*," *Degré Second*, 12 (November, 1989), 39–44.

"Isabelle"
Dethurens, Pascal. "Palimpseste et herméneutique dans 'Isabelle' ou l'art de la fugue," *Bull des Amis*, 18 (1990), 321–342.
Goulet, Alain. "Le Bovarysme, fausse monnaie de Gérard," *Bull des Amis*, 18 (1990), 267–291.
Mahieu, Raymond. "Les Inconnues giddienes: D'Isabelle à Gertrude," *Bull des Amis*, 18 (1990), 293–307.
Meyer, Alain. "La Ruine du manoir et l'adieu au romanesque," *Bull des Amis*, 18 (1990), 253–265.

Segrestaa, Jean-Noël. " 'Isabelle,' construction, déconstruction d'un mythe," *Bull des Amis*, 18 (1990), 239–252.

"The Pastoral Symphony"

Apter, Emily S. *André Gide* . . . , 133–134.

Britton, Celia. "Fiction, Fact, and Madness: Intertextual Relations among Gide's Female Characters," in Worton, Michael, and Judith Still, Eds. *Intertextuality* . . . , 159–175.

Cancalon, Elaine D. " 'La Symphonie pastorale': Voix dérivées voie à la dérive," *Bull des Amis*, 17 (April–July, 1989), 253–257.

Kadish, Doris. "Journal de la nature et nature de journal dans 'La Symphonie pastorale,' " *Bull des Amis*, 17 (April–July, 1989), 267–276.

Walker, David H. *André Gide*, 60–79.

"Robert"

Apter, Emily S. *André Gide* . . . , 146–148.

"Theseus"

Apter, Emily S. *André Gide* . . . , 111–114.

ELLEN GILCHRIST

"Anna, Part I"

Bolsteri, Margaret J. "Ellen Gilchrist's Characters and the Southern Woman's Experience: Rhoda Manning's Double Bind and Anna Hand's Creativity," *New Orleans R*, 15, i (1988), 9.

"Revenge"

Bolsteri, Margaret J. "Ellen Gilchrist's Characters . . . ," 7–9.

CHARLOTTE PERKINS GILMAN

"The Crux"

Showalter, Elaine. *Sexual Anarchy* . . . , 197–198.

"The Giant Wistaria"

+Fleenor, Julian E. "The Gothic Prism: Charlotte Perkins Gilman's Gothic Stories and Her Autobiography," in Meyering, Sheryl L., Ed. *Charlotte Perkins Gilman* . . . , 124.

"The Rocking Chair"

+Fleenor, Julian E. "The Gothic Prism . . . ," 120–123.

"The Yellow Wallpaper"

Boa, Elizabeth. "Creepy-Crawlies: Gilman's 'The Yellow Wallpaper' and Kafka's 'The Metamorphosis,' " *Paragraph*, 13, i (1990), 19–29.

Feldstein, Richard. "Reader, Text, and Ambiguous Referentiality in 'The Yellow Wallpaper,' " in Feldstein, Richard, and Judith Roof, Eds. *Feminism* . . . , 269–279.

+Fleenor, Julian E. "The Gothic Prism . . . ," 232–233; rpt. Meyering, Sheryl L., Ed. *Charlotte Perkins Gilman* . . . , 123–124.

Girgus, Sam B. *Desire and the Political Unconscious* . . . , 133–134.
Hadas, Pamela W. "Madness and Medicine," *Lit & Medicine*, 9 (1990), 181–193.
Haney-Peritz, Janice. "Monumental Feminism and Literature's Ancestral House: Another Look at 'The Yellow Wallpaper,' " *Women's Stud*, 12, ii (1986), 113–128; rpt. Meyering, Sheryl L., Ed. *Charlotte Perkins Gilman* . . . , 95–107.
Hill, Mary A. "Charlotte Perkins Gilman: A Feminist Struggle with Womanhood," *Massachusetts R*, 21 (1980), 511–512; rpt. Meyering, Sheryl L., Ed. *Charlotte Perkins Gilman* . . . , 36–37.
Johnson, Barbara. "Is Female to Male as Ground Is to Figure?" in Feldstein, Richard, and Judith Roof, Eds. *Feminism* . . . , 259–260.
Johnson, Greg. "Gilman's Gothic Allegory: Rage and Redemption in 'The Yellow Wallpaper,' " *Stud Short Fiction*, 26 (1989), 521–530.
Kasmer, Lisa. "Charlotte Perkins Gilman's 'The Yellow Wall Paper': A Symptomatic Reading," *Lit & Psych*, 36, iii (1990), 1–15.
Kennard, Jean E. "Convention Coverage or How to Read Your Own Life," *New Lit Hist*, 8, i (1981), 68–88; rpt. Meyering, Sheryl L., Ed. *Charlotte Perkins Gilman* . . . , 75–94.
King, Jeannette, and Pam Morris. "On Not Reading Between the Lines: Models of Reading in 'The Yellow Wallpaper,' " *Stud Short Fiction*, 26 (1989), 23–32.
Lane, Ann J. *To "Herland" and Beyond* . . . , 124–132.
Lanser, Susan S. "Feminist Criticism, 'The Yellow Wallpaper,' and the Politics of Color in America," *Feminist Stud*, 15 (1989), 415–441.
Post, Stephen L. "His and Hers: Mental Breakdown as Depicted by Evelyn Waugh and Charlotte Perkins Gilman," *Lit & Medicine*, 9 (1990), 172–180.
Shumaker, Conrad. " 'Too Terribly Good To Be Printed': Charlotte Perkins Gilman's 'The Yellow Wallpaper,' " *Am Lit*, 57 (1985), 588–599; rpt. Meyering, Sheryl L., Ed. *Charlotte Perkins Gilman* . . . , 65–74.
Wagner-Martin, Linda. "Gilman's 'The Yellow Wallpaper': A Centenary," in Meyering, Sheryl L., Ed. *Charlotte Perkins Gilman* . . . , 51–64.

GEORGE GISSING

"The Mysterious Portrait"

Selig, Robert L. "Three Stories by George Gissing: Lost Tales from Chicago," *Engl Lit Transition*, 33 (1990), 278–280.

"The Picture"

Selig, Robert L. "Three Stories . . . ," 280.

"The Portrait"

Selig, Robert L. "Three Stories . . . ," 277–278.

GAIL GODWIN

"A Sorrowful Woman"

Halisky, Linda H. "Redeeming the Irrational: The Inexplicable Heroines of 'A Sorrowful Woman' and 'To Room Nineteen,' " *Stud Short Fiction*, 27 (1990), 45–48.

TOM GODWIN

"The Cold Equation"

Huntington, John. *Rationalizing Genius* . . . , 79–85.

Wolfe, Gary K. "Frontiers in Space," in Mogen, David, Mark Busby, and Paul Bryant, Eds. *The Frontier Experience* . . . , 257–259.

NIKOLAI GOGOL

"The Carriage"

Brown, William E. *A History . . . Romantic Period*, IV, 305–306.

"Christmas Eve"

Natov, Nadine. "The Supernatural in Bulgakov and Gogol," in Mandelker, Amy, and Robert Reeder, Eds. *The Supernatural* . . . , 253–254.

"The Diary of a Madman"

Brown, William E. *A History . . . Romantic Period*, IV, 302–305.

Grayson, Jane, and Faith Wigzell. *Nikolay Gogol* . . . , 50–62.

McElroy, Bernard. . . . *Modern Grotesque*, 120–121.

"The Government Inspector"

Grayson, Jane, and Faith Wigzell. *Nikolay Gogol* . . . , 10–15.

"Ivan Fyodorovich Shponka and His Aunt"

Brown, William E. *A History . . . Romantic Period*, IV, 273.

Rancour-Laferriere, Daniel. "Šponka's Dream Interpreted," *Slavic & East European J*, 33 (1989), 358–372.

"A May Night"

Grayson, Jane, and Faith Wigzell. *Nikolay Gogol* . . . , 25–28.

"The Nevsky Prospect"

Brown, William E. *A History . . . Romantic Period*, IV, 294–298.

Waszink, Paul M. "The Representation of Synchrony in Gogol's 'Nevskij Prospekt,' " *Wiener Slawistischer Almanach*, 24 (1989), 43–64.

"The Nose"

Brown, William E. *A History . . . Romantic Period*, IV, 306–311.

Chances, Ellen B. *Conformity's Children* . . . , 104–105.

Grayson, Jane, and Faith Wigzell. *Nikolay Gogol* . . . , 64–78.

Holquist, Michael. "From Body-Talk to Biography: The Chronobiological Bases of Narrative," *Yale J Criticism*, 3, i (1989), 1–35.

"Old-World Landowners"
Brown, William E. *A History . . . Romantic Period*, IV, 276–277.

"The Overcoat"
Brown, William E. *A History . . . Romantic Period*, IV, 316–323.
Peace, Richard. "Gogol and Psychological Realism: 'Shinel,' " in Freeborn, Richard, R. R. Milner-Gulland, and Charles A. Ward, Eds. *Russian and Slavic Literature*, 63–91.
Peppard, Victor. "Who Stole Whose Overcoat and Whose Text Is It?" *So Atlantic R*, 55, i (1990), 63–80.
Sherman, Joseph. " 'God and the Tsar': Ironic Ambiguity and Restorative Laughter in Gogol's 'Overcoat' and Sholem Aleykhem's 'On Account of a Hat,' " in Monday, Henrietta, Ed. *The Waking Sphinx . . .*, 59–82.

"The Portrait"
Brown, William E. *A History . . . Romantic Period*, IV, 298–302.

"The Quarrel Between Ivan Ivanovich and Ivan Nikiforovich"
Brown, William E. *A History . . . Romantic Period*, IV, 287–291.
Kornblatt, Judith D. "Legacy or Travesty: The Mystic Cossack Heroes of Gogol and Babel," *Selected Proceedings of the Kentucky Foreign Language Conference, Slavic Section*, 6, i (1989–1990), 9–10.

"St. John's Eve"
Natov, Nadine. "The Supernatural . . . ," 254.

"The Sorochintsy Fair"
Grayson, Jane, and Faith Wigzell. *Nikolay Gogol . . .*, 19–25.

"Taras Bulba"
Brown, William E. *A History . . . Romantic Period*, IV, 277–282.
Kornblatt, Judith D. "Legacy or Travesty . . . ," 8–9.

"A Terrible Vengeance"
Natov, Nadine. "The Supernatural . . . ," 254–255.

"Viy"
Brown, William E. *A History . . . Romantic Period*, IV, 283–287.
Grayson, Jane, and Faith Wigzell. *Nikolay Gogol . . .*, 30–31.
Natov, Nadine. "The Supernatural . . . ," 255.

EDUARDO GOLIGORSKY

"Orden jerárquicos"
Simpson, Amelia S. *Detective Fiction . . .*, 145–146.

JOSÉ LUIS GONZÁLEZ

"La carte"
Ramos, Mary Jo. "El desplazamiento del jíbaro en tres cuentos de José Luis González," *Americas R*, 17, iii (1989), 101–103.

"Despojo"
Ramos, Mary Jo. "El desplazamiento . . . ," 99–101.

"En el fondo del caño hay un negrito"
Ramos, Mary Jo. "El desplazamiento . . . ," 103–105.

ADRIANO GONZÁLEZ LEÓN

"El arco en el cielo"
Ramos, Elías A. *El cuento venezolano* . . . , 138–139.

"En el lago"
Ramos, Elías A. *El cuento venezolano* . . . , 131–132.

"Ensalmo para Vicente Cunarrosa"
Ramos, Elías A. *El cuento venezolano* . . . , 51–52.

"Fatima o las llamas"
Ramos, Elías A. *El cuento venezolano* . . . , 117–118.

"Los invisible fuegos"
Ramos, Elías A. *El cuento venezolano* . . . , 50–51.

"Madam Clotilde"
Ramos, Elías A. *El cuento venezolano* . . . , 139–140.

"Los pasos de rigor"
Ramos, Elías A. *El cuento venezolano* . . . , 132.

"Ruidos de tablas"
Ramos, Elías A. *El cuento venezolano* . . . , 97–99.

"Las voces lejanas"
Ramos, Elías A. *El cuento venezolano* . . . , 117.

NADINE GORDIMER

"Africa Emergent"
Trump, Martin. "What Time Is This for a Woman? An Analysis of Nadine Gordimer's Short Fiction," in Clayton, Cherry, Ed. *Women and Writing* . . . , 203.

"The Catch"
Eckstein, Barbara J. *The Language of Fiction* . . . , 120–122.
Head, Dominic. "Positive Isolation and Productive Ambiguity in Nadine Gordimer's Short Stories," *J Short Story Engl*, 15 (Autumn, 1990), 19–21.

"A Chip of Glass Ruby"
Trump, Martin. "What Time Is This . . . ," 200–202.

"A City of the Dead, A City of the Living"
Eckstein, Barbara J. *The Language of Fiction* . . . , 135–136.

"Crimes of Conscience"
Head, Dominic. "Positive Isolation . . . ," 26–28.

"Good Climate, Friendly Inhabitants"
Trump, Martin. "What Time Is This . . . ," 194–196.

"Is There Nowhere Else Where We Can Meet?"
Devoize, Jeanne. "Elements of Narrative Technique in Nadine Gordimer's 'Is There Nowhere Else Where We Can Meet?' " *J Short Story Engl*, 15 (Autumn, 1990), 11–16.
Trump, Martin. "What Time Is This . . . ," 187–189.
Wheeler, Kathleen. "Nadine Gordimer: Irony and the Politics of Style," *J Short Story Engl*, 15 (Autumn, 1990), 86–90.

"Open House"
Trump, Martin. "What Time Is This . . . ," 202–203.

"Six Feet of the Country"
Eckstein, Barbara J. *The Language of Fiction* . . . , 126–131.
Trump, Martin. "What Time Is This . . . ," 190–194.

"The Smell of Death and Flowers"
Trump, Martin. "What Time Is This . . . ," 194.

"Some Monday for Sure"
Head, Dominic. "Positive Isolation . . . ," 21–22.
Trump, Martin. "What Time Is This . . . ," 199–200.

"Something for the Time Being"
Eckstein, Barbara J. *The Language of Fiction* . . . , 131–134.
Trump, Martin. "What Time Is This . . . ," 196–199.

"Something Out There"
Link, Viktor. "The Unity of 'Something Out There,' " *J Short Story Engl*, 15 (Autumn, 1990), 31–39.
Mazurek, Raymond A. "Gordimer's 'Something Out There' and Ndebele's *'Fools' and Other Stories:* The Politics of Literary Form," *Stud Short Fiction*, 26 (1989), 72–75.
Newman, Judie. "Nadine Gordimer and the Naked Southern Ape: 'Something Out There,' " *J Short Story Engl*, 15 (Autumn, 1990), 55–73.

"The Termitary"
Louvel, Lilian. "Divided Space, a Reading of Nadine Gordimer's Short Story 'The Termitary,' " *J Short Story Engl*, 15 (Autumn, 1990), 41–53.

"The Train from Rhodesia"
Trump, Martin. "What Time Is This . . . ," 189–190.
Wheeler, Kathleen. "Nadine Gordimer . . . ," 79–82.

CAROLINE GORDON

"All Lovers Love the Spring"
Makowsky, Veronica A. *Caroline Gordon* . . . , 170–171.

"The Brilliant Leaves"
Makowsky, Veronica A. *Caroline Gordon* . . . , 134–136.

"The Captive"
Makowsky, Veronica A. *Caroline Gordon* . . . , 107–109.
Waldron, Ann. *Close Connections* . . . , 98–99.

"Emmanuele, Emmanuele"
Makowsky, Veronica A. *Caroline Gordon* . . . , 200–202.

"The Enemy"
Makowsky, Veronica A. *Caroline Gordon* . . . , 131–132.

"The Forest of the South"
Makowsky, Veronica A. *Caroline Gordon* . . . , 169–170.

"Hear the Nightingale Sing" [originally "Chain Ball Lightning"]
Makowsky, Veronica A. *Caroline Gordon* . . . , 168–169.

"Her Quaint Honor" [originally "Frankie and Thomas and Bud Avery"]
Makowsky, Veronica A. *Caroline Gordon* . . . , 149–150.

"The Ice House"
Makowsky, Veronica A. *Caroline Gordon* . . . , 100–101.

"The Last Day in the Field"
Makowsky, Veronica A. *Caroline Gordon* . . . , 124–125.
Sullivan, Walter. *"In Praise of Bloody Sports"* . . . , 106–108.

"The Long Day"
Makowsky, Veronica A. *Caroline Gordon* . . . , 90–91.

"Mr. Powers"
Makowsky, Veronica A. *Caroline Gordon* . . . , 99–100.

"Old Red"
Brown, Ashley. "Caroline Gordon's 'Old Red,' " *Southern Q*, 28, iii (1990), 53–62.
Makowsky, Veronica A. *Caroline Gordon* . . . , 116–117.
Waldron, Ann. *Close Connections* . . . , 120.

"The Olive Garden"
Makowsky, Veronica A. *Caroline Gordon* . . . , 116–117.

"One More Time"
Makowsky, Veronica A. *Caroline Gordon* . . . , 131.

"The Petrified Woman"
Makowsky, Veronica A. *Caroline Gordon* . . . , 183–184.

"The Presence"
Makowsky, Veronica A. *Caroline Gordon* . . . , 185–186.

DANIIL GRANIN

"Bison"
Shneidman, N. N. *Soviet Literature* . . . , 58–59.

"The Track Is Still Visible"
Shneidman, N. N. *Soviet Literature* . . . , 123–124.

RUSSELL GRAY [BRUNO FISCHER]

"Plague of the Black Passion"
Lachman, Marvin. "Religious Cults and Mystery," in Breen, Jon L., and Martin Greenberg, Eds. *Synod of Sleuths* . . . , 88–89.

ANNA KATHARINE GREEN

"The Grotto Spectre"
Maida, Patricia D. *Mother of Detective Fiction* . . . , 76–77.

"The Hermit of — Street"
Maida, Patricia D. *Mother of Detective Fiction* . . . , 93–94.

"The House of Mist"
Maida, Patricia D. *Mother of Detective Fiction* . . . , 86–87.

"Midnight in Beauchamp Row"
Maida, Patricia D. *Mother of Detective Fiction* . . . , 42–43.

"The Second Bullet"
Maida, Patricia D. *Mother of Detective Fiction* . . . , 75–76.

"Shall He Wed Her?"
Maida, Patricia D. *Mother of Detective Fiction* . . . , 96–97.

"Staircase at the Heart's Delight"
Maida, Patricia D. *Mother of Detective Fiction* . . . , 43–45.

"Violet's Own"
Maida, Patricia D. *Mother of Detective Fiction* . . . , 77.

JULIEN GREEN

"Leviathan"
Ziegler, Robert. "(L)imitations of Silence: The Implications of Reader Exclusion in Julien Green's 'Léviathan: La Traversée inutile,' " *Stud Short Fiction*, 27 (1990), 339–345.

GRAHAM GREENE

"Across the Bridge"
Schöneich, Christoph. "Alive and Suffering: Graham Greene's 'Across the Bridge,' " in Diedrich, Maria, and Christoph Schöneich, Eds. *Studien zur Englischen und Amerikanischen Prosa* . . . , 46–58.
Schulz, Volker. *Das kurzepische Werk* . . . , 87–89.

"Alas, Poor Maling"
Schulz, Volker. *Das kurzepische Werk* . . . , 51–53.

"Awful When You Think of It"
Schulz, Volker. *Das kurzepische Werk* . . . , 195–199.

"The Basement Room"
Miller, R. H. *Understanding Graham Greene*, 150–152.
Schulz, Volker. *Das kurzepische Werk* . . . , 80–83.

"The Blessing"
Schulz, Volker. *Das kurzepische Werk* . . . , 99–100.

"The Blue Film"
Schulz, Volker. *Das kurzepische Werk* . . . , 204–209.

"Brother"
Schulz, Volker. *Das kurzepische Werk* . . . , 109–110.

"The Case for the Defense"
Schulz, Volker. *Das kurzepische Werk* . . . , 86–87.

"Chagrin in Three Parts"
Schulz, Volker. *Das kurzepische Werk* . . . , 100–101.

"A Chance for Mr. Lever"
Schulz, Volker. *Das kurzepische Werk* . . . , 76–78.

"Cheap in August"
Schulz, Volker. *Das kurzepische Werk* . . . , 89–90.

"Church Militant"
Schulz, Volker. *Das kurzepische Werk* . . . , 114–115.

"A Day Saved"
Schulz, Volker. *Das kurzepische Werk* . . . , 125–127.

"Dear Dr. Falkenheim"
Schulz, Volker. *Das kurzepische Werk* . . . , 107–108.

"The Destructors"
McCartney, J. F. "Politics in Graham Greene's 'The Destructors,' " *Southern Hum R*, 12 (1978), 31–41.
Miller, R. H. *Understanding Graham Greene*, 152–155.
Ower, J. "Dark Parable: History and Theology in Graham Greene's 'The Destructors,' " *Cithara*, 15, i (1975), 69–78.
Schulz, Volker. *Das kurzepische Werk* . . . , 127–133.

"A Discovery in the Woods"
Schulz, Volker. *Das kurzepische Werk* . . . , 70–71.

"Doctor Crombie"
Schulz, Volker. *Das kurzepische Werk* . . . , 200–203.

"Dream of a Strange Land"
Schulz, Volker. *Das kurzepische Werk* . . . , 76–78.

"A Drive in the Country"
Schulz, Volker. *Das kurzepische Werk* . . . , 96–98.

"The End of the Party"
Schulz, Volker. *Das kurzepische Werk* . . . , 231–239.

"The Hint of an Explanation"
Bayley, John. "Graham Greene: The Short Stories," in Meyer, Jeffrey, Ed. *Graham Greene* . . . , 94–98.
Schulz, Volker. *Das kurzepische Werk* . . . , 57–59.

"I Spy"
Schulz, Volker. *Das kurzepische Werk* . . . , 104–105.

"The Innocent"
Schulz, Volker. *Das kurzepische Werk* . . . , 209–212.

"The Invisible Japanese Gentleman"
Schulz, Volker. *Das kurzepische Werk* . . . , 116–118.

"Jubilee"
Schulz, Volker. *Das kurzepische Werk* . . . , 102–104.

"A Little Place off the Edgeware Road"
Schulz, Volker. *Das kurzepische Werk* . . . , 46–47.

"May We Borrow Your Husband?"
Schulz, Volker. *Das kurzepische Werk* . . . , 245–261.

"Men at Work"
Schulz, Volker. *Das kurzepische Werk* . . . , 192–195.

"Mortmain"
Schulz, Volker. *Das kurzepische Werk* . . . , 240–245.

"The Overnight Bag"
Schulz, Volker. *Das kurzepische Werk* . . . , 118–119, 172–173.

"Proof Positive"
Schulz, Volker. *Das kurzepische Werk* . . . , 43–44.

"The Second Death"
Schulz, Volker. *Das kurzepische Werk* . . . , 45–46.

"A Shocking Accident"
Schulz, Volker. *Das kurzepische Werk* . . . , 78–80.

"Special Duties"
Schulz, Volker. *Das kurzepische Werk* . . . , 101–102.

"Two Gentle People"
Schulz, Volker. *Das kurzepische Werk* . . . , 212–230.

"Under the Garden"
Schulz, Volker. *Das kurzepische Werk* . . . , 83–86.

"A Visit to Morin"
Bayley, John. "Graham Greene . . . ," 98–99.
Duran, L. "Graham Greene's 'A Visit to Morin,' " *Clergy R*, 59 (1974), 643–647.
Schulz, Volker. *Das kurzepische Werk* . . . , 119–122.

"When Greek Meets Greek"
Schulz, Volker. *Das kurzepische Werk* . . . , 53–57.

IRINA GREKOVA [ELENA SERGEEVNA VENCEL]

"The Faculty"
Shneidman, N. N. *Soviet Literature* . . . , 173–174.

"The Hotel Manager"
Barker, Adele. "Women Without Men in the Writings of Contemporary Soviet Women Writers," in Rancour-Laferriere, Daniel, Ed. *Russian Literature* . . . , 435–439.
Shneidman, N. N. *Soviet Literature* . . . , 172–173.

"Ladies Hairdresser"
Barker, Adele. "Women Without Men . . . ," 439.

"The Ship of Widows"
Shneidman, N. N. *Soviet Literature* . . . , 174–176.

FRANZ GRILLPARZER

"The Poor Player"
Nicolai, Ralf R. "Grillparzers 'Der arme Spielmann': Eine Deutung," *Literaturwissenschaftliches Jahrbuch*, 29 (1988), 63–84.

ALFONSO GROSSO

"Carboneo"
Fernández Jiménez, Juan. "Temática social andaluza en los cuentos de Alfonso Grosso," in Menchacatorre, Félix, Ed. *Ensayos de literatura . . .*, 160.

"Germinal"
Fernández Jiménez, Juan. "Temática social andaluza . . .," 158–159.

AMADIS MA. GUERRERO

"The Children of the City"
Dimalanta, Ophelia A. "City Fiction: Manila, a Way of Life and Art," in Villacorta, Wilfrido V., Isagani R. Cruz, and Ma. Lourdes Brillantes, Eds. *Manila . . .*, 258.

"Click of the Camera"
Dimalanta, Ophelia A. "City Fiction . . .," 286.

"Clock Watchers"
Dimalanta, Ophelia A. "City Fiction . . .," 286.

MARY GUERRERO

"Para el día de la muerte"
Ramos, Elías A. *El cuento venezolano . . .*, 32–33.

"El paseo"
Ramos, Elías A. *El cuento venezolano . . .*, 119–120.

P. J. HAASBROEK

"An Anatomy Lesson"
Trump, Martin. "Afrikaner Literature and the South African Liberation Struggle," *J Commonwealth Lit*, 25, i (1990), 58–59.

"Two Terrorists"
Trump, Martin. "Afrikaner Literature . . .," 57–58.

DONALD HALL

"The First Woman"
Yahnke, Robert E., and Richard M. Eastman. *Aging in Literature* . . . , 43–44.

"The Ideal Bakery"
Yahnke, Robert E., and Richard M. Eastman. *Aging in Literature* . . . , 43.

EDMOND HAMILTON

"Crashing Suns"
Panshin, Alexel, and Cory Panshin. *The World Beyond* . . . , 216–219.

RON HANSEN

"Red-Letter Day"
Yahnke, Robert E., and Richard M. Eastman. *Aging in Literature* . . . , 44–45.

HAO RAN

"Longevity"
Liu Bai-sha. "The Hero Image in Hao Ran's Writings," in Malmqvist, Göran, Ed. *Modern Chinese Literature* . . . , 201–202.

"Miracle Grass"
Liu Bai-sha. "The Hero Image . . . ," 202.

THOMAS HARDY

"Barbara of the House of Grebe"
Wright, T. R. *Hardy and the Erotic*, 94–95.

"A Changed Man"
Wright, T. R. *Hardy and the Erotic*, 101–102.

"The Distracted Preacher"
Wright, T. R. *Hardy and the Erotic*, 92–93.

"The Fiddler of the Reels"
Wright, T. R. *Hardy and the Erotic*, 97–98.

"An Imaginative Woman"
Wright, T. R. *Hardy and the Erotic*, 98–99.

"On the Western Circuit"
Wright, T. R. *Hardy and the Erotic*, 99–101.

"The Romantic Adventures of a Milkmaid"
Wright, T. R. *Hardy and the Erotic*, 103–104.

"The Waiting Supper"
Wright, T. R. *Hardy and the Erotic*, 102–103.

"The Withered Arm"
Wright, T. R. *Hardy and the Erotic*, 90–91.

HARRY HARRISON

"Brave Newer World"
Stover, Leon. *Harry Harrison*, 78.

"By the Falls"
Stover, Leon. *Harry Harrison*, 77–78.

"A Criminal Act"
Stover, Leon. *Harry Harrison*, 75–76.

"From Fanaticism, or for Reward"
Stover, Leon. *Harry Harrison*, 52–53.

"K-Factor"
Stover, Leon. *Harry Harrison*, 46–47.

"Mute Milton"
Stover, Leon. *Harry Harrison*, 77.

"Rescue Operation"
Stover, Leon. *Harry Harrison*, 39–44.

EPELI HAU'OFA

"The Glorious Pacific War"
Edmond, Rod. " 'Kiss my arse!': Epeli Hau'ofa and the Politics of Laughter," *J Commonwealth Lit*, 25, i (1990), 144–145.

"The Wages of Sin"
Edmond, Rod. " 'Kiss my arse!' . . . ," 144.

GERHART HAUPTMANN

"Signalman Thiel"
Rock, David G. "Interior Landscapes: Narrative Perspective in Hauptmann's 'Bahnwärter Thiel,' " *Mod Langs*, 70 (1989), 211–219.

W. T. HAWLEY

"The Unknown, or Lays of the Forest"
MacDonald, Mary Lu. "Red & White Men; Black, White & Grey Hats," *Canadian Lit*, 124–125 (1990), 99.

NATHANIEL HAWTHORNE

"Alice Doane's Appeal"
Berlant, Lauren. "America, Post-Utopia: Body, Landscape, and National Fantasy in Hawthorne's *Native Land*," *Arizona Q*, 44, iv (1989), 30–45.
+Downing, David. "Beyond Convention: The Dynamics of Imagery and Response in Nathaniel Hawthorne's Early Sense of Evil," in Cady, Edwin H., and Louis J. Budd, Eds. *On Hawthorne* . . . , 185–193.
Levine, Robert. *Conspiracy and Romance* . . . , 117–118.
Wagenknecht, Edward. *Nathaniel Hawthorne* . . . , 188–189.

"The Ambitious Guest"
Wagenknecht, Edward. *Nathaniel Hawthorne* . . . , 189.

"The Artist of the Beautiful"
Bromell, Nicholas K. " 'The Bloody Hand' of Labor: Three Stories by Hawthorne," *Am Q*, 42 (1990), 550–552.
Crisman, William. " 'The Snow Image' as Key to Hawthorne's Biotechnology Tales," *Am Transcendental Q*, 3, N.S. (1989), 180–181.
Harshbarger, Scott. "Bugs and Butterflies: Conflict and Transcendence in 'The Artist of the Beautiful' and 'The Apple-Tree Table,' " *Stud Short Fiction*, 26 (1989), 186–189.
Wagenknecht, Edward. *Nathaniel Hawthorne* . . . , 190–192.
Wohlpart, A. James. "The Status of the Artist in Hawthorne's 'The Artist of the Beautiful,' " *Am Transcendental Q*, 3, N.S. (1989), 242–256.

"The Birthmark"
Bromell, Nicholas K. " 'The Bloody Hand' . . . ," 552–553.
Crisman, William. " 'The Snow Image' as Key . . . ," 182–183.
Eckstein, Barbara. "Hawthorne's 'The Birthmark': Science and Romance as Belief," *Stud Short Fiction*, 26 (1989), 511–519.
Haggerty, George E. *Gothic Fiction* . . . , 113–115.
Johnson, Barbara. "Is Female to Male as Ground Is to Figure?" in Feldstein, Richard, and Judith Roof, Eds. *Feminism* . . . , 258–259.
Limon, John. *The Place of Fiction* . . . , 126–130.
Luedtke, Luther. *Nathaniel Hawthorne* . . . , 159–160.
Wagenknecht, Edward. *Nathaniel Hawthorne* . . . , 38–41.
Westbrook, Ellen E. "Probable Improbabilities: Verisimilar Romance in Hawthorne's 'The Birthmark,' " *Am Transcendental Q*, 3, N.S. (1989), 203–217.

"The Canterbury Pilgrims"
Wagenknecht, Edward. *Nathaniel Hawthorne* . . . , 192.

"The Celestial Railroad"
Wagenknecht, Edward. *Nathaniel Hawthorne* . . . , 193.

"Dr. Heidegger's Experiment"
Wagenknecht, Edward. *Nathaniel Hawthorne* . . . , 194–195.

"Drowne's Wooden Image"
Bromell, Nicholas. " 'The Bloody Hand' . . . ," 553–556.
Crisman, William. " 'The Snow Image' as Key . . . ," 181–182.
Luedtke, Luther. *Nathaniel Hawthorne* . . . , 168–171.
Wagenknecht, Edward. *Nathaniel Hawthorne* . . . , 195–196.
Wutz, Michael. "Hawthorne's Drowne: *Felix Culpa* Exculpated," *Stud Am Fiction*, 18 (1990), 99–109.

"Earth's Holocaust"
Wagenknecht, Edward. *Nathaniel Hawthorne* . . . , 196.

"Edward Randolph's Portrait"
Wagenknecht, Edward. *Nathaniel Hawthorne* . . . , 34–35.

"Egotism; or, The Bosom Serpent"
Matsusaka, Hitoshi. "Hawthorne's 'Egotism' and the Ambiguous Snake," *Chu-Shikoku Stud Am Lit*, 26 (June, 1990), 1–9.
Wagenknecht, Edward. *Nathaniel Hawthorne* . . . , 197–198.

"Endicott and the Red Cross"
Levine, Robert. *Conspiracy and Romance* . . . , 122–123.
Wagenknecht, Edward. *Nathaniel Hawthorne* . . . , 23–25.

"Ethan Brand"
Wagenknecht, Edward. *Nathaniel Hawthorne* . . . , 41–50.

"Feathertop"
Schirmeister, Pamela. *The Consolations* . . . , 56–63.
Westbrook, Ellen E. "Exposing the Verisimilar: Hawthorne's 'Wakefield' and 'Feathertop,' " *Arizona Q*, 45, iv (1989), 12–21.

"The Gentle Boy"
+Dauner, Louise. "The 'Case' of Tobias Pearson: Hawthorne and the Ambiguities," in Cady, Edwin H., and Louis J. Budd, Eds. *On Hawthorne* . . . , 24–32.
+Gross, Seymour L. "Hawthorne's Revision of 'The Gentle Boy,' " in Cady, Edwin H., and Louis J. Budd, Eds. *On Hawthorne* . . . , 39–51.
Levine, Robert. *Conspiracy and Romance* . . . , 125–126.
Luedtke, Luther. *Nathaniel Hawthorne* . . . , 93–103.
Wagenknecht, Edward. *Nathaniel Hawthorne* . . . , 29–32.

"The Gray Champion"
Levine, Robert. *Conspiracy and Romance* . . . , 120–122.
Wagenknecht, Edward. *Nathaniel Hawthorne* . . . , 21–23.

"The Great Carbuncle"
Limon, John. *The Place of Fiction* . . . , 121–125.
Wagenknecht, Edward. *Nathaniel Hawthorne* . . . , 198–199.

"The Great Stone Face"
Wagenknecht, Edward. *Nathaniel Hawthorne* . . . , 199–200.

"The Hall of Fantasy"
Levine, Robert. *Conspiracy and Romance* . . . , 129–130.

"The Hollow of the Three Hills"
Berlant, Lauren. "America, Post-Utopia . . . ," 28–30.
+Downing, David. "Beyond Convention . . . ," 180–185.

"Howe's Masquerade"
Wagenknecht, Edward. *Nathaniel Hawthorne* . . . , 33–34.

"Lady Eleanore's Mantle"
Wagenknecht, Edward. *Nathaniel Hawthorne* . . . , 35–36.

"The Lily's Quest"
Wagenknecht, Edward. *Nathaniel Hawthorne* . . . , 201.

"The Man of Adamant"
Wagenknecht, Edward. *Nathaniel Hawthorne* . . . , 201–202.

"The Maypole of Merry Mount"
Levine, Robert. *Conspiracy and Romance* . . . , 124–125.
Miller, John N. " 'The Maypole of Merry Mount': Hawthorne's Festive Irony," *Stud Short Fiction*, 26 (1989), 111–123.
Wagenknecht, Edward. *Nathaniel Hawthorne* . . . , 25–29.
Weltzien, Alan O. "The Picture of History in 'The May-Pole of Merry Mount,' " *Arizona Q*, 45, i (1989), 29–48.

"The Minister's Black Veil"
Haggerty, George E. *Gothic Fiction* . . . , 110–112.
Wagenknecht, Edward. *Nathaniel Hawthorne* . . . , 202–203.

"Mr. Higginbotham's Catastrophe"
Wagenknecht, Edward. *Nathaniel Hawthorne* . . . , 203–204.

"Monsieur du Miroir"
Auerbach, Jonathan. *The Romance of Failure* . . . , 76–79.

"My Kinsman, Major Molineux"
Canaan, Howard. " 'My Kinsman, Major Molineux' and the Romantic Dilemma," *Mid-Hudson Lang Stud*, 12, ii (1989), 40–54.
Girgus, Sam B. *Desire and the Political Unconscious* . . . , 56–59.
Haggerty, George E. *Gothic Fiction* . . . , 108–109.
Leverenz, David. *Manhood* . . . , 231–239.
Lewis, Paul. *Comic Effects* . . . , 91–93.
Miller, John N. "The Pageantry of Revolt in 'My Kinsman, Major Molineux,' " *Stud Am Fiction*, 17 (1989), 51–64.
Wagenknecht, Edward. *Nathaniel Hawthorne* . . . , 66–72.

"The New Adam and Eve"
Wagenknecht, Edward. *Nathaniel Hawthorne* . . . , 204–205.

"Old Esther Dudley"
Wagenknecht, Edward. *Nathaniel Hawthorne* . . . , 36–38.

"Peter Goldthwaite's Treasure"
Wagenknecht, Edward. *Nathaniel Hawthorne* . . . , 206.

"The Prophetic Pictures"
Wagenknecht, Edward. *Nathaniel Hawthorne* . . . , 206–207.

"Rappaccini's Daughter"
Chappell, Charles. "Pietro Baglioni's Motives for Murder in 'Rappaccini's Daughter,' " *Stud Am Fiction*, 18 (1990), 55–63.
Haggerty, George E. *Gothic Fiction* . . . , 115–135.
Hazlett, John D. "Re-Reading 'Rappaccini's Daughter': Giovanni

and the Seduction of the Transcendental Reader," *ESQ: J Am Renaissance*, 35, i (1989), 43–68.
Limon, John. *The Place of Fiction* . . . , 130–132.
Luedtke, Luther. *Nathaniel Hawthorne* . . . , 174–181.
Pahl, Dennis. *Architects of the Abyss* . . . , 59–70.
+Rosenberry, Edward H. "Hawthorne's Allegory of Science: 'Rappaccini's Daughter,' " in Cady, Edwin H., and Louis J. Budd, Eds. *On Hawthorne* . . . , 106–113.
Wagenknecht, Edward. *Nathaniel Hawthorne* . . . , 50–57.

"Roger Malvin's Burial"
Hochberg, Shifra. "Etymology and the Significance of Names in 'Roger Malvin's Burial,' " *Stud Short Fiction*, 26 (1989), 317–321.
+McIntosh, James. "Nature and Frontier in 'Roger Malvin's Burial,' " in Cady, Edwin H., and Louis J. Budd, Eds. *On Hawthorne* . . . , 245–261.
Wagenknecht, Edward. *Nathaniel Hawthorne* . . . , 207–208.

"The Shaker Bridal"
Wagenknecht, Edward. *Nathaniel Hawthorne* . . . , 192–193.

"The Snow Image"
Crisman, William. " 'The Snow Image' as Key . . . ," 171–179.
Wagenknecht, Edward. *Nathaniel Hawthorne* . . . , 209–210.

"Wakefield"
Laffrado, Laura. " 'Far and Momentary Glimpses': Hawthorne's Treatment of Mrs. Wakefield," *Bucknell R*, 31, ii (1988), 34–44.
Manning, Susan. *The Puritan-Provincial Vision* . . . , 116–118.
Westbrook, Ellen E. "Exposing the Verisimilar . . . ," 1–12.

"The Wives of the Dead"
Wagenknecht, Edward. *Nathaniel Hawthorne* . . . , 211–212.

"Young Goodman Brown"
Girgus, Sam B. *Desire and the Political Unconscious* . . . , 59–66.
Haggerty, George E. *Gothic Fiction* . . . , 112–113.
+Levin, David. "Shadows of Doubt: Specter Evidence in Hawthorne's 'Young Goodman Brown,' " in Cady, Edwin H., and Louis J. Budd, Eds. *On Hawthorne* . . . , 114–122.
Levine, Robert. *Conspiracy and Romance* . . . , 127–129.
Manning, Susan. *The Puritan-Provincial Vision* . . . , 97–101.
Wagenknecht, Edward. *Nathaniel Hawthorne* . . . , 57–66.
Zanger, Jules. " 'Young Goodman Brown' and 'A White Heron': Correspondences and Illuminations," *Papers Lang & Lit*, 26 (1990), 346–357.

HAYYIM [HAIM] HAZAZ

"Rahamim"
Alter, Robert, Ed. *Modern Hebrew Literature*, 253–256.

"Revolutionary Chapters"
Roskies, David G. "The Rape of the Shtetl," in Roskies, David G., Ed. *The Literature of Destruction* . . . , 281–282.

"The Sermon"
Alter, Robert, Ed. *Modern Hebrew Literature*, 267–270.

BESSIE HEAD

"The Collector of Treasures"
Chetin, Sara. "Myth, Exile, and the Female Condition: Bessie Head's *The Collector of Treasures*," *J Commonwealth Lit*, 24, i (1989), 134–135.

"The Deep River: A Story of the Ancient Tribal Migration"
Chetin, Sara. "Myth, Exile . . . ," 115–118.

"Heaven Is Not Closed"
Chetin, Sara. "Myth, Exile . . . ," 119–120.

"Hunting"
Chetin, Sara. "Myth, Exile . . . ," 136–137.

"Jacob: The Story of a Faith-Healing Priest"
Chetin, Sara. "Myth, Exile . . . ," 123–127.

"Kgotla"
Chetin, Sara. "Myth, Exile . . . ," 131–132.

"Life"
Chetin, Sara. "Myth, Exile . . . ," 127–129.

"Look for a Rain God"
Chetin, Sara. "Myth, Exile . . . ," 130–131.

"Snapshots at a Wedding"
Chetin, Sara. "Myth, Exile . . . ," 132–133.

"The Special One"
Chetin, Sara. "Myth, Exile . . . ," 133–134.

"The Village Exile"
Chetin, Sara. "Myth, Exile . . . ," 121–123.

"The Wind and the Boy"
Chetin, Sara. "Myth, Exile . . . ," 132.

"Witchcraft"
Chetin, Sara. "Myth, Exile . . . ," 127–129.

LAFCADIO HEARN

"The Reconciliation"
Hirakawa, Sukehiro. "Was She Really Reconciled? Ghost Wife Stories in Chinese, Korean, Japanese and American Literatures," *Tamkang R*, 18, i–iv (Autumn, 1987—Summer, 1988), 188–192.

JOHN HEARNE

"The Lost Country"
Kusgen, Reinhardt. "John Hearne's 'The Lost Country': A Caribbean Version of the American Dream," in Stummer, Peter O., Ed. *The Story Must Be Told . . .* , 77–85.

CHRISTOPHER HEIN

"Drachenblut"
Roberts, David. "Surface and Depth: Christopher Hein's 'Drachenblut,' " *Germ Q*, 63 (1990), 478–489.

ROBERT HEINLEIN

"By His Bootstraps"
Panshin, Alexel, and Cory Panshin. *The World Beyond . . .* , 399–401.

"Coventry"
Panshin, Alexel, and Cory Panshin. *The World Beyond . . .* , 376–377.

"Magic, Inc."
Panshin, Alexel, and Cory Panshin. *The World Beyond . . .* , 373–380.

"Misfit"
Panshin, Alexel, and Cory Panshin. *The World Beyond . . .* , 369–371.

"The Roads Must Roll"
Huntington, John. *Rationalizing Genius . . .* , 74–79.

JOSEPH HELLER

"Castle of Snow"
Seed, David. . . . *Against the Grain*, 17–21.

"I Don't Love You Anymore"
Seed, David. . . . *Against the Grain*, 14–15.

"McAdam's Log"
Seed, David. . . . *Against the Grain*, 19–21.

MARK HELPRIN

"A Dove of the East"
Greenstein, Michael. "Jewish Pegasus," *Jewish Book Forum*, 45 (1990), 52–53.

ANTONIO HELÚ

"El Fistol de Corbata"
Simpson, Amelia S. *Detective Fiction* . . . , 83–84.

ERNEST HEMINGWAY

"After the Storm"
Stoltfus, Ben. "Hemingway's 'After the Storm': A Lacanian Reading," in Benson, Jackson J., Ed. *New Critical Approaches* . . . , 48–57.

"An Alpine Idyll"
Gajdusek, Robert E. " 'An Alpine Idyll': The Sun-Struck Mountain Vision and the Necessary Valley Journey," in Beegel, Susan F., Ed. *Hemingway's Neglected Short Fiction* . . . , 163–183.

"Banal Story"
+Kvam, Wayne. "Hemingway's 'Banal Story,' " in Benson, Jackson J., Ed. *New Critical Approaches* . . . , 215–223.
Monteiro, George. "The Writer on Vocation: Hemingway's 'Banal Story,' " in Beegel, Susan F., Ed. *Hemingway's Neglected Short Fiction* . . . , 141–147.

"The Battler"
Flora, Joseph M. *Ernest Hemingway* . . . , 56–57.
+Monteiro, George. " 'This Is My Pal Bugs': Ernest Hemingway's 'The Battler,' " in Benson, Jackson J., Ed. *New Critical Approaches* . . . , 224–228.
Strychacz, Thomas. "Dramatization of Manhood in Hemingway's *In Our Time* and *The Sun Also Rises,*" *Am Lit*, 61 (1989), 251–252.

"Big Two-Hearted River"
Benoit, Raymond. "The Complete Walker: Food & Lodging in Hemingway's 'Big Two-Hearted River,' " *Notes Contemp Lit*, 20, iii (1990), 10–12.
Bredahl, A. Carl. *New Ground* . . . , 74–76.
Flora, Joseph M. *Ernest Hemingway* . . . , 51–60.
Godden, Richard. *Fiction of Capital* . . . , 43–47.
+Hoffman, Steven K. "*Nada* and the Clean, Well-Lighted Place: The Unity of Hemingway's Short Fiction," in Benson, Jackson J., Ed. *New Critical Approaches* . . . , 185–186.
McDowell, Nicholas. *Hemingway*, 42–45.
Schmidt, Susan. "Ecological Renewal Images in Hemingway's 'Big Two-Hearted River': Jack Pines and Fisher King," *Hemingway R*, 9, ii (1990), 142–144.
Strychacz, Thomas. "Dramatization . . . ," 252–255.

"Black Ass at the Cross Roads"
Flora, Joseph M. *Ernest Hemingway* . . . , 102–104.

"The Butterfly and the Tank"
Flora, Joseph M. *Ernest Hemingway* . . . , 93.
Johnston, Kenneth G. " 'The Butterfly and the Tank': Casualties of War," *Stud Short Fiction*, 26 (1989), 183–186.

Josephs, Allen. "Hemingway's Spanish Civil War Stories, or the Spanish Civil War as Reality," in Beegel, Susan F., Ed. *Hemingway's Neglected Short Fiction* . . . , 321–322.

"A Canary for One"

Flora, Joseph M. *Ernest Hemingway* . . . , 36–39.

Harding, Brian. "Ernest Hemingway: Men with, or Without, Women," in Massa, Ann, Ed. *American Declarations* . . . , 110–112.

"The Capital of the World"

Cooper, Stephen. "Illusion and Reality: 'The Capital of the World,' " in Beegel, Susan F., Ed. *Hemingway's Neglected Short Fiction* . . . , 303–311.

"Cat in the Rain"

+Bennett, Warren. "The Poor Kitty and the Padrone and the Tortoise-shell Cat in 'Cat in the Rain,' " in Benson, Jackson J., Ed. *New Critical Approaches* . . . , 245–256.

+Holmesland, Oddvar. "Structuralism and Interpretation: Ernest Hemingway's 'Cat in the Rain,' " in Benson, Jackson J., Ed. *New Critical Approaches* . . . , 58–72.

"A Clean, Well-Lighted Place"

Bennett, Warren. "The Characterization and Dialogue Problem in Hemingway's 'A Clean, Well-Lighted Place,' " *Hemingway R*, 9, ii (1990), 94–122.

Flora, Joseph M. *Ernest Hemingway* . . . , 19–25.

+Hoffman, Steven K. "*Nada* and the Clean, Well-Lighted Place . . . ," 172–173, 176–178.

Stanton, Edward F. *Hemingway and Spain* . . . , 132–139.

"Cross-Country Snow"

Flora, Joseph M. *Ernest Hemingway* . . . , 41–43.

"A Day's Wait"

Flora, Joseph M. *Ernest Hemingway* . . . , 44–46.

Gajdusek, Linda. "Up and Down: Making Connections in 'A Day's Wait,' " in Beegel, Susan F., Ed. *Hemingway's Neglected Short Fiction* . . . , 291–302.

"The Denunciation"

Flora, Joseph M. *Ernest Hemingway* . . . , 92–93.

+Johnston, Kenneth G. "Hemingway's 'The Denunciation': The Aloof American," in Benson, Jackson J., Ed. *New Critical Approaches* . . . , 257–265.

"The Doctor and the Doctor's Wife"

Flora, Joseph M. *Ernest Hemingway* . . . , 18–19.

Strychacz, Thomas. "Dramatization . . . ," 249–250.

"The End of Something"

Flora, Joseph M. *Ernest Hemingway* . . . , 29–30.

"The Faithful Bull"

Flora, Joseph M. *Ernest Hemingway* . . . , 111–112.

"Fathers and Sons"
Flora, Joseph M. *Ernest Hemingway* . . . , 46–51.
Lewis, Robert W. " 'Long Time Ago Good, Now No Good': Hemingway's Indian Stories," in Benson, Jackson J., Ed. *New Critical Approaches* . . . , 205–206.
+McCann, Richard. "To Embrace or Kill: 'Fathers and Sons,' " in Benson, Jackson J., Ed. *New Critical Approaches* . . . , 266–274.
Strong, Paul. "Gathering the Pieces and Filling in the Gaps: Hemingway's 'Fathers and Sons,' " *Stud Short Fiction*, 26 (1989), 49–58.

"Fifty Grand"
Flora, Joseph M. *Ernest Hemingway* . . . , 131–133.
+Weeks, Robert P. "Wise-Guy Narrator and Trickster Out-Tricked in Hemingway's 'Fifty Grand,' " in Benson, Jackson J., Ed. *New Critical Approaches* . . . , 275–281.

"The Gambler, the Nun, and the Radio"
Bovey, Seth. "The Western Code of Hemingway's Gambler," *No Dakota Q*, 58, iii (1990), 87–93.
Fleming, Robert E. "American Nightmare: Hemingway and the West," *Midwest Q*, 30 (1989), 364–366.
Flora, Joseph M. *Ernest Hemingway* . . . , 69–74.
+Hoffman, Steven K. "*Nada* and the Clean, Well-Lighted Place . . . ," 182–183, 189–190.
+Whittle, Amberys R. "A Reading of Hemingway's 'The Gambler, the Nun, and the Radio,' " in Benson, Jackson J., Ed. *New Critical Approaches* . . . , 282–287.

"Get a Seeing-Eye Dog"
Flora, Joseph M. *Ernest Hemingway* . . . , 113–117.
Hannum, Howard L. "Hemingway's Tales of 'The Real Dark,' " in Beegel, Susan F., Ed. *Hemingway's Neglected Short Fiction* . . . , 339–350.

"The Good Lion"
Flora, Joseph M. *Ernest Hemingway* . . . , 110–111.

"Great News from the Mainland"
Flora, Joseph M. *Ernest Hemingway* . . . , 107–108.

"Hills Like White Elephants"
Consigney, Scott. "Hemingway's 'Hills Like White Elephants,' " *Explicator*, 48, i (1989), 54–55.
Flora, Joseph M. *Ernest Hemingway* . . . , 33–35.
Hays, Peter L. *Ernest Hemingway*, 55–56.
Kelly, Lionel. "Hemingway and Fitzgerald: Two Short Stories," in Hanson, Clare, Ed. *Re-reading* . . . , 98–104.
Lanier, Doris. "The Bittersweet Taste of Absinthe in Hemingway's 'Hills Like White Elephants,' " *Stud Short Fiction*, 26 (1989), 279–288.
+Smiley, Pamela. "Gender-Linked Miscommunication in 'Hills Like White Elephants,' " in Benson, Jackson J., Ed. *New Critical Approaches* . . . , 288–299.

Wilt, Judith. *Abortion, Choice . . .*, 103–105.

"Homage to Switzerland"
Flora, Joseph M. *Ernest Hemingway . . .*, 43–44.
Nakjavani, Erik. "Repetition as Design and Intention: Hemingway's 'Homage to Switzerland,' " in Beegel, Susan F., Ed. *Hemingway's Neglected Short Fiction . . .*, 263–282.
Reynolds, Michael S. " 'Homage to Switzerland': Einstein's Train Stops at Hemingway's Station," in Beegel, Susan F., Ed. *Hemingway's Neglected Short Fiction . . .*, 256–262.

"I Guess Everything Reminds You of Something"
Flora, Joseph M. *Ernest Hemingway . . .*, 105–107.

"In Another Country"
Flora, Joseph M. *Ernest Hemingway . . .*, 153–156.
Harding, Brian. "Ernest Hemingway . . . ," 112–113.

"Indian Camp"
Hays, Peter L. *Ernest Hemingway*, 43–44.
Hillenaar, Henk. "Hemingway: Sémiotique et interprétation," *Neophilologus*, 73 (1989), 183–188.
Lewis, Robert W. " 'Long Time Ago Good . . . ,' " 202–203.
+Meyers, Jeffrey. "Hemingway's Primitivism and 'Indian Camp,' " in Benson, Jackson J., Ed. *New Critical Approaches . . .*, 300–308.
Sonne, Harly, and Christian Grambye. "Narrativité et représentation psychologique," *Neophilologus*, 73 (1989), 162–182.
Strychacz, Thomas. "Dramatization . . . ," 247–249.

"The Killers"
+Fleming, Robert E. "Hemingway's 'The Killers': The Map and the Territory," in Benson, Jackson J., Ed. *New Critical Approaches . . .*, 309–313.
Hays, Peter L. *Ernest Hemingway*, 54–55.
+Hoffman, Steven K. "*Nada* and the Clean, Well-Lighted Place . . . ," 178–179.
Monteiro, George. "The Hit in Summit: Ernest Hemingway's 'The Killers,' " *Hemingway R*, 8, ii (1989), 40–42.

"Language with Figures"
Flora, Joseph M. *Ernest Hemingway . . .*, 96–98.

"The Last Good Country"
+Johnson, David R. " 'The Last Good Country': Again the End of Something," in Benson, Jackson J., Ed. *New Critical Approaches . . .*, 314–320.

"The Light of the World"
Fleming, Robert E. "Myth or Reality: 'The Light of the World' as Initiation Story," in Beegel, Susan F., Ed. *Hemingway's Neglected Short Fiction . . .*, 283–290.
Flora, Joseph M. *Ernest Hemingway . . .*, 66–69.
Hannum, Howard L. "Nick Adams and the Search for Light," *Stud*

Short Fiction, 23 (1986), 9–13; rpt. Benson, Jackson J., Ed. *New Critical Approaches* . . . , 321–330.
Lewis, Robert W. " 'Long Time Ago Good . . . ,' " 204–205.

"A Man of the World"
Fleming, Robert E. "American Nightmare . . . ," 369–370.
Flora, Joseph M. *Ernest Hemingway* . . . , 112–113.
Hannum, Howard L. "Hemingway's Tales . . . ," 339–350.

"The Mercenaries"
Glatstein, Mimi R. " 'The Mercenaries': A Harbinger of Vintage Hemingway," in Beegel, Susan F., Ed. *Hemingway's Neglected Short Fiction* . . . , 19–30.

"Mr. and Mrs. Elliot"
Smith, Paul. "From the Waste Land to the Garden with the Elliots," in Beegel, Susan F., Ed. *Hemingway's Neglected Short Fiction* . . . , 123–129.

"The Mother of a Queen"
Brenner, Gerry. "From 'Sepi Jingan' to 'Mother of a Queen': Hemingway's Three Epistemologic Formulas for Short Fiction," in Benson, Jackson J., Ed. *New Critical Approaches* . . . ," 165–169.

"My Old Man"
Sipiora, Phillip. "Ethical Narration in 'My Old Man,' " in Beegel, Susan F., Ed. *Hemingway's Neglected Short Fiction* . . . , 43–60.

"A Natural History of the Dead"
Stetler, Charles, and Gerald Locklin. " 'A Natural History of the Dead' as Metafiction," in Beegel, Susan F., Ed. *Hemingway's Neglected Short Fiction* . . . , 247–253.

"Night Before Battle"
Flora, Joseph M. *Ernest Hemingway* . . . , 93–95.
Josephs, Allen. "Hemingway's Spanish Civil War Stories . . . ," 322.

"Nobody Ever Dies"
Edgerton, Larry. " 'Nobody Ever Dies!': Hemingway's *Fifth* Story of the Spanish Civil War," *Arizona Q*, 38, ii (1983), 135–147; rpt. Benson, Jackson J., Ed. *New Critical Approaches* . . . , 331–340.
Flora, Joseph M. *Ernest Hemingway* . . . , 98–99.

"Now I Lay Me"
Flora, Joseph M. *Ernest Hemingway* . . . , 55–56.
Harding, Brian. "Ernest Hemingway . . . ," 113–114.
+Hoffman, Steven K. "*Nada* and the Clean, Well-Lighted Place . . . ," 180–181.
Nakjavani, Erik. "Emotional Disorder and the Order of Things: Nick Adams in Italy," in Lewis, Robert W., Ed. "*Hemingway in Italy*" . . . , 191–197.

"The Old Man and the Sea"
Hays, Peter L. *Ernest Hemingway*, 102–109.
McDowell, Nicholas. *Hemingway*, 90–93.
Timms, David. "Contrasts in Form: Hemingway's 'The Old Man and

the Sea' and Faulkner's 'The Bear,' " in Lee, A. Robert, Ed. *The Modern American Novella*, 97–112.

Van Woensel, Maurice. "Hemingway's 'Old Man': An Agnostic Agonistes," *Estudios Anglo-Americanos*, 12–13 (1988–1989), 51–57.

Yahnke, Robert E., and Richard M. Eastman. *Aging in Literature* . . . , 12.

"Old Man at the Bridge"

Flora, Joseph M. *Ernest Hemingway* . . . , 90–92.

Lambadaridou, E. A. "Ernest Hemingway's Message to Contemporary Man," *Hemingway R*, 9, ii (1990), 146–154.

"One Reader Writes"

Flora, Joseph M. *Ernest Hemingway* . . . , 61–64.

"Out of Season"

Adair, William. "Hemingway's 'Out of Season': The End of the Line," in Benson, Jackson J., Ed. *New Critical Approaches* . . . , 341–346.

Flora, Joseph M. *Ernest Hemingway* . . . , 30–33.

Steinke, James. " 'Out of Season' and Hemingway's Neglected Discovery: Ordinary Actuality," in Beegel, Susan F., Ed. *Hemingway's Neglected Short Fiction* . . . , 61–73.

Sylvester, Bickford. "Hemingway's Italian *Waste Land*: The Complex Unity of 'Out of Season,' " in Beegel, Susan F., Ed. *Hemingway's Neglected Short Fiction* . . . , 75–98.

"A Pursuit Race"

Putnam, Ann. "Waiting for the End in Hemingway's 'A Pursuit Race,' " in Beegel, Susan F., Ed. *Hemingway's Neglected Short Fiction* . . . , 185–194.

"The Sea Change"

Bennett, Warren. " 'That's Not Very Polite': Sexual Identity in Hemingway's 'The Sea Change,' " in Beegel, Susan F., Ed. *Hemingway's Neglected Short Fiction* . . . , 225–245.

+Fleming, Robert E. "Perversion and the Writer in 'The Sea Change,' " in Benson, Jackson J., Ed. *New Critical Approaches* . . . , 347–352.

"Sepi Jingan"

Brenner, Gerry. "From 'Sepi Jingan' to 'Mother of a Queen' . . . ," 157–159.

"The Short Happy Life of Francis Macomber"

Baym, Nina. " 'Actually, I Felt Sorry for the Lion,' " in Benson, Jackson J., Ed. *New Critical Approaches* . . . , 112–120.

Cheatham, George. "The Unhappy Life of Robert Wilson," *Stud Short Fiction*, 26 (1989), 341–345.

Flora, Joseph M. *Ernest Hemingway* . . . , 74–81.

Gaillard, Theodore L. "Hemingway's 'The Short Happy Life of Francis Macomber,' " *Explicator*, 47, iii (1989), 44–47.

Hays, Peter L. *Ernest Hemingway*, 84–86.

+Hoffman, Steven K. "*Nada* and the Clean, Well-Lighted Place . . . ," 186–187.

"A Simple Enquiry"

Brenner, Gerry. "A Semiotic Inquiry into Hemingway's 'A Simple Enquiry,' " in Beegel, Susan F., Ed. *Hemingway's Neglected Short Fiction* . . . , 195–207.

"The Snows of Kilimanjaro"

Fleming, Robert E. "American Nightmare . . . ," 366–367.

Flora, Joseph M. *Ernest Hemingway* . . . , 81–88.

Galinsky, Hans. "Beobachtungen zum Wortschatz von Hemingways 'The Snows of Kilimanjaro,' " in Bauer, Gero, Franz K. Stanzel, and Franz Zaic, Eds. *Festschrift: Prof. Dr. Herbert Koziol* . . . , 87–104.

Hays, Peter L. *Ernest Hemingway*, 86–88.

+Hoffman, Steven K. "*Nada* and the Clean, Well-Lighted Place . . . ," 187–188.

"Soldier's Home"

Bredahl, A. Carl. *New Ground* . . . , 73–74.

"Today Is Friday"

Flora, Joseph M. *Ernest Hemingway* . . . , 24–25.

"The Undefeated"

Flora, Joseph M. *Ernest Hemingway* . . . , 174–177.

Hays, Peter L. *Ernest Hemingway*, 55–56.

"Under the Ridge"

Flora, Joseph M. *Ernest Hemingway* . . . , 95–96.

Josephs, Allen. "Hemingway's Spanish Civil War Stories . . . ," 322–324.

"Up in Michigan"

Hays, Peter L. *Ernest Hemingway*, 82–84.

+Petry, Alice H. "Coming of Age in Hortons Bay: Hemingway's 'Up in Michigan,' " in Benson, Jackson J., Ed. *New Critical Approaches* . . . , 353–359.

Swartzlander, Susan. "Uncle Charles in Michigan," in Beegel, Susan F., Ed. *Hemingway's Neglected Short Fiction* . . . , 31–40.

"A Very Short Story"

Donaldson, Scott. " 'A Very Short Story' as Therapy," in Beegel, Susan F., Ed. *Hemingway's Neglected Short Fiction* . . . , 99–105.

Scholes, Robert. "Decoding Papa: 'A Very Short Story,' " in his *Semiotics and Interpretation*, 110–129; rpt. Benson, Jackson J., Ed. *New Critical Approaches* . . . , 33–47.

"A Way You'll Never Be"

+Hoffman, Steven K. "*Nada* and the Clean, Well-Lighted Place . . . ," 181.

Nakjavani, Erik. "Emotional Disorder . . . ," 197–199.

Scaffela, Frank. "The Way It Never Was on the Piave," in Lewis, Robert W., Ed. *"Hemingway in Italy"* . . . , 181–188.

"Wine of Wyoming"
Fleming, Robert E. "American Nightmare . . . ," 363–364.
Flora, Joseph M. *Ernest Hemingway* . . . , 65–66.
+Martin, Lawrence H. "Crazy in Sheridan: Hemingway's 'Wine of Wyoming' Reconsidered," in Benson, Jackson J., Ed. *New Critical Approaches* . . . , 360–372.
Stoneback, H. R. " 'Mais Je Reste Catholique': Communion, Betrayal, and Aridity in 'Wine of Wyoming,' " in Beegel, Susan F., Ed. *Hemingway's Neglected Short Fiction* . . . , 209–224.

FELISBERTO HERNÁNDEZ

"El Balcón"
Díaz, José P. "Felisberto Hernández: una conciencia que se rehúsa a la existencia," in Hernández, Felisberto. *Obras completas* . . . , IV, 110–112.

"El caballo perdido"
Díaz, José P. "Felisberto Hernández . . . ," 97–105.

ALFONSO HERNÁNDEZ CATÁ

"Cámara oscura"
Cabrera, Rosa M. "Simbolos y claves en los cuentos de Alfonso Hernández Catá," in Neumeister, Sebastián, Ed. *Actas del IX Congreso* . . . , II, 494–495.

"El mal barquero"
Cabrera, Rosa M. "Simbolos y claves . . . ," 494.

"Los Muebles"
Cabrera, Rosa M. "Simbolos y claves . . . ," 496–497.

JOHN HERSEY

"The Death of Buchanan Walsh"
Sanders, David. *John Hersey Revisited*, 103–104.

"A Fable South of Cancer"
Sanders, David. *John Hersey*, 51–53.
———. *John Hersey Revisited*, 35–36.

"Fling"
Sanders, David. *John Hersey Revisited*, 105–106.

"God's Typhoon"
Sanders, David. *John Hersey Revisited*, 104–105.

"Peggety's Parcel of Shortcomings"
Sanders, David. *John Hersey Revisited*, 37.

"The Pen"
Sanders, David. *John Hersey Revisited*, 34.

"Requiescat"
Sanders, David. *John Hersey Revisited*, 103–104.

"A Short Wait"
Sanders, David. *John Hersey Revisited*, 36–37.

"Why Were You Sent Out Here?"
Sanders, David. *John Hersey Revisited*, 34–35.

HERMANN HESSE

"The City"
Stelzig, Eugene L. *Hermann Hesse's Fiction* . . . , 113–114.

"The Cyclone"
Stelzig, Eugene L. *Hermann Hesse's Fiction* . . . , 114.

"The Homecoming"
Stelzig, Eugene L. *Hermann Hesse's Fiction* . . . , 111–113.

"Journey to the East"
Mileck, Joseph. *Hermann Hesse* . . . , 34–35.
Stelzig, Eugene L. *Hermann Hesse's Fiction* . . . , 239–250.

"Klein and Wagner"
Stelzig, Eugene L. *Hermann Hesse's Fiction* . . . , 162–169.

"Klingsor's Last Summer"
Stelzig, Eugene L. *Hermann Hesse's Fiction* . . . , 169–173.

"The Latin Scholar"
Stelzig, Eugene L. *Hermann Hesse's Fiction* . . . , 109.

"The Poet"
Banãles, Victoria. "Diversidad y congruencia: Los ríos de Rulfo, Benét, Guimarães Rosa y Hesse," *Romance Lang Annual*, 1 (1989), 375–376.

"Robert Aghion"
Stelzig, Eugene L. *Hermann Hesse's Fiction* . . . , 114–117.

"Siddhartha"
Decloedt, Leopold R. G. " 'Siddhartha: Eine indische Dichtung': Die kunstlerische Darstellung einer Selbstfindung," *Germanistische Mitteilungen*, 30 (1989), 9–21.
Mileck, Joseph. *Hermann Hesse* . . . , 30–31.
Stelzig, Eugene L. *Hermann Hesse's Fiction* . . . , 173–187.
Verma, Kamal D. "The Nature and Perception of Reality in Hermann Hesse's 'Siddhartha,' " *So Asian R*, 11–12 (July, 1988), 1–10.

"Walter Kömpff"
Stelzig, Eugene L. *Hermann Hesse's Fiction* . . . , 110–111.

JOSÉ HIERRO

"Boceto"
Corona Marzol, Gonzalo. "Entre prosa y poetía: Varios cuentos de José Hierro escritos en la década de los años cincuenta," in Fonquerne, Yves-René, and Aurora Egido, Eds. *Formas breves* . . . , 269–270.

"El obstinado"
Corona Marzol, Gonzalo. "Entre prosa y poetía . . . ," 277–280.

"El parque"
Corona Marzol, Gonzalo. "Entre prosa y poetía . . . ," 280–281.

JOANNA HIGGINS

"The Courtship of Widow Sobcek"
Yahnke, Robert E., and Richard M. Eastman. *Aging in Literature* . . . , 45.

HIRABAYASHI HATSUMOSUKE

"The Artificial Human Being"
Matthew, Robert. *Japanese Science Fiction* . . . , 17.

HO FEI

"A Big Family"
Hsia, C. T. "Residual Femininity: Women in Chinese Communist Fiction," in Birch, Cyril, Ed. *Chinese Communist Literature*, 171–172.

JACK HODGINS

"The Concert Stages of Europe"
Vauthier, Simone. "Reader's Squint: An Approach to Jack Hodgins' *The Barclay Family Theatre*," in Nischik, Reingard M., and Barbara Korte, Eds. *Modes of Narrative* . . . , 155–159.

"Ladies and Gentlemen"
Vauthier, Simone. "Reader's Squint . . . ," 155–159.

KARL VON HOERSCHELMANN

"Affar"
Pachmuss, Temira. "The Fantastic in Hoerschelmann," in Mandelker, Amy, and Robert Reeder, Eds. *The Supernatural* . . . , 319.

"The Crossing"
Pachmuss, Temira. "The Fantastic . . . ," 320–321.

"The Crystals"
Pachmuss, Temira. "The Fantastic . . . ," 318–319.

"In One of the Neighboring Worlds"
Pachmuss, Temira. "The Fantastic . . . ," 318.

"The Mermaid"
Pachmuss, Temira. "The Fantastic . . . ," 322.

"Suicide"
Pachmuss, Temira. "The Fantastic . . . ," 321–322.

"Thought"
Pachmuss, Temira. "The Fantastic . . . ," 326.

E[RNEST] T[HEODOR] A[MADEUS] HOFFMANN

"The Entail"
Gerrekens, Louis. "Von erzählerische Erinnerung und literarischer Anamnese Eine Untersuchung zu E. T. A. Hoffmann: 'Das Majorat,' " *Études Germaniques*, 45, ii (1990), 157–183.

"The Golden Pot"
Reh, Albert M. *Literatur und Psychologie*, 204–211.

"The Hermit Serapion"
Ziolkowski, Theodore. *German Romanticism . . .* , 207–210.

"Mademoiselle de Scudery"
Wermer, Johannes. "Was treibt Cardillac? Ein Goldschmied auf Abwegen," *Wirkendes Wort*, 40, i (1990), 32–38.

"The Mines of Falun"
Wight, Doris T. "Masochism, Mourning, Melancholia: A Freudian Interpretation of E. T. A. Hoffmann's Tale 'The Mines of Falun,' " *Germ Notes*, 21, iii–iv (1990), 49–55.
Ziolkowski, Theodore. *German Romanticism . . .* , 253–257.

HUGO VON HOFMANNSTHAL

"Horseman's Story" [same as "The Rider's Story"]
Gray, Richard T. "The Hermeneut(r)ic(k) of the Psychic Narrative: Freud's 'Das Unheimliche' and Hofmannsthal's 'Reitergeschichte,' " *Germ Q*, 62 (1989), 473–488.
Kamla, Thomas A. "The Aestheticism—Decadence Dialectic in Hofmannsthal's 'Reitergeschichte,' " *Orbis Litterarum*, 44 (1989), 327–340.

"Reminiscence of Beautiful Days"
Flanell-Friedman, Donald. "Rebirth in Venice: Hugo von Hofmannsthal's 'Erinnerung Schöner Tage,' " *Stud Short Fiction*, 26 (1989), 17–21.

DAVID HOGAN [FRANK GALLAGHER]

"The Leaping Trout"
Rohmann, Gerd. "David Hogan's Irish Civil War Story 'The Leaping Trout,' " *J Short Story Engl*, 12 (Spring, 1989), 79–85.

JAMES HOGG

"The Hunt of Eildon"
Bloedé, Barbara. "The Witchcraft Tradition in Hogg's Tales and Verse," *Stud Hogg*, 1 (1990), 92.

"The Witches of Traquair"
Bloedé, Barbara. "The Witchcraft Tradition . . . ," 92–96.

EDUARDO LADISLAU HOLMBERG

"Un periódica liberal"
Marún, Giaconda. "Historia y ficción en el cuento inédito de Eduardo L. Holmberg: 'Un periódica liberal,' " *Discurso literario*, 7 (1990), 377–385.

"El ruiseñor y el artista"
Marún, Giaconda. " 'El ruiseñor y el artista' (1876): un temprano cuento modernista argentino," *Río de la Plata*, 2 (1982), 107–116.

HOSHI SHIN'ICHI

"The Age of Money"
Matthew, Robert. *Japanese Science Fiction* . . . , 68–69.

"The Black Stick"
Matthew, Robert. *Japanese Science Fiction* . . . , 188–189.

"Bokkochan"
Matthew, Robert. *Japanese Science Fiction* . . . , 110–111.

"A Certain Neurosis"
Matthew, Robert. *Japanese Science Fiction* . . . , 147–149.

"The Charm"
Matthew, Robert. *Japanese Science Fiction* . . . , 135–136.

"The Crew"
Matthew, Robert. *Japanese Science Fiction* . . . , 64–65.

"The Deep-Laid Plan"
Matthew, Robert. *Japanese Science Fiction* . . . , 78–79.

"The Dwarf"
Matthew, Robert. *Japanese Science Fiction* . . . , 162–163, 198–200.

"The First Day of an Apprenticeship"
Matthew, Robert. *Japanese Science Fiction* . . . , 98–99.

"The Flower of Prosperity"
Matthew, Robert. *Japanese Science Fiction* . . . , 75–77.

"The God of Fortune"
Matthew, Robert. *Japanese Science Fiction* . . . , 72–73.

"The God of Television"
Matthew, Robert. *Japanese Science Fiction* . . . , 60–62.

"The God with the Laughing Face"
Matthew, Robert. *Japanese Science Fiction* . . . , 71–72.

"The Grand Design"
Matthew, Robert. *Japanese Science Fiction* . . . , 79–80.

"Hey, Come Out of It!"
Matthew, Robert. *Japanese Science Fiction* . . . , 90–91.

"The Investigators"
Matthew, Robert. *Japanese Science Fiction* . . . , 202.

"Just Before Going to Bed"
Matthew, Robert. *Japanese Science Fiction* . . . , 161–162.

"The Last Day"
Matthew, Robert. *Japanese Science Fiction* . . . , 63–64.

"The Law of Leaps"
Matthew, Robert. *Japanese Science Fiction* . . . , 45–47.

"Let Us Decry Evil"
Matthew, Robert. *Japanese Science Fiction* . . . , 143–144.

"The Love Key"
Matthew, Robert. *Japanese Science Fiction* . . . , 159–160.

"The Malcontent"
Matthew, Robert. *Japanese Science Fiction* . . . , 94–96.

"The Man in White Uniform"
Matthew, Robert. *Japanese Science Fiction* . . . , 214–215.

"The Matches"
Matthew, Robert. *Japanese Science Fiction* . . . , 132–133.

"The Meddlers"
Matthew, Robert. *Japanese Science Fiction* . . . , 131–132.

"The Mirror"
Matthew, Robert. *Japanese Science Fiction* . . . , 141–143.

"Mood Insurance"
Matthew, Robert. *Japanese Science Fiction* . . . , 81–82.

"The Negotiations"
Matthew, Robert. *Japanese Science Fiction* . . . , 139.

"The New Company President"
Matthew, Robert. *Japanese Science Fiction* . . . , 177–178.

"The Night We Lost a Friend"
Matthew, Robert. *Japanese Science Fiction* . . . , 93, 94.

"The Oath"
Matthew, Robert. *Japanese Science Fiction* . . . , 64.

"On a Dim Planet"
Matthew, Robert. *Japanese Science Fiction* . . . , 149–150.

"The Patient"
Matthew, Robert. *Japanese Science Fiction* . . . , 155.

"Peter Pan's Island"
Matthew, Robert. *Japanese Science Fiction* . . . , 84–85.

"Profits Guaranteed"
Matthew, Robert. *Japanese Science Fiction* . . . , 65–66.

"Reluctance"
Matthew, Robert. *Japanese Science Fiction* . . . , 165–167.

"The Safety Device"
Matthew, Robert. *Japanese Science Fiction* . . . , 163–165.

"The Secretary on the Shoulder"
Matthew, Robert. *Japanese Science Fiction* . . . , 155–158.

"The Shack Dweller"
Matthew, Robert. *Japanese Science Fiction* . . . , 62–63.

"A Shortage of Staff"
Matthew, Robert. *Japanese Science Fiction* . . . , 140–141.

"The Small Society"
Matthew, Robert. *Japanese Science Fiction* . . . , 69–70.

"Space Checkpoint"
Matthew, Robert. *Japanese Science Fiction* . . . , 91–93.

"The Stubborn Fellow"
Matthew, Robert. *Japanese Science Fiction* . . . , 144.

"Symptoms"
Matthew, Robert. *Japanese Science Fiction* . . . , 154–155.

"With Souvenirs in Their Hands"
Matthew, Robert. *Japanese Science Fiction* . . . , 203.

HOSHIDA SAMPEI

"The Construction of the Earth's Central City"
Matthew, Robert. *Japanese Science Fiction* . . . , 28–29.

WILLIAM DEAN HOWELLS

"The Angel of the Lord" [originally "At Third Hand: A Psychological Inquiry"]
Crowley, John W. *The Mask of Fiction* . . . , 149–152.

"A Difficult Case"
Crowley, John W. *The Mask of Fiction* . . . , 138–145.

"Editha"
Crowley, John W. *The Mask of Fiction* . . . , 30–34, 39–40.

"His Apparition"
Crowley, John W. *The Mask of Fiction* . . . , 145–147.

"Though One Rose from the Dead"
Crowley, John W. *The Mask of Fiction* . . . , 152–155.

HSI JUNG

"Corduroy"
Hsia, C. T. "Residual Femininity: Women in Chinese Communist Fiction," in Birch, Cyril, Ed. *Chinese Communist Literature*, 160–161.

HSIAO HUNG [same as XIAO HONG or ZHANG NAIYING]

"At the Foot of the Mountain"
Dunsing, Charlotte. "Xiao Hong," in Slupski, Zbigniew, Ed. *A Selective Guide* . . . , II, 205–206.

"A Cry in the Wilderness"
Dunsing, Charlotte. "Xiao Hong," 205.

"The Family Outsider"
Goldblatt, Howard. "Xiao Hong," in Slupski, Zbigniew, Ed. *A Selective Guide* . . . , II, 203–204.

"Flight from Danger"
Dunsing, Charlotte. "Xiao Hong," 206–207.

"Vague Expectations"
Dunsing, Charlotte. "Xiao Hong," 206.

HU YEPIN

"The Fool"
Ptak, Roderich. "Hu Yepin," in Slupski, Zbigniew, Ed. *A Selective Guide* . . . , II, 74–75.

HUANG CHUNMING

"A Flower in the Rainy Night"
Wang, David D. "Female Consciousness in Modern Chinese Male Fiction," in Duke, Michael S., Ed. *Modern Chinese Women Writers* . . . , 250–251.

"Sayonara, Good-By"
Wang, David D. "Female Consciousness . . . ," 250.

W[ILLIAM] H[ENRY] HUDSON

"Dead Man's Plack"
Miller, David. *W. H. Hudson* . . . , 164–168.

"Marta Riquelme"
Frederick, Bonnie. "Reading the Warning: The Reader and the Image of the Captive Woman," *Chasqui*, 18, ii (1989), 8.
Miller, David. *W. H. Hudson* . . . , 131–135.

"An Old Thorn"
Miller, David. *W. H. Hudson* . . . , 169–172.

"El Ombú"
Miller, David. *W. H. Hudson* . . . , 126–131.

"The Story of a Piebald Horse"
Miller, David. *W. H. Hudson* . . . , 124–125.

ISABEL HUGGAN

"Sawdust"
Potvin, Liza. "*The Elizabeth Stories* and Women's Autobiographical Strategies," *Stud Canadian Lit*, 14, ii (1989), 3–7.

LANGSTON HUGHES

"Berry"
Miller, R. Baxter. *The Art and Imagination* . . . , 103–104.

"Big Round World"
Miller, R. Baxter. *The Art and Imagination* . . . , 110–112.

"Father and Son"
Hathaway, Heather. " 'Maybe Freedom Lies in Hating': Miscegenation and the Oedipal Conflict," in Yaeger, Patricia, and Beth Kowaleski-Wallace, Eds. *Refiguring the Father* . . . , 153–167.

"Lynn Clarisse"
Miller, R. Baxter. *The Art and Imagination* . . . , 115–117.

"Shadow of the Blues"
Miller, R. Baxter. *The Art and Imagination* . . . , 112–115.

"Slave on the Block"
+Roberts, Edgar V., and Henry E. Jacobs. *Instructor's Manual* . . . , 2nd ed., 77–78.

RICHARD HUGHES

"Diary of a Steerage Passenger"
Morgan, Paul B. "*A Moment of Time*: The Short Stories of Richard Hughes," *New Welsh R*, 1, ii (1988), 60–61.

"The Ghost"
Morgan, Paul B. "*A Moment of Time* . . . ," 58–59.

"Locomotive"
Morgan, Paul B. "*A Moment of Time* . . . ," 58.

"Martha"
Morgan, Paul B. "*A Moment of Time* . . . ," 61–62.

"A Moment of Time"
Morgan, Paul B. "*A Moment of Time* . . . ," 60.

"The Vanishing Man"
Morgan, Paul B. "*A Moment of Time* . . . ," 60.

WILLIAM HUMPHREY

"A Good Indian"
Tebeaux, Elizabeth. "Irony as Art: The Short Fiction of William Humphrey," *Stud Short Fiction*, 26 (1989), 327–328.

"A Job of the Plains"
Tebeaux, Elizabeth. "Irony as Art . . . ," 324–325.

"Patience of a Saint"
Tebeaux, Elizabeth. "Irony as Art . . . ," 329–330.

"Report Cards"
Tebeaux, Elizabeth. "Irony as Art . . . ," 330–332.

MARY HUNTER

"The Return of Mr. Willis"
Graulich, Melody. " 'O Beautiful for Spacious Guys': An Essay on the 'Legitimate Inclinations of the Sexes,' " in Mogen, David, Mark Busby, and Paul Bryant, Eds. *The Frontier Experience* . . . , 190–191.

ZORA NEALE HURSTON

"The Gilded Six-Bits"
Jarrett, Mary. "The Idea of Audience in the Short Stories of Zora Neale Hurston and Alice Walker," *J Short Story Engl*, 12 (Spring, 1989), 34–35.

"Isis"
Jarrett, Mary. "The Idea of Audience . . . ," 36–37.

JULIAN HUXLEY

"The Tissue-Culture King"
Parrinder, Patrick. "Scientists in Science Fiction: Enlightenment and After," in Garnett, Rhys, and R. J. Ellis, Eds. *Science Fiction Roots* . . . , 72–73.

HWANG SUN-WON

"Masks"
Holman, Martin. "Introduction," *The Book of Masks . . .* [by Hwang Sun-won], xiii–xiv.

"Old Man Hwang"
Holman, Martin. "Introduction," xi.

"Shadows"
Holman, Martin. "Introduction," xi–xii.

IKUSHIMA JIRO

"The Generation Revolution"
Matthew, Robert. *Japanese Science Fiction . . .*, 105–106.

WASHINGTON IRVING

"The Adventure of the German Student"
+Ringe, Donald A. "Irving's Use of the Gothic Mode," in Aderman, Ralph M., Ed. *Critical Essays on Washington Irving*, 212–213.

"Dolph Heyliger"
+Ringe, Donald A. " . . . Gothic Mode," 210–211.

"The Legend of Sleepy Hollow"
Leary, Lewis. "Washington Irving," in Rubin, Louis D., Ed. *The Comic Imagination . . .*, 75–76; rpt. Aderman, Ralph M., Ed. *Critical Essays on Washington Irving*, 201–202.

"Rip Van Winkle"
Leary, Lewis. "Washington Irving," 74–75; rpt. Aderman, Ralph M., Ed. *Critical Essays on Washington Irving*, 201–202.

CHRISTOPHER ISHERWOOD

"An Evening at the Bay"
Schwerdt, Lisa M. *Isherwood's Fiction . . .*, 52–53.

"Gems of Belgian Architecture"
Schwerdt, Lisa M. *Isherwood's Fiction . . .*, 20–22.

VSEVOLOD IVANOV

"Farbige Winde"
Jensen, Peter A. "Der Text als Teil der Welt: Vsevolod Ivanovs Erzählung 'Farbige Winde,' " in Schmid, Wolf, Ed. *Mythos in der Slawischen Moderne*, 293–325.

ENRIQUE IZAGUIRRE

"La noche y el sumario"
Ramos, Elías A. *El cuento venezolano . . .*, 99–100.

SHIRLEY JACKSON

"The Lottery"
Coulthard, A. R. "Jackson's 'The Lottery,' " *Explicator*, 48 (1990), 226–228.
Schaub, Danielle. "Shirley Jackson's Use of Symbols in 'The Lottery,' " *J Short Story Engl*, 14 (Spring, 1990), 79–86.

C[YRIL] L[IONEL] R[OBERT] JAMES

"La Divina Pastora"
Sander, Reinhard W. *The Trinidad Awakening . . .*, 93–94.
"Revolution"
Sander, Reinhard W. *The Trinidad Awakening . . .*, 92–93.
"Triumph"
Sander, Reinhard W. *The Trinidad Awakening . . .*, 92–93.
"Turner's Prosperity"
Sander, Reinhard W. *The Trinidad Awakening . . .*, 49–50.

HENRY JAMES

"The Altar of the Dead"
Bronfen, Elisabeth. "Dialogue with the Dead: The Deceased Beloved as Muse," in Barreca, Regina, Ed. *Sex and Death . . .*, 253–254.
Smythe, Karen. " 'The Altar of the Dead': James's Grammar of Grieving," *Engl Stud Canada*, 16 (1990), 315–324.
"The Aspern Papers"
Auerbach, Jonathan. *The Romance of Failure . . .*, 134–144.
Bell, Millicent. " 'The Aspern Papers': The Unvisitable Past," *Henry James R*, 10, ii (1989), 120–127.
Church, Joseph. "Writing and the Dispossession of Woman in 'The Aspern Papers,' " *Am Imago*, 47 (1990), 23–42.
Rivkin, Julie. "Speaking with the Dead: Ethics and Representation in 'The Aspern Papers,' " *Henry James R*, 10, ii (1989), 135–141.
"The Author of 'Beltraffio' "
Auerbach, Jonathan. *The Romance of Failure . . .*, 131–134.
Chapman, Sara S. . . . *Writer as Hero*, 28–34.
Gardaphe, Fred L. "The Echoes of 'Beltraffio': Reading Italy in Henry James's 'The Author of "Beltraffio," ' " *Romance Lang Annual*, 1 (1989), 121–127.

Vickers, Craig E., and Robert T. Backus. "James's 'The Author of "Beltrafio," ' " *Explicator*, 48 (1990), 188–189.

"The Beast in the Jungle"

Birje-Patil, J. "T. S. Eliot's 'Portrait of a Lady' and Henry James's 'The Beast in the Jungle': Echoes and Correspondences," in Singh, Amritjit, and K. Ayyappa Paniker, Eds. *The Magic Circle* . . . , 114–121.

Cavell, Stanley. "Postscript (1989): To Whom It May Concern," *Critical Inquiry*, 16 (1990), 248–289.

Engelberg, Edward. *Elegiac Fictions* . . . , 129–132.

Fike, Matthew A. "James's 'The Beast in the Jungle,' " *Explicator*, 47, iii (1989), 18–21.

+Gargano, James W. "Imagery as Action in 'The Beast in the Jungle,' " in Hocks, Richard A. . . . *A Study of the Short Fiction*, 160–171.

Gray, Larry A. "Sibyls, Seekers, and the Sacred Founts in the Tales of Henry James," *Henry James R*, 11 (1990), 189–192.

Irwin, Michael. "Henry James and the Vague *Nouvelle*," in Lee, A. Robert, Ed. *The Modern American Novella*, 22–23.

Przybylowicz, Donna. "The 'Lost Stuff of Consciousness': The Priority of Futurity and the Deferral of Desire in 'The Beast in the Jungle,' " in Singh, Amritjit, and K. Ayyappa Paniker, Eds. *The Magic Circle* . . . , 85–113.

Sedgwick, Eva K. "The Beast in the Closet: James and the Writing of Homosexual Panic," in Showalter, Elaine, Ed. *Speaking of Gender*, 256–265.

Van Leer, David. "The Beast of the Closet: Homosociality and Pathology of Manhood," *Critical Inquiry*, 15 (1989), 587–605.

"The Bench of Desolation"

Cameron, Sharon. *Thinking* . . . , 165–166.

Hocks, Richard A. . . . *A Study of the Short Fiction*, 89–91.

Lyons, Richard S. "Ironies of Loss in *The Finer Grain*," *Henry James R*, 11 (1990), 206–207.

"The Birthplace"

McDonald, Henry. "Nietzsche Contra Derrida: Two Views of Henry James's 'The Birthplace,' " *Henry James R*, 11 (1990), 133–148.

"The Coxon Fund"

Chapman, Sara S. . . . *Writer as Hero*, 69–76.

Haggerty, George E. *Gothic Fiction* . . . , 141–142.

"Crapy Cornelia"

Lyons, Richard S. "Ironies of Loss . . . ," 204–205.

"Daisy Miller"

Fogel, Daniel M. . . . *Comedy of Manners*, 25–86.

Hocks, Richard A. . . . *A Study of the Short Fiction*, 31–35.

Irwin, Michael. "Henry James . . . ," 15–17.

Page, Philip. "Daisy Miller's Parasol," *Stud Short Fiction*, 27 (1990), 591–600.

Shaw, W. David. *Victorians and Mystery* . . . , 132–136.

Wilkinson, Myler. "Henry James and the Ethical Moment," *Henry James R*, 11 (1990), 158–163.

"The Death of the Lion"

Chapman, Sara S. . . . *Writer as Hero*, 63–68.

"De Grey: A Romance"

Akiyama, Masayuki. "Sanyūtei Enchō, Ch'ü Yu, and Henry James: Stories of the Supernatural," *Tamkang R*, 18, i–iv (Autumn, 1987—Summer, 1988), 155–157.

"The Diary of a Man of Fifty"

Engelberg, Edward. *Elegiac Fictions* . . . , 127–128.

Gray, Larry A. "Sibyls, Seekers . . . ," 196.

"The Figure in the Carpet"

Auerbach, Jonathan. *The Romance of Failure* . . . , 144–158.

Chapman, Sara S. . . . *Writer as Hero*, 85–92.

Hocks, Richard A. . . . *A Study of the Short Fiction*, 51–54.

Martin, W. R., and Warren U. Ober. "After *Guy Domville*: Henry James's 'Glasses' and 'The Figure in the Carpet,' " *Engl Stud Africa*, 33, i (1990), 27–36.

"Four Meetings"

Hocks, Richard A. . . . *A Study of the Short Fiction*, 19–25.

"Gabrielle de Bergerac"

Fussell, Edwin S. *The French Side* . . . , 218–220.

"The Ghostly Rental"

Martin, W. R., and Warren U. Ober. "Captain Diamond and Old Hickory: Realities and Ambivalence in Henry James's 'The Ghostly Rental,' " *Stud Short Fiction*, 26 (1989), 1–9.

"Glasses"

Martin, W. R., and Warren U. Ober. "After *Guy Domville* . . . ," 27–36.

"The Great Good Place"

Hocks, Richard A. . . . *A Study of the Short Fiction*, 75–77.

"Greville Fane"

Chapman, Sara S. . . . *Writer as Hero*, 47–53.

Hocks, Richard A. . . . *A Study of the Short Fiction*, 42–48.

"In the Cage"

Basoff, Bruce. "Turning the Tables: The Stories of Henry James," *Études Anglaises*, 43 (1990), 286–287.

Hocks, Richard A. . . . *A Study of the Short Fiction*, 56–60.

Irwin, Michael. "Henry James . . . ," 23–28.

Walton, Priscilla L. " 'Everything . . . might mean almost anything': Absence and Creativity in James's 'In the Cage,' " *No Dakota Q*, 53, iii (1990), 35–43.

"An International Episode"

Hocks, Richard A. . . . *A Study of the Short Fiction*, 26–29.

"The Jolly Corner"

Haggerty, George E. *Gothic Fiction* . . . , 157–168.

Stock, R. D. *The Flutes of Dionysus* . . . , 312–313.

"A Landscape Painter"
Gray, Larry A. "Sibyls, Seekers . . . ," 195.

"The Last of the Valerii"
Clark, Michael. "The Hermes in Henry James's 'The Last of the Valerii,' " *Henry James R*, 10 (1989), 210–213.
Miller, J. Hillis. *Versions of Pygmalion*, 211–243.

"The Lesson of the Master"
Chapman, Sara S. . . . *Writer as Hero*, 37–46.
Hocks, Richard A. . . . *A Study of the Short Fiction*, 50–51.
Milliman, Craig A. "The Dangers of Fiction: Henry James's 'The Lesson of the Master,' " *Stud Short Fiction*, 27 (1990), 81–88.

"The Liar"
Funston, Judith. "James's Portrait of the Artist as Liar," *Stud Short Fiction*, 26 (1989), 431–438.
Gray, Larry A. "Sibyls, Seekers . . . ," 196–197.
Hocks, Richard A. . . . *A Study of the Short Fiction*, 39–42.
Stanzel, Franz K. "Wanderlung und Verwandlung eines Lügners: 'The Liar' von Henry James," in Herget, Winfried, Klaus P. Jochum, and Ingeborg Weber, Eds. *Theorie und Praxis* . . . , 283–293.

"Madame de Mauves"
Fussell, Edwin S. *The French Side* . . . , 220–225.
Hocks, Richard A. . . . *A Study of the Short Fiction*, 14–19.

"The Madonna of the Future"
Engelberg, Edward. *Elegiac Fictions* . . . , 128–129.
Hocks, Richard A. . . . *A Study of the Short Fiction*, 12–13.
Shackleford, Lynne P. "Michelangelo, Henry James's Artistic Hero in 'The Madonna of the Future,' " *Am Notes & Queries*, 3, N.S. (1990), 110–113.

"Maud-Evelyn"
Bronfen, Elisabeth. "Dialogue with the Dead . . . ," 254–256.

"The Middle Years"
Chapman, Sara S. . . . *Writer as Hero*, 54–60.

"Miss Gunton of Poughkeepsie"
Hocks, Richard A. . . . *A Study of the Short Fiction*, 72–73.

"Mona Montravers"
Lyons, Richard S. "Ironies of Loss . . . ," 204.

"The Next Time"
Chapman, Sara S. . . . *Writer as Hero*, 77–84.

"Osborne's Revenge"
Gray, Larry A. "Sibyls, Seekers . . . ," 195.

"Owen Wingate"
Haggerty, George E. *Gothic Fiction* . . . , 145–150.

"Pandora"
Friedl, Bettina. "The Misreading of 'Daisy Miller' as Re-vision: Henry James's 'Pandora,' " in Singh, Amritjit, and K. Ayyappa Paniker, Eds. *The Magic Circle* . . . , 8–20.

Irwin, Michael. "Henry James . . . ," 18–19.

"The Point of View"
Hocks, Richard A. . . . *A Study of the Short Fiction*, 29–31.

"The Private Life"
Auslander, Adrienne. *Andromeda's Chains* . . . , 132–134.

"The Pupil"
Gray, Larry A. "Sibyls, Seekers . . . ," 197–198.
Hocks, Richard A. . . . *A Study of the Short Fiction*, 61–69.

"The Real Right Thing"
Chapman, Sara S. . . . *Writer as Hero*, 104–105.

"The Real Thing"
Basoff, Bruce. "Turning the Tables . . . ," 290.
Grover, P. J. "Realism, Representation and 'The Real Thing,' " in Singh, Amritjit, and K. Ayyappa Paniker, Eds. *The Magic Circle* . . . , 122–131.
Hocks, Richard A. . . . *A Study of the Short Fiction*, 49–50.
Lackey, Kris. "Art and Class in 'The Real Thing,' " *Stud Short Fiction*, 26 (1989), 190–192.

"A Round of Visits"
Hocks, Richard A. . . . *A Study of the Short Fiction*, 91–105.
Lyons, Richard S. "Ironies of Loss . . . ," 205–206.

"The Siege of London"
Fussell, Edwin S. *The French Side* . . . , 229–232.

"The Story in It"
Chapman, Sara S. . . . *Writer as Hero*, 106–107.
Vieilledent, Catherine. "Literary Pornographics: Henry James's Politics of Suppression," *Henry James R*, 10 (1989), 185–196.

"A Tragedy of Error"
Fussell, Edwin S. *The French Side* . . . , 216–218.

"The Tree of Knowledge"
Gray, Larry A. "Sibyls, Seekers . . . ," 198–199.

"The Turn of the Screw"
Beidler, Peter G. *Ghosts, Demons, and Henry James* . . . , 187–221.
Fleming, Bruce E. "Floundering About in Silence: What the Governess Couldn't Say," *Stud Short Fiction*, 26 (1989), 135–143.
+Goetz, William R. "The 'Frame' of 'The Turn of the Screw': Framing the Reader In," in Hocks, Richard A. . . . *A Study of the Short Fiction*, 155–159.
Haggerty, George E. *Gothic Fiction* . . . , 150–157.
Heller, Terry. . . . *Bewildered Vision*, 54–140.
Hocks, Richard A. . . . *A Study of the Short Fiction*, 78–80.
Hurst, Mary J. *The Voice of the Child* . . . , 48–56.
Krieg, Joann P. "A Question of Value: Culture and Cognition in 'The Turn of the Screw,' " in Singh, Amritjit, and K. Ayyappa Paniker, Eds. *The Magic Circle* . . . , 132–145.
McMaster, Graham. "Henry James and India: A Historical Reading of 'The Turn of the Screw,' " *Clio*, 18, i (1988), 23–40.

Miller, Karl. *Authors*, 5–9.
Pecora, Vincent P. *Self and Form* . . . , 176–194.
Shaw, W. David. *Victorians and Mystery* . . . , 136–140.
Stock, R. D. *The Flutes of Dionysus* . . . , 313–315.
Wilkinson, Myler. "Henry James . . . ," 163–166.

"The Velvet Glove"
Fussell, Edwin S. *The French Side* . . . , 232–236.
Lyons, Richard S. "Ironies of Loss . . . ," 203–204.

"Washington Square"
Griffin, Susan M. "The Jamesian Body: Two Oral Tales," *Victorian Institute J*, 17 (1989), 125–139.
Rasmussen, Barbara. "Re-Producing 'James': Marxism, Phallocentrism and 'Washington Square,' " *J Am Stud*, 23, i (1989), 63–67.
Zacharias, Greg W. "Henry James' Style in 'Washington Square,' " *Stud Am Fiction*, 18 (1990), 207–224.

M[ONTAGUE] R[HODES] JAMES

"Oh, Whistle, and I'll Come to You, My Lad"
Joshi, S. T. *The Weird Tale*, 135–136.

ENRIQUE JARAMILLO LEVI

"El agua"
Zlotchew, Clark M. "Metáforas de la creación literaria en tres cuentos de Enrique Jaramillo Levi," *Alba de América*, 8, xiv–xv (1990), 141–144.

"Luna de hiel"
Zlotchew, Clark M. "Metáforas de la creación . . . ," 144–145.

"El punto de referencia"
Zlotchew, Clark M. "Metáforas de la creación . . . ," 145–146.

FRANCISCO JAVIER YÁNEZ

"Conciencia y realidad"
Ramos, Elías A. *El cuento venezolano* . . . , 124–125.

BARBARA JEFFERIS

"The Drover's Wife"
Arens, Werner. "The Ironical Fate of 'The Drover's Wife': Four Versions from Henry Lawson (1892) to Barbara Jefferis (1980)," in Stummer, Peter O., Ed. *The Story Must Be Told* . . . , 129–131.

GEORGE JESSOP

"Extracts from the Correspondence of Mr. Miles Grogan"
Fanning, Charles. *The Irish Voice . . .*, 184–185.

"The Rise and Fall of the 'Irish Aigle' "
Fanning, Charles. *The Irish Voice . . .*, 183–184.

SARAH ORNE JEWETT

"Along Shore"
Sherman, Sarah W. *Sarah Orne Jewett . . .*, 235–236.

"An Autumn Holiday"
Sherman, Sarah W. *Sarah Orne Jewett . . .*, 67–68.

"The Christmas Ghost"
Sherman, Sarah W. *Sarah Orne Jewett . . .*, 58–63.

"The Dunnet Shepherdess"
Sherman, Sarah W. *Sarah Orne Jewett . . .*, 236–239.

"For Country Girls"
Sherman, Sarah W. *Sarah Orne Jewett . . .*, 75–76.

"The Foreigner"
Church, Joseph. "Absent Mothers and Anxious Daughters: Facing Ambivalence in Jewett's 'The Foreigner,' " *Essays Lit*, 17, i (1990), 52–68.
Sherman, Sarah W. *Sarah Orne Jewett . . .*, 239–246.

"The Queen's Twin"
Roman, Judith A. . . . *The Spirit of Charles Street*, 157–158.
Sherman, Sarah W. *Sarah Orne Jewett . . .*, 246–255.

"A White Heron"
Donovan, Josephine. *After the Fall . . .*, 13–15, 119–120.
Heller, Terry. "The Rhetoric of Communion in Jewett's 'A White Heron,' " *Colby Q*, 26 (1990), 182–194.
Kadota, Linda K. "Women, Linguistics, and 'A White Heron,' " *Chu-Shikoku Stud Am Lit*, 26 (June, 1990), 21–26.
Zanger, Jules. " 'Young Goodman Brown' and 'A White Heron': Correspondences and Illuminations," *Papers Lang & Lit*, 26 (1990), 346–357.

"William's Wedding"
Sherman, Sarah W. *Sarah Orne Jewett . . .*, 258–265.

RUTH PRAWER JHABVALA

"Desecration"
Sucher, Laurie. *The Fiction of Ruth Prawer Jhabvala . . .*, 77–97.

"An Experience of India"
Sucher, Laurie. *The Fiction of Ruth Prawer Jhabvala . . .*, 40–44.

"Expiation"
Sucher, Laurie. *The Fiction of Ruth Prawer Jhabvala* . . . , 221–227.

"Farid and Farida"
Sucher, Laurie. *The Fiction of Ruth Prawer Jhabvala* . . . , 201–202.

"Grandmother"
Sucher, Laurie. *The Fiction of Ruth Prawer Jhabvala* . . . , 164–167.

"The Housewife"
Sucher, Laurie. *The Fiction of Ruth Prawer Jhabvala* . . . , 69–76.

"Passion"
Sucher, Laurie. *The Fiction of Ruth Prawer Jhabvala* . . . , 28–29.

"A Spiritual Call"
Sucher, Laurie. *The Fiction of Ruth Prawer Jhabvala* . . . , 44–47.

"A Summer by the Sea"
Sucher, Laurie. *The Fiction of Ruth Prawer Jhabvala* . . . , 202–205.

JIANG GUANGCI [GUANGCHI]

"On the Yalu River"
Wedell-Wedellsborg, Anne. "Jiang Guangci," in Slupski, Zbigniew, Ed. *A Selective Guide* . . . , II, 76.

NICK JOAQUÍN

"Doña Jerónima"
Oloroso, Laura S. "Nick Joaquín and His Brightly Burning Prose Works," in Manuud, Antonio G., Ed. *Brown Heritage* . . . , 775–777.

"Guardia de Honor"
Bernad, Miguel A. *Bamboo and the Greenwood Tree* . . . , 56–58.

"The Mass of St. Sylvester"
Bernad, Miguel A. *Bamboo and the Greenwood Tree* . . . , 65–66.

"The Summer Solstice"
Bernad, Miguel A. *Bamboo and the Greenwood Tree* . . . , 58–60.

"Three Generations"
Bernad, Miguel A. *Bamboo and the Greenwood Tree* . . . , 62–63.

JOSEPHINE JOHNSON

"Old Harry"
Yahnke, Robert E., and Richard M. Eastman. *Aging in Literature* . . . , 45–46.

ELIZABETH JOLLEY

"Adam's Bride"
José, Nicholas. "Possibilities of Love in Recent Australian Stories," in Stummer, Peter O., Ed. *The Story Must Be Told* . . . , 139–140.

JAMES JOYCE

"After the Race"
Henke, Suzette A. *James Joyce* . . . , 24–25.
Kershner, R. B. . . . *Chronicles of Disorder*, 71–79.

"Araby"
Barta, Peter I. "Munkácsy's *Ecce Homo* and Joyce's 'Araby,' " *New Hungarian Q*, 31 (Summer, 1990), 134–137.
Henke, Suzette A. *James Joyce* . . . , 19–21.
Kershner, R. B. . . . *Chronicles of Disorder*, 46–60.
Leonard, Garry M. "The Question and the Quest: The Story of Mangan's Sister," *Mod Fiction Stud*, 35 (1989), 459–477.
Pecora, Vincent P. *Self and Form* . . . , 238–239.

"The Boarding House"
Gillespie, Michael P. *Reading the Book* . . . , 31–33.
Henke, Suzette A. *James Joyce* . . . , 26–29.
Kershner, R. B. . . . *Chronicles of Disorder*, 89–93.

"Clay"
Henke, Suzette A. *James Joyce* . . . , 33–35.
Kershner, R. B. . . . *Chronicles of Disorder*, 104–110.
Owens, Cóilín. " 'Clay' (1): Irish Folklore," *James Joyce Q*, 27 (1990), 337–352.
———. " 'Clay' (3): The Mass of Mary and All the Saints," *James Joyce Q*, 28 (1990), 257–267.

"Counterparts"
Gillespie, Michael P. *Reading the Book* . . . , 34–36.
Henke, Suzette A. *James Joyce* . . . , 32–33.
Kershner, R. B. . . . *Chronicles of Disorder*, 101–104.
Restuccia, Frances L. *Joyce and the Law* . . . , 5–6.

"The Dead"
Barolsky, Paul. "Joyce's Distant Music," *Virginia Q R*, 65 (1989), 111–119.
Bramsbäck, Birgit. "James Joyce and the Divided Irish Cultural Heritage: Glimpses from *Dubliners* and *A Portrait of the Artist as a Young Man*," in Bramsbäck, Birgit, Ed. *Homage to Ireland* . . . , 21–24.
Cowart, David. "From Nuns' Island to Monkstown: Celibacy, Concupiscence, and Sterility in 'The Dead,' " *James Joyce Q*, 26 (1989), 499–504.
Doherty, Gerald. "Shades of Difference: Tropic Transformations in James Joyce's 'The Dead,' " *Style*, 23 (1989), 225–237.
Dunleavy, Janet E. "The Ectoplasmic Truthteller of 'The Dead,' "

in Ben-Merre, Diana A., and Maureen Murphy, Eds. *James Joyce . . .*, 1–10.
Flood, Jeanne A. "The Sow That Eats Her Farrow: Gender and Politics," in Ben-Merre, Diana A., and Maureen Murphy, Eds. *James Joyce . . .*, 70–76.
Harty, John. "Joyce's 'The Dead,' " *Explicator*, 47, iii (1989), 35–37.
Henke, Suzette A. *James Joyce . . .*, 42–49.
Kershner, R. B. . . . *Chronicles of Disorder*, 138–150.
Norris, Margot. "Stifled Back Answers: The Gender Politics of Art in Joyce's 'The Dead,' " *Mod Fiction Stud*, 35 (1989), 479–503.
Pecora, Vincent P. *Self and Form . . .*, 227–238.
Rix, Walter T. "James Joyce's 'The Dead': The Symbolist Inspiration and Its Narrative Reflection," in Allen, Michael, and Angela Wilcox, Eds. *Critical Approaches . . .*, 146–165.
Rutelli, Romana. "Sublime epifanico in un segmento di 'The Dead,' " *Strumenti Critici*, 61 (1989), 357–364.
Sisson, Annette. "Constructing the Human Conscience in Joyce's *Dubliners*," *Midwest Q*, 30 (1989), 495–502.

"An Encounter"
Degnan, James P. "The Encounter in Joyce's 'An Encounter,' " *Twentieth Century Lit*, 35 (1989), 89–93.
Kershner, R. B. . . . *Chronicles of Disorder*, 31–46.

"Eveline"
Gillespie, Michael P. *Reading the Book . . .*, 21–22.
Henke, Suzette A. *James Joyce . . .*, 21–24.
Kershner, R. B. . . . *Chronicles of Disorder*, 60–71.
Scholes, Robert. *Semiotics and Interpretation*, 87–108.

"Grace"
Henke, Suzette A. *James Joyce . . .*, 39–41.
Kershner, R. B. . . . *Chronicles of Disorder*, 130–138.

"Ivy Day in the Committee Room"
Henke, Suzette A. *James Joyce . . .*, 38–39.
Kershner, R. B. . . . *Chronicles of Disorder*, 118–124.

"A Little Cloud"
Henke, Suzette A. *James Joyce . . .*, 29–32.
Kershner, R. B. . . . *Chronicles of Disorder*, 96–101.
Restuccia, Frances L. *Joyce and the Law . . .*, 4–5.
Sisson, Annette. "Constructing the Human Conscience . . . ," 506–511.

"A Mother"
Henke, Suzette A. *James Joyce . . .*, 40–41.
Kershner, R. B. . . . *Chronicles of Disorder*, 124–130.

"A Painful Case"
Henke, Suzette A. *James Joyce . . .*, 35–37.
Kershner, R. B. . . . *Chronicles of Disorder*, 110–117.
Knapp, Bettina L. *Machine, Metaphor . . .*, 29–45.

Sisson, Annette. "Constructing the Human Conscience . . . ," 502–506.

"The Sisters"

Albert, Leonard. "Gnomonology: James Joyce's 'The Sisters,' " *James Joyce Q*, 27 (1990), 353–364.

Bierman, Robert. "Joyce's 'The Sisters,' " *Explicator*, 48 (1990), 274–275.

Dettmar, Kevin J. "From Interpretation to 'Intrepidation': Joyce's 'The Sisters' as a Precursor of the Postmodern Mystery," in Walker, Ronald G., and June M. Frazer, Eds. *The Cunning Craft* . . . , 149–165.

Geary, Edward A. "Undecidability in Joyce's 'The Sisters,' " *Stud Short Fiction*, 26 (1989), 305–310.

Henke, Suzette A. *James Joyce* . . . , 14–19.

Kershner, R. B. . . . *Chronicles of Disorder*, 22–31.

Korninger, Siegfried. "Artistic Integration in Joyce's *Dubliners*," in Bauer, Gero, Franz K. Stanzel, and Franz Zaic, Eds. *Festschrift: Prof. Dr. Herbert Koziol* . . . , 147–168.

Leonard, Garry M. "The Free Man's Journal: The Making of His[$]tory in Joyce's 'The Sisters,' " *Mod Fiction Stud*, 36 (1990), 455–482.

Schork, R. Joseph. "Liturgical Irony in Joyce's 'The Sisters,' " *Stud Short Fiction*, 26 (1989), 193–197.

"Two Gallants"

Henke, Suzette A. *James Joyce* . . . , 25–26.

Ingersoll, Earl G. "Irish Jokes: A Lacanian Reading of Short Stories by James Joyce, Flann O'Brien, and Bryan MacMahon," *Stud Short Fiction*, 27 (1990), 239–241.

Kershner, R. B. . . . *Chronicles of Disorder*, 79–88.

Mirza, Shikoh M. "Narration and Theme in James Joyce's 'Two Gallants,' " *Aligarh Crit Misc*, 21, i (1989), 101–111.

JU CHIH-CHUAN [same as RU ZHIJUAN]

"A Promise Is Kept"

Hsia, C. T. "Residual Femininity: Women in Chinese Communist Fiction," in Birch, Cyril, Ed. *Chinese Communist Literature*, 170.

"The Warmth of Spring"

Hsia, C. T. "Residual Femininity . . . ," 168–170.

FRANZ KAFKA

"The Bridge"

Koelb, Clayton. "The Turn of the Trope: Kafka's 'Die Brücke,' " *Mod Austrian Lit*, 22, i (1989), 57–70.

"The Burrow"

McElroy, Bernard. . . . *Modern Grotesque*, 62–63.

+Sussman, Henry. "The All-Embracing Metaphor: Reflections on 'The Burrow,' " in Gross, Ruth V., Ed. *Critical Essays* . . . , 130–152.

———. *Afterimages of Modernity* . . . , 195–196.

"The Cares of a Family Man"

Ehrich-Haefeli, Verena. "Bewegungensenergien in Psyche und Text: Zu Kafkas 'Odradek,' " *Zeitschrift für Deutsche Philologie*, 109 (1990), 238–252.

"A Country Doctor"

Bernheimer, Charles. "Kafka's 'Ein Landarzt': The Poetics of *Nachträglichkeit*," *J Kafka Soc Am*, 11, i–ii (1987), 4–8.

Golomb-Brecman, Etti. "No Roses Without Thorns: Ambivalences in Kafka's 'A Country Doctor,' " *Am Imago*, 46 (1989), 77–84.

Koelb, Clayton. *Kafka's Rhetoric* . . . , 195–207.

Mailloux, Peter. *A Hesitation before Birth* . . . , 389–390.

Midgley, David. "The Word and the Spirit: Explorations of the Irrational in Kafka, Döblin, and Musil," in Collier, Peter, and Judy Davies, Eds. *Modernism* . . . , 117–119.

Whitlark, James S. "Kafka's 'A Country Doctor' as Neoromantic Fairy Tale," in Saciuk, Olena H., Ed. *The Shape of the Fantastic* . . . , 43–49.

"Description of a Struggle"

Koelb, Clayton. *Kafka's Rhetoric* . . . , 182–195.

Sandbank, Shimon. *After Kafka* . . . , 17–20.

Sussman, Henry. *Afterimages of Modernity* . . . , 75–81.

"The Giant Mole"

McElroy, Bernard. . . . *Modern Grotesque*, 43–44.

"Give It Up!"

+Politzer, Heinz. " 'Give It Up!': A Discourse on Method," in Gross, Ruth V., Ed. *Critical Essays* . . . , 53–73.

"A Hunger Artist"

Del Caro, Adrian. "Denial versus Affirmation: Kafka's 'Ein Hungerkünstler' as a Paradigm of Freedom," *Mod Austrian Lit*, 22, i (1989), 35–56.

Ginsburg, Ruth. "Karneval und Fasten: Exzess und Mangel in der Sprache des Körpers," *Poetica*, 21, i–ii (1989), 26–42.

McElroy, Bernard. . . . *Modern Grotesque*, 53–54.

Mailloux, Peter. *A Hesitation before Birth* . . . , 500–502.

Norris, Margot. "Sadism and Masochism in 'In the Penal Colony' and 'A Hunger Artist,' " in Anderson, Mark, Ed. *Reading Kafka* . . . , 170–186.

+Roberts, Edgar V., and Henry E. Jacobs. *Instructor's Manual* . . . , 2nd ed., 78–79.

"The Hunter Gracchus"

Möbus, Frank. "Theoderich, Julia und die Jakobsleiter: Franz Kafkas Erzählfragmente zum 'Jäger Gracchus,' " *Zeitschrift für Deutsche Philologie*, 109 (1990), 253–271.

Phillips, K. J. *Dying Gods* . . . , 50–54.

"In the Penal Colony"

Beckmann, Martin. "Franz Kafka's Erzählung 'In der Strafkolonie': Ein Deutungsversuch," *Wirkendes Wort*, 39 (1989), 375–392.
Bogue, Ronald. *Deleuze and Guattari*, 112–113.
Detweiler, Robert. *Breaking the Fall* . . . , 131–136.
Horn, Peter. " 'Ein eigentümlicher Apparat' im Blick eines Forschungsreisenden: Zur anthropologischen Methode Kafkas 'In der Strafkolonie,' " *Acta Germanica*, 19 (1988), 49–78.
Koelb, Clayton. *Kafka's Rhetoric* . . . , 66–69.
McElroy, Bernard. . . . *Modern Grotesque*, 55–61.
Mailloux, Peter. *A Hesitation before Birth* . . . , 350–352.
Norris, Margot. "Sadism and Masochism . . . ," 170–186.
+Weinstein, Arnold. "Kafka's Writing Machine: Metamorphosis in the Penal Colony," in Gross, Ruth V., Ed. *Critical Essays* . . . , 120–130.

"Jackals and Arabs"

Koelb, Clayton. *Kafka's Rhetoric* . . . , 22–27.

"Josephine the Singer"

Rickels, Laurence A. "Musicphantoms: 'Uncanned' Conceptions of Music from Josephine the Singer to Mickey Mouse," *SubStance*, 18, i (1989), 3–6.

"The Judgment"

Engelberg, Edward. *Elegiac Fictions* . . . , 158–162.
McElroy, Bernard. . . . *Modern Grotesque*, 36–39.
Mailloux, Peter. *A Hesitation before Birth* . . . , 263–266.

"Metamorphosis"

Barry, Thomas F. "On the Parasite Metaphor in Kafka's 'The Metamorphosis,' " *West Virginia Univ Philol Papers*, 35 (1989), 65–73.
Boa, Elizabeth. "Creepy-Crawlies: Gilman's 'The Yellow Wallpaper' and Kafka's 'The Metamorphosis,' " *Paragraph*, 13, i (1990), 19–29.
Bogue, Ronald. *Deleuze and Guattari*, 110–113.
Bouson, J. Brooks. *The Empathic Reader* . . . , 51–63; rpt. Gross, Ruth V., Ed. *Critical Essays* . . . , 191–205.
Engelberg, Edward. *Elegiac Fictions* . . . , 93–96.
Kempf, Franz. "Kafka und der Expressionismus: 'Die Verwandlung,' " *Seminar*, 26, iv (1990), 327–341.
Mailloux, Peter. *A Hesitation before Birth* . . . , 272–275.
Sandbank, Shimon. *After Kafka* . . . , 20–28.
Sweeney, Kevin. "Competing Theories of Identity in Kafka's 'The Metamorphosis,' " *Mosaic*, 23, iv (1990), 23–35.

"The New Advocate"

Schomaker, G. "Deformation eines klassischen Motivs: Anmerkungen zu einem Text von Franz Kafka 'Der neue Advokat,' " *Germanistische Mitteilungen*, 31 (1990), 23–29.

"An Old Page" [same as "An Old Manuscript"]
Koelb, Clayton. *Kafka's Rhetoric* . . . , 24–26.

"A Report to an Academy"
Avni, Ora. *The Resistance of Reference* . . . , 116–121, 159–174.

"The Silence of the Sirens"
Koelb, Clayton. *Kafka's Rhetoric* . . . , 93–95.
Mykyta, Larysa. "Kafka's Siren-Text," *J Kafka Soc Am*, 11, i–ii (1987), 44–51.

"The Top"
Koelb, Clayton. *Kafka's Rhetoric* . . . , 117–119.

KANG ZHUO [MAO JICHANG]

"My Two Landlords"
Beyer, John. "Kang Zhuo," in Slupski, Zbigniew, Ed. *A Selective Guide* . . . , II, 80–82.

VALENTIN KATAEV

"The Dry Estuary"
Shneidman, N. N. *Soviet Literature* . . . , 73.

"The Sleeping Man"
Shneidman, N. N. *Soviet Literature* . . . , 72–73.

"Werther Has Already Been Written"
Shneidman, N. N. *Soviet Literature* . . . , 66–68.

KAWABATA YASUNARI

"The Ring"
Palmer, Thom. "The Asymmetrical Garden: Discovering Yasunari Kawabata," *Southwest R*, 74, iii (1989), 399.

KAYAMA SHIGERU

"The Reminiscences of Oran Pendek"
Matthew, Robert. *Japanese Science Fiction* . . . , 37–38.

"The Revenge of Oran Pendek"
Matthew, Robert. *Japanese Science Fiction* . . . , 37–38.

GOTTFRIED KELLER

"Herr Jacques"
Hart, Gail K. *Readers and Their Fictions* . . . , 86–90.

"Der Narr auf Manegg"
Hart, Gail K. *Readers and Their Fictions* . . . , 92.

"A Village Romeo and Juliet"
Hart, Gail K. *Readers and Their Fictions* . . . , 60–84.

DANIEL KEYES

"Flowers for Algernon"
Huntington, John. *Rationalizing Genius* . . . , 65–68.

DANIIL KHARMS [DANIIL IVANOVICH YUVACHEV]

"Connection"
Shukman, Ann. "Toward a Poetics of the Absurd: The Prose Writings of Daniil Kharms," in Kelly, Catriona, Michael Makin, and Donald Shepherd, Eds. *Discontinuous Discourses* . . . , 68–69.

"Rehabilitation"
Shukman, Ann. "Toward a Poetics . . . ," 64–65.

"The Start of a Very Nice Summer's Day"
Shukman, Ann. "Toward a Poetics . . . ," 65.

"The Story"
Shukman, Ann. "Toward a Poetics . . . ," 63–64.

"What Happened on the Street"
Shukman, Ann. "Toward a Poetics . . . ," 66.

KIGI KOTARO

"Angioskiaphobia"
Matthew, Robert. *Japanese Science Fiction* . . . , 30–31.

GRACE KING

"Bayou L'Ombre"
Taylor, Helen. *Gender, Race, and Region* . . . , 61–64.

"Bonne Maman"
Elfenbein, Anna S. *Women on the Color Line* . . . , 88–92.

"The Drama of Evening"
Taylor, Helen. *Gender, Race, and Region* . . . , 52–53, 55–56.

"La Grande Demoiselle"
DeJean, Joan. "Critical Creolization: Grace King and Writing on French in the American South," in Humphries, Jefferson, Ed. *Southern Literature* . . . , 120.

"The Little Convent Girl"
DeJean, Joan. "Critical Creolization . . . ," 122–123.
Elfenbein, Anna S. *Women on the Color Line* . . . , 108–116.

"Mademoiselle Coralie"
Taylor, Helen. *Gender, Race, and Region* . . . , 78–80.

"Madrilène"
Elfenbein, Anna S. *Women on the Color Line* . . . , 82–88.

"Monsieur Motte"
DeJean, Joan. "Critical Creolization . . . ," 115–120.
Elfenbein, Anna S. *Women on the Color Line* . . . , 92–106.
Taylor, Helen. *Gender, Race, and Region* . . . , 50–52.

THOMAS KING

"Bingo Bigbear and the Tie-and-Choke Bone Game"
Petrone, Penny. *Native Literature* . . . , 146–147.

"Joe the Painter and the Deer Island"
Atwood, Margaret. "A Double-Bladed Knife: Subversive Laughter in Two Stories by Thomas King," *Canadian Lit*, 124–125 (1990), 244–247.

"One Good Story, That One"
Atwood, Margaret. "A Double-Bladed Knife . . . ," 247–250.

RUDYARD KIPLING

"Beyond the Pale"
Crook, Nora. *Kipling's Myth* . . . , 115–118.
McBratney, John. "Lovers Beyond the Pale: Images of Indian Women in Kipling's Tales of Miscegenation," *Works & Days*, 8, i (1990), 19–21, 24–31.
Paffard, Mark. *Kipling's Indian Fiction*, 49–50.

"The Bridge Builders"
Kaye, M. M. "Introduction," *Picking Up Gold* . . . [by Rudyard Kipling], 15–18.
Paffard, Mark. *Kipling's Indian Fiction*, 121–123.
Ramachandran, C. N. "Kipling as the Chronicler of the Empire: Ambivalences and Archetypes," *Lit Criterion*, 22, iv (1987), 14–15.

"The Brushwood Boy"
Crook, Nora. *Kipling's Myth* . . . , 14–15.
Paffard, Mark. *Kipling's Indian Fiction*, 58–60.
Poole, Adrian. "Kipling's Upper Case," in Mallett, Phillip, Ed. *Kipling Considered*, 155–156.

"The City of Dreadful Night"
McBratney, John. "Lovers Beyond the Pale . . . ," 22–23.

"The Comprehension of Private Copper"
Crook, Nora. *Kipling's Myth . . .*, 108–109.

"A Conference of the Powers"
Poole, Adrian. "Kipling's Upper Case," 127–128.

"The Conversion of Aurelian McGoggin"
Poole, Adrian. "Kipling's Upper Case," 147–148.
Seymour-Smith, Martin. *Rudyard Kipling*, 107–110.

"Dayspring Mishandled"
Mallett, Phillip. "Kipling and the Hoax," in Mallett, Phillip, Ed. *Kipling Considered*, 103–113.
Seymour-Smith, Martin. *Rudyard Kipling,* 258–263.

"A Deal in Cotton"
Crook, Nora. *Kipling's Myth . . .*, 47–49.

"The Disturber of Traffic"
Crook, Nora. *Kipling's Myth . . .*, 4–7.
Paffard, Mark. *Kipling's Indian Fiction*, 124–125.

"The Dog Hervey"
Musgrove, Sydney. " 'When 'Omer smote 'is bloomin' lyre,' " in Gibson, Colin, Ed. *Art and Society . . .*, 192–193.

"The Eye of Allah"
Coates, John. "Memories of Mansura: The 'Tints and Textures' of Kipling's Late Art in 'The Eye of Allah,' " *Mod Lang R*, 85 (1990), 555–569.
Crook, Nora. *Kipling's Myth . . .*, 93–94.

"The Finest Story in the World"
Lyon, John. "Half-Written Tales: Kipling and Conrad," in Mallett, Phillip, Ed. *Kipling Considered*, 128–129.

"The Flag of the Country"
Gilmour, Robin. "*Stalky & Co.*: Revising the Code," in Mallett, Phillip, Ed. *Kipling Considered*, 30–31.

"The Fumes of the Heart"
Leenerts, Cynthia. "Kipling's Fumes of the Heart: An Introduction to *The Eyes of Asia*," *Lit Criterion*, 25, ii (1990), 16–18.

"The Gardener"
Seymour-Smith, Martin. *Rudyard Kipling*, 354–355.

"Georgie Porgie"
Paffard, Mark. *Kipling's Indian Fiction*, 58–59.

"Gloriana"
Crook, Nora. *Kipling's Myth . . .*, 123–124.

"An Habitation Enforced"
Trotter, David. "Kipling's England: The Edwardian Years," in Mallett, Phillip, Ed. *Kipling Considered*, 67–69.

"The Head of the District"
Paffard, Mark. *Kipling's Indian Fiction*, 40–43.
Seymour-Smith, Martin. *Rudyard Kipling*, 169–171.

"His Private Honour"
Paffard, Mark. *Kipling's Indian Fiction*, 64–65.

"His Wedded Wife"
Crook, Nora. *Kipling's Myth . . .*, 89–91.
Seymour-Smith, Martin. *Rudyard Kipling*, 86–87.

"The House Surgeon"
Seymour-Smith, Martin. *Rudyard Kipling*, 340–341.

"How Fear Came"
Paffard, Mark. *Kipling's Indian Fiction*, 93–96.

"In Ambush"
Mallett, Phillip. "Kipling and the Hoax," 99–101.

"The Incarnation of Krishna Mulvaney"
Paffard, Mark. *Kipling's Indian Fiction*, 67–68.

"Kidnapped"
Paffard, Mark. *Kipling's Indian Fiction*, 46–47.

"Letting in the Jungle"
Paffard, Mark. *Kipling's Indian Fiction*, 94–96.

"Lispeth"
Seymour-Smith, Martin. *Rudyard Kipling*, 69–70.

"The Lost Legion"
Kaye, M. M. "Introduction," 112–115.

"Love-o'-Women"
Paffard, Mark. *Kipling's Indian Fiction*, 67–74.

"The Madness of Private Ortheris"
Paffard, Mark. *Kipling's Indian Fiction*, 62–64.

"A Madonna of the Trenches"
Crook, Nora. *Kipling's Myth . . .*, 157–168.
Seymour-Smith, Martin. *Rudyard Kipling*, 355–357.

"The Man Who Would Be King"
Mallett, Phillip. "Kipling and the Hoax," 102–106.
Paffard, Mark. *Kipling's Indian Fiction*, 76–79.

"Mary Postgate"
Crook, Nora. *Kipling's Myth . . .*, 124–147.
Hanson, Clare. "Limits and Renewals: The Meaning of Form in the Stories of Rudyard Kipling," in Mallett, Phillip, Ed. *Kipling Considered*, 88–91.
Poole, Adrian. "Kipling's Upper Case," 151–152.
Seymour-Smith, Martin. *Rudyard Kipling*, 219–220.

"A Matter of Fact"
Crook, Nora. *Kipling's Myth . . .*, 44–47.

"Mrs. Bathurst"
Crook, Nora. *Kipling's Myth . . .*, 61–86.
Lodge, David. " 'Mrs. Bathurst': Indeterminacy in Modern Narrative," in Mallett, Phillip, Ed. *Kipling Considered*, 71–84.
Seymour-Smith, Martin. *Rudyard Kipling*, 310–321.

"My Son's Wife"
Crook, Nora. *Kipling's Myth* . . . , 153–155.
Musgrove, Sydney. " 'When 'Omer smote 'is bloomin' lyre,' " 190–192.

"On Greenhow Hill"
Paffard, Mark. *Kipling's Indian Fiction*, 50–54.

"Pig"
Crook, Nora. *Kipling's Myth* . . . , 41–44.

"The Record of Badalia Herodsfoot"
Paffard, Mark. *Kipling's Indian Fiction*, 116–119.

"Red Dog"
Paffard, Mark. *Kipling's Indian Fiction*, 94–96.

"A Retired Gentleman"
Leenerts, Cynthia. "Kipling's Fumes . . . ," 11–16.

"Sea Constables"
Lyon, John. "Half-Written Tales . . . ," 132–133.

"The Strange Ride of Morrowbie Jukes"
Crook, Nora. *Kipling's Myth* . . . , 94–107.

"The Tender Achilles"
Mallett, Phillip. "Kipling and the Hoax," 106–108.

"Thrown Away"
Lyon, John. "Half-Written Tales . . . ," 117–118.
Ramachandran, C. N. "Kipling as the Chronicler . . . ," 15.

"The Tomb of His Ancestors"
Poole, Adrian. "Kipling's Upper Case," 154–155.
Ramachandran, C. N. "Kipling as the Chronicler . . . ," 16.

"A Trooper of Horse"
Leenerts, Cynthia. "Kipling's Fumes . . . ," 18–20.

"Uncovenanted Mercies"
Mason, Philip. " 'Uncovenanted Mercies': The Last of Kipling's Collected Stories," *Kipling J*, 63 (June, 1989), 11–16.

"The Village That Voted the Earth Was Flat"
Crook, Nora. *Kipling's Myth* . . . , 49–53.

"The Vortex"
Crook, Nora. *Kipling's Myth* . . . , 53–58.

"A Wayside Comedy"
Paffard, Mark. *Kipling's Indian Fiction*, 34–36.

"William the Conqueror"
Poole, Adrian. "Kipling's Upper Case," 148–149.

"Wireless"
Seymour-Smith, Martin. *Rudyard Kipling*, 321–325.

"The Wish House"
Crook, Nora. *Kipling's Myth* . . . , 119–120.

"Without Benefit of Clergy"
McBratney, John. "Lovers Beyond the Pale . . . ," 19–21, 24–31.
Paffard, Mark. *Kipling's Indian Fiction*, 97–100.

"The Woman in His Life"
Seymour-Smith, Martin. *Rudyard Kipling*, 357–358.

"Wressley of the Foreign Service"
Ramachandran, C. N. "Kipling as the Chronicler . . . ," 14.

ITSIK KIPNIS

"Months and Days"
Roskies, David G. "The Rape of the Shtetl," in Roskies, David G., Ed. *The Literature of Destruction* . . . , 282–283.

KITA MORIO

"A Vacant Piece of Ground"
Matthew, Robert. *Japanese Science Fiction* . . . , 54–55.

KIZU TORA

"The Wedding Shrouded in Grey"
Matthew, Robert. *Japanese Science Fiction* . . . , 19–20.

HEINRICH VON KLEIST

"The Beggar Woman of Locarno"
Wilpert, Gero von. "Der Ausrutcher des Bettelweibes von Locarno: 'Capriccio con fuoco,' " *Seminar*, 26 (1990), 283–293.

"The Duel"
Jacobs, Carl. *Uncontainable Romanticism* . . . , 159–170.
Schubert, Ernst, and Ernst Osterkamp. " 'Der Zweikampf': Ein mittelalterliches Ordal und seine Vergegenwartigung bei Heinrich von Kleist," *Kleist-Jahrbuch 1988–1989*, 280–308.

"The Foundling"
Jacobs, Carl. *Uncontainable Romanticism* . . . , 176–179.

"The Marquise of O—"
Huszar Allen, Marguerite de. "Denial and Acceptance: Narrative Patterns in Thomas Mann's 'Die Betrogene' and Kleist's 'Die Marquise von O—,' " *Germ R*, 64 (1989), 121–128.
Pfeiffer, Joachim. "Die wiedergefundene Ordnung: Literaturpsychologische Anmerkungen zu Kleists 'Die Marquise von O—,' " *Jahrbuch für Internationale Germanistik*, 19, i (1987), 36–53.

"Michael Kohlhaas"
Koelb, Clayton. "Incorporating the Text: Kleist's 'Michael Kohlhaas,' " *PMLA*, 105 (1990), 1098–1107.

DAMON FRANCIS KNIGHT

"Country of the Kind"
Huntington, John. *Rationalizing Genius* . . . , 167–170.

KOMATSU SAKYO

"Adam's Descendants"
Matthew, Robert. *Japanese Science Fiction* . . . , 48.

"The Age of Models"
Matthew, Robert. *Japanese Science Fiction* . . . , 47–48.

"The American Wall"
Matthew, Robert. *Japanese Science Fiction* . . . , 221–223.

"And Everybody Stopped Work"
Matthew, Robert. *Japanese Science Fiction* . . . , 73–74.

"A Blue Sky"
Matthew, Robert. *Japanese Science Fiction* . . . , 88–89.

"The Child in the Dark"
Matthew, Robert. *Japanese Science Fiction* . . . , 101–102.

"The Construction of a New Capital"
Matthew, Robert. *Japanese Science Fiction* . . . , 100–101.

"The Fourteenth Day in April"
Matthew, Robert. *Japanese Science Fiction* . . . , 233–234.

"The Grand Strategy for Adoption as Sons"
Matthew, Robert. *Japanese Science Fiction* . . . , 218–219.

"The Harmonica"
Matthew, Robert. *Japanese Science Fiction* . . . , 104–105.

"Judgment on Man"
Matthew, Robert. *Japanese Science Fiction* . . . , 87–88.

"The Man Who Hated Young Girls"
Matthew, Robert. *Japanese Science Fiction* . . . , 113–114.

"The Mother of a Strange Child"
Matthew, Robert. *Japanese Science Fiction* . . . , 213.

"Oh, for Quiet in the Woods!"
Matthew, Robert. *Japanese Science Fiction* . . . , 49–50.

"Perfect Crimes"
Matthew, Robert. *Japanese Science Fiction* . . . , 49.

"A Quiet Corridor"
Matthew, Robert. *Japanese Science Fiction* . . . , 89–90.

"The Sound of Chasing Feet"
Matthew, Robert. *Japanese Science Fiction* . . . , 102–103.

"The Theatre of Fate"
Matthew, Robert. *Japanese Science Fiction* . . . , 50–51.

"There Was No War"
Matthew, Robert. *Japanese Science Fiction* . . . , 212–213.

KONO NORIO

"Locomotives in the Field"
Matthew, Robert. *Japanese Science Fiction* . . . , 178–179.

MARIA KONOPNICKA

"My Aunt"
Eber, Irene. *Voices from Afar* . . . , 55.

CYRIL KORNBLUTH

"The Marching Morons"
Huntington, John. *Rationalizing Genius* . . . , 61–64.

KOZAKAI FUBOKU

"The Love Curve"
Matthew, Robert. *Japanese Science Fiction* . . . , 16–17.

HENRY KREISEL

"Chassidic Song"
Greenstein, Michael. *Third Solitudes* . . . , 5–6.

ALEXANDER KRON

"The Captain of the Merchant Fleet"
Shneidman, N. N. *Soviet Literature* . . . , 122–123.

VLADIMIR KRUPIN

"The Fortieth Day"
Shneidman, N. N. *Soviet Literature* . . . , 53–54.

"Handbell"
Shneidman, N. N. *Soviet Literature* . . . , 53.

KUZE JURAN

"The Animal Kingdom Under the Earth"
Matthew, Robert. *Japanese Science Fiction . . .*, 33–34.

MARISA LABOZZETTA

"Making the Wine"
Yahnke, Robert E., and Richard M. Eastman. *Aging in Literature . . .*, 47–48.

TOMMASO LANDOLFI

"Gogol's Wife"
Capek-Habekovic, Romana. "Fantastic and Grotesque Symmetry in Landolfi's 'La moglie di Gogol,' " in Mancini, Albert N., Paolo A. Giordano, and Anthony J. Tamburri, Eds. *Italiana 1988*, 181–187.

ROSE WILDER LANE

"Old Maid"
Holtz, William. "Rose Wilder Lane's Old Home Town," *Stud Short Fiction*, 26 (1989), 482.

LAO SHE [SHU QINGCHUN]

"Black Li and White Li"
Lee, Leo O. "Lao She's 'Black Li and White Li': A Reading in Psychological Structure," in Huters, Theodore, Ed. . . . *Modern Chinese Short Story*, 22–36.

"The Crescent Moon"
Vohra, Ranbir. *Lao She . . .*, 121–125.

"Death-Bearing Lances"
Almberg, Shiu-Pang. "Lao She," in Slupski, Zbigniew, Ed. *A Selective Guide . . .*, II, 91–92.

"Firm of Long Standing"
Almberg, Shiu-Pang. "Lao She," 90–91.

"The Glasses"
Slupski, Zbigniew. "Lao She," in Slupski, Zbigniew, Ed. *A Selective Guide . . .*, II, 83–84.

"Liu's Compound"
Vohra, Ranbir. *Lao She . . .*, 117–119.

"On Duty"
Slupski, Zbigniew. "Lao She," 86.

"A Story I Have Heard"
Almberg, Shiu-Pang. "Lao She," 89–90.

RING LARDNER

"Haircut"
Cervo, Nathan. "Lardner's 'Haircut,' " *Explicator*, 47, ii (1989), 47–48.
Phelan, James. "Narrative Discourse, Literary Character, and Ideology," in Phelan, James, Ed. *Reading Narrative* . . . , 132–138.

PAZ LATORENA

"Desire"
Santillan-Castrence, P. "The Period of Apprenticeship," in Manuud, Antonio G., Ed. *Brown Heritage* . . . , 556–557.

MARGARET LAURENCE

"A Bird in the House"
Scott, Jamie S. "Self-Writing, Self-Transcendence, Commemoration: Margaret Laurence's *A Bird in the House*," *J Short Story Engl*, 12 (Spring, 1989), 92–94, 102.
"The Drummer of All the World"
Richards, David. " 'Leave the Dead some room to dance!': Margaret Laurence and Africa," in Nicholson, Colin, Ed. *Critical Approaches* . . . , 24–25.
"The Half Husky"
Scott, Jamie S. "Self-Writing . . . ," 97–99.
"Horses of the Night"
Scott, Jamie S. "Self-Writing . . . ," 95–97.
"Jericho's Brick Battlements"
Scott, Jamie S. "Self-Writing . . . ," 99–101.
"The Loons"
Easingwood, Peter. "The Realism of Laurence's Semi-Autobiographical Fiction," in Nicholson, Colin, Ed. *Critical Approaches* . . . , 124–125.
Scott, Jamie S. "Self-Writing . . . ," 94–95.
"The Mask of the Bear"
Scott, Jamie S. "Self-Writing . . . ," 91–92.
"The Sound of Singing"
Scott, Jamie S. "Self-Writing . . . ," 88–89.
"To Set Our House in Order"
Grabes, Herbert. "Creating to Dissect: Strategies of Character Portrayal and Evaluation in Short Stories by Margaret Laurence,

Alice Munro, and Mavis Gallant," in Nischik, Reingard M., and Barbara Korte, Eds. *Modes of Narrative* . . . , 120–122.
Scott, Jamie S. "Self-Writing . . . ," 89–91.

MARY LAVIN

"At Sallygap"
Thompson, Richard J. *Everlasting Voices* . . . , 91–92.

"A Cup of Tea"
Thompson, Richard J. *Everlasting Voices* . . . , 85.

"Frail Vessel"
Thompson, Richard J. *Everlasting Voices* . . . , 86–87.

"Happiness"
Thompson, Richard J. *Everlasting Voices* . . . , 89–90.

"In the Middle of the Field"
Thompson, Richard J. *Everlasting Voices* . . . , 89.

"A Memory"
Thompson, Richard J. *Everlasting Voices* . . . , 94–96.

"The Sand Castle"
Thompson, Richard J. *Everlasting Voices* . . . , 92.

"The Small Bequest"
Thompson, Richard J. *Everlasting Voices* . . . , 86, 88–89.

"Trastevere"
Thompson, Richard J. *Everlasting Voices* . . . , 87–88.

"The Widow's Son"
Thompson, Richard J. *Everlasting Voices* . . . , 93–94.

"A Woman Friend"
Thompson, Richard J. *Everlasting Voices* . . . , 82–83.

D. H. LAWRENCE

"The Blind Man"
Marcus, Phillip. " 'A Healed Whole Man': Frazer, Lawrence and Blood Consciousness," in Fraser, Robert, Ed. *Sir James Frazer* . . . , 240–242.

"The Captain's Doll"
McDowell, Frederick P. W. " 'The Individual in His Pure Singleness': Theme and Symbol in 'The Captain's Doll,' " in Squires, Michael, and Keith Cushman, Eds. *The Challenge* . . . , 143–157.

"The Daughters of the Vicar" [originally "Two Marriages"]
Kiely, Robert. "Out on Strike: The Language and Power of the Working Class in Lawrence's Fiction," in Squires, Michael, and Keith Cushman, Eds. *The Challenge* . . . , 97–99.

"England, My England"

Blayac, Alain. "Guerre et guerres dans 'England, My England,' " in Katz-Roy, Ginette, Ed. *Études lawrenciennes*, II, 17–38.

Padhi, Bibhu. *D. H. Lawrence* . . . , 37–42.

"The Flying Fish"

Roy, Ginette. "Tel un poisson dans l'eau: du léthal au foetal dans 'The Flying Fish,' " in Katz-Roy, Ginette, Ed. *Études lawrenciennes*, I, 59–72.

"The Fox"

Nelson, Jane A. "The Familial Isotopy in 'The Fox,' " in Squires, Michael, and Keith Cushman, Eds. *The Challenge* . . . , 129–141.

Padhi, Bibhu. *D. H. Lawrence* . . . , 89–92.

Renner, Stanley. "Sexuality and the Unconscious: Psychosexual Drama and Conflict in 'The Fox,' " *D. H. Lawrence R*, 21 (1989), 245–273.

Sinzelle, Claude. "Skinning the Fox: A Masochist's Delight," in Preston, Peter, and Peter Hoare, Eds. . . . *Modern World*, 161–179.

Stewart, Jack F. "Totem and Symbol in 'The Fox' and 'St. Mawr,' " *Stud Hum*, 16, ii (1989), 84–98.

Whelan, P. T. "The Hunting Metaphor in 'The Fox' and Other Works," *D. H. Lawrence R*, 21 (1990), 275–290.

"The Horse Dealer's Daughter"

Daleski, H. M. "Life as a Four-Letter Word: A Contemporary View of Lawrence and Joyce," in Preston, Peter, and Peter Hoare, Eds. . . . *Modern World*, 100–101.

Fraustino, Daniel. "Psychic Rebirth and Christian Imagery in D. H. Lawrence's 'The Horse-Dealer's Daughter,' " *J Evolutionary Psych*, 9, i–ii (1989), 105–108.

Meyers, Jeffrey. "D. H. Lawrence and Tradition: 'The Horse Dealer's Daughter,' " *Stud Short Fiction*, 26 (1989), 346–351.

Padhi, Bibhu. *D. H. Lawrence* . . . , 85–88.

"Love Among the Haystacks"

Chatman, Seymour. "The 'Rhetoric' of 'Fiction,' " in Phelan, James, Ed. *Reading Narrative* . . . , 46–47.

"The Lovely Lady"

Aquien, Pascal. "Le visage et la voix dans 'The Lovely Lady,' " in Katz-Roy, Ginette, Ed. *Études lawrenciennes*, II, 71–80.

"The Man Who Died" [originally "The Escaped Cock"]

Conway, James C. *D. H. Lawrence* . . . , 237–253.

Padhi, Bibhu. *D. H. Lawrence* . . . , 207–211.

Phillips, K. J. *Dying Gods* . . . , 150–153.

Wallace, M. Elizabeth. "The Circling Hawk: Philosophy of Knowledge in Polanyi and Lawrence," in Squires, Michael, and Keith Cushman, Eds. *The Challenge* . . . , 115–117.

"The Man Who Loved Islands"

Alexandre-Garner, Corinne. " 'The Man Who Loved Islands' ou l'effacement de la trace," in Katz-Roy, Ginette, Ed. *Études lawrenciennes*, II, 91–106.

Padhi, Bibhu. *D. H. Lawrence* . . . , 203–206.

"Monkey Nuts"
Marcus, Phillip. " 'A Healed Whole Man' . . . ," 242–243.

"The Prussian Officer" [originally "Honour and Arms"]
Marcus, Phillip. " 'A Healed Whole Man' . . . ," 236–238.
Padhi, Bibhu. *D. H. Lawrence* . . . , 190–193.

"The Rocking-Horse Winner"
Padhi, Bibhu. *D. H. Lawrence* . . . , 50–52.

"St. Mawr"
Padhi, Bibhu. *D. H. Lawrence* . . . , 64–71.
Stewart, Jack F. "Totem and Symbol . . . ," 84–98.

"Samson and Delilah"
Naugrette, Jean-Pierre. "L'homme ligoté: variations sur 'Samson and Delilah,' " in Katz-Roy, Ginette, Ed. *Études lawrenciennes*, II, 37–49.

"A Sick Collier"
Kiely, Robert. "Out on Strike . . . ," 92–93.

"Strike Pay"
Kiely, Robert. "Out on Strike . . . ," 93–94.

"The Thorn in the Flesh"
Conway, James C. *D. H. Lawrence* . . . , 156–166.

"The Woman Who Rode Away"
Balbert, Peter. *D. H. Lawrence* . . . , 109–132.
Padhi, Bibhu. *D. H. Lawrence* . . . , 200–203.
Phillips, K. J. *Dying Gods* . . . , 146–150.
Ruffinelli, Jorge. *El otro México* . . . , 102–106.
Wallace, M. Elizabeth. "The Circling Hawk . . . ," 114–115.

HENRY LAWSON

"The Drover's Wife"
Arens, Werner. "The Ironical Fate of 'The Drover's Wife': Four Versions from Henry Lawson (1892) to Barbara Jefferis (1980)," in Stummer, Peter O., Ed. *The Story Must Be Told* . . . , 120–123.

STEPHEN LEACOCK

"The Extraordinary Entanglement"
Lynch, Gerald. "Religion and Romance in Mariposa," in Staines, David, Ed. *Stephen Leacock* . . . , 91.

"The Fore-Ordained Attachment"
Lynch, Gerald. "Religion and Romance . . . ," 91–92.

"The Hostelry of Mr. Smith"
Lynch, Gerald. "Religion and Romance . . . ," 84–85.

"The Mariposa Bank Mystery"
Lynch, Gerald. "Religion and Romance . . . ," 92.

"The Ministrations"
Lynch, Gerald. "Religion and Romance . . . ," 86–87.

DAVID LEAVITT

"Territory"
Klarer, Mario. "Homoerotische 'Trigonometrie': Zu David Leavitts 'Territory,' " *Forum Homo*, 7 (1989), 51–69.

ALBERTO LEDUC

"Divina!"
Pavón, Alfredo. "De la violencia en los modernistas," in Pavón, Alfredo, Ed. *Paquette: Cuento* . . . , 76–77.

"Fragatita"
Pavón, Alfredo. "De la violencia . . . ," 74–76.

VERNON LEE [VIOLET PAGET]

"Amour Dure"
Christensen, Peter G. "The Burden of History in Vernon Lee's Ghost Story 'Amour Dure,' " *Stud Hum*, 16, i (1989), 33–43.
Tracy, Robert. "Loving You All Ways: Vamp, Vampires, Necrophiles and Necrofilles in Nineteenth-Century Fiction," in Barreca, Regina, Ed. *Sex and Death* . . . , 47–48.

"Oke of Okehurst, or, The Phantom Lover"
Tracy, Robert. "Loving You All Ways . . . ," 48.

JOSEPH SHERIDAN LE FANU

"An Account of Some Strange Disturbances in Aungier Street"
Melada, Ivan. *Sheridan Le Fanu*, 120–122.

"The Bride of Carrivarah"
Melada, Ivan. *Sheridan Le Fanu*, 16–17.

"Carmilla"
Coughlan, Patricia. "Doubles, Shadows, Sedan-Chairs and the Past: The 'Ghost Stories' of J. S. Le Fanu," in Allen, Michael, and Angela Wilcox, Eds. *Critical Approaches* . . . , 30–31.
Melada, Ivan. *Sheridan Le Fanu*, 99–101.
Tracy, Robert. "Loving You All Ways: Vamps, Vampires, Necrophiles and Necrofilles in Nineteenth-Century Fiction," in Barreca, Regina, Ed. *Sex and Death* . . . , 38–42.

"Dickon the Devil"
Melada, Ivan. *Sheridan Le Fanu*, 108–109.

"The Drunkard's Dream"
Melada, Ivan. *Sheridan Le Fanu*, 20–21.

"The Evil Guest"
Melada, Ivan. *Sheridan Le Fanu*, 69–72.

"The Familiar" [originally titled "The Watcher"]
Melada, Ivan. *Sheridan Le Fanu*, 97–98.

"Green Tea"
Carroll, Noël. *The Philosophy of Horror*, 147–148.
Melada, Ivan. *Sheridan Le Fanu*, 94–97.

"The Haunted Baronet"
Coughlan, Patricia. "Doubles, Shadows . . . ," 31–32, 37–39.
Melada, Ivan. *Sheridan Le Fanu*, 18–21.

"Justice Harbottle"
Melada, Ivan. *Sheridan Le Fanu*, 97–98.

"The Last Heir of Castle Connor"
Melada, Ivan. *Sheridan Le Fanu*, 15–16.

"Laura Silver Bell"
Melada, Ivan. *Sheridan Le Fanu*, 112–113.

"My Aunt Margaret's Adventure"
Melada, Ivan. *Sheridan Le Fanu*, 122–124.

"The Mysterious Lodger"
Melada, Ivan. *Sheridan Le Fanu*, 117–120.

"Passage in the Secret History of an Irish Countess"
Melada, Ivan. *Sheridan Le Fanu*, 21–23.

"The Room in the Dragon Volant"
Melada, Ivan. *Sheridan Le Fanu*, 98–99.

"A Strange Event in the Life of Schalken the Painter"
Coughlan, Patricia. "Doubles, Shadows . . . ," 26–28.
Melada, Ivan. *Sheridan Le Fanu*, 18–20.
Swafford, James. "Tradition and Guilt in Le Fanu's 'Schalken the Painter,' " *Canadian J Irish Stud*, 14, ii (1989), 48–59.
Tracy, Robert. "Loving You All Ways . . . ," 36–38.

"Ultor de Lacy"
Melada, Ivan. *Sheridan Le Fanu*, 109–110.

"The Vision of Tom Chuff"
Melada, Ivan. *Sheridan Le Fanu*, 114–116.

"The White Cat of Drumgunniol"
Coughlan, Patricia. "Doubles, Shadows . . . ," 36.
Melada, Ivan. *Sheridan Le Fanu*, 111.

"Wicked Captain Walshawe of Wauling"
Melada, Ivan. *Sheridan Le Fanu*, 113–114.

URSULA K. LE GUIN

"An die Musik"
Cummins, Elizabeth. *Understanding Ursula K. Le Guin*, 148–149.

"The Forest"
Cummins, Elizabeth. *Understanding Ursula K. Le Guin*, 137–138.

"The Fountains"
Cummins, Elizabeth. *Understanding Ursula K. Le Guin*, 135–136.

"The New Atlantis"
Cummins, Elizabeth. *Understanding Ursula K. Le Guin*, 166–172.

"The Ones Who Walk Away from Omelas"
Collins, Jerre. "Leaving Omelas: Questions of Faith and Understanding," *Stud Short Fiction*, 27 (1990), 525–535.

"The Road East"
Cummins, Elizabeth. *Understanding Ursula K. Le Guin*, 144–145.

"Sur"
Brown, Barbara. "Feminist Myth in Le Guin's 'Sur,' " *Mythlore*, 16, iv (1990), 56–59.

"A Week in the Country"
Cummins, Elizabeth. *Understanding Ursula K. Le Guin*, 146–148.

"Winter's King"
Cummins, Elizabeth. *Understanding Ursula K. Le Guin*, 73–74.

FRITZ LEIBER

"Coming Attractions"
Huntington, John. *Rationalizing Genius . . .* , 104–107.

"Sanity"
Panshin, Alexel, and Cory Panshin. *The World Beyond . . .* , 612–615.

MURRAY LEINSTER

"First Contact"
Huntington, John. *Rationalizing Genius . . .* , 116–119.
Panshin, Alexel, and Cory Panshin. *The World Beyond . . .* , 617–618.

"Sidewise in Time"
Panshin, Alexel, and Cory Panshin. *The World Beyond . . .* , 243–244.
Pierce, John J. *Great Themes of Science Fiction . . .* , 176–177.

JOHN LENNON

"Araminta Ditch"
Kaplan, Louis P. "Lennon's Larfter: Treating 'Araminta Ditch,' " *Mod Fiction Stud*, 36 (1990), 529–534.

JESÚS ALBERTO LÉON

"La amistad"
Ramos, Elías A. *El cuento venezolano . . .* , 83–84.

"Distancia"
Ramos, Elías A. *El cuento venezolano* . . . , 52–53, 140–141.

"Gesta"
Ramos, Elías A. *El cuento venezolano* . . . , 58–60.

"Martingala"
Ramos, Elías A. *El cuento venezolano* . . . , 42–43.

"Otra memoria"
Ramos, Elías A. *El cuento venezolano* . . . , 125–126.

A. LEONOV

"Out of the Mist"
Starikova, Elizaveta. "The Sociological Aspects of Contemporary 'Village Prose,' " *Soviet Stud Lit*, 26, i (1989–1990), 53–54.

"A Remote Place"
Starikova, Elizaveta. "The Sociological Aspects . . . ," 53.

"Ulkhan and Kriazhik"
Starikova, Elizaveta. "The Sociological Aspects . . . ," 54–55.

MIKHAIL LERMONTOV

"Bela"
Bagby, L. "Narrative Double-Voicing in Lermontov's *A Hero of Our Time*," *Slavic & East European J*, 22 (1978), 268–270.
Barratt, Andrew, and A. D. P. Briggs. *A Wicked Irony* . . . , 10–29.
Gregg, R. "The Cooling of Pechorin: The Skull Beneath the Skin," *Slavic R*, 43 (1984), 392–393.
Marsh, Cynthia. "Lermontov and the Romantic Tradition: The Function of Landscape in *A Hero of Our Time*," *Slavonic & East European R*, 66, i (1988), 37–42.
Mersereau, John. *Mikhail Lermontov*, 81–95.
Reed, W. L. *Meditations* . . . , 122–124.
Rosenshield, Gary. "Fatalism in *A Hero of Our Time*: Cause or Commonplace," in Mandelker, Amy, and Robert Reeder, Eds. *The Supernatural* . . . , 85–86.

"The Fatalist"
Bagby, L. "Narrative Double-Voicing . . . ," 281–283.
Barratt, Andrew, and A. D. P. Briggs. *A Wicked Irony* . . . , 105–122.
Faletti, Heidi E. "Elements of the Demonic in the Character of Pechorin in Lermontov's *A Hero of Our Time*," *Forum Mod Lang Stud*, 14 (1978), 370–371.
Freeborn, Richard. *The Rise of the Russian Novel*, 70–72.
Gregg, R. "The Cooling of Pechorin . . . ," 391–392.
Marsh, Cynthia. "Lermontov and the Romantic Tradition . . . ," 46.
Mersereau, John. *Mikhail Lermontov*, 132–143.
Reed, W. L. *Meditations* . . . , 129–130.
Rosenshield, Gary. "Fatalism in *A Hero of Our Time* . . . , 92–94.

Turner, C. J. G. *Pechorin* . . . , 55–62.

"The Journal"
Bagby, L. "Narrative Double-Voicing . . . ," 272–273.
Freeborn, Richard. *The Rise of the Russian Novel*, 60–61.

"Maksim Maksimych"
Bagby, L. "Narrative Double-Voicing . . . ," 270–272.
Barratt, Andrew, and A. D. P. Briggs. *A Wicked Irony* . . . , 30–42.
Freeborn, Richard. *The Rise of the Russian Novel*, 53–55.
Gregg, R. "The Cooling of Pechorin . . . ," 394–398.
Marsh, Cynthia. "Lermontov and the Romantic Tradition . . . ," 37–43.
Mersereau, John. *Mikhail Lermontov*, 96–104.
Reed, W. L. *Meditations* . . . , 124–125.
Turner, C. J. G. *Pechorin* . . . , 11–19.

"Princess Mary"
Arian, I. "Some Aspects of Lermontov's *A Hero of Our Time*," *Forum Mod Lang Stud*, 4 (1968), 367–370.
Bagby, L. "Narrative Double-Voicing . . . ," 274–281.
Barratt, Andrew, and A. D. P. Briggs. *A Wicked Irony* . . . , 66–104.
Freeborn, Richard. *The Rise of the Russian Novel*, 61–70.
Gregg, R. "The Cooling of Pechorin . . . ," 390–391.
Marsh, Cynthia. "Lermontov and the Romantic Tradition . . . ," 44–45.
Mersereau, John. *Mikhail Lermontov*, 113–131.
Reed, W. L. *Meditations* . . . , 126–129.
Rosenshield, Gary. "Fatalism in *A Hero of Our Time* . . . ," 87–91, 94–96.
Turner, C. J. G. *Pechorin* . . . , 26–43.

"Taman"
Arian, I. "Some Aspects . . . ," 27–29.
Bagby, L. "Narrative Double-Voicing . . . ," 273–274.
Barratt, Andrew, and A. D. P. Briggs. *A Wicked Irony* . . . , 43–65.
Freeborn, Richard. *The Rise of the Russian Novel*, 56–60.
Gregg, R. "The Cooling of Pechorin . . . ," 389–390.
Marsh, Cynthia. "Lermontov and the Romantic Tradition . . . ," 42–44.
Mersereau, John. *Mikhail Lermontov*, 105–112.
Peace, R. A. "The Role of 'Taman' in Lermontov's *Geroy nashegc vremeni*," *Slavonic & East European R*, 45 (1967), 12–29.
Reed, W. L. *Meditations* . . . , 125–126.
Turner, C. J. G. *Pechorin* . . . , 23–24.

DORIS LESSING

"The Black Madonna"
DaCrema, Joseph J. "Lessing's 'The Black Madonna,' " *Explicator*, 47, iii (1989), 55–58.

"The De Wets Come to Kloof Grange"
Chennells, Anthony. "Reading Doris Lessing's Rhodesian Stories in Zimbabwe," in Sprague, Claire, Ed. *In Pursuit of Doris Lessing* . . . , 34.

"Hunger"
Chennells, Anthony. " . . . Rhodesian Stories in Zimbabwe," 35–38.

" 'Leopard' George"
Chennells, Anthony. " . . . Rhodesian Stories in Zimbabwe," 27–30.

"The Old Chief Mshlanga"
Chennells, Anthony. " . . . Rhodesian Stories in Zimbabwe," 32–33.
+Roberts, Edgar V., and Henry E. Jacobs. *Instructor's Manual* . . . , 2nd ed., 80–81.

"A Room"
Tiger, Virginia. " 'Taking Hands and Dancing in (Dis)unity': Story to Storied in Doris Lessing's 'To Room Nineteen' and 'A Room,' " *Mod Fiction Stud*, 36 (1990), 428–431.

"A Sunset on the Veld"
Chennells, Anthony. " . . . Rhodesian Stories in Zimbabwe," 32.

"To Room Nineteen"
Halisky, Linda H. "Redeeming the Irrational: The Inexplicable Heroines of 'A Sorrowful Woman' and 'To Room Nineteen,' " *Stud Short Fiction*, 27 (1990), 48–54.
Tiger, Virginia. " 'Taking Hands . . . ,' " 424–428.
Watson, Irene G. "Lessing's 'To Room Nineteen,' " *Explicator*, 47, iii (1989), 54–55.

"Winter in July"
Chennells, Anthony. " . . . Rhodesian Stories in Zimbabwe," 31–32.

NORMAN LEVINE

"The Playground"
Greenstein, Michael. *Third Solitudes* . . . , 74–76.

HENRY CLAY LEWIS

"Seeking a Location"
Watts, Edward. "In the Midst of a Noisome Swamp: The Landscape of Henry Clay Lewis," *Southern Lit J*, 22, ii (1990), 122.

WYNDHAM LEWIS

"The Bull Gun"
Murray, Robert E. "Wyndham Lewis and His Fiction of the First World War," *J Short Story Engl*, 14 (Spring, 1990), 56–58.

"Cantleman's Spring Mate"
Murray, Robert E. "Wyndham Lewis . . . ," 49–52.

"The French Poodle"
Caracciolo, Peter L. " 'Carnival of Mass-Murder': The Frazer Origins of Wyndham Lewis's *The Childermass*," in Fraser, Robert, Ed. *Sir James Frazer* . . . , 212–214.
Murray, Robert E. "Wyndham Lewis . . . ," 47–49.

"The King of the Trenches"
Murray, Robert E. "Wyndham Lewis . . . ," 54–56.

"Mr. Zagreus and the Split-Man"
Caracciolo, Peter L. " 'Carnival of Mass-Murder' . . . ," 216.

"The War Baby"
Murray, Robert E. "Wyndham Lewis . . . ," 52–54.

LI ANG [SHI SHUDUAN]

"Dark Night"
Yeh, Michelle. "Shapes of Darkness: Symbols in Li Ang's 'Dark Night,' " in Duke, Michael S., Ed. *Modern Chinese Women Writers* . . . , 78–95.

LI CHUN

"Mother and Daughter"
Hsia, C. T. "Residual Femininity: Women in Chinese Communist Fiction," in Birch, Cyril, Ed. *Chinese Communist Literature*, 171.

"The Story of Li Shuang-shuang"
Hsia, C. T. "Residual Femininity . . . ," 170–171.
Shih, C. W. "Co-operatives and Communes in Chinese Communist Fiction," in Birch, Cyril, Ed. *Chinese Communist Literature*, 202–203.

LI JIANWU

"In the Countryside"
Pollard, David. "Li Jianwu," in Slupski, Zbigniew, Ed. *A Selective Guide* . . . , II, 97–98.

"The Shadow of Death"
Pollard, David. "Li Jianwu," 98–99.

LI QIAO

"Dancing Together"
Wang, David D. "Female Consciousness in Modern Chinese Male Fiction," in Duke, Michael S., Ed. *Modern Chinese Women Writers* . . . , 252.

"Phallophobia"
Wang, David D. "Female Consciousness . . . ," 252–253.

LI WEI-LUN

"Love"
Hsia, C. T. "Residual Femininity: Women in Chinese Communist Fiction," in Birch, Cyril, Ed. *Chinese Communist Literature*, 173.

ENRIQUE LIHN

"Huacho y Pochocha"
Pérez-Fernández, Francisco. "Notas para una lectura de 'Huacho y Pochocha' de Enrique Lihn," *Inti*, 31, iii (1990), 89–96.

LIN CHIN-LAN

"New Life"
Hsia, C. T. "Residual Femininity: Women in Chinese Communist Fiction," in Birch, Cyril, Ed. *Chinese Communist Literature*, 172–173.

LING SHUHUA

"After Drinking"
Chow, Rey. "Virtuous Transactions: A Reading of Three Stories by Ling Shuhua," *Mod Chinese Lit*, 4, i–ii (1988), 82–84.

"Amah Yang"
Pollard, David. "Ling Shuhua," in Slupski, Zbigniew, Ed. *A Selective Guide* . . . , II, 101–102.

"Embroidered Pillows"
Chow, Rey. "Virtuous Transactions . . . ," 76–79.

"The Night of Midautumn Festival"
Chow, Rey. "Virtuous Transactions . . . ," 79–82.

"The Send-Off"
Pollard, David. "Ling Shuhua," 102–103.

"Ying"
Eide, Elisabeth. "Ling Shuhua," in Slupski, Zbigniew, Ed. *A Selective Guide* . . . , II, 105.

"Young Brother"
Eide, Elisabeth. "Ling Shuhua," 104–105.

GORDON LISH

"For Rupert"
Seabrook, David. " 'What we write about when we write about Gordon Lish,' " in Clarke, Graham, Ed. *The New American Writing* . . . , 125–126.

"Guilt"
Seabrook, David. " 'What we write about . . . ,' " 135–136.

"The Psoriasis Diet"
Seabrook, David. " 'What we write about . . . ,' " 125.

CLARICE LISPECTOR

"The Chicken"
Lastinger, Valerie C. "Humor in a New Reading of Clarice Lispector," *Hispania*, 72 (1989), 132–133, 134, 136.

"The Daydream of a Drunken Housewife" [same as " . . . Drunken Woman"]
Lastinger, Valerie C. "Humor in a New Reading . . . ," 133.

"The Dinner"
Lastinger, Valerie C. "Humor in a New Reading . . . ," 135.

"Happy Birthday" [same as "Happy Anniversary"]
Lastinger, Valerie C. "Humor in a New Reading . . . ," 132.

"The Imitation of the Rose"
Helena, Lucia. "Genre and Gender in Clarice Lispector's 'The Imitation of the Rose,' " *Style*, 24 (1990), 215–227.

"Love"
Clark, Maria. "Facing the Other in Clarice Lispector's Short Story 'Amor,' " *Letras Femeninas*, 15, i–ii (1990), 13–20.

"Mystery in São Cristóvão"
DiAntonio, Robert E. *Brazilian Fiction* . . . , 37–42.

"The Smallest Woman in the World"
Lastinger, Valerie C. "Humor in a New Reading . . . ," 131–132.
Rosenberg, Judith. "Taking Her Measurements: Clarice Lispector and 'The Smallest Woman in the World,' " *Critique S*, 30, ii (1989), 71–76.

LIU CHEN

"Big Sister Ch'un"
Hsia, C. T. "Residual Femininity: Women in Chinese Communist Fiction," in Birch, Cyril, Ed. *Chinese Communist Literature*, 163–164.

LIU PIN-YEN

"Our Paper's Inside News "
Hsia, C. T. "Residual Femininity: Women in Chinese Communist Fiction," in Birch, Cyril, Ed. *Chinese Communist Literature*, 177–179.

PENELOPE LIVELY

"Corruption"
Yvard, Pierre. "*Pack of Cards*, a Theme and a Technique," *J Short Story Engl*, 13 (Autumn, 1989), 109–110.

"Miss Carleton and the Pop Concert"
Yvard, Pierre. "*Pack of Cards* . . . ," 105–106.

JACK LONDON

"A Daughter of the Aurora"
Tavernier-Courbin, Jacqueline. "Social Myth as Parody in Jack London's Northern Tales," *Thalia*, 9, ii (1987), 4–5.

"The Great Interrogation"
Tavernier-Courbin, Jacqueline. "Social Myth . . . ," 7–8.

"The House of Pride"
Reesman, Jeanne C. "Knowledge and Identity in Jack London's Hawaiian Fiction," *Jack London Newsletter*, 19 (1986), 92.

"A Hyperborean Brew"
Tavernier-Courbin, Jacqueline. "Social Myth . . . ," 10–11.

"Keesh, the Son of Keesh"
Tavernier-Courbin, Jacqueline. "Social Myth . . . ," 11–13.

"Koolau the Leper"
Reesman, Jeanne C. "Knowledge and Identity . . . ," 92–93.

"The Marriage of Lit-Lit"
Tavernier-Courbin, Jacqueline. "Social Myth . . . ," 5–6.

"The Master of Mysteries"
Tavernier-Courbin, Jacqueline. "Social Myth . . . ," 9–10.

"Shin Bones"
Reesman, Jeanne C. "Knowledge and Identity . . . ," 93.

"The Son of the Wolf"
Tavernier-Courbin, Jacqueline. "Social Myth . . . ," 8–9.

"The Story of Jees-Uck"
Tavernier-Courbin, Jacqueline. "Social Myth . . . ," 7.

"To Build a Fire"
McIntyre, John C. "Horacio Quiroga and Jack London Compared: 'A la deriva,' 'El hombre muerto,' and 'To Build a Fire,' " *New Comparison*, 7 (1987), 143–159.

"The Water Baby"
Reesman, Jeanne C. "Knowledge and Identity . . . ," 93–94.

"The Wife of a King"
Tavernier-Courbin, Jacqueline. "Social Myth . . . ," 5.

JUDY LOPATIN

"Budapest Dangereux"
Siegle, Robert. *Suburban Ambush* . . . , 371–372.

"Krystal Goes Mystical"
Siegle, Robert. *Suburban Ambush* . . . , 370.

"Modern Romances"
Siegle, Robert. *Suburban Ambush* . . . , 367–368.

"Our Perfect Partners"
Siegle, Robert. *Suburban Ambush* . . . , 373–374.

"A Phantasm, A Bird—"
Siegle, Robert. *Suburban Ambush* . . . , 370–371.

"Trixie Taylor, Hospital Nurse"
Siegle, Robert. *Suburban Ambush* . . . , 369–370.

LILITH LORRAINE [MARY MAUDE WRIGHT]

"Into the 28th Century"
Donawerth, Jane. "Lilith Lorraine: Feminist Socialist Writer in the Pulps," *Sci-Fiction Stud*, 17 (1990), 254–256.

H. P. LOVECRAFT

"The Call of Cthulhu"
Burleson, Donald R. *Lovecraft* . . . , 77–85.
Cannon, Peter. "The Late Francis Wayland Thurston of Boston: Lovecraft's Last Dilettante," *Lovecraft Stud*, 19–20 (Fall, 1989), 32, 39.
Carroll, Noël. *The Philosophy of Horror*, 81–83.

"The Cats of Ulthar"
Burleson, Donald R. *Lovecraft* . . . , 39–48.

"The Colour Out of Space"
Burleson, Donald R. *Lovecraft* . . . , 106–117.
Mariconda, Steven J. "The Subversion of Sense in 'The Colour out of Space,' " *Lovecraft Stud*, 19–20 (Fall, 1989), 20–22.

"The Dunwich Horror"
Burleson, Donald R. *Lovecraft* . . . , 118–132.
Joshi, S. T. *The Weird Tale*, 188–189.

"From Beyond"
Joshi, S. T. *The Weird Tale*, 201–202.

"The Green Meadow"
Dziemianowicz, Stefan. " 'The Green Meadow' and 'The Willows': Lovecraft, Blackwood, and a Peculiar Coincidence," *Lovecraft Stud*, 19–20 (Fall, 1989), 33–39.

"The Haunter of the Dark"
Burleson, Donald R. *Lovecraft* . . . , 147–155.

"Herbert West—Reanimator"
Joshi, S. T. *The Weird Tale*, 186–187.

"The Horror at Red Hook"
Joshi, S. T. *The Weird Tale*, 222–223.

"The Lurking Fear"
Joshi, S. T. *The Weird Tale*, 221–222.

"The Music of Erich Zann"
Burleson, Donald R. *Lovecraft* . . . , 67–76.

"The Nameless City"
Burleson, Donald R. *Lovecraft* . . . , 49–57.

"The Outsider"
Burleson, Donald R. *Lovecraft* . . . , 58–66.

"Pickman's Model"
Anderson, James. " 'Pickman's Model': H. P. Lovecraft's Model of Terror," *Lovecraft Stud*, 22–23 (1990), 15–21.
Burleson, Donald R. *Lovecraft* . . . , 86–93.
Carroll, Noël. *The Philosophy of Horror*, 115–116.

"The Rats in the Wall"
Stock, R. D. *The Flutes of Dionysus* . . . , 373–374.

"The Shadow out of Time"
Joshi, S. T. *The Weird Tale*, 209–210.

"The Shadow over Innsmouth"
Burleson, Donald R. *Lovecraft* . . . , 133–146.
Joshi, S. T. *The Weird Tale*, 223–224.
Stock, R. D. *The Flutes of Dionysus* . . . , 374–376.

"The Shunned House"
Joshi, S. T. *The Weird Tale*, 180–181.

"The Statement of Randolph Carter"
Burleson, Donald R. *Lovecraft* . . . , 17–27.

"The Strange High House in the Mist"
Burleson, Donald R. *Lovecraft* . . . , 94–105.

"The Temple"
Joshi, S. T. *The Weird Tale*, 181–182.

"The Terrible Old Man"
Burleson, Donald R. *Lovecraft* . . . , 28–38.

"The Thing on the Doorstep"
Joshi, S. T. *The Weird Tale*, 208–209.

"The Whisper in Darkness"
Joshi, S. T. *The Weird Tale*, 202–203.

MALCOLM LOWRY

"The Forest Path to the Spring"
Bock, Martin. *Crossing the Shadow-Line* . . . , 130–131.

"Lunar Caustic"
Newton, Norman. "The Loxodromic Curve: A Study of 'Lunar Caustic' by Malcolm Lowry," *Canadian Lit*, 126, i (1990), 65–86.

LU LING [XU SIYU]

"In Search of Love"
Denton, Kirk. "Lu Ling," in Slupski, Zbigniew, Ed. *A Selective Guide* . . . , II, 108.

"The Way of Wang Bingquan"
Huters, Theodore T. "Lu Ling," in Slupski, Zbigniew, Ed. *A Selective Guide* . . . , II, 110–111.

LU XING'ER

"Dazixiang Quietly Blooms"
Leung, Lai-fong. "In Search of Love and Self: The Image of Young Female Intellectuals in Post-Mao Women's Fiction," in Duke, Michael S., Ed. *Modern Chinese Women Writers* . . . , 143–144.

"Oh, Blue Bird"
Leung, Lai-fong. "In Search of Love and Self . . . ," 145–146.

LU XÜN [LU HSÜN or CHOU SHU-JEN]

"Diary of a Madman"
Anderson, Marston. *The Limits* . . . , 82–83.
Brown, Carolyn. "The Paradigm of the Iron House: Shouting and Silence in Lu Xün's Short Stories," *Chinese Lit*, 6, i–ii (1984), 117.
Huters, Theodore. "Blossoms in the Snow: Lu Xün and the Dilemma of Modern Chinese Literature," *Mod China*, 10, i (1984), 61–62.
Pollard, David. "Lu Xün," in Slupski, Zbigniew, Ed. *A Selective Guide* . . . , II, 114.
Wang, Alfred A. "Lu Xün and Maxine Hong Kingston: Medicine as a Symbol in Chinese and Chinese American Literature," *Lit & Med*, 8 (1989), 5–8.

"A Happy Family"
Anderson, Marston. *The Limits* . . . , 86.

"In the Tavern" [same as "In the Wineshop" or "Upstairs in the Wineshop"]
Huters, Theodore. "Blossoms in the Snow . . . ," 69–70.

"Kong Yiji"
Huters, Theodore. "Blossoms in the Snow . . . ," 62–63.
Pollard, David. "Lu Xün," 116–117.

"The Loner"
Lyell, William A. "Introduction," *"Diary of a Madman" and Other Stories* [by Lu Xün], xxxvi.

"Medicine"
Anderson, Marston. *The Limits . . .*, 87–88.
Brown, Carolyn. "The Paradigm . . .," 114–115.
Huters, Theodore. "Blossoms in the Snow . . .," 60–61.
Pollard, David. "Lu Xün," 115–116.
Wang, Alfred A. "Lu Xün and Maxine Hong Kingston . . .," 8–10.

"The Misanthrope"
Brown, Carolyn. "The Paradigm . . .," 116.

"My Old Home"
Huters, Theodore. "Blossoms in the Snow . . .," 63–64.
Pollard, David. "Lu Xün," 117–118.

"New Year's Sacrifice"
Anderson, Marston. *The Limits . . .*, 88–89.
Brown, Carolyn. "The Paradigm . . .," 103–108.
Huters, Theodore. "Blossoms in the Snow . . .," 66–67.

"Regret of the Past"
Brown, Carolyn. "The Paradigm . . .," 115–116.

"The True Story of Ah Q"
Anderson, Marston. *The Limits . . .*, 63–64, 80–82.
Huang, Martin W. "The Inescapable Predicament: The Narrator and His Discourse in 'The True Story of Ah Q,' " *Mod China*, 16 (1990), 430–449.
Lyell, William A. "Introduction," xxxvi–xxxvii.
Pollard, David. "Lu Xün," 118–120.

"Upstairs in a Wineshop"
Lyell, William A. "Introduction," xxxii–xxxvi.

LU YIN [HUANG YING]

"A Certain Person's Melancholy"
Gálik, Marián. "Lu Yin," in Slupski, Zbigniew, Ed. *A Selective Guide . . .*, II, 129.

"Friends on the Seashore"
Gálik, Marián. "Lu Yin," 128–129.

LUO SHU

"Widow with a Living Husband"
Wan Chun-yee. "Luo Shu," in Slupski, Zbigniew, Ed. *A Selective Guide . . .*, II, 132–134.

MA FENG

"Marriage"
Hsia, C. T. "Residual Femininity: Women in Chinese Communist Fiction," in Birch, Cyril, Ed. *Chinese Communist Literature*, 162–163.

CARSON McCULLERS

"Art and Mr. Mahoney"
Carr, Virginia S. . . . *Carson McCullers*, 155–156.

"The Ballad of the Sad Café"
Carr, Virginia S. . . . *Carson McCullers*, 53–69.
Chamlee, Kenneth D. "Cafés and Community in Three Carson McCullers Novels," *Stud Am Fiction*, 18 (1990), 236–238.
Messent, Michael. "Continuity and Change in the Southern Novella," in Lee, A. Robert, Ed. *The Modern American Novella*, 132–134.

"Breath from the Sky"
Carr, Virginia S. . . . *Carson McCullers*, 139.

"Correspondence"
Carr, Virginia S. . . . *Carson McCullers*, 152–153.

"Court in the West Eighties"
Carr, Virginia S. . . . *Carson McCullers*, 145–146.

"The Haunted Boy"
Carr, Virginia S. . . . *Carson McCullers*, 151–152.

"Instant of the Hour After"
Carr, Virginia S. . . . *Carson McCullers*, 156–157.

"Like That"
Carr, Virginia S. . . . *Carson McCullers*, 136–137.

"Madame Zilensky and the King of Finland"
Carr, Virginia S. . . . *Carson McCullers*, 147–149.

"Poldi"
Carr, Virginia S. . . . *Carson McCullers*, 146–147.

"The Sojourners"
Carr, Virginia S. . . . *Carson McCullers*, 149–150.

"The Sucker"
Carr, Virginia S. . . . *Carson McCullers*, 131–132.

"A Tree, A Rock, A Cloud"
Carr, Virginia S. . . . *Carson McCullers*, 129.

"Untitled Piece"
Carr, Virginia S. . . . *Carson McCullers*, 143–145.

"Who Has Seen the Wind?"
Carr, Virginia S. . . . *Carson McCullers*, 159–160.

"Wunderkind"
Carr, Virginia S. . . . *Carson McCullers*, 133–135.

D. R. MacDONALD

"Of One Kind"
Yahnke, Robert E., and Richard M. Eastman. *Aging in Literature* . . . , 49.

"Poplars"
Yahnke, Robert E., and Richard M. Eastman. *Aging in Literature* . . . , 48.

"Work"
Yahnke, Robert E., and Richard M. Eastman. *Aging in Literature* . . . , 48–49.

JOHN McGAHERN

"The Beginning of an Idea"
Quinn, Antoinette. "Varieties of Disenchantment: Narrative Technique in John McGahern's Short Stories," *J Short Story Engl*, 13 (Autumn, 1989), 81.

"Bomb Box"
Kennedy, Eileen. "Sons and Fathers in John McGahern's Short Stories," in Brophy, James D., and Eamon Grennan, Eds. *New Irish Writing* . . . , 66–67.

"Faith, Hope, and Charity"
Kennedy, Eileen. "Sons and Fathers . . . ," 68–69.

"Gold Watch"
Kennedy, Eileen. "Sons and Fathers . . . ," 70–71.
Quinn, Antoinette. "Varieties of Disenchantment . . . ," 86–87.

"High Ground"
Bradbury, Nicola. "High Ground," in Hanson, Clare, Ed. *Re-reading* . . . , 93–96.
Kennedy, Eileen. "Sons and Fathers . . . ," 72–73.

"Old-Fashioned"
Kennedy, Eileen. "Sons and Fathers . . . ," 72.

"Parachutes"
Bradbury, Nicola. "High Ground," 88–93.
Quinn, Antoinette. "Varieties of Disenchantment . . . ," 87–89.

"Sierra Leone"
Kennedy, Eileen. "Sons and Fathers . . . ," 71–72.

"A Slip-Up"
Johnston, Dillon. "Next to Nothing: Uses of the Otherworld in Modern Irish Literature," in Brophy, James D., and Eamon Grennan, Eds. *New Irish Writing* . . . , 127–128.

"The Stoat"
Kennedy, Eileen. "Sons and Fathers . . . ," 67.

"Wheels"
Kennedy, Eileen. "Sons and Fathers . . . ," 69–70.

"The Wine Breath"
Johnston, Dillon. "Next to Nothing . . . ," 126–127.

PATRICK McGRATH

"Ambrose Syme"
Siegle, Robert. *Suburban Ambush* . . . , 300–301.

"The Angel"
Siegle, Robert. *Suburban Ambush* . . . , 308–309.

"The Arnold Crombeck Story"
Siegle, Robert. *Suburban Ambush* . . . , 307–308.

"The Black Hand of the Raj"
Siegle, Robert. *Suburban Ambush* . . . , 306–307.

"Blood and Water"
Siegle, Robert. *Suburban Ambush* . . . , 304–305.

"Blood Disease"
Siegle, Robert. *Suburban Ambush* . . . , 305–306.

"The Boot's Tale"
Siegle, Robert. *Suburban Ambush* . . . , 311.

"The E(rot)ic Potato"
Siegle, Robert. *Suburban Ambush* . . . , 310–311.

"Marmilion"
Siegle, Robert. *Suburban Ambush* . . . , 309–310.

"The Skewer"
Siegle, Robert. *Suburban Ambush* . . . , 301–304.

JOAQUIM MARÍA MACHADO DE ASSIS

"Canción de esponsale"
Bosi, Alfredo. "Prólogo," *Cuentos* [by Joaquim M. Machado de Assis], xxv–xxvi.

"Doña Benedicta"
Bosi, Alfredo. "Prólogo," xxv.

"The Mirror"
Bosi, Alfredo. "Prólogo," xxiii–xxiv.
Dixon, Paul B. "Feedback, Strange Loops and Machado de Assis's 'O espelho,' " *Romance Q*, 36 (1989), 213–221.

"Noche de Almirante"
Bosi, Alfredo. "Prólogo," xxix–xxxi.

"Padre contra madre"
Bosi, Alfredo. "Prólogo," xxiv–xxv.

"El Secreto del bonzo"
Bosi, Alfredo. "Prólogo," xxi–xxii.

"La Serenísima República"
Bosi, Alfredo. "Prólogo," xx–xxi.

"Unos brazos"
Bosi, Alfredo. "Prólogo," xxi.

"Verba Testamentaria"
Bosi, Alfredo. "Prólogo," xxvi–xxvii.

ARTHUR MACHEN

"The Great God Pan"
Joshi, S. T. *The Weird Tale*, 20–22.

"The White People"
Stock, R. D. *The Flute of Dionysus . . .* , 336–337.

NORMAN MACLEAN

"A River Runs Through It"
Lojek, Helen. "Casting Flies and Recasting Myths with Norman Maclean," *Western Am Lit*, 25, ii (1990), 145–156.

ALISTAIR MacLEOD

"The Boat"
Nicholson, Colin. " 'The Tuning of Memory': Alistair MacLeod's Short Stories," *Recherches Anglaises et Nord-Américaines*, 20 (1987), 86–90.

"The Closing Down of Summer"
Nicholson, Colin. " 'The Tuning of Memory' . . . ," 90–92.

"In the Fall"
Nicholson, Colin. " 'The Tuning of Memory' . . . ," 86.

"The Vastness of the Dark"
Nicholson, Colin. " 'The Tuning of Memory' . . . ," 86.

"Vision"
Davidson, Arnold E. "Blindness and Second Sight in Alistair MacLeod's 'Vision,' " *J Short Story Engl*, 12 (Spring, 1989), 21–31.

BRYAN MacMAHON

"Exile's Return"
Ingersoll, Earl G. "Irish Jokes: A Lacanian Reading of Short Stories by James Joyce, Flann O'Brien, and Bryan MacMahon," *Stud Short Fiction*, 27 (1990), 243–245.

D'ARCY McNICKLE

"Snowfall"
Purdy, John L. *Word Ways* . . . , 109–112.

A. G. McNUTT

"Chunkey's Fight with the Panthers"
Fisher, Benjamin F. "Devils and Devilishness in Comic Yarns of the Old Southwest," *ESQ: J Am Renaissance*, 36 (1990), 49–51.

MANUEL V. MAGALLANES

"Guasina"
Ramos, Elías A. *El cuento venezolano* . . . , 85–86.

"Juan Adrián"
Ramos, Elías A. *El cuento venezolano* . . . , 80.

"El llanto del labriego"
Ramos, Elías A. *El cuento venezolano* . . . , 48–49.

"El mensaje inesperado"
Ramos, Elías A. *El cuento venezolano* . . . , 80–81.

"Nuestro hijo"
Ramos, Elías A. *El cuento venezolano* . . . , 54–55.

"Paradoja"
Ramos, Elías A. *El cuento venezolano* . . . , 81–82.

"La verdad de la sangre"
Ramos, Elías A. *El cuento venezolano* . . . , 55.

"El viejo Blas Macias"
Ramos, Elías A. *El cuento venezolano* . . . , 49.

MAURICIO MAGDALENO

"El héroe de Peñuelas"
Barrientos, Juan José. "Un tema de Mauricio Magdaleno y Roa Bastos y una figura del relato," in Neumeister, Sebastián, Ed. *Actas del IX Congreso* . . . , II, 457–461.

MAKI ITSUMA

"7.03 Hours"
Matthew, Robert. *Japanese Science Fiction* . . . , 32–33.

BERNARD MALAMUD

"Angel Levine"
Ochshorn, Kathleen G. . . . *Bernard Malamud's Hero*, 75–77.
Solotaroff, Robert. *Bernard Malamud* . . . , 37–38.

"An Apology"
Solotaroff, Robert. *Bernard Malamud* . . . , 64–66.

"Behold the Key"
Ochshorn, Kathleen G. . . . *Bernard Malamud's Hero*, 71–74.
Solotaroff, Robert. *Bernard Malamud* . . . , 59–60.

"The Bill"
Ochshorn, Kathleen G. . . . *Bernard Malamud's Hero*, 68–69.
Solotaroff, Robert. *Bernard Malamud* . . . , 48–52.

"Black Is My Favorite Color"
Ochshorn, Kathleen G. . . . *Bernard Malamud's Hero*, 124–127.
Solotaroff, Robert. *Bernard Malamud* . . . , 80–82.

"A Choice of Profession"
Ochshorn, Kathleen G. . . . *Bernard Malamud's Hero*, 129–132.
Solotaroff, Robert. *Bernard Malamud* . . . , 84–85.

"The Cost of Living"
Ochshorn, Kathleen G. . . . *Bernard Malamud's Hero*, 120–121.
Solotaroff, Robert. *Bernard Malamud* . . . , 71–75.

"The Death of Me"
Ochshorn, Kathleen G. . . . *Bernard Malamud's Hero*, 127–129.
Solotaroff, Robert. *Bernard Malamud* . . . , 75–77.

"An Exorcism"
Solotaroff, Robert. *Bernard Malamud* . . . , 121–122.

"The First Seven Years"
Ochshorn, Kathleen G. . . . *Bernard Malamud's Hero*, 53–55.
Solotaroff, Robert. *Bernard Malamud* . . . , 18–25.

"The German Refugee"
Kremer, S. Lillian. *Witness Through Imagination* . . . , 82–83.
Lasher, Lawrence M. "Narrative Strategy in Malamud's 'The German Refugee,' " *Stud Am Jewish Lit*, 9, i (1990), 73–83.
Ochshorn, Kathleen G. . . . *Bernard Malamud's Hero*, 139–140.
Solotaroff, Robert. *Bernard Malamud* . . . , 82–84.

"The Girl of My Dreams"
Ochshorn, Kathleen G. . . . *Bernard Malamud's Hero*, 55–57.

"Glass Blower of Venice"
Buchen, Irving H. "Malamud's Italian Progress: Art and Bisexuality," *Mod Lang Stud*, 20, ii (1990), 72–75.

Solotaroff, Robert. *Bernard Malamud . . .*, 110–113.

"Idiots First"

Ochshorn, Kathleen G. . . . *Bernard Malamud's Hero*, 116–120.
Solotaroff, Robert. *Bernard Malamud . . .*, 67–71.

"In Kew Gardens"

Solotaroff, Robert. *Bernard Malamud . . .*, 118.

"In Retirement"

Ochshorn, Kathleen G. . . . *Bernard Malamud's Hero*, 232–234.
Yahnke, Robert E., and Richard M. Eastman. *Aging in Literature . . .*, 49–50.

"The Jewbird"

Greenstein, Michael. "Jewish Pegasus," *Jewish Book Forum*, 45 (1990), 49–50.
Ochshorn, Kathleen G. . . . *Bernard Malamud's Hero*, 136–138.
Solotaroff, Robert. *Bernard Malamud . . .*, 77–80.

"The Lady of the Lake"

Kremer, S. Lillian. *Witness Through Imagination . . .*, 83–86.
Ochshorn, Kathleen G. . . . *Bernard Malamud's Hero*, 57–59.
Solotaroff, Robert. *Bernard Malamud . . .*, 60–62.

"The Last Mohican"

Ahokas, Pirjo. "Through the Ghetto to Giotto: The Process of Inner Transformation in Malamud's 'Last Mohican,' " *Am Stud Scandinavia*, 19 (1987), 57–69.
Buchen, Irving H. "Malamud's Italian Progress . . .," 64–66.
Kremer, S. Lillian. *Witness Through Imagination . . .*, 87–90.
Solotaroff, Robert. *Bernard Malamud . . .*, 54–59.

"The Letter"

Ochshorn, Kathleen G. . . . *Bernard Malamud's Hero*, 230–232.
Solotaroff, Robert. *Bernard Malamud . . .*, 122–123.

"Life Is Better Than Death"

Ochshorn, Kathleen G. . . . *Bernard Malamud's Hero*, 132.
Solotaroff, Robert. *Bernard Malamud . . .*, 87–89.

"The Loan"

Kremer, S. Lillian. *Witness Through Imagination . . .*, 82.
+May, Charles E. "The Bread of Tears: Malamud's 'The Loan,' " in Solotaroff, Robert. *Bernard Malamud . . .*, 170–172.
Ochshorn, Kathleen G. . . . *Bernard Malamud's Hero*, 69–71.

"A Lost Grave"

Solotaroff, Robert. *Bernard Malamud . . .*, 114–115.

"The Magic Barrel"

Ochshorn, Kathleen G. . . . *Bernard Malamud's Hero*, 59–63.
Solotaroff, Robert. *Bernard Malamud . . .*, 35–37.

"The Maid's Shoes"

Ochshorn, Kathleen G. . . . *Bernard Malamud's Hero*, 121–124.
Solotaroff, Robert. *Bernard Malamud . . .*, 85–87.

"Man in the Drawer"
Ochshorn, Kathleen G. . . . *Bernard Malamud's Hero*, 225–230.
Solotaroff, Robert. *Bernard Malamud* . . . , 128–130.

"The Mourners"
Ochshorn, Kathleen G. . . . *Bernard Malamud's Hero*, 63–65.
Solotaroff, Robert. *Bernard Malamud* . . . , 34–35.
Yahnke, Robert E., and Richard M. Eastman. *Aging in Literature* . . . , 49.

"My Son the Murderer"
Ochshorn, Kathleen G. . . . *Bernard Malamud's Hero*, 240–244.
Solotaroff, Robert. *Bernard Malamud* . . . , 125–127.

"Naked Nude"
Solotaroff, Robert. *Bernard Malamud* . . . , 94–99.

"Notes from a Lady at a Dinner Party"
Ochshorn, Kathleen G. . . . *Bernard Malamud's Hero*, 237–240.
Solotaroff, Robert. *Bernard Malamud* . . . , 127–128.

"Pictures of the Artist"
Buchen, Irving H. "Malamud's Italian Progress . . . ," 71–72.
Solotaroff, Robert. *Bernard Malamud* . . . , 104–109.

"A Pimp's Revenge"
Buchen, Irving H. "Malamud's Italian Progress . . . ," 68–71.
Solotaroff, Robert. *Bernard Malamud* . . . , 99–104.

"The Place Is Different Now"
Solotaroff, Robert. *Bernard Malamud* . . . , 11–16.

"The Prison"
Ochshorn, Kathleen G. . . . *Bernard Malamud's Hero*, 67–68.
Solotaroff, Robert. *Bernard Malamud* . . . , 52–54.

"Rembrandt's Hat"
Ochshorn, Kathleen G. . . . *Bernard Malamud's Hero*, 234–237.

"The Silver Crown"
Ochshorn, Kathleen G. . . . *Bernard Malamud's Hero*, 220–225.
Solotaroff, Robert. *Bernard Malamud* . . . , 123–127.

"Still Life"
Solotaroff, Robert. *Bernard Malamud* . . . , 90–94.

"A Summer's Reading"
Ochshorn, Kathleen G. . . . *Bernard Malamud's Hero*, 74–75.
Solotaroff, Robert. *Bernard Malamud* . . . , 43–47.

"Take Pity"
Ochshorn, Kathleen G. . . . *Bernard Malamud's Hero*, 65–67.
Solotaroff, Robert. *Bernard Malamud* . . . , 38–42.

"The Talking Horse"
+Burch, Beth and Paul W. "Myth on Myth: Bernard Malamud's 'The Talking Horse,' " in Solotaroff, Robert. *Bernard Malamud* . . . , 176–180.
Ochshorn, Kathleen G. . . . *Bernard Malamud's Hero*, 244–246.
Solotaroff, Robert. *Bernard Malamud* . . . , 130–133.

"A Wig"
Solotaroff, Robert. *Bernard Malamud* . . . , 119–120.

HÉCTOR MALAVÉ MATA

"La noche ingrima"
Ramos, Elías A. *El cuento venezolano* . . . , 96.

EDUARDO MALLEA

"Anabella y yo"
Jaime-Ramírez, Helios. "Vivificación del tiempo y el espacio en el Mallea de los años veintre," *Río de la Plata*, 4–6 (1987), 199–200.

"Seis poemas a Georgia"
Jaime-Ramírez, Helios. "Vivificación del tiempo . . . ," 201–202.

"Sonata de soledad"
Jaime-Ramírez, Helios. "Vivificación del tiempo . . . ," 200–201.

BARRY MALZBERG

"Final War"
Spark, Alasdair. "Vietnam: The War in Science Fiction," in Davies, Philip J., Ed. *Science Fiction* . . . , 121.

THOMAS MANN

"Anecdote"
Lesér, Esther H. *Thomas Mann's Short Fiction* . . . , 155–156.

"At the Prophet's"
Lesér, Esther H. *Thomas Mann's Short Fiction* . . . , 139–143.

"The Black Swan"
Lesér, Esther H. *Thomas Mann's Short Fiction* . . . , 210–216.

"Blood of the Walsungs"
Lesér, Esther H. *Thomas Mann's Short Fiction* . . . , 146–155.
Whiton, John. "Thomas Mann's 'Wälsungenblut': Implications of the Revised Ending," *Seminar*, 25, i (1989), 37–48.

"Death"
Lesér, Esther H. *Thomas Mann's Short Fiction* . . . , 31–33.

"Death in Venice"
Bouson, J. Brooks. *The Empathic Reader* . . . , 105–117.
Fickert, Kurt. "Truth and Fiction in 'Der Tod in Venedig,' " *Germ Notes*, 21, i–ii (1990), 25–31.
Hayes, Tom, and Lee Quinby. "The Aporia of Bourgeois Art: Desire in Thomas Mann's 'Death in Venice,' " *Criticism*, 3, ii (1989), 159–177.

Lesér, Esther H. *Thomas Mann's Short Fiction* . . . , 161–180.
Oppenheimer, Fred E. "Auf den Spuren Gustav Aschenbachs: Schlusselfiguren zu Gustav Aschenbach in Thomas Manns 'Der Tod in Venedig,' " in López Criado, Fidel, Ed. *Studies in Modern and Classical Languages* . . . , 145–153.
Pütz, Peter. "Der Ausbruch aus der Negativität: Das Ethos im 'Tod in Venedig,' " *Thomas Mann Jahrbuch*, 1 (1988), 1–11.
Slochower, Harry. "Thomas Mann's 'Death in Venice,' " *Am Imago*, 46 (1989), 255–279.
Stock, R. D. *The Flutes of Dionysus* . . . , 357–359.
Yahnke, Robert E., and Richard M. Eastman. *Aging in Literature* . . . , 50–51.

"The Dilettante"
Lesér, Esther H. *Thomas Mann's Short Fiction* . . . , 44–54.

"Disillusionment"
Felder, Paul. " 'Die Betrogene,' 'Unverkennbar von mir,' " *Thomas Mann Jahrbuch*, 3 (1990), 118–138.
Huszar Allen, Marguerite de. "Denial and Acceptance: Narrative Patterns in Thomas Mann's 'Die Betrogene' and Kleist's 'Die Marquise von O—,' " *Germ R*, 64 (1989), 121–128.
Lesér, Esther H. *Thomas Mann's Short Fiction* . . . , 34–37.
Northcote-Bade, James. " 'Noch einmal also dies': Zur Bedeutung von Thomas Manns 'letzter Liebe' im Spatwerk," *Thomas Mann Jahrbuch*, 3 (1990), 139–148.

"Disorder and Early Sorrow"
Hoffmeister, Werner. "Thomas Manns 'Unordnung und fruhe Leid': Neue Gesellschaft, neue Geselligkeit," *Monatshefte*, 82, ii (1990), 157–176.

"Fallen"
Lesér, Esther H. *Thomas Mann's Short Fiction* . . . , 22–27.

"The Fight Between Jappe and Do Escobar"
Lesér, Esther H. *Thomas Mann's Short Fiction* . . . , 158–160.

"The Hungry Ones"
Lesér, Esther H. *Thomas Mann's Short Fiction* . . . , 107–110.

"The Infant Prodigy'"
Cervo, Nathan A. "Civilization as Spent Culture: Mann's 'Infant Prodigy' and Spengler's *Decline*," *Mosaic*, 23, i (1990), 73–86.
Lesér, Esther H. *Thomas Mann's Short Fiction* . . . , 135–139.

"The Law"
Lesér, Esther H. *Thomas Mann's Short Fiction* . . . , 207–210.

"Little Herr Friedemann"
Lesér, Esther H. *Thomas Mann's Short Fiction* . . . , 38–44.

"Mario and the Magician"
Lesér, Esther H. *Thomas Mann's Short Fiction* . . . , 192–198.

"Railway Accident"
Lesér, Esther H. *Thomas Mann's Short Fiction* . . . , 156–158.

"Tobias Mindernickel"
Lesér, Esther H. *Thomas Mann's Short Fiction* . . . , 55–58.

"Tonio Kröger"
Argullol, Rafael. "Decadencia y condenación: El artista moderno en la obra de Thomas Mann," *Cuadernos Hispanoamericanos*, 479 (May, 1990), 41–47.
Lesér, Esther H. *Thomas Mann's Short Fiction* . . . , 110–160.

"The Transposed Heads"
Lesér, Esther H. *Thomas Mann's Short Fiction* . . . , 198–207.
Murti, Kamakshi P. "Parodie und Trivialisierung als Schreibvarianten beim Leser-Autor: Versuch eines paradigmatischen Modells für die Indienrezeption bei Thomas Mann und Hermann Hesse," *Colloquia Germanica*, 22 (1989), 222–243.

"Tristan"
Lesér, Esther H. *Thomas Mann's Short Fiction* . . . , 83–102.

"Vision"
Lesér, Esther H. *Thomas Mann's Short Fiction* . . . , 20–22.

"The Wardrobe"
Lesér, Esther H. *Thomas Mann's Short Fiction* . . . , 62–66.

"The Weary Hours"
Lesér, Esther H. *Thomas Mann's Short Fiction* . . . , 143–146.

"The Will to Happiness"
Lesér, Esther H. *Thomas Mann's Short Fiction* . . . , 27–30.

KATHERINE MANSFIELD [KATHERINE BEAUCHAMP]

"The Garden Party"
Marek, Jayne. "Class-Consciousness and Self-Consciousness in Katherine Mansfield's 'The Garden Party,' " *Postscript*, 7 (1990), 35–43.

"The Luftbad"
Parkin-Gounelas, Ruth. "Katherine Mansfield's Piece of Pink Wool: Feminine Signification in 'The Luftbad,' " *Stud Short Fiction*, 27 (1990), 501–504.

"Miss Brill"
Mandel, Miriam B. "Reductive Imagery in 'Miss Brill,' " *Stud Short Fiction*, 26 (1989), 473–477.

"Prelude" [previously "The Aloe" but originally "Mary"]
Morrow, Patrick. "Katherine Mansfield and World War I," in Bevan, David, Ed. *Literature and War*, 41–42.

"Something Childish but Very Natural"
Parkin-Gounelas, Ruth. "Katherine Mansfield's Piece of Pink Wool . . . ," 498–500.

"The Woman at the Store" [originally, in shorter form, "Millie"]
Carrera-Suarez, Isabel. "A Gendered Bush: Mansfield and Australian Drovers' Wives," *Australian Lit Stud*, 15, ii (1991), 140–148.

MAO DUN [same as MAO TUNG or SHEN YEN-PING]

"Algae"
Feuerwerker, Yi-tsi Mei. "The Dialectics of Struggle: Ideology and Realism in Mao Dun's 'Algae,' " in Huters, Theodore, Ed. . . . *Modern Chinese Short Story*, 51–73.

"Creation"
Anderson, Marston. *The Limits* . . . , 180–182.
Kubin, Wolfgang. "Mao Dun," in Slupski, Zbigniew, Ed. *A Selective Guide* . . . , II, 135–136.

"Disillusionment"
Anderson, Marston. *The Limits* . . . , 192–195.

"The Little Witch"
Gálik, Marián. "On the Social and Literary Context in Modern Chinese Literature of the 1920's and 1930's," in Malmqvist, Göran, Ed. *Modern Chinese Literature* . . . , 11–16.

"Pursuit"
Anderson, Marston. *The Limits* . . . , 129–131.

"Vacillation"
Anderson, Marston. *The Limits* . . . , 138–142.

DAMBUDZO MARECHERA

"The Slow Sound of His Feet"
Riemerschneider, Dieter. "Short Fiction from Zimbabwe," *Research African Lit*, 20 (1989), 406–407.

JUAN MARIN

"Anonymous Heroes"
Swain, James O. *Juan Marin* . . . , 76–77.

"As the Ship Was Sinking"
Swain, James O. *Juan Marin* . . . , 68–69.

"At the Colonial Club"
Swain, James O. *Juan Marin* . . . , 71.

"Black Port"
Swain, James O. *Juan Marin* . . . , 72–73.

"Captain Ulrici's Promise"
Swain, James O. *Juan Marin* . . . , 70.

"The Falling of the Sky"
Swain, James O. *Juan Marin* . . . , 77.

"A Flight into Mystery"
Swain, James O. *Juan Marin* . . . , 65.

"Hole Haven"
Swain, James O. *Juan Marin* . . . , 67–68.

"The Hunchback"
Swain, James O. *Juan Marin* . . . , 69–70.

"Julian Aranda's Death"
Swain, James O. *Juan Marin* . . . , 79–80.

"Lazarus"
Swain, James O. *Juan Marin* . . . , 74.

"The Man at the Funeral"
Swain, James O. *Juan Marin* . . . , 66.

"The Man from Midnight"
Swain, James O. *Juan Marin* . . . , 70–71.

"The Manhunt"
Swain, James O. *Juan Marin* . . . , 75–76.

"Nuptial"
Swain, James O. *Juan Marin* . . . , 66–67.

"Pacific Ocean"
Swain, James O. *Juan Marin* . . . , 73.

"Percival Lawrence's Crime"
Swain, James O. *Juan Marin* . . . , 79.

"Pop's Club"
Swain, James O. *Juan Marin* . . . , 69.

PAZ MARQUEZ-BENITEZ

"Dead Stars"
Santillan-Castrence, P. "The Period of Apprenticeship," in Manuud, Antonio G., Ed. *Brown Heritage* . . . , 550–552.

"A Night in the Hills"
Santillan-Castrence, P. "The Period of Apprenticeship," 552.

ANTONIO MÁRQUEZ-SALAS

"Crepúsculo"
Ramos, Elías A. *El cuento venezolano* . . . , 48.

"El hombre y su verde caballo"
Ramos, Elías A. *El cuento venezolano* . . . , 47–48.

JUAN MARSÉ

"El fantasma del Cine Roxy"
Sherzer, William M. "Textual Autobiography in 'Historia de detectives' and 'El fantasma del Cine Roxy,' " in Brown, Frieda S., et al. [3], Eds. *Rewriting the Good Fight . . .*, 89–94.

"Historia de detectives"
Sherzer, William M. "Textual Autobiography . . .," 83–89.

JOSÉ MARTÍ

"Los zapaticos de rosa"
Cánovas Pérez, Alejandro. "El narrador y el espacio en 'Los zapaticos de rosa,' " *Universidad,* 231 [n.d.], 57–73.

CARMEN MARTÍN GAITE

"Un día de libertad"
Jordan, Barry. *Writing and Politics . . .*, 74.

PEPE MARTÍNEZ DE LA VEGA

"El secreto de la lata de sardinas"
Simpson, Amelia S. *Detective Fiction . . .*, 87–88.

BOBBIE ANN MASON

"Drawing Names"
Brinkmeyer, Robert H. "Finding One's History: Bobbie Ann Mason and Contemporary Southern Literature," *Southern Lit J*, 19, ii (1987), 23–24.
Underwood, Karen. "Mason's 'Drawing Names,' " *Explicator*, 48 (1990), 231–232.

"Nancy Culpepper"
Arnold, Edwin T. "Falling Apart and Staying Together: Bobbie Ann Mason and Leon Driskell Explore the State of the Modern Family," *Appalachian J*, 12, ii (1985), 138–139.
Morphew, G. O. "Downhome Feminists in *'Shiloh' and Other Stories*," *Southern Lit J*, 22, iii (1989), 47–48.

"Offerings"
Morphew, G. O. "Downhome Feminists . . .," 46–47.

"Old Things"
Morphew, G. O. "Downhome Feminists . . .," 45–46.

"Residents and Transients"
Arnold, Edwin T. "Falling Apart . . .," 137.
Morphew, G. O. "Downhome Feminists . . .," 48–49.

"The Retreat"
Giannone, Richard. "Bobbie Ann Mason and the Recovery of Mystery," *Stud Short Fiction*, 27 (1990), 558–561.
Morphew, G. O. "Downhome Feminists . . . ," 42–44.

"The Rookers"
Arnold, Edwin T. "Falling Apart . . . ," 136–137.

"Shiloh"
Brinkmeyer, Robert H. "Finding One's History . . . ," 24–26.
Giannone, Richard. ". . . Recovery of Mystery," 555–558.
Henning, Barbara. "Minimalism and the American Dream: 'Shiloh' by Bobbie Ann Mason and 'Preservation' by Raymond Carver," *Mod Fiction Stud*, 35 (1989), 689–698.
Morphew, G. O. "Downhome Feminists . . . ," 44–45.
Sullivan, Walter. *"In Praise of Bloody Sports"* . . . , 42–43.

"Third Monday"
Giannone, Richard. ". . . Recovery of Mystery," 561–564.

FRANCISCO MASSIANI

"Cuando las hojas de la noche esperan que todos duerman, para crecer"
Ramos, Elías A. *El cuento venezolano* . . . , 133–134.

"Mamá se pone triste"
Ramos, Elías A. *El cuento venezolano* . . . , 121–122.

"Yo soy un tipo"
Ramos, Elías A. *El cuento venezolano* . . . , 43.

RICHARD MATHESON

"Born of Man and Woman"
Huntington, John. *Rationalizing Genius* . . . , 126–128.

JACK MATTHEWS

"The Eternal Mortgage"
Yahnke, Robert E., and Richard M. Eastman. *Aging in Literature* . . . , 51–52.

"First the Leg and Last the Heart"
Yahnke, Robert E., and Richard M. Eastman. *Aging in Literature* . . . , 51.

ANA MARÍA MATUTE

"Happiness"
Parra, Nathalie. "Filomena o el deseo de vivir: 'La felicidad,' un relato de Ana María Matute," *Ventanal*, 14 (1988), 211–215.

GUY DE MAUPASSANT

"Bed No. 29"
Abamine, E. P. "German-French Sexual Encounters of the Franco-Prussian War in the Fiction of Guy de Maupassant," *Coll Lang Assoc J*, 32 (1989), 323–334.

"A Cock Crowed"
Schapira, Charlotte. "Maupassant: Présentation des personnages et narration impersonnelle," *Neophilologus*, 73 (1989), 45–51.

"A Country Excursion"
Grisé, Catherine. "A Source of the Nightingale Symbol in Maupassant's 'Une Partie de campagne,' " *Romance Notes*, 29 (1989), 221–226.

"The Horla"
Harris, Trevor A. Le V. *Maupassant in the Hall of Mirrors . . .*, 168–176.

"Little Roque" [same as "Little Louise Roque"]
Schapira, Charlotte. "Maupassant . . . ," 49–50.
Stivale, Charles J. "Duty, Desire, and Dream: Maupassant's 'La Petite Roque,' " *J Narrative Technique*, 20, ii (1990), 120–133.

"The Lock of Hair"
Maddox, Donald. "Veridiction, Verifiction, Verifactions: Reflections on a Methodology," *New Lit Hist*, 20 (1989), 661–677.

"Madame Tellier's House"
Dickson, Colin. "Théorie et pratique de la clôture: l'example de Maupassant dans 'La Maison Tellier,' " *French R*, 64, i (1990), 42–53.

"Mademoiselle Fifi"
Abamine, E. P. "German-French Sexual Encounters . . . ," 326–327.

"The Piece of String"
Greimas, Algirdas L. "Description and Narrativity: 'The Piece of String,' " *New Lit Hist*, 20 (1989), 614–626.

"Tallow Ball"
Abamine, E. P. "German-French Sexual Encounters . . . ," 325–326.
Baguley, David B. *Naturalist Fiction . . .*, 147–149.
Schapira, Charlotte. "Maupassant . . . ," 46–47.

FRANÇOIS MAURIAC

"Conte de Noël"
Griffin, Richard. "Mauriac and the Art of the Short Story," in Flower, John E., and Bernard C. Smith, Eds. *François Mauriac . . .*, 83–84.

"Coups de couteau"
Griffin, Richard. "Mauriac and the Art . . . ," 86–91.

"Le Démon de la connaissance"
Griffin, Richard. "Mauriac and the Art . . . ," 81–83.

"Insomnie"
Griffin, Richard. "Mauriac and the Art . . . ," 85–86.

"Thérèse Desqueyroux"
Kidd, William. "Oedipal and Pre-Oedipal Elements in 'Thérèse Desqueyroux,' " in Flower, John E., and Bernard C. Smith, Eds. *François Mauriac* . . . , 25–45.
McGrath, Susan M. "François Mauriac's 'Thérèse Desqueyroux,' " *Cincinnati Romance R*, 9 (1990), 76–86.
Scott, Malcolm. *The Struggle for the Soul* . . . , 193–198.

"Le visiteur nocturne"
Griffin, Richard. "Mauriac and the Art . . . ," 79–81.

PERCIVAL C. MAYNARD

"His Last Fling"
Sander, Reinhard W. *The Trinidad Awakening* . . . , 66–67.

"His Right of Possession"
Sander, Reinhard W. *The Trinidad Awakening* . . . , 59–61.

HERMAN MELVILLE

"The Apple-Tree Table"
Harshbarger, Scott. "Bugs and Butterflies: Conflict and Transcendence in 'The Artist of the Beautiful' and 'The Apple-Tree Table,' " *Stud Short Fiction*, 26 (1989), 186–189.

"Bartleby the Scrivener"
Barnett, Louise K. " 'Truth Is Voiceless': Speech and Silence in Melville's *Piazza Tales*," *Papers Lang & Lit*, 25 (1989), 63–65.
Grenberg, Bruce L. *Some Other World* . . . , 165–176.
Jay, Gregory S. *America the Scrivener* . . . , 19–27.
McCall, Dan. *The Silence of Bartleby*, 47–52.
McCarthy, Paul. *"The Twisted Mind"* . . . , 100–104.
Manning, Susan. *The Puritan-Provincial Vision* . . . , 102–105.
Mitchell, Thomas R. "Dead Letters and Dead Men: Narrative Purpose in 'Bartleby the Scrivener,' " *Stud Short Fiction*, 27 (1990), 329–338.

"The Bell Tower"
MacPherson, Jay. "Waiting for Shiloh: Transgression and Fall in Melville's 'The Bell-Tower,' " in Graham, Kenneth W., Ed. *Gothic Fictions* . . . , 245–258.

"Benito Cereno"
Anderson, Douglas. *A House Undivided* . . . , 133–136.
Barnett, Louise K. " 'Truth Is Voiceless' . . . ," 61–62.
Grenberg, Bruce L. *Some Other World* . . . , 158–165.

Jay, Gregory S. *America the Scrivener* . . . , 335–336.
Leverenz, David. *Manhood* . . . , 93–97.
Levine, Robert. *Conspiracy and Romance* . . . , 165–168.
McCarthy, Paul. *"The Twisted Mind"* . . . , 104–108.
Manning, Susan. *The Puritan-Provincial Vision* . . . , 131–132.

"Billy Budd"
+Adler, Joyce S. " 'Billy Budd' and Melville's Philosophy of War," in Milder, Robert, Ed. *Critical Essays* . . . , 156–172.
Baris, Sharon. "Melville's Dansker: The Absent Damsel in 'Billy Budd,' " in Spolsky, Ellen, Ed. *The Uses of Adversity* . . . , 153–173.
Bellis, Peter J. *No Mysteries* . . . , 187–190.
+Berthoff, Warner. " 'Certain Phenomenal Men': The Example of 'Billy Budd,' " in Milder, Robert, Ed. *Critical Essays* . . . , 74–88.
+Bowen, Merlin. "[Captain Vere and the Weakness of Expediency]," in Milder, Robert, Ed. *Critical Essays* . . . , 61–74.
+Brodtkorb, Paul. "The Definitive 'Billy Budd': 'But Aren't It All Sham?' " in Milder, Robert, Ed. *Critical Essays* . . . , 114–127.
+Fogle, Richard H. " 'Billy Budd': The Order of the Fall," in Milder, Robert, Ed. *Critical Essays* . . . , 50–61.
Girgus, Sam B. *Desire and the Political Unconscious* . . . , 95–101.
Goodwyn, Cary. "How to Read Republicanism: An Analysis of Melville's 'Billy Budd, Sailor (An Inside Narrative),' " *Am Transcendental Q*, 4, N.S. (1990), 239–255.
Grenberg, Bruce L. *Some Other World* . . . , 192–211.
+Hurtgen, James. "Melville: *Billy Budd* and the Context of Political Rule," in Milder, Robert, Ed. *Critical Essays* . . . , 173–185.
+Ives, C. B. " 'Billy Budd' and the Articles of War," in Milder, Robert, Ed. *Critical Essays* . . . , 88–94.
+Johnson, Barbara. "Melville's Fist: The Execution of 'Billy Budd,' " in her *The Critical Difference* . . . , 79–109; rpt. Milder, Robert, Ed. *Critical Essays* . . . , 185–199.
Levine, Robert. *Conspiracy and Romance* . . . , 228–230.
McCarthy, Paul. *"The Twisted Mind"* . . . , 127–134.
McElroy, John H. "The Uncompromising Truth of 'Billy Budd': Its Miraculous Climax," *Christianity & Lit*, 38, iii (1989), 47–62.
McIntosh, James. " 'Billy Budd, Sailor': Melville's Last Romance," in Milder, Robert, Ed. *Critical Essays* . . . , 223–237.
Milder, Robert. "Melville's Late Poetry and 'Billy Budd': From Nostalgia to Transcendence," *Philol Q*, 66, iv (1987), 493–507; rpt. Milder, Robert, Ed. *Critical Essays* . . . , 212–223.
Pahl, Dennis. *Architects of the Abyss* . . . , 81–100.
Parker, Hershel. *Reading "Billy Budd,"* 97–162.
+Rathbun, John W. " 'Billy Budd' and the Limits of Perception," in Milder, Robert, Ed. *Critical Essays* . . . , 94–106.
+Reich, Charles A. "The Tragedy of Justice in 'Billy Budd,' " in Milder, Robert, Ed. *Critical Essays* . . . , 127–143.
Samson, John. *White Lies* . . . , 211–230.
+Schiffman, Joseph. "Melville's Final Stage, Irony: A Re-

examination of 'Billy Budd' Criticism," in Milder, Robert, Ed. *Critical Essays . . .*, 46–50.
Shapiro, Alan. "The Flexible Rule: An Essay on the Ethical Imagination," *TriQuarterly*, 76 (1989), 166–185.
+Stern, Milton R. "Introduction," *Billy Budd, Sailor (An Inside Narrative)*, in Milder, Robert, Ed. *Critical Essays . . .*, 143–156.
Thomas, Brook. " 'Billy Budd' and the Judgment of Silence," *Bucknell R*, 27 (1982), 51–78; rpt. Milder, Robert, Ed. *Critical Essays . . .*, 199–211.
+Watson, E. L. Grant. "Melville's Testament of Acceptance," in Milder, Robert, Ed. *Critical Essays . . .*, 41–45.
+Willett, Ralph W. "Nelson and Vere: Hero and Victim in 'Billy Budd, Sailor,' " in Milder, Robert, Ed. *Critical Essays . . .*, 107–114.
Zuckert, Catherine H. *Natural Right . . .*, 112–121.

"Cock-A-Doodle-Doo!"
Young, Philip. "Experimental Melville: 'Cockeye-Doodle-Dee!' " *Am Transcendental Q*, 4, N.S. (1990), 343–351.

"The Encantadas"
Barnett, Louise K. " 'Truth Is Voiceless' . . . ," 60–61.
Brecht, Katherine M. "A Significantly Named Ship in 'The Encantadas,' " *Melville Soc Extracts*, 78 (September, 1989), 12.
Dunphy, Mark. "Melville's Turning of the Darwinian Table in 'The Encantadas,' " *Melville Soc Extracts*, 79 (November, 1989), 14.
Eutsler, Nellvena D. "Melville's 'Encantadas': A View from the Rock," *Mount Olive R*, 3 (Spring, 1989), 22–28.
Grenberg, Bruce L. *Some Other World . . .*, 152–158.
Levine, Robert. *Conspiracy and Romance . . .*, 196–197.
McCarthy, Paul. *"The Twisted Mind" . . .*, 98–100.
Manning, Susan. *The Puritan-Provincial Vision . . .*, 120–121.
Schirmeister, Pamela. *The Consolations . . .*, 113–126.

"The Lightning-Rod Man"
Young, Philip. "Melville in the Berkshire Bishopric: 'The Lightning-Rod Man,' " *Coll Lit*, 16 (1989), 201–210.

"The Paradise of Bachelors and the Tartarus of Maids"
Girgus, Sam B. *Desire and the Political Unconscious . . .*, 93–95.
Paglia, Camille. *Sexual Personae . . .*, 590–593.
Weigman, Robyn. "Melville's Geography of Gender," *Am Lit Hist*, 1 (1989), 735–753.

"The Piazza"
Schirmeister, Pamela. *The Consolations . . .*, 126–136.

"Poor Man's Pudding and Rich Man's Crumbs"
Hiltner, Judith R. "Melville and the Limits of Charity," *Tennessee Philol Bull*, 26 (1989), 60–62.

ALFRED H. MENDES

"Afternoon in Trinidad"
Sander, Reinhard W. *The Trinidad Awakening . . .*, 56–58.

"Her Chinaman's Way"
Sander, Reinhard W. *The Trinidad Awakening* . . . , 61–64.

DURANGO MENDOZA

"Summer Water and Shirley"
Benzinger, Edith, and G. Richard Benzinger. "The Two Worlds of Durango Mendoza's 'Summer Water and Shirley,' " *Stud Short Fiction*, 27 (1990), 587–590.

GUILLERMO MENESES

"La mano junto al muro"
Ramos, Elías A. *El cuento venezolano* . . . , 122–123.

PROSPER MÉRIMÉE

"The Blue Room"
Carpenter, Scott D. "Diversions in Reading: Esthetics and Mérimée's 'La Chambre bleu,' " *French Forum*, 14 (1989), 303–310.

"Carmen"
Segal, Naomi. *Narcissus and Echo* . . . , 35–51.

"Venus of Ille"
Avni, Ora. *The Resistance of Reference* . . . , 178–202.

JUDITH MERRIL

"That Only a Mother"
Huntington, John. *Rationalizing Genius* . . . , 100–104.

ABRAHAM MERRITT

"Through the Dragon Glass"
Panshin, Alexel, and Cory Panshin. *The World Beyond* . . . , 148–149.

JOHN METCALF

"The Teeth of My Father"
Rooke, Constance. *Fear of the Open Heart* . . . , 157–162.

CONRAD FERDINAND MEYER

"Gustav Adolf's Page"
Hart, Gail K. "The Facts of Fiction: C. F. Meyer's Dismantling of Facticity," *Seminar*, 26 (1990), 225–230.

"Der Schuss von Kanzel"
Hart, Gail K. "The Facts of Fiction . . . ," 232–234.

"The Sufferings of a Boy"
Hart, Gail K. "The Facts of Fiction . . . ," 230–232.

C. D. MINNI

"El Dorado"
Walter, Jean-Claude. "La Quête de l'identifé dans *Other Selves* de C. D. Minni," *Recherches Anglaises et Nord-Américaines*, 20 (1987), 98–99, 100.

"Roots"
Walter, Jean-Claude. "La Quête de l'identifé . . . ," 97–98, 99–100.

STEPHEN MINOT

"Small Point Bridge"
Yahnke, Robert E., and Richard M. Eastman. *Aging in Literature* . . . , 52–53.

"The Tide and Isaac Bates"
Yahnke, Robert E., and Richard M. Eastman. *Aging in Literature* . . . , 52.

GABRIEL MIRÓ

"Estampas del faro"
Altisent, Marta E. " 'Estampas del faro' o el cuento lírico de Gabriel Miró," in Neumeister, Sebastián, Ed. *Actas del IX Congreso* . . . , II, 111–121.

MISHIMA YUKIO

"Patriotism"
Wolfe, Peter. *Yukio Mishima*, 41–42.

"Seventeen"
Napier, Susan J. "Death and the Emperor: Mishima, Ōe, and the Politics of Betrayal," *J Asian Stud*, 48, i (1989), 74–79.

S. WEIR MITCHELL

"The Case of George Dedlow"
Journet, Debra. "Phantom Limbs and 'Body-Ego': S. Weir Mitchell's 'George Dedlow,' " *Mosaic*, 23, i (1990), 87–99.

MARY L. MOLESWORTH

"Mrs. Farquhar's Old Lady"
Beidler, Peter G. *Ghosts, Demons, and Henry James* . . . , 116–117.

"The Shadow in the Moonlight"
Beidler, Peter G. *Ghosts, Demons, and Henry James* . . . , 118–119.

"Unexplained"
Beidler, Peter G. *Ghosts, Demons, and Henry James* . . . , 117–118.

C[ATHERINE] L. MOORE

"Shambleau"
Pearson, Jacqueline. "Where No Man Has Gone Before: Sexual Politics and Women's Science Fiction," in Davies, Philip J., Ed. *Science Fiction* . . . , 11–12.

"Yvala"
Pearson, Jacqueline. "Where No Man Has Gone Before . . . ," 12–13.

GEORGE MOORE

"Julia Cahill's Curse"
Martin, Augustine. "Julia Cahill, Father McTurnan, and the Geography of Nowhere," in Welch, Robert, and Suheil Badi Bushrui, Eds. . . . *Art of Criticism*, 98–102.

"A Letter to Rome"
Martin, Augustine. "Julia Cahill . . . ," 105–111.

"A Play-House in the Waste"
Martin, Augustine. "Julia Cahill . . . ," 102–105.

FRANK MOORHOUSE

"The Drover's Wife"
Arens, Werner. "The Ironical Fate of 'The Drover's Wife': Four Versions from Henry Lawson (1892) to Barbara Jefferis (1980)," in Stummer, Peter O., Ed. *The Story Must Be Told* . . . , 126–129.

"The Everlasting Secret Family"
José, Nicholas. "Possibilities of Love in Recent Australian Stories," in Stummer, Peter O., Ed. *The Story Must Be Told* . . . , 140–141.

ALBERTO MORAVIA

"Arrivederci"
Meter, Helmut. "Moravias *Racconti romani* und das Problem der römischen Identität," *Romanistisches Jahrbuch*, 38 (1987), 170–171.

"La donna nella casa del doganiere"
Massi Albanese, Carolina. "Realtà, mito e favola nella recente publicazione di Alberto Moravia: *La cosa* e altri racconti," *Revista Letras* (Paraná, Brazil), 33 (1984), 7–8.

"The Fantastic"
Meter, Helmut. "Moravias *Racconti romani* . . . ," 168–169.

"Rain in May"
Meter, Helmut. "Moravias *Racconti romani* . . . ," 169–170.

"Romulus and Remus"
Meter, Helmut. "Moravias *Racconti romani* . . . ," 176–177.

"The Thinker"
Meter, Helmut. "Moravias *Racconti romani* . . . ," 171–172.

"Il tuono liberatore"
Massi Albanese, Carolina. "Realtà, mito . . . ," 6–7.

JOSÉ MORENO COLMENÁREZ

"Prontuario"
Ramos, Elías A. *El cuento venezolano* . . . , 110–111.

WILLIAM MORRIS

"A Dream"
Kirchhoff, Frederick. *William Morris* . . . , 39–43.

"Frank's Sealed Letter"
Kirchhoff, Frederick. *William Morris* . . . , 44–46.

"Gertha's Lovers"
Kirchhoff, Frederick. *William Morris* . . . , 46–49.

"Golden Wings"
Kirchhoff, Frederick. *William Morris* . . . , 43–44.

"The Hollow Land"
Kirchhoff, Frederick. *William Morris* . . . , 50–57.

"Lindenborg"
Kirchhoff, Frederick. *William Morris* . . . , 50.

"The Story of an Unknown Land"
Kirchhoff, Frederick. *William Morris* . . . , 32–39.

"Svend and His Brethren"
Kirchhoff, Frederick. *William Morris* . . . , 49–50.

"The Widow's House by Great Water"
Timo, Helen A. " 'The Widow's House by Great Water': A Literary Enigma," *J William Morris Soc*, 7, ii (1989), 7–15.

DANIEL DAVID MOSES

"Gramma's Doing"
Petrone, Penny. *Native Literature* . . . , 147.

BORIS MOZHAEV

"One and a Half Square Metres"
Shneidman, N. N. *Soviet Literature* . . . , 59.

MOHAMMED MRABET

"The Beach Café"
Dawood, Ibrahim. "Mohammed Mrabet's Fiction of Alienation," *World Lit Today*, 64 (1990), 260.

"Chico"
Dawood, Ibrahim. " . . . Fiction of Alienation," 266–267.

"The Voice"
Dawood, Ibrahim. " . . . Fiction of Alienation," 266.

HÉCTOR MÚJICA

"Comité central"
Ramos, Elías A. *El cuento venezolano* . . . , 101–102.

"La mosca"
Ramos, Elías A. *El cuento venezolano* . . . , 110.

"La O cruzada de tiza blanca"
Ramos, Elías A. *El cuento venezolano* . . . , 82–83.

"El tigre"
Ramos, Elías A. *El cuento venezolano* . . . , 70.

"Los tres testimonios"
Ramos, Elías A. *El cuento venezolano* . . . , 100–101.

CHARLES MUNGOSHI

"Shadows on the Wall"
Riemenschneider, Dieter. "Short Fiction from Zimbabwe," *Research African Lit*, 20 (1989), 404–405.

"Who Will Stop the Dark?"
Yahnke, Robert E., and Richard M. Eastman. *Aging in Literature* . . . , 53–54.

ALICE MUNRO

"Age of Faith"
Carrington, Ildikó de Papp. *Controlling the Uncontrollable* . . . , 81–82.
Rasporich, Beverly J. *Dance of the Sexes* . . . , 46, 47.

"At the Other Place"
Carrington, Ildikó de Papp. *Controlling the Uncontrollable* . . . , 35–38.

"Baptizing"
Carrington, Ildikó de Papp. *Controlling the Uncontrollable* . . . , 86–93.

"Bardon Bus"
Carrington, Ildikó de Papp. *Controlling the Uncontrollable* . . . , 148–153.
Rasporich, Beverly J. *Dance of the Sexes* . . . , 70–74.

"A Basket of Strawberries"
Carrington, Ildikó de Papp. *Controlling the Uncontrollable* . . . , 18–20.

"The Beggar Maid"
Carrington, Ildikó de Papp. *Controlling the Uncontrollable* . . . , 131–134.
Rooke, Constance. *Fear of the Open Heart* . . . , 48.

"Boys and Girls"
Carrington, Ildikó de Papp. *Controlling the Uncontrollable* . . . , 76–77.
Goldman, Marlene. "Penning in the Bodies: The Construction of Gendered Subjects in Alice Munro's 'Boys and Girls,' " *Stud Canadian Lit*, 15, i (1990), 62–75.
Rasporich, Beverly J. *Dance of the Sexes* . . . , 35–39.

"Changes and Ceremonies"
Carrington, Ildikó de Papp. *Controlling the Uncontrollable* . . . , 119–120.

"Characters"
Carrington, Ildikó de Papp. *Controlling the Uncontrollable* . . . , 24–25.

"Circle of Prayer"
Carrington, Ildikó de Papp. *Controlling the Uncontrollable* . . . , 65–66.

"Connection"
Carrington, Ildikó de Papp. *Controlling the Uncontrollable* . . . , 27–28.
Rasporich, Beverly J. *Dance of the Sexes* . . . , 74–75.
Rocard, Marcienne. "L'Art et la necessité de la connexion dans 'Connexion' d'Alice Munro," *Recherches Anglaises et Nord-Américaines*, 20 (1987), 109–115.

"The Dimensions of the Shadow"
Carrington, Ildikó de Papp. *Controlling the Uncontrollable* . . . , 19–20.

"Dulse"
Carrington, Ildikó de Papp. *Controlling the Uncontrollable* . . . , 146–148.
Rooke, Constance. *Fear of the Open Heart* . . . , 48–50.

"Epilogue: The Photographer"
Carrington, Ildikó de Papp. *Controlling the Uncontrollable* . . . , 93–94.
Quatermaine, Peter. " 'Living on the Surface': Versions of Real Life in Alice Munro's *Lives of Girls and Women*," *Recherches Anglaises et Nord-Américaines*, 20 (1987), 121–125.

"Eskimo"
Carrington, Ildikó de Papp. *Controlling the Uncontrollable* . . . , 159–162.

"Executioners"
Carrington, Ildikó de Papp. *Controlling the Uncontrollable* . . . , 48–51.

"The Ferguson Girls Must Never Marry"
Carrington, Ildikó de Papp. *Controlling the Uncontrollable* . . . , 95–98.

"Fits"
Hanly, Charles. "Autobiography and Creativity: Alice Munro's Story 'Fits,' " in Stich, K. R., Ed. *Reflections* . . . , 163–174.
Howells, Coral A. "Alice Munro's Art of Indeterminacy: *The Progress of Love*," in Nischik, Reingard M., and Barbara Korte, Eds. *Modes of Narrative* . . . , 146–148.

"The Flats Road"
Carrington, Ildikó de Papp. *Controlling the Uncontrollable* . . . , 77–78.
Quatermaine, Peter. " 'Living on the Surface' . . . ," 117–121.

"Half a Grapefruit"
Daziron, Hélaine. "The Anatomy of Embedding in Alice Munro's 'Half a Grapefruit,' " *Recherches Anglaises et Nord-Américaines*, 20 (1987), 103–107.

"Hard Luck Stories"
Carrington, Ildikó de Papp. *Controlling the Uncontrollable* . . . , 153–155.

"Heirs of the Living Body"
Carrington, Ildikó de Papp. *Controlling the Uncontrollable* . . . , 78–81.
Rooke, Constance. *Fear of the Open Heart* . . . , 44–45.

"Home"
Carrington, Ildikó de Papp. *Controlling the Uncontrollable* . . . , 193–196.

"How I Met My Husband"
Hamdson, Robert. "Johnny Panic and the Pleasures of Disruption," in Hanson, Clare, Ed. *Re-reading* . . . , 70–72.

"Images"
Carrington, Ildikó de Papp. *Controlling the Uncontrollable* . . . , 73–76.
Rooke, Constance. *Fear of the Open Heart* . . . , 46.

"Jesse and Meribeth" [originally "Secrets Between Friends"]
Carrington, Ildikó de Papp. *Controlling the Uncontrollable* . . . , 128–131.

"Labor Day Dinner"
Carrington, Ildikó de Papp. *Controlling the Uncontrollable* . . . , 155–158.
Rooke, Constance. *Fear of the Open Heart* . . . , 51.

"Lichen"
Carrington, Ildikó de Papp. *Controlling the Uncontrollable* . . . , 162–165.
Rooke, Constance. *Fear of the Open Heart* . . . , 50–51.

"Lives of Girls and Women"
Carrington, Ildikó de Papp. *Controlling the Uncontrollable* . . . , 82–85, 87–88.

"Marrakesh"
Carrington, Ildikó de Papp. *Controlling the Uncontrollable* . . . , 116–117.

"Material"
Carrington, Ildikó de Papp. *Controlling the Uncontrollable* . . . , 28–29.
Hamdson, Robert. " . . . Pleasures of Disruption," 74–78.

"Memorial"
Carrington, Ildikó de Papp. *Controlling the Uncontrollable* . . . , 56–59.
Hamdson, Robert. " . . . Pleasures of Disruption," 79–81.

"Meneseteung"
Carrington, Ildikó de Papp. *Controlling the Uncontrollable* . . . , 214–215.

"Miles City, Montana"
Carrington, Ildikó de Papp. *Controlling the Uncontrollable* . . . , 68–70.

"Mischief"
Carrington, Ildikó de Papp. *Controlling the Uncontrollable* . . . , 134–138.

"Mrs. Cross and Mrs. Kidd"
Daziron, Hélaine. "Of Beasts and Stones: 'Mrs. Cross and Mrs. Kidd,' " *Commonwealth Essays & Studs*, 11, ii (1989), 75–82.
Yahnke, Robert E., and Richard M. Eastman. *Aging in Literature* . . . , 54.

"Simon's Luck" [originally "Emily"]
Carrington, Ildikó de Papp. *Controlling the Uncontrollable* . . . , 138–140.

"Something I've Been Meaning to Tell You"
Carrington, Ildikó de Papp. *Controlling the Uncontrollable* . . . , 112–116.
Rooke, Constance. *Fear of the Open Heart* . . . , 47.

"The Spanish Lady"
Carrington, Ildikó de Papp. *Controlling the Uncontrollable* . . . , 111–112.

"Spelling"
Rooke, Constance. *Fear of the Open Heart* . . . , 52–53.

"Sunday Afternoon"
Carrington, Ildikó de Papp. *Controlling the Uncontrollable* . . . , 103–105.

"Tell Me Yes or No"
Carrington, Ildikó de Papp. *Controlling the Uncontrollable* . . . , 109–110.

"Thanks for the Ride"
Carrington, Ildikó de Papp. *Controlling the Uncontrollable* . . . , 107–109.

"Walker Brothers Cowboys"
Carrington, Ildikó de Papp. *Controlling the Uncontrollable* . . . , 71–73.
Rasporich, Beverly J. *Dance of the Sexes* . . . , 130–132.

"Walking on Water"
Carrington, Ildikó de Papp. *Controlling the Uncontrollable* . . . , 117–122.
Hamdson, Robert. " . . . Pleasures of Disruption," 82–85.

"White Dump"
Carrington, Ildikó de Papp. *Controlling the Uncontrollable* . . . , 170–176.
Howells, Coral A. "Alice Munro's Art . . . ," 148–149.
Rooke, Constance. *Fear of the Open Heart* . . . , 51–52.

"Who Do You Think You Are?"
Grabes, Herbert. "Creating to Dissect: Strategies of Character Portrayal and Evaluation in Short Stories by Margaret Laurence, Alice Munro, and Mavis Gallant," in Nischik, Reingard M., and Barbara Korte, Eds. *Modes of Narrative* . . . , 122–124.

"Wild Swans"
Carrington, Ildikó de Papp. *Controlling the Uncontrollable* . . . , 124–128.

"Winter Wind"
Carrington, Ildikó de Papp. *Controlling the Uncontrollable* . . . , 189–190.

"Wood"
Carrington, Ildikó de Papp. *Controlling the Uncontrollable* . . . , 63–65.

IRIS MURDOCH

"Something Special"
Dezure, Deborah. "The Perceiving Self as Gatekeeper: Choice in Iris Murdoch's 'Something Special,' " *Stud Short Fiction*, 27 (1990), 211–220.

ROBERT MUSIL

"The Temptation of Silent Veronica"
Midgley, David. "The Word and the Spirit: Explorations of the Irrational in Kafka, Döblin, and Musil," in Collier, Peter, and Judy Davies, Eds. *Modernism* . . . , 117–119.

VLADIMIR NABOKOV

"Bachmann"
Boyd, Brian. . . . *The Russian Years*, 235–236.

"Breaking the News"
Boyd, Brian. . . . *The Russian Years*, 405–406.

"A Busy Man"
Boyd, Brian. . . . *The Russian Years*, 371–372.

"Christmas"
Boyd, Brian. . . . *The Russian Years*, 71–72.

"The Circle"
Boyd, Brian. . . . *The Russian Years*, 404–405.

"Cloud, Castle, Lake" [originally "Cloud, Lake, Tower"]
Elms, Alan C. "Cloud, Castle, Claustrum: Nabokov as a Freudian in Spite of Himself," in Rancour-Laferriere, Daniel, Ed. *Russian Literature* . . . , 353–368.
Shawen, Edgar M. "Motion and Stasis: Nabokov's 'Cloud, Castle, Lake,' " *Stud Short Fiction*, 27 (1990), 379–383.

"The Fight"
Boyd, Brian. . . . *The Russian Years*, 242–243.

"Lik"
Boyd, Brian. . . . *The Russian Years*, 493–494.

"Music"
Boyd, Brian. . . . *The Russian Years*, 377–378.

"A Nursery Tale"
Boyd, Brian. . . . *The Russian Years*, 259–260.

"The Potato Elf"
Boyd, Brian. . . . *The Russian Years*, 229–230.

"Recruiting"
Toker, Leona. *Nabokov* . . . , 22–23.

"The Return of Chorb"
Boyd, Brian. . . . *The Russian Years*, 249–250.

"Signs and Symbols"
Toker, Leona. *Nabokov* . . . , 214–215.

"Sounds"
Boyd, Brian. . . . *The Russian Years*, 217–218.

"Spring in Fialta"
Boyd, Brian. . . . *The Russian Years*, 426–427.

"Terror"
Boyd, Brian. . . . *The Russian Years*, 261–262.

"The Thunderstorm"
Boyd, Brian. . . . *The Russian Years*, 233–234.

"The Vane Sisters"
Toker, Leona. *Nabokov* . . . , 9–10.

"Vasily Shishkov"
Boyd, Brian. . . . *The Russian Years*, 509–510.

YURI NAGIBIN

"Patience"
Shneidman, N. N. *Soviet Literature* . . . , 35–36.

V[IDIADHAR] S[URAJPRASAD] NAIPAUL

"The Baker's Story"
Kelly, Richard. *V. S. Naipaul*, 34–35.

"A Christmas Story"
Kelly, Richard. *V. S. Naipaul*, 33–34.

"The Enemy"
Kelly, Richard. *V. S. Naipaul*, 29–31.

"A Flag on the Island"
Kelly, Richard. *V. S. Naipaul*, 84–89.

"The Heart"
Kelly, Richard. *V. S. Naipaul*, 32–33.

"In a Free State"
Kelly, Richard. *V. S. Naipaul*, 108–119.

"My Aunt Gold Teeth"
Kelly, Richard. *V. S. Naipaul*, 28–29.

"Tell Me Who to Kill"
Kelly, Richard. *V. S. Naipaul*, 107–108.

NAOKI SANJUGO

"The Robot and the Weight of the Bed"
Matthew, Robert. *Japanese Science Fiction* . . . , 20–21.

GLORIA NAYLOR

"The Two"
Smith, Barbara. "The Truth That Never Hurts: Black Lesbians in Fiction in the 1980s," in Braxton, Joanne M., and Andrée N. McLaughlin, Eds. *Wild Women* . . . , 225–230.

NJABULOS NDEBELE

"Fools"
Mazurek, Raymond A. "Gordimer's 'Something Out There' and Ndebele's *'Fools' and Other Stories*: The Politics of Literary Form," *Stud Short Fiction*, 26 (1989), 77–79.

"The Test"
Mazurek, Raymond A. " . . . Politics of Literary Form," 76.

"Uncle"
Mazurek, Raymond A. " . . . Politics of Literary Form," 76–77.

GÉRARD DE NERVAL [GÉRARD LABRUNIE]

"The King of Bicêtre"
Avni, Ora. *The Resistance of Reference* . . . , 202–229.

"Sylvie"
Segal, Naomi. *Narcissus and Echo* . . . , 123–137.

J. DAVID NIGHTINGALE

"The Nursing Home"
Yahnke, Robert E., and Richard M. Eastman. *Aging in Literature* . . . , 55.

HUGH NISSENSON

"The Blessing"
Berger, Alan L. "Holiness and Holocaust: The Jewish Writing of Hugh Nissenson," *Jewish Book Forum*, 45 (1990), 9–10.

"The Crazy Old Man"
Berger, Alan L. "Holiness and Holocaust . . . ," 21.

"Forcing the End"
Berger, Alan L. "Holiness and Holocaust . . . ," 19.

"Going Up"
Berger, Alan L. "Holiness and Holocaust . . . ," 14.

"The Groom of Zlota Street"
Berger, Alan L. "Holiness and Holocaust . . . ," 13.

"In the Reign of Peace"
Berger, Alan L. "Holiness and Holocaust . . . ," 21–22.

"Lamentation"
Berger, Alan L. "Holiness and Holocaust . . . ," 15–16.

"The Law"
Berger, Alan L. "Holiness and Holocaust . . . ," 13–14.

"The Prisoner"
Berger, Alan L. "Holiness and Holocaust . . . ," 11–12.

"The Throne of Good"
Berger, Alan L. "Holiness and Holocaust . . . ," 20–21.

"The Well"
Berger, Alan L. "Holiness and Holocaust . . . ," 19.

NOMURA KŌDŌ

"Murder by Soundwave"
Matthew, Robert. *Japanese Science Fiction* . . . , 31–32.

LESLIE NORRIS

"My Uncle's Story"
Yahnke, Robert E., and Richard M. Eastman. *Aging in Literature* . . . , 55–56.

PHILLIP FRANCIS NOWLAN

"The Airlords of Han"
Panshin, Alexel, and Cory Panshin. *The World Beyond* . . . , 215–216.

"Armegeddon—2419 A.D."
Panshin, Alexel, and Cory Panshin. *The World Beyond* . . . , 214–215.

STANLEY NYAMFUKUDZA

"Aftermaths"
Riemenschneider, Dieter. "Short Fiction from Zimbabwe," *Research African Lit*, 20 (1989), 407–408.

JOYCE CAROL OATES

"Accomplished Desires"
Trachtenberg, Stanley. "Desire, Hypocrisy, and Ambition in Academe: Joyce Carol Oates's *Hungry Ghosts*," in Siegel, Ben, Ed. *The American Writer* . . . , 48.

"Archways"
Cunningham, Frank R. "The Enclosure of Identity in the Early Stories," in Pearlman, Mickey, Ed. *American Women* . . . , 12–13.
Trachtenberg, Stanley. "Desire, Hypocrisy . . . ," 46–47.

"By the River"
Cunningham, Frank R. "The Enclosure . . . ," 21–22.

"The Dead"
Trachtenberg, Stanley. "Desire, Hypocrisy . . . ," 48–49.

"Democracy in America"
Trachtenberg, Stanley. "Desire, Hypocrisy . . . ," 41–42.

"A Descriptive Catalog"
Trachtenberg, Stanley. "Desire, Hypocrisy . . . ," 43–44.

"Did You Ever Slip on Red Blood?"
Cunningham, Frank R. "The Enclosure . . . ," 21.

"Edge of the World"
Cunningham, Frank R. "The Enclosure . . . ," 13–14.

"An Encounter with the Blind"
Cunningham, Frank R. "The Enclosure . . . ," 15–17.

"Happy Onion"
Cunningham, Frank R. "The Enclosure . . . ," 18–19.

"In the Autumn of the Year"
Trachtenberg, Stanley. "Desire, Hypocrisy . . . ," 50.

"In the Region of Ice"
Trachtenberg, Stanley. "Desire, Hypocrisy . . . ," 47.

"Magna Mater"
Trachtenberg, Stanley. "Desire, Hypocrisy . . . ," 49–50.

"Master Race"
Dörfel, Hanspeter. "Images of Germany and the Germans in Some of Joyce Carol Oates' Short Stories," in Freese, Peter, Ed. *Germany and German Thought* . . . , 272–276.
Zapf, Hubert. "Aesthetic Experience and Ideological Critique in Joyce Carol Oates's 'Master Race,' " *Int'l Fiction R*, 16, i (1989), 48–55.

"My Warszawa: 1980"
Dörfel, Hanspeter. "Images of Germany . . . ," 269–271.

"The Narcotic"
Cunningham, Frank R. "The Enclosure . . . ," 20–21.

"Our Wall"
Dörfel, Hanspeter. "Images of Germany . . . ," 277–278, 280–281.

"Pastoral Blood"
Cunningham, Frank R. "The Enclosure . . . ," 20.

"Puzzle"
Cunningham, Frank R. "The Enclosure . . . ," 25.

"Rewards of Fame"
Trachtenberg, Stanley. "Desire, Hypocrisy . . . ," 44–45.

"Stigmata"
Cunningham, Frank R. "The Enclosure . . . ," 14–15.

"A Theory of Knowledge"
Yahnke, Robert E., and Richard M. Eastman. *Aging in Literature* . . . , 56–57.

"Through the Looking Glass"
Trachtenberg, Stanley. "Desire, Hypocrisy . . . ," 47–48.

"The Transformation of Vincent Scoville"
Trachtenberg, Stanley. "Desire, Hypocrisy . . . ," 45–46.

"Up from Slavery"
Trachtenberg, Stanley. "Desire, Hypocrisy . . . ," 42–43.

"What Death with Love Should Have to Do"
Cunningham, Frank R. "The Enclosure . . . ," 11–12.

"Where Are You Going, Where Have You Been?"
Coulthard, A. R. "Joyce Carol Oates's 'Where Are You Going, Where Have You Been?' " *Stud Short Fiction*, 26 (1989), 505–510.
Easterly, Joan. "The Shadow of a Satyr in Oates's 'Where Are You Going, Where Have You Been?' " *Stud Short Fiction*, 27 (1990), 537–543.

EDNA O'BRIEN

"The Doll"
Carriker, Kitti. "Edna O'Brien's 'The Doll': A Narrative of Abjection," *Notes Mod Irish Lit*, 1 (1989), 6–13.

FLANN O'BRIEN

"The Martyr's Crown"
Ingersoll, Earl G. "Irish Jokes: A Lacanian Reading of Short Stories by James Joyce, Flann O'Brien, and Bryan MacMahon," *Stud Short Fiction*, 27 (1990), 241–243.

SILVINA OCAMPO

"Autobiography of Irene"
Klingenberg, Patricia N. "The Twisted Mirror: The Fantastic Stories of Silvina Ocampo," *Letras Femeninas*, 13, i–ii (1987), 69–70.

"La casa de azúcar"
Klingenberg, Patricia N. "The Twisted Mirror . . . ," 72–73.

"El cuaderno"
Klingenberg, Patricia N. "The Twisted Mirror . . . ," 72.

"El diario de Porfiria Bernal"
Klingenberg, Patricia N. "The Feminine 'I': Silvina Ocampo's Fantasies of the Subject," *Romance Lang Annual*, 1 (1989), 488–494.

"La familia Linio Milagro"
Klingenberg, Patricia N. "The Twisted Mirror . . . ," 68–69.

"Malva'"
Klingenberg, Patricia N. "The Twisted Mirror . . . ," 76–77.

"Los objetos"
Klingenberg, Patricia N. "The Twisted Mirror . . . ," 71.

"El pecado mortal"
Araüjo, Helena. "Erotismo y perversión en un cuento de Silvina Ocampo," *Río de la Plata*, 1 (1985), 141–145.

"Siesta en el cedro"
Klingenberg, Patricia N. "The Twisted Mirror . . . ," 67–68.

"El vestido de terciopelo"
Klingenberg, Patricia N. "The Twisted Mirror . . . ," 74–76.

FLANNERY O'CONNOR

"The Artificial Nigger"
Bonney, William. "The Moral Structure of Flannery O'Connor's *A Good Man Is Hard to Find*," *Stud Short Fiction*, 27 (1990), 349–350.
Brinkmeyer, Robert H. *The Art & Vision* . . . , 73–83.
Giannone, Richard. *Flannery O'Connor* . . . , 87–97.
Magistrale, Tony. "Patterns of Spiritual Revelation in the Stories of Flannery O'Connor," *Lamar J Hum*, 12, i (1986), 57.
Stock, R. D. *The Flutes of Dionysus* . . . , 393–394.
Yahnke, Robert E., and Richard M. Eastman. *Aging in Literature* . . . , 57.

"The Barber"
Brinkmeyer, Robert H. *The Art & Vision* . . . , 50–53.

"A Circle of Fire"
Giannone, Richard. *Flannery O'Connor* . . . , 81–87.

"The Comforts of Home"
Giannone, Richard. *Flannery O'Connor* . . . , 193–201.
Winn, Harbour. "*Everything That Rises Must Converge*: O'Connor's Seven-Story Cycle," *Renascence*, 42 (1990), 200–202.

"The Displaced Person"
Giannone, Richard. *Flannery O'Connor* . . . , 101–113.

"The Enduring Chill"
Andreas, James. " 'If It's a Symbol, to Hell with It': The Medieval Gothic Style of Flannery O'Connor in *Everything That Rises Must Converge*," *Christianity & Lit*, 38, ii (1989), 30–31.
Brinkmeyer, Robert H. *The Art & Vision* . . . , 83–89, 149–152.
Giannone, Richard. *Flannery O'Connor* . . . , 185–193.
Stock, R. D. *The Flutes of Dionysus* . . . , 392–393.
Winn, Harbour. " . . . Seven-Story Cycle," 199–200.

"Everything That Rises Must Converge"
Andreas, James. " 'If It's a Symbol . . . ,' " 28–29.
Brinkmeyer, Robert H. *The Art & Vision* . . . , 68–72, 149–152.
Giannone, Richard. *Flannery O'Connor* . . . , 160–166.
Winn, Harbour. " . . . Seven-Story Cycle," 192–195.

"The Geranium"
Giannone, Richard. *Flannery O'Connor* . . . , 234–239.

"Good Country People"
Brinkmeyer, Robert H. *The Art & Vision* . . . , 145–149.
Giannone, Richard. *Flannery O'Connor* . . . , 62–69.
McElroy, Bernard. . . . *Modern Grotesque*, 140–141.

"A Good Man Is Hard to Find"
Brinkmeyer, Robert H. *The Art & Vision* . . . , 160–162, 180–185.
Burns, Margie. "A Good Rose Is Hard to Find: 'Southern Gothic' as Social Dislocation in Faulkner and O'Connor," *Works & Days*, 6, i–ii (1988), 185–201.
Church, Joseph. "An Abuse of the Imagination in Flannery O'Connor's 'A Good Man Is Hard to Find,' " *Notes Contemp Lit*, 20, iii (1990), 8–10.
Currie, Sheldon. "A Good Grandmother Is Hard to Find: Story as Exemplum," *Antigonish R*, No. 81–82 (1990), 147–156.
Desmond, John F. "Sign of the Times: Lancelot and the Misfit," *Flannery O'Connor Bull*, 18 (1989), 91–98.
Giannone, Richard. *Flannery O'Connor* . . . , 46–54.
Ochshorn, Kathleen G. "A Cloak of Grace: Contradictions in 'A Good Man Is Hard to Find,' " *Stud Am Fiction*, 18 (1990), 113–117.
+Roberts, Edgar V., and Henry E. Jacobs. *Instructor's Manual* . . . , 2nd ed., 81–82.
Vipond, Diane. "Flannery O'Connor's World Without Pity," *Notes Contemp Lit*, 20, ii (1990), 8–9.

"Greenleaf"
Giannone, Richard. *Flannery O'Connor* . . . , 166–175.
Phillips, K. J. *Dying Gods* . . . , 75–81.
Stock, R. D. *The Flutes of Dionysus* . . . , 391–392.
Winn, Harbour. " . . . Seven-Story Cycle," 195–197.

"Judgement Day"
Giannone, Richard. *Flannery O'Connor* . . . , 239–247.

"The Lame Shall Enter First"
Andreas, James. " 'If It's a Symbol . . . ," 31–32.
Brinkmeyer, Robert H. *The Art & Vision* . . . , 91–98.

Giannone, Richard. *Flannery O'Connor* . . . , 201–210.
Magistrale, Tony. "O'Connor's 'The Lame Shall Enter First,' " *Explicator*, 47, iii (1989), 58–61.
Winn, Harbour. " . . . Seven-Story Cycle," 202–203.

"A Late Encounter with the Enemy"
Giannone, Richard. *Flannery O'Connor* . . . , 97–101.
Yahnke, Robert E., and Richard M. Eastman. *Aging in Literature* . . . , 57–58.

"The Life You Save May Be Your Own"
Giannone, Richard. *Flannery O'Connor* . . . , 54–60.
Ragen, Brian A. *A Wreck on the Road* . . . , 96–105.

"Parker's Back"
Andreas, James. " 'If It's a Symbol . . . ,' " 32–33.
Giannone, Richard. *Flannery O'Connor* . . . , 220–231.
Ragen, Brian A. *A Wreck on the Road* . . . , 26–53.
Stock, R. D. *The Flutes of Dionysus* . . . , 388–389.

"The Patridge Festival"
Brinkmeyer, Robert H. *The Art & Vision* . . . , 152–157.

"Revelation"
Giannone, Richard. *Flannery O'Connor* . . . , 213–220.
Winn, Harbour. " . . . Seven-Story Cycle," 203–208.

"The River"
Behrendt, Stephen C. "Knowledge and Innocence in Flannery O'Connor's 'The River,' " *Stud Am Fiction*, 17 (1989), 143–155.
Giannone, Richard. *Flannery O'Connor* . . . , 71–76.
Sexton, Mark S. "Flannery O'Connor's Presentation of Vernacular Religion in 'The River,' " *Flannery O'Connor Bull*, 18 (1989), 1–12.

"A Stroke of Good Fortune"
Giannone, Richard. *Flannery O'Connor* . . . , 60–62.

"A Temple of the Holy Ghost"
Bonney, William. "The Moral Structure . . . ," 348–349.
Giannone, Richard. *Flannery O'Connor* . . . , 76–81.

"The Train"
Brinkmeyer, Robert H. *The Art & Vision* . . . , 53–55.

"The Turkey"
Powers, Douglas. "Ruller McFarney's Cutting Loose," *Flannery O'Connor Bull*, 18 (1989), 70–78.

"A View of the Woods"
Giannone, Richard. *Flannery O'Connor* . . . , 175–181.
Winn, Harbour. " . . . Seven-Story Cycle," 197–199.

FRANK O'CONNOR [MICHAEL O'DONOVAN]

"An Act of Charity"
Hildebidle, John. *Five Irish Writers* . . . , 107–108.

"The American Wife"
Hildebidle, John. *Five Irish Writers* . . . , 181–182.

"Don Juan's Temptation"
Hildebidle, John. *Five Irish Writers* . . . , 187–188.
Murphy, Kate. "Grappling with the World," *Twentieth Century Lit*, 36 (1990), 333.

"The Face of Evil"
Murphy, Kate. "Grappling . . . ," 318–321.

"First Confession"
Roberts, Edgar V., and Henry E. Jacobs. *Instructor's Manual* . . . , 2nd ed., 82–83.

"First Love"
Murphy, Kate. "Grappling . . . ," 327–328.

"The Frying Pan"
Hildebidle, John. *Five Irish Writers* . . . , 182–183.
Murphy, Kate. "Grappling . . . ," 340–341.

"The Grand Vizier's Daughter"
Hildebidle, John. *Five Irish Writers* . . . , 205–206.

"Guests of the Nation"
Hildebidle, John. *Five Irish Writers* . . . , 179–181.
Murphy, Kate. "Grappling . . . ," 322–323.
Renner, Stanley. "The Theme of Hidden Powers: Fate vs. Human Responsibility in 'Guests of the Nation,' " *Stud Short Fiction*, 27 (1990), 371–377.
Thompson, Richard J. *Everlasting Voices* . . . , 19–22.

"The Holy Door"
Thompson, Richard J. *Everlasting Voices* . . . , 28–29.

"The Impossible Marriage"
Hildebidle, John. *Five Irish Writers* . . . , 173–177.

"In the Train"
Thompson, Richard J. *Everlasting Voices* . . . , 22–23.

"Jo"
Murphy, Kate. "Grappling . . . ," 323–325.

"The Lady of the Sagas"
Hildebidle, John. *Five Irish Writers* . . . , 189–190.
Murphy, Kate. "Grappling . . . ," 330–331.

"Laughter"
Murphy, Kate. "Grappling . . . ," 325–327.

"The Little Mother"
Hildebidle, John. *Five Irish Writers* . . . , 192–195.

"Lonely Rock"
Murphy, Kate. "Grappling . . . ," 333–334.

"The Long Road to Ummera"
Murphy, Kate. "Grappling . . . ," 334–335.
Thompson, Richard J. *Everlasting Voices* . . . , 25–26.

"The Luceys"
Thompson, Richard J. *Everlasting Voices* . . . , 26.

"The Mad Lomasneys"
Murphy, Kate. "Grappling . . . ," 331.
Thompson, Richard J. *Everlasting Voices* . . . , 26–27.

"The Majesty of the Law"
Murphy, Kate. "Grappling . . . ," 338.
Thompson, Richard J. *Everlasting Voices* . . . , 23–24.

"The Masculine Principle'"
Murphy, Kate. "Grappling . . . ," 329–330.

"News for the Church"
Hildebidle, John. *Five Irish Writers* . . . , 186–187.

"Peasants"
Murphy, Kate. "Grappling . . . ," 338–339.

"The Sorcerer's Apprentice"
Murphy, Kate. "Grappling . . . ," 330.

"Uprooted"
Thompson, Richard J. *Everlasting Voices* . . . , 27.

"The Weeping Children"
Hildebidle, John. *Five Irish Writers* . . . , 203–204.

WELMA ODENDAAL

"Dry-Nurse"
Trump, Martin. "Afrikaner Literature and the South African Liberation Struggle," *J Commonwealth Lit*, 25, i (1990), 59–61.

ŌE KENZABURŌ

"The Day He Himself Shall Wipe My Tears Away"
Napier, Susan J. "Death and the Emperor: Mishima, Ōe, and the Politics of Betrayal," *J Asian Stud*, 48, i (1989), 82–85.

"Seventeen"
Napier, Susan J. "Death and the Emperor . . . ," 74–79.

SEAN O'FAOLAIN

"A Broken World"
Thompson, Richard J. *Everlasting Voices* . . . , 45–46.

"Dividends"
Thompson, Richard J. *Everlasting Voices* . . . , 39–40, 55–57.

"The Faithless Wife"
Thompson, Richard J. *Everlasting Voices* . . . , 58–59.

"Foreign Affairs"
Hildebidle, John. *Five Irish Writers* . . . , 165–166.

LIAM O'FLAHERTY

"The Wild Goat's Kid"
Thompson, Richard J. *Everlasting Voices* . . . , 75–76.

SEUMAS O'KELLY

"Cruiskeen Lawn"
Gallagher, Monique. "Full Stuff, False Stuff, Fool's Stuff from Dublin: Myles of Falstaffian Blather," *Cycnos*, 5 (1989), 63–69.

"The Weaver's Grave: A Story of Old Men"
Cooley, Elizabeth. "Seumas O'Kelly's 'The Weaver's Grave': What Lies Beneath 'A Story of Old Men,' " *Stud Short Fiction*, 26 (1989), 453–462.

OKURI CHUTARO

"The Adventure in the Pacific Plughole"
Matthew, Robert. *Japanese Science Fiction* . . . , 34–35.

FRANCISCO M. DE OLAGUÍBEL

"El crimen de Margarita"
Pavón, Alfredo. "De la violencia en los modernistas," in Pavón, Alfredo, Ed. *Paquette: Cuento* . . . , 83–84.

IURIĬ [YURY] KARLOVICH OLESHA

"Al'debaran"
Peppard, Victor. *The Poetics* . . . , 66–67.

"The Chain"
Peppard, Victor. *The Poetics* . . . , 99–103.

"The Cherry Pit" [same as "The Cherry Stone"]
Naydan, Michael M. "Intimations of Biblical Myth and the Creative Process in Jurij Oleša's 'Višnevaja kostočka,' " *Slavic & East European J*, 33 (1989), 373–385.
Peppard, Victor. *The Poetics* . . . , 65–66.

"Liompa"
Peppard, Victor. *The Poetics* . . . , 104–110.

TILLIE OLSEN

"I Stand Here Ironing"
Bauer, Helen P. " 'A child of anxious, not proud love': Mother and Daughter in Tillie Olsen's 'I Stand Here Ironing,' " in Pearlman, Mickey, Ed. *Mother Puzzles* . . . , 34–39.
+Roberts, Edgar V., and Henry E. Jacobs. *Instructor's Manual* . . . , 2nd ed., 84–85.

"Tell Me a Riddle"
Banks, Joanne T. "Death Labors," *Lit & Med*, 9 (1990), 162–171.
Connelly, Julia E. "The Whole Story," *Lit & Med*, 9 (1990), 150–161.
Trensky, Anne. "The Unnatural Silences of Tillie Olsen," *Stud Short Fiction*, 27 (1990), 509–516.
Yahnke, Robert E., and Richard M. Eastman. *Aging in Literature* . . . , 58–59.

JUAN CARLOS ONETTI

"The Album"
Benedetti, Mario. *Crítica cómplice*, 27.

"Dreaded Hell"
Benedetti, Mario. *Crítica cómplice*, 27–28.

"A Dream Come True"
Benedetti, Mario. *Crítica cómplice*, 21–22.

"Esbjerg, on the Coast"
Benedetti, Mario. *Crítica cómplice*, 24.

"The Knight of the Rose"
Benedetti, Mario. *Crítica cómplice*, 27.

"Welcome, Bob"
Benedetti, Mario. *Crítica cómplice*, 24.

YOLANDA OREAMUNO

"High Valley"
Gold, Janet. "Feminine Space and the Discourse of Silence: Yolanda Oreamuno, Elena Poniatowska, and Luisa Valenzuela," in Valis, Noël, and Carol Maiser, Eds. *In the Feminine Mode* . . . , 196–198.

GEORGE ORWELL

"Animal Farm"
Crick, Bernard. *Essays on Politics* . . . , 170–179.

GILBERT OSKABOOSE

"The Serpent's Egg"
Petrone, Penny. *Native Literature* . . . , 146.

OUYANG SHAN [YANG FENGQI]

"Tomorrow's Artist"
Wedell-Wedellsborg, Anne. "Ouyang Shan," in Slupski, Zbigniew, Ed. *A Selective Guide* . . . , II, 143–144.

AMOS OZ

"Before His Time"
Alter, Robert, Ed. *Modern Hebrew Literature*, 329–332.

"The Hill of Evil Counsel"
Cohen, Joseph. *Voices of Israel* . . . , 165–167.

"Late Love"
Cohen, Joseph. *Voices of Israel* . . . , 164.

"Longing"
Cohen, Joseph. *Voices of Israel* . . . , 166–167.

"Mr. Levi"
Cohen, Joseph. *Voices of Israel* . . . , 165–166.

CYNTHIA OZICK

"Bloodshed"
Kielsky, Vera E. *Inevitable Exiles* . . . , 79–92.
Kremer, S. Lillian. *Witness Through Imagination* . . . , 246–249.

"The Dock-Witch"
Kielsky, Vera E. *Inevitable Exiles* . . . , 116–130.

"An Education"
Kielsky, Vera E. *Inevitable Exiles* . . . , 167–176.

"Envy; or Yiddish in America"
Kielsky, Vera E. *Inevitable Exiles* . . . , 151–166.
Kremer, S. Lillian. *Witness Through Imagination* . . . , 237–239.

"Levitation"
Greenstein, Michael. "Jewish Pegasus," *Jewish Book Forum*, 45 (1990), 53–54.
Kielsky, Vera E. *Inevitable Exiles* . . . , 67–78.
Kremer, S. Lillian. *Witness Through Imagination* . . . , 249–252.

"A Mercenary"
Kielsky, Vera E. *Inevitable Exiles* . . . , 47–66.
Kremer, S. Lillian. *Witness Through Imagination* . . . , 244–246.

"The Pagan Rabbi"
Kielsky, Vera E. *Inevitable Exiles* . . . , 103–114.

"The Shawl"
Scrafford, Barbara. "Nature's Silent Scream: A Commentary on Cynthia Ozick's 'The Shawl,' " *Critique S*, 31, i (1989), 11–15.

"The Suitcase"
Borchers, Hans. "The Difficulty of Imagining Germany: Some Observations on the Work of Cynthia Ozick," in Freese, Peter, Ed. *Germany and German Thought* . . . , 285–292.
Kielsky, Vera E. *Inevitable Exiles* . . . , 31–45.
Kremer, S. Lillian. *Witness Through Imagination* . . . , 239–243.

"Virility"
Kielsky, Vera E. *Inevitable Exiles* . . . , 135–149.

PA CHIN [same as BA JIN or LI FEIGAN]

"Dog"
Lancashire, Douglas. "Ba Jin," in Slupski, Zbigniew, Ed. *A Selective Guide* . . . , II, 34.

"The Garden of Rest"
Lang, Olga. *Pa Chin and His Writings* . . . , 212–213.

"God"
Lancashire, Douglas. "Ba Jin," 29.

"Life-giving Herb"
Shih, Vincent Y. C. "Enthusiast and Escapist: Writers of the Older Generation," in Birch, Cyril, Ed. *Chinese Communist Literature*, 104–106.

"Man: A Nightmare"
Lancashire, Douglas. "Ba Jin," 30–31.

"My Tears"
Lancashire, Douglas. "Ba Jin," 32–33.

"Spirit: An Autobiography"
Lancashire, Douglas. "Ba Jin," 30.

LEWIS PADGETT [CATHERINE L. MOORE and HENRY KUTTNER]

"Deadlock"
Panshin, Alexel, and Cory Panshin. *The World Beyond* . . . , 592–594.

"Mimsy Were the Borogoves"
Huntington, John. *Rationalizing Genius* . . . , 128–130.
Panshin, Alexel, and Cory Panshin. *The World Beyond* . . . , 596–600.

"The Proud Robot"
Panshin, Alexel, and Cory Panshin. *The World Beyond* . . . , 603–605.

ANTONIA PALACIOS

"Continente de yerbas"
Ramos, Elías A. *El cuento venezolano* . . . , 126–127.

GRACE PALEY

"At That Time, or The History of a Joke"
Isaacs, Neil D. *Grace Paley* . . . , 78–79.
Lyons, Bonnie. "Grace Paley's Jewish Miniatures," *Stud Am Jewish Lit*, 8, i (1989), 30.
Taylor, Jacqueline. *Grace Paley* . . . , 62–63.

"The Burdened Man"
Isaacs, Neil D. *Grace Paley* . . . , 51–52.
Taylor, Jacqueline. *Grace Paley* . . . , 102.

"Come On, Ye Sons of Art"
Isaacs, Neil D. *Grace Paley* . . . , 45–46.

"The Contest"
Isaacs, Neil D. *Grace Paley* . . . , 22–24.
Taylor, Jacqueline. *Grace Paley* . . . , 102.

"A Conversation with My Father"
Aarons, Victoria. "A Perfect Marginality: Public and Private Telling in the Stories of Grace Paley," *Stud Short Fiction*, 27 (1990), 41–43.
Eckstein, Barbara J. *The Language of Fiction* . . . , 148–149.
Isaacs, Neil D. *Grace Paley* . . . , 60–62.
Taylor, Jacqueline. *Grace Paley* . . . , 69–73.

"Debts"
Isaacs, Neil D. *Grace Paley* . . . , 37–38.
Taylor, Jacqueline. *Grace Paley* . . . , 99–100.

"Distance"
Isaacs, Neil D. *Grace Paley* . . . , 39–41.
Taylor, Jacqueline. *Grace Paley* . . . , 111–112.

"Dreamer in a Dead Language"
Eckstein, Barbara J. "Grace Paley's Community: Gradual Epiphanies in the Meantime," in Sorkin, Adam J., Ed. *Politics and the Muse* . . . , 135.
Isaacs, Neil D. *Grace Paley* . . . , 67–71.
Taylor, Jacqueline. *Grace Paley* . . . , 59–61.

"Enormous Changes at the Last Minute"
Isaacs, Neil D. *Grace Paley* . . . , 52–55.
Taylor, Jacqueline. *Grace Paley* . . . , 82–83.

"The Expensive Moment"
Isaacs, Neil D. *Grace Paley* . . . , 74–76.

"Faith in a Tree"
Eckstein, Barbara J. "Grace Paley's Community . . . ," 132.
———. *The Language of Fiction* . . . , 142–145.
Isaacs, Neil D. *Grace Paley* . . . , 47–50.
Lyons, Bonnie. " . . . Jewish Miniatures," 29.
Taylor, Jacqueline. *Grace Paley* . . . , 120–122.

"Faith in the Afternoon"
Isaacs, Neil D. *Grace Paley* . . . , 41–42.

"The Floating Truth"
Isaacs, Neil D. *Grace Paley . . .*, 32–35.

"Friends"
Isaacs, Neil D. *Grace Paley . . .*, 77–78.
Lyons, Bonnie. " . . . Jewish Miniatures," 29–30.
Taylor, Jacqueline. *Grace Paley . . .*, 32–33.

"Gloomy Tunes"
Isaacs, Neil D. *Grace Paley . . .*, 42–44.

"Goodbye and Good Luck"
Eckstein, Barbara J. "Grace Paley's Community . . .," 126.
Isaacs, Neil D. *Grace Paley . . .*, 8–12.
Lyons, Bonnie. " . . . Jewish Miniatures," 27–28.
+Roberts, Edgar V., and Henry E. Jacobs. *Instructor's Manual . . .*, 2nd ed., 85–86.
Taylor, Jacqueline. *Grace Paley . . .*, 73–75.

"The Immigrant Story"
Isaacs, Neil D. *Grace Paley . . .*, 63–64.
Taylor, Jacqueline. *Grace Paley . . .*, 102–103.

"In the Garden"
Isaacs, Neil D. *Grace Paley . . .*, 71–72.

"In Time Which Made a Monkey of Us All"
Eckstein, Barbara J. "Grace Paley's Community . . .," 129–130.
Isaacs, Neil D. *Grace Paley . . .*, 27–32.

"An Interest in Life"
Eckstein, Barbara J. "Grace Paley's Community . . .," 126–127.
Isaacs, Neil D. *Grace Paley . . .*, 16–19.
Taylor, Jacqueline. *Grace Paley . . .*, 76–77.

"An Irrevocable Diameter"
Isaacs, Neil D. *Grace Paley . . .*, 19–21.

"Lavinia: An Old Story"
Taylor, Jacqueline. *Grace Paley . . .*, 27–28.

"Listening"
Isaacs, Neil D. *Grace Paley . . .*, 91–93.
Taylor, Jacqueline. *Grace Paley . . .*, 89–90.

"The Little Girl"
Isaacs, Neil D. *Grace Paley . . .*, 58–60.

"Living"
Isaacs, Neil D. *Grace Paley . . .*, 44–45.

"The Long-Distance Runner"
Eckstein, Barbara J. "Grace Paley's Community . . .," 132–133.
The Language of Fiction . . ., 145–148.
Isaacs, Neil D. *Grace Paley . . .*, 65–67.
Taylor, Jacqueline. *Grace Paley . . .*, 26–27.

"The Loudest Voice"
Isaacs, Neil D. *Grace Paley . . .*, 21–22.
Taylor, Jacqueline. *Grace Paley . . .*, 63–66.

"Love"
Eckstein, Barbara J. "Grace Paley's Community . . . ," 134–135.
Isaacs, Neil D. *Grace Paley* . . . , 68–69.
Taylor, Jacqueline. *Grace Paley* . . . , 85–88.

"A Man Told Me the Story of His Life"
Isaacs, Neil D. *Grace Paley* . . . , 84–85.

"Midrash on Happiness"
Isaacs, Neil D. *Grace Paley* . . . , 93–94.
Taylor, Jacqueline. *Grace Paley* . . . , 105–106.

"Mother"
Taylor, Jacqueline. *Grace Paley* . . . , 104.

"Northeast Playground"
Isaacs, Neil D. *Grace Paley* . . . , 56–58.
Taylor, Jacqueline. *Grace Paley* . . . , 98–99.

"The Pale Pink Roast"
Eckstein, Barbara J. "Grace Paley's Community . . . ," 126.
Isaacs, Neil D. *Grace Paley* . . . , 13–16.
Taylor, Jacqueline. *Grace Paley* . . . , 76.

"Politics"
Aarons, Victoria. "Talking Lives: Storytelling and Renewal in Grace Paley's Short Fiction," *Stud Am Jewish Lit*, 9, i (1990), 26–27.
Isaacs, Neil D. *Grace Paley* . . . , 56.

"Ruth and Edie"
Isaacs, Neil D. *Grace Paley* . . . , 83–84.
Taylor, Jacqueline. *Grace Paley* . . . , 18–19.

"Samuel"
Isaacs, Neil D. *Grace Paley* . . . , 50–51.
Taylor, Jacqueline. *Grace Paley* . . . , 100–102.

"Somewhere Else"
Eckstein, Barbara J. "Grace Paley's Community . . . ," 136–137.
———. *The Language of Fiction* . . . , 149–153.
Isaacs, Neil D. *Grace Paley* . . . , 73–74.

"The Story Hearer"
Aarons, Victoria. "Talking Lives . . . ," 27–28.
Isaacs, Neil D. *Grace Paley* . . . , 85–87.
Taylor, Jacqueline. *Grace Paley* . . . , 88–89.

"A Subject of Childhood"
Eckstein, Barbara J. "Grace Paley's Community . . . ," 128.
Isaacs, Neil D. *Grace Paley* . . . , 26–27.
Taylor, Jacqueline. *Grace Paley* . . . , 79–80.

"This Is a Story about My Friend George, the Toy Inventor"
Isaacs, Neil D. *Grace Paley* . . . , 87–89.
Taylor, Jacqueline. *Grace Paley* . . . , 103–104.

"The Used-Boy Raisers"
Eckstein, Barbara J. *The Language of Fiction* . . . , 138–142.
Isaacs, Neil D. *Grace Paley* . . . , 25–26.

Lyons, Bonnie. " . . . Jewish Miniatures," 28–29.
Taylor, Jacqueline. *Grace Paley* . . . , 77–79.

"Wants"
Eckstein, Barbara J. "Grace Paley's Community . . . ," 130.
Isaacs, Neil D. *Grace Paley* . . . , 37–38.

"A Woman Young and Old"
Isaacs, Neil D. *Grace Paley* . . . , 12–13.

"Zagrowsky Tells"
Aarons, Victoria. "Talking Lives . . . ," 23–24.
Isaacs, Neil D. *Grace Paley* . . . , 89–91.
Taylor, Jacqueline. *Grace Paley* . . . , 118–119.

BREECE D'J PANCAKE

"In the Dry"
High, Ellesa C. "A Lost Generation: The Appalachia of Breece D'J Pancake," *Appalachian J*, 13, i (1985), 36–37.

"Trilobites"
High, Ellesa C. "A Lost Generation . . . ," 37–38.

EMILIA PARDO BAZÁN

"The Earrings"
Durham, Carolyn R. "Subversion in Two Short Stories by Emilia Pardo Bazán," *Letras Peninsulares*, 2, i (1988), 60–63.

"La novia fiel"
Tolliver, Joyce. "Knowledge, Desire, and Syntactic Empathy in Pardo Bazán's 'La novia fiel,' " *Hispania*, 7 (1989), 909–918.

"Possession"
Durham, Carolyn R. "Subversion . . . ," 58–60.

AMÉRICO PAREDES

"The Hammon and the Beans"
Saldívar, Ramón. *Chicano Narrative* . . . , 50–55.

"Over the Waves Is Out"
Saldívar, Ramón. *Chicano Narrative* . . . , 55–60.

ESDRAS PARRA

"Deserción"
Ramos, Elías A. *El cuento venezolano* . . . , 137.

"El insurgente"
Ramos, Elías A. *El cuento venezolano* . . . , 115.

"La llegada del fin"
Ramos, Elías A. *El cuento venezolano* . . . , 129–130.

"Parte de un ser encorría aún el otro territorio"
Ramos, Elías A. *El cuento venezolano* . . . , 114–115.

"Perseo"
Ramos, Elías A. *El cuento venezolano* . . . , 127–128.

BATISTAI PARWADA

"A Story of War"
Riemenschneider, Dieter. "Short Fiction from Zimbabwe," *Research African Lit*, 20 (1989), 408–409.

BORIS PASTERNAK

"The Apelles Mark"
Barnes, Christopher. *Boris Pasternak* . . . , I, 194–197.

"Suboctave Story"
Barnes, Christopher. *Boris Pasternak* . . . , I, 219–221.

WALTER PATER

"Apollo in Picardy"
Dellamora, Richard. *Masculine Desire* . . . , 186–192.

"Denys l'Auxerrois"
Dellamora, Richard. *Masculine Desire* . . . , 180–186.

"Emerald Uthwart"
Shuter, William F. "The Arrested Narrative of 'Emerald Uthwart,' " *Nineteenth-Century Lit*, 45 (1990), 1–25.

CESARE PAVESE

"The Blind"
O'Healy, Áine. *Cesare Pavese*, 100–101.

"A Certainty"
O'Healy, Áine. *Cesare Pavese*, 89.

"The Corn Field"
O'Healy, Áine. *Cesare Pavese*, 88–89.

"Discharged"
O'Healy, Áine. *Cesare Pavese*, 45–46.

"The Evil Eye"
O'Healy, Áine. *Cesare Pavese*, 57–58.

"Festival Night"
O'Healy, Áine. *Cesare Pavese*, 53–55.

"Festivities"
O'Healy, Áine. *Cesare Pavese*, 92–93.

"First Love"
O'Healy, Áine. *Cesare Pavese*, 55–56.

"The Flood"
O'Healy, Áine. *Cesare Pavese*, 103–104.

"The Hermit"
O'Healy, Áine. *Cesare Pavese*, 90.

"Honeymoon"
O'Healy, Áine. *Cesare Pavese*, 50.

"The Idol"
O'Healy, Áine. *Cesare Pavese*, 50–51.

"The Intruder"
O'Healy, Áine. *Cesare Pavese*, 52.

"The Island"
O'Healy, Áine. *Cesare Pavese*, 104.

"Jailbirds"
O'Healy, Áine. *Cesare Pavese*, 52–53.

"Job Sickness"
O'Healy, Áine. *Cesare Pavese*, 94–95.

"The Leather Jacket"
O'Healy, Áine. *Cesare Pavese*, 91–92.

"The Road"
O'Healy, Áine. *Cesare Pavese*, 101.

"The Sea"
O'Healy, Áine. *Cesare Pavese*, 90–91.

"Sea Foam"
O'Healy, Áine. *Cesare Pavese*, 102–103.

"A Secret History"
O'Healy, Áine. *Cesare Pavese*, 93–94.

"Suicide"
O'Healy, Áine. *Cesare Pavese*, 51.

"The Wheat Field"
O'Healy, Áine. *Cesare Pavese*, 56–57.

NIKOLAY PAVLOV

"The Name Day Party"
Mersereau, John. "The Chorus and Spear Carriers of Russian Romantic Fiction," in Freeborn, Richard, R. R. Milner-Gulland, and Charles A. Ward, Eds. *Russian and Slavic Literature*, 57; rpt. in his *Russian Romantic Fiction*, 240–241.

"Yataghan"
Mersereau, John. "The Chorus . . . ," 58–59; rpt. in his *Russian Romantic Fiction*, 241–243.

CARLOS PAZ GARCÍA

"Andanzas de un guerrillero"
Ratcliff, Dillwyn F. *Venezuelan Prose Fiction*, 212–213.

"Cuento futurista"
Ratcliff, Dillwyn F. *Venezuelan Prose Fiction*, 209.

"El ingeniero"
Ratcliff, Dillwyn F. *Venezuelan Prose Fiction*, 208–209.

"Juan Rodríguez"
Ratcliff, Dillwyn F. *Venezuelan Prose Fiction*, 212.

"La venganza"
Ratcliff, Dillwyn F. *Venezuelan Prose Fiction*, 211.

YITZHAK [ITZHAK] LEIB PERETZ

"The Mad Talmudist"
Frieden, Ken. "Psychological Depth in I. L. Peretz' *Familiar Scenes*," *Jewish Book Annual*, 47 (1989–1990), 147–149.

"The Messenger"
Frieden, Ken. "Psychological Depth . . . ," 146–147.

"Scenes from Limbo"
Alter, Robert, Ed. *Modern Hebrew Literature*, 42–43.

"A Weaver's Love"
Eber, Irene. *Voices from Afar* . . . , 86.

EMILIANO PÉREZ CRUZ

"Todos tienen premio, todos"
Dávila Gutiérrez, Joel. "Tres cuentos mejicanos, tres," in Pavón, Alfredo, Ed. *Paquette: Cuento* . . . , 154–155, 156–157.

BENITO PÉREZ GALDÓS

"La novela en el tranvía"
Gilman, Stephen. *Galdós and the Art* . . . , 201–202.
Smith, Alan. "Los relatos fantásticos de Galdós," in *Actas del Tercer Congreso Internacional de Estudios Galdosianos*, II, 226–233.

CRISTINA PERI ROSSI

"El museo de los esfuerzos inutiles"
Araújo, Helena. "Simbología y poder femenino en algunos personajes de Cristina Peri Rossi," *Plural*, 205 (October, 1988), 26–29.

FERDINANDO ANTÓNIO NOGUEIRA PESSOA

"The Anarchist Banker"
Sapega, Ellen. "On Logical Contradictions and Contradictory Logic: Ferdinando Pessoa's 'O Banqueiro Anarquista,' " *Luso-Brazilian R*, 26, i (1989), 111–117.

MARY PETERSON

"The Carved Table"
Robb, Kenneth A. "Point of View in Mary Peterson's 'The Carved Table,' " *Notes Contemp Lit*, 19, i (1989), 4–5.

LJUDMILA PETRUŠEVSKAJA

"Across the Fields"
Barker, Adele. "Women Without Men in the Writings of Soviet Women Writers," in Rancour-Laferriere, Daniel, Ed. *Russian Literature* . . . , 445.

"History of Clarissa"
Barker, Adele. "Women Without Men . . . ," 445–447.

"Nets and Traps"
Barker, Adele. "Women Without Men . . . ," 444–445.

"The Talker"
Barker, Adele. "Women Without Men . . . ," 444.

RICARDO PIGLIA

"Homage to Roberto Arlt"
Simpson, Amelia S. *Detective Fiction* . . . , 59–60.

"La loca y el relato del crimen"
Simpson, Amelia S. *Detective Fiction* . . . , 152–155.

BORIS PIL'NYAK [BORIS ANDREEVICH VOGAU]

"About Sevka"
Browning, Gary. *Boris Pilniak* . . . , 95–96.

"Along the Old Road"
Browning, Gary. *Boris Pilniak* . . . , 104–105.

"Big Heart"
  Browning, Gary. *Boris Pilniak* . . . , 158–159.

"Birth of Man"
  Browning, Gary. *Boris Pilniak* . . . , 178–181.

"A Complete Life" [originally "Over the Ravine"]
  Browning, Gary. *Boris Pilniak* . . . , 97–98.

"Country Roads"
  Browning, Gary. *Boris Pilniak* . . . , 112–114.

"Damp Mother Earth"
  Browning, Gary. *Boris Pilniak* . . . , 143–147.

"Death Beckons"
  Browning, Gary. *Boris Pilniak* . . . , 102–103.

"Deaths"
  Browning, Gary. *Boris Pilniak* . . . , 98–99.

"Earth on Her Hands"
  Browning, Gary. *Boris Pilniak* . . . , 163–164.

"Forest Dacha" [originally "Spring Floods"]
  Browning, Gary. *Boris Pilniak* . . . , 100–102.

"Grand Slam"
  Browning, Gary. *Boris Pilniak* . . . , 177–178.

"The Heirs"
  Browning, Gary. *Boris Pilniak* . . . , 111–112.

"Ivan Moscow"
  Browning, Gary. *Boris Pilniak* . . . , 161–163.
  Maloney, Philip. "Anarchism and Bolshevism in the Works of Boris Pilnyak," *Russian R*, 23 (1973), 46–47.

"Machines and Wolves"
  Browning, Gary. *Boris Pilniak* . . . , 131–141.

"Mahogany"
  Browning, Gary. *Boris Pilniak* . . . , 164–166.
  Maloney, Philip. "Anarchism and Bolshevism . . . ," 51–52.

"A Monastery Legend"
  Browning, Gary. *Boris Pilniak* . . . , 106–107.

"Nenashin"
  Browning, Gary. *Boris Pilniak* . . . , 130–131.

"Old House"
  Browning, Gary. *Boris Pilniak* . . . , 141–142.

"Settlers in Remote Places"
  Browning, Gary. *Boris Pilniak* . . . , 181–182.

"Speranza"
  Browning, Gary. *Boris Pilniak* . . . , 127–130.

"Spilled Time"
  Browning, Gary. *Boris Pilniak* . . . , 142–143.

"Swindlers"
Browning, Gary. *Boris Pilniak* . . . , 150–151.

"Tale of the Unextinguished Moon"
Browning, Gary. *Boris Pilniak* . . . , 152–158.
Frankel, Edith R. "A Note on Pil'nyak's 'Tale of the Unextinguished Moon,' " *Soviet Stud*, 24, iv (1973), 350–353.

"Things"
Browning, Gary. *Boris Pilniak* . . . , 103–104.

"A Thousand Years"
Browning, Gary. *Boris Pilniak* . . . , 109–111.

"Varangian Times"
Browning, Gary. *Boris Pilniak* . . . , 107–109.

"Without a Name"
Browning, Gary. *Boris Pilniak* . . . , 159–160.

"Zavoloch'e"
Browning, Gary. *Boris Pilniak* . . . , 147–150.

VIRGILIO PIÑERA

"El baile"
Torres, Carmen L. *La cuentística de Virgilio Piñera* . . . , 52–53.

"La boda"
Torres, Carmen L. *La cuentística de Virgilio Piñera* . . . , 56–58.

"La cena"
Torres, Carmen L. *La cuentística de Virgilio Piñera* . . . , 100–101.

"El comercio"
Torres, Carmen L. *La cuentística de Virgilio Piñera* . . . , 55–56.

"El conflicto"
Torres, Carmen L. *La cuentística de Virgilio Piñera* . . . , 74–75.

"La gran escalera del Palacio Legislativo"
Torres, Carmen L. *La cuentística de Virgilio Piñera* . . . , 58–59.

"Interludio"
Torres, Carmen L. *La cuentística de Virgilio Piñera* . . . , 75–76.

"La locomotora"
Torres, Carmen L. *La cuentística de Virgilio Piñera* . . . , 77.

"El muñeco"
Torres, Carmen L. *La cuentística de Virgilio Piñera* . . . , 64–70.

"El parque"
Torres, Carmen L. *La cuentística de Virgilio Piñera* . . . , 53–55.

"Las partes"
Torres, Carmen L. *La cuentística de Virgilio Piñera* . . . , 91–92.

"Un parto insospechado"
Torres, Carmen L. *La cuentística de Virgilio Piñera* . . . , 73–74.

"El señor Ministro"
Torres, Carmen L. *La cuentística de Virgilio Piñera* . . . , 60–64.

"La transformación"
Torres, Carmen L. *La cuentística de Virgilio Piñera* . . . , 72–73.

"El viage"
Torres, Carmen L. *La cuentística de Virgilio Piñera* . . . , 71–72.

PING [BING] HSIN [XIN]—[same as HSIE/XIE WAN-YING]

"Chuang-hung's Elder Sister"
Boušková, Marcela. "The Stories of Ping Hsin," in Prušek, Jaroslav, Ed. . . . *Modern Chinese Literature*, 116, 121–125.

"The Difference"
Tian Luoluo and M. Henri Day. "Bing Xin," in Slupski, Zbigniew, Ed. *A Selective Guide* . . . , II, 39–40.

"The First Dinner Party"
Eide, Elisabeth. "Bing Xin," in Slupski, Zbigniew, Ed. *A Selective Guide* . . . , II, 41–42.
Tian Luoluo and M. Henri Day. "Bing Xin," 38.

"One Year Away from Home"
Boušková, Marcela. "The Stories . . . ," 115.

"Our Lady's Drawing Room"
Boušková, Marcela. "The Stories . . . ," 116–117.

"The Paternal Aunt"
Tian Luoluo and M. Henri Day. "Bing Xin," 38.

"The Smile"
Boušková, Marcela. "The Stories . . . ," 115.

"Three Years"
Tian Luoluo and M. Henri Day. "Bing Xin," 38–39.

"Two Families"
Boušková, Marcela. "The Stories . . . ," 116.

DAVID PINSKI

"Rabbi Akiba's Temptation"
Eber, Irene. *Voices from Afar* . . . , 59–60.

JULIO PLANCHART

"La familia de la Marca del Valle"
Ratcliff, Dillwyn F. *Venezuelan Prose Fiction*, 113–114.

SYLVIA PLATH

"The Daughters of Blossom Street" [originally "This Earth Our Hospital"]
Greene, Sally. "Fathers and Daughters in Sylvia Plath's 'Blossom Street,' " *Stud Am Fiction*, 18 (1990), 225–231.
Stevenson, Anne. *Bitter Fame* . . . , 143–144.

"The Fifty-ninth Bear"
Stevenson, Anne. *Bitter Fame* . . . , 160–161.

"Johnny Panic and the Bible of Dreams"
Hamdson, Robert. "Johnny Panic and the Pleasures of Disruption," in Hanson, Clare, Ed. *Re-reading* . . . , 73–74.
Stevenson, Anne. *Bitter Fame* . . . , 141–143.

EDGAR ALLAN POE

"The Assignation"
Pahl, Dennis. *Architects of the Abyss* . . . , 25–40.
Punter, David. "Edgar Allan Poe: Tales of Dark Heat," in Bloom, Clive, Brian Docherty, Jane Gibb, and Keith Shand, Eds. *Nineteenth-Century Suspense* . . . , 9–10; rpt. in Punter, David. *The Romantic Unconscious* . . . , 158–159.

"Berenice"
Paglia, Camille. *Sexual Personae* . . . , 574–575.
Punter, David. "Edgar Allan Poe . . . ," 4–6; rpt. in his *The Romantic Unconscious* . . . , 154–156.
Weissberg, Lilian. "In Search of Truth and Beauty: Allegory in 'Berenice' and 'The Domain of Arnheim,' " in Fisher, Benjamin F., Ed. *Poe and His Times* . . . , 67–70.

"The Black Cat"
Aberbach, David. *Surviving Trauma* . . . , 144–145.
Auerbach, Jonathan. *The Romance of Failure* . . . , 39–45.
Campos, Cecy B. "O Fantástico em 'The Black Cat,' " *Estudios Anglo-Americanos*, 12–13 (1988–1989), 45–50.
Foster, Dennis A. "Re-Poe Man: A Problem of Pleasure," *Arizona Q*, 46, iv (1990), 8–9.
Lewis, Paul. "Poe's Humor: A Psychological Analysis," *Stud Short Fiction*, 26 (1989), 538–539.
———. *Comic Effects* . . . , 134–135.

"The Cask of Amontillado"
Punter, David. "Edgar Allan Poe . . . ," 2–4; rpt. in his *The Romantic Unconscious* . . . , 151–154.
White, Patrick. " 'The Cask of Amontillado': A Case for the Defense," *Stud Short Fiction*, 26 (1989), 550–555.

"The Colloquy of Monos and Una"
Limon, John. *The Place of Fiction* . . . , 105–106.

"The Conversation of Eiros and Charmion"
Limon, John. *The Place of Fiction* . . . , 104–105.

"A Descent into the Maelström"
Bock, Martin. *Crossing the Shadow-Line* . . . , 52–53.
Bonesio, Louisa. "Il sublime iniziatico," *Cenobio*, 38 (1989), 295–308.
Limon, John. *The Place of Fiction* . . . , 79–81.
Paglia, Camille. *Sexual Personae* . . . , 575–576.
Seaman, Robert E. "Lacan, Poe, and the Descent of the Self," *Texas Stud Lit & Lang*, 31 (1989), 196–214.

"The Domain of Arnheim"
Michael, John. "Narration and Reflection: The Search for Grounds in Poe's 'The Power of Words' and 'The Domain of Arnheim,' " *Arizona Q*, 45, iii (1989), 1–22.
Weissberg, Lilian. "In Search of Truth and Beauty . . . ," 70–73.

"Eleonora"
Fisher, Benjamin F. " 'Eleonora': Poe and Madness," in Fisher, Benjamin F., Ed. *Poe and His Times* . . . , 178–188.

"The Facts in the Case of M. Valdemar"
Auerbach, Jonathan. *The Romance of Failure* . . . , 64–67.
Lewis, Paul. "Poe's Humor . . . ," 541–542.
———. *Comic Effects* . . . , 138–139.

"The Fall of the House of Usher"
Auerbach, Jonathan. *The Romance of Failure* . . . , 47–51.
Brennan, Matthew C. "Poe's Gothic Sublimity: Prose Style, Painting, and Mental Boundaries in 'The Fall of the House of Usher,' " *J Evolutionary Psych*, 11 (1990), 353–359.
———. "Turnerian Topography: The Paintings of Roderick Usher," *Stud Short Fiction*, 27 (1990), 605–607.
Foster, Dennis A. "Re-Poe Man . . . ," 10–14.
Jay, Gregory S. *America the Scrivener* . . . , 177–183.
Johansen, Ib. "The Madness of the Text: Deconstruction of Narrative Logic in 'Usher,' 'Berenice,' and 'Doctor Tarr and Professor Fether,' " *Poe Stud*, 22, i (1989), 3–6.
Jordan, Cynthia S. *Second Stories* . . . , 149–153.
Pahl, Dennis. *Architects of the Abyss* . . . , 3–24.
Sloane, David E. "Usher's Nervous Fever: The Meaning of Medicine in 'The Fall of the House of Usher,' " in Fisher, Benjamin F., Ed. *Poe and His Times* . . . , 146–153.
Thompson, G. R. "Locke, Kant, and Gothic Fiction: A Further Word on the Indeterminism of Poe's 'Usher,' " *Stud Short Fiction*, 26 (1989), 547–550.
Tombleson, Gary E. "Poe's 'Fall of the House of Usher' as Archetypal Gothic: Literary and Archetypal Analogs of Cosmic Unity," *Nineteenth-Century Contexts*, 12, ii (1988), 83–106.

"The Gold Bug"
Foster, Dennis A. "Re-Poe Man . . . ," 14–18.
Kronick, Joseph G. "Edgar Allan Poe: The Error of Reading and the Reading of Error," *Lit & Psych*, 35, iii (1989), 36–38.

"Hop-Frog"
Lewis, Paul. "Poe's Humor . . . ," 535–536.
Lucas, Doreen M. "Poe's Theatre in 'King Pest' and 'Hop Frog,' " *J Short Story Engl*, 14 (Spring, 1990), 25–40.

"The Imp of the Perverse"
Foster, Dennis A. "Re-Poe Man . . . ," 9–10.

"King Pest"
Lucas, Doreen M. "Poe's Theatre . . . ," 25–40.

"The Landscape Garden"
Mantion, Jean-Rémy. "Le Pas des anges dans 'Le Jardin-Paysages' d'Edgar Allan Poe," *Littérature*, 61 (February, 1986), 65–75.

"Ligeia"
Graef, Ortwin de. "The Eye of the Text: Two Short Stories by Edgar Allan Poe," *Mod Lang Notes*, 104 (1989), 1099–1123.
Gruesser, John C. " 'Ligeia' and Orientalism," *Stud Short Fiction*, 26 (1989), 145–149.
Jordan, Cynthia S. *Second Stories* . . . , 135–139.
Kagle, Steven E. "The Corpse Within Us," in Fisher, Benjamin F., Ed. *Poe and His Times* . . . , 119–127.
Lewis, Paul. "Poe's Humor . . . ," 537.
———. *Comic Effects* . . . , 132–134.
Paglia, Camille. *Sexual Personae* . . . , 573–574.

"The Man of the Crowd"
Auerbach, Jonathan. *The Romance of Failure* . . . , 27–35.
Bloom, Clive. "Capitalising on Poe's Detective: The Dollars and Sense of Nineteenth-Century Detective Fiction," in Bloom, Clive, Brian Docherty, Jane Gibb, and Keith Shand, Eds. *Nineteenth-Century Suspense* . . . , 15–17.
Manning, Susan. *The Puritan-Provincial Vision* . . . , 118–119.

"The Man That Was Used Up"
Graef, Ortwin de. "The Eye of the Text . . . ," 1099–1123.

"MS. Found in a Bottle"
Bock, Martin. *Crossing the Shadow-Line* . . . , 54–56.

"The Masque of the Red Death"
Manning, Susan. *The Puritan-Provincial Vision* . . . , 122–123.
Paglia, Camille. *Sexual Personae* . . . , 576–577.
Slick, Richard D. "Poe's 'The Masque of the Red Death,' " *Explicator*, 47, ii (1989), 24–26.
Zapf, Hubert. "Entropic Imagination in Poe's 'The Masque of the Red Death,' " *Coll Lit*, 16 (1989), 211–218.

"Morella"
Jay, Gregory S. *America the Scrivener* . . . , 187–192.

"The Murders in the Rue Morgue"
Creswell, Catherine J. "Poe's Philosophy of Aesthetics and Ratiocination: Compositions of Death in 'The Murders in the Rue Morgue,' " in Walker, Ronald G., and June M. Frazer, Eds. *The Cunning Craft* . . . , 38–54.

Kronick, Joseph G. "Edgar Allan Poe . . . ," 34–35.
Limon, John. *The Place of Fiction* . . . , 96–99.
Martin, Terry J. "Detection, Imagination, and the Introduction to 'The Murders in the Rue Morgue,' " *Mod Lang Stud*, 19, iv (1989), 31–45.
Sweeney, S. E. "Locked Rooms: Detective Fiction, Narrative Theory, and Self-Reflexivity," in Walker, Ronald G., and June M. Frazer, Eds. *The Cunning Craft* . . . , 1–14.

"The Mystery of Marie Roget"
Brand, Dana. "From the *Flâneur* to the Detective: Interpreting the City of Poe," in Bennett, Tony, Ed. *Popular Fiction* . . . , 226–228.
Roth, Martin. "Mysteries of 'The Mystery of Marie Roget,' " *Poe Stud*, 22 (1989), 27–34.

"The Narrative of Arthur Gordon Pym"
Billy, Ted. "Providence and Chaos in 'The Narrative of Arthur "Goddin" Pym,' " *J Evolutionary Psych*, 9 (1989), 126–133.
Bock, Martin. *Crossing the Shadow-Line* . . . , 56–58.
Kronick, Joseph G. "Edgar Allan Poe . . . ," 33–34.
Lewis, Paul. "Poe's Humor . . . ," 539–541.
———. *Comic Effects* . . . , 135–136.
Paglia, Camille. *Sexual Personae* . . . , 579–580.
Pahl, Dennis. *Architects of the Abyss* . . . , 41–56.
Watkins, G. K. *God and Circumstance* . . . , 115–175.

"The Pit and the Pendulum"
Paglia, Camille. *Sexual Personae* . . . , 577–578.
Punter, David. "Edgar Allan Poe . . . ," 7–8; rpt. in his *The Romantic Unconscious* . . . , 156–157.

"The Power of Words"
Michael, John. "Narration and Reflection . . . ," 1–22.

"The Premature Burial"
Auerbach, Jonathan. *The Romance of Failure* . . . , 58–60.
Engel, Leonard W. "Claustrophobia, the Gothic Enclosure, and Poe," *Clues*, 10, ii (1989), 107–117.
Foster, Dennis A. "Re-Poe Man . . . ," 3–6.
Lewis, Paul. "Poe's Humor . . . ," 536.

"The Purloined Letter"
Blythe, Hal, and Charlie Sweet. "The Reader as Poe's Ultimate Dupe in 'The Purloined Letter,' " *Stud Short Fiction*, 26 (1989), 311–315.
Hull, Richard. " 'The Purloined Letter': Poe's Detective Story Versus Panoptic Foucaultian Theory," *Style*, 24 (1990), 201–214.
Jay, Gregory S. *America the Scrivener* . . . , 198–204.
Kronick, Joseph G. "Edgar Allan Poe . . . ," 27–33.
Limon, John. *The Place of Fiction* . . . , 101–104.

"The System of Dr. Tarr and Professor Fether"
Johansen, Ib. "The Madness of the Text . . . ," 6–7.

"A Tale of the Ragged Mountains"
Kopley, Richard. "Poe's *Pym*-Esque 'A Tale of the Ragged Mountains,' " in Fisher, Benjamin F., Ed. *Poe and His Times* . . . , 167–177.

"The Tell-Tale Heart"
Auerbach, Jonathan. *The Romance of Failure* . . . , 45–47.
Bynum, Paige M. " 'Observe How Healthily—How Calmly I Can Tell You the Whole Story': Moral Insanity and Edgar Allan Poe's 'The Tell-Tale Heart,' " in Amrine, Frederick, Ed. *Literature and Science* . . . , 141–152.
Foster, Dennis A. "Re-Poe Man . . . ," 6–7.
Sussman, Henry. "A Note on the Public and the Private in Literature: The Literature of 'Acting Out,' " *Mod Lang Notes*, 104 (1989), 597–611.

"The Unparalleled Adventures of One Hans Pfaall"
Bennett, Maurice J. " 'Visionary Wings': Art and Metamorphosis in Edgar Allan Poe's 'Hans Pfaall,' " in Fisher, Benjamin F., Ed. *Poe and His Times* . . . , 76–87.
Brody, Selma B. "The Source and Significance of Poe's Use of Axote in 'Hans Pfaall,' " *Sci-Fiction Stud*, 17, i (1990), 60–63.
Panshin, Alexel, and Cory Panshin. *The World Beyond* . . . , 33–35.

"Van Kempelen and His Discovery"
Auerbach, Jonathan. *The Romance of Failure* . . . , 67–70.

"William Wilson"
Auerbach, Jonathan. *The Romance of Failure* . . . , 76–79.
Manning, Susan. *The Puritan-Provincial Vision* . . . , 84–88.
Ware, Tracy. "The Two Stories of 'William Wilson,' " *Stud Short Fiction*, 26 (1989), 43–48.

"X-ing a Paragrab"
Perkins, Leroy, and Joseph A. Dupras. "Mystery and Meaning in Poe's 'X-ing a Paragrab,' " *Stud Short Fiction*, 27 (1990), 489–494.

FREDERIK POHL

"The Gold at the Starbow's End"
Pierce, John J. *Great Themes of Science Fiction* . . . , 31–32.

SYRIA POLETTI

"Bad Luck"
Schiminovich, Flora. "Two Argentine Female Writers Perfect the Art of Detection: María Angélica Bosco and Syria Poletti," *R*, 42, i (1990), 20.

"Red in the Salt Pit"
Schiminovich, Flora. "Two Argentine Female Writers . . . ," 19–20.

ELENA PONIATOWSKA

"Cine Prado"

Zielina, María. "La falsa percepción de la realidad en 'Cine Prado,' " in López González, Aralia, Amelia Malagamba, and Elena Urrutia, Eds. *Mujer y literatura* . . . , 87–91.

"Happiness"

Gold, Janet. "Feminine Space and the Discourse of Silence: Yolanda Oreamuno, Elena Poniatowska, and Luisa Valenzuela," in Valis, Noël, and Carol Maiser, Eds. *In the Feminine Mode* . . . , 199–200.

"The Inventory"

Poot Herrera, Sandra. "La 'Flor de Lis,' Códice y huella de Elena Poniatowska," in López González, Aralia, Amelia Malagamba, and Elena Urrutia, Eds. *Mujer y literatura* . . . , 101–104.

KATHERINE ANNE PORTER

"Flowering Judas"

Titus, Mary E. "The 'Booby Trap' of Love: Artist and Sadist in Katherine Anne Porter's Mexican Fiction," *J Mod Lit*, 16 (1990), 619–622.

"The Grave"

Cheatham, George. "Death and Repetition in Porter's Miranda Stories," *Am Lit*, 61 (1989), 612–617.

———. "The Rabbit and the Dove: Death and Repetition in Porter's 'The Grave,' " *Pubs Arkansas Philol Assoc*, 15 (1989), 166–175.

Erdim, Esim. "The Ring or the Dove: The New Woman in Katherine Anne Porter's Fiction," in Diedrich, Maria, and Dorothy F. Hornung, Eds. *Women and War* . . . , 58–61.

"The Jilting of Granny Weatherall"

Harder, Worth T. "Granny and Ivan: Katherine Anne Porter's Mirror for Tolstoy," *Renascence*, 42 (1990), 149–156.

Laman, Barbara. "Porter's 'The Jilting of Granny Weatherall,' " *Explicator*, 48 (1990), 279–281.

"The Lovely Legend"

Titus, Mary E. "The 'Booby Trap' of Love . . . ," 627–629.

"The Martyr"

Titus, Mary E. "The 'Booby Trap' of Love . . . ," 626–627.

"Old Mortality"

Cheatham, George. "Death and Repetition . . . ," 617–621.

Erdim, Esim. "The Ring or the Dove . . . ," 56–57.

Messent, Peter. "Continuity and Change in the Southern Novella," in Lee, A. Robert, Ed. *The Modern American Novella*, 126–131.

"Pale Horse, Pale Rider"

Cheatham, George. "Death and Repetition . . . ," 621–624.

"Theft"
Erdim, Esim. "The Ring or the Dove . . . ," 55–56.

"Virgin Violeta"
Titus, Mary E. "The 'Booby Trap' of Love . . . ," 623–626.

ESTELA PORTILLO TRAMBLEY

"The Burning"
Daghistany, Ann. "The Shaman, Light and Dark," in Dennis, Philip, and Wendell Aycock, Eds. *Literature and Anthropology*, 293–297.

CHAIM POTOK

"The Dark Place Inside"
Kremer, S. Lillian. *Witness Through Imagination* . . . , 301–302.

NANCY POTTER

"A Private Space"
Yahnke, Robert E., and Richard M. Eastman. *Aging in Literature* . . . , 59.

"A Short Vacation"
Yahnke, Robert E., and Richard M. Eastman. *Aging in Literature* . . . , 59.

JOE POYER

"Null Zone"
Franklin, H. Bruce. "The Vietnam War as American Science Fiction and Fantasy," *Sci-Fiction Stud*, 17 (1990), 344–345.

AUGUSTUS PRINCEPS

"A Man of Sentiment in the Mofussil"
Stilz, Gerhard. "Plain Tales before Kipling: Anglo-Indian Short Prose of the 1830s," in Stummer, Peter O., Ed. *The Story Must Be Told* . . . , 96.

ALEXANDER PROKHANOV

"The Grey Soldier"
Shneidman, N. N. *Soviet Literature* . . . , 152.

ROY L. PROSTERMAN

"Peace Probe"
Franklin, H. Bruce. "The Vietnam War as American Science Fiction and Fantasy," *Sci-Fiction Stud*, 17 (1990), 347–348.

BOLESLAW PRUS

"Lichens"
Eber, Irene. *Voices from Afar* . . . , 54.

"Outpost"
Eber, Irene. *Voices from Afar* . . . , 73.

ALEXANDER PUSHKIN

"The Coffinmaker"
Brown, William E. *A History* . . . *Romantic Period*, III, 207–208.

"Egyptian Nights"
Brown, William E. *A History* . . . *Romantic Period*, III, 211–212.

"Mistress into Maid"
Brown, William E. *A History* . . . *Romantic Period*, III, 206–207.

"The Queen of Spades"
Brown, William E. *A History* . . . *Romantic Period*, III, 218–224.
Chances, Ellen B. *Conformity's Children* . . . , 41–42.
Mersereau, John. "The Nineteenth Century: Romanticism, 1820–40," in Moser, Charles H., Ed. . . . *Russian Literature*, 175–177.

"The Shot"
Brown, William E. *A History* . . . *Romantic Period*, III, 201–203.
Davydov, Sergej. " 'The Shot' by Aleksandr Pushkin and Its Trajectories," in Clayton, J. Douglas, Ed. *Issues in Russian Literature* . . . , 62–74.
Mersereau, John. "The Nineteenth Century . . . ," 172–173.

"The Snowstorm"
Brown, William E. *A History* . . . *Romantic Period*, III, 203–204.

"The Stationmaster"
Brown, William E. *A History* . . . *Romantic Period*, III, 204–206.

THOMAS PYNCHON

"Entropy"
Dugdale, John. *Thomas Pynchon* . . . , 54–75.
Kuehl, John. *Alternate Worlds* . . . , 252–255.
Olster, Stacey. *Reminiscence* . . . , 102–103.
Slade, Joseph W. *Thomas Pynchon*, 15–22.

"Low-lands"
Slade, Joseph W. *Thomas Pynchon*, 8–15.

"Mortality and Mercy in Vienna"
Dugdale, John. *Thomas Pynchon* . . . , 17–37.
Olster, Stacey. *Reminiscence* . . . , 87–88.
Slade, Joseph W. *Thomas Pynchon*, 3–8.

"The Secret Integration"
Barnett, Stuart. "Refused Readings: Narrative and History in 'The Secret Integration,' " *Pynchon Notes*, 22–23 (Spring–Fall, 1988), 79–85.
Olster, Stacey. *Reminiscence* . . . , 77–78.
Slade, Joseph W. *Thomas Pynchon*, 22–27.

"The Small Rain"
Slade, Joseph W. *Thomas Pynchon*, 1–3.

"Under the Rose"
Dugdale, John. *Thomas Pynchon* . . . , 85–87.
Olster, Stacey. *Reminiscence* . . . , 79–80.
Zamora, Lois P. *Writing the Apocalypse* . . . , 55–56.

QIAN ZHONGSHU

"The Cat"
Slupski, Zbigniew. "Some Points of Contact Between *Rulin waishi* and Modern Chinese Fiction," in Malmqvist, Göran, Ed. *Modern Chinese Literature* . . . , 135–136.
———. "Qian Zhongshu," in Slupski, Zbigniew, Ed. *A Selective Guide* . . . , II, 145–146.

"Inspiration"
Slupski, Zbigniew. "Qian Zhongshu," 146–147.

QIU DONG-PING

"Below Maoshan"
Gotz, Michael. "The Pen as Sword: Wartime Stories of Qiu Dong-ping," in *La Littérature chinoise* . . . , 104–108.

ARTHUR QUILLER-COUCH

"The Roll-Call on the Reef"
Schork, R. J. "The Holy Word," *Stud Short Fiction*, 27 (1990), 603–604.

JOSÉ MARÍA DE QUINTO

"Atardecer sin tabernas"
Jordan, Barry. *Writing and Politics* . . . , 76.

"Noche de agosto"
Jordan, Barry. *Writing and Politics* . . . , 76.

"Noviembre en los huesos"
Jordan, Barry. *Writing and Politics* . . . , 75–76.

ELENA QUIROGA

"Plácida la joven"
Zatlin, Phyllis. "Childbirth with Fear: Bleeding to Death Softly," *Letras Femeninas*, 16, i–ii (1990), 39–41.

HORACIO QUIROGA

"The Dead Man"
McIntyre, John C. "Horacio Quiroga and Jack London Compared: 'A la deriva,' 'El hombre muerto,' and 'To Build a Fire,' " *New Comparison*, 7 (1989), 143–145.

"Drifting"
McIntyre, John C. "Horacio Quiroga and Jack London Compared . . . ," 143–159.

"La lengua"
Askeland, Jon. "Fantasía, juego y metáfora: Un estudio comparativo de 'La lengua' y de 'El Zapallo que se hizo cosmos,' " *Río de la Plata*, 4–6 (1987), 237–244.

JAN RABIE

"Drought"
Trump, Martin. "Afrikaner Literature and the South African Liberation Struggle," *J Commonwealth Lit*, 25, i (1990), 52–53.

"The Great Trek"
Trump, Martin. "Afrikaner Literature . . . ," 53–55.

"White on Black"
Trump, Martin. "Afrikaner Literature . . . ," 55.

ALEXANDER ZISKIND RABINOWITZ

"The Decree Has Been Rescinded"
Wallenrod, Reuben. . . . *Modern Israel*, 20–21.

"In the World of Creation"
Wallenrod, Reuben. . . . *Modern Israel*, 21–22.

RACHILDE [MARGUERITE VALETTE]

"L'Araignée de cristal"
Ziegler, Robert E. "Fantasies of Partial Selves in Rachilde's *Le Démon de l'absurde*," *Nineteenth-Century French Stud*, 19 (1990), 124–126.

"La Dent"
Ziegler, Robert E. "Fantasies of Partial Selves . . . ," 126–128.
"Le Mains"
Ziegler, Robert E. "Fantasies of Partial Selves . . . ," 128–129.

MANUEL RAMOS OTERO

"La última plena"
Mullen, Edward. "Interpreting Puerto Rico's Cultural Myths: Rosario Ferré and Manuel Ramos Otero," *Americas R*, 17, iii (1989), 94–96.

RAN IKUJIRO

"The Brainwave Controller"
Matthew, Robert. *Japanese Science Fiction* . . . , 35.

PAULO CELSO RANGEL

"Depoimento"
Simpson, Amelia S. *Detective Fiction* . . . , 164–167.

VALENTIN GRIGOREVICH RASPUTIN

"Baikal, Baikal"
Shneidman, N. N. *Soviet Literature* . . . , 105.
"I Can't"
Shneidman, N. N. *Soviet Literature* . . . , 103–104.
"Live and Love a Lifetime"
Polowy, Teresa. *The Novellas* . . . , 212–213.
"Natasha"
Polowy, Teresa. *The Novellas* . . . , 206–208.
Shneidman, N. N. *Soviet Literature* . . . , 107.
"What Shall I Tell the Crow?"
Polowy, Teresa. *The Novellas* . . . , 209–211.
"You Live and Love"
Shneidman, N. N. *Soviet Literature* . . . , 102–103.

AARON REUBENI

"At the Wall"
Wallenrod, Reuben. . . . *Modern Israel*, 23–24.

ALFONSO REYES

"La cena"
Ramirez L., Edelmira. "Lo fantastico en 'La cena,' " in *Asedio a Alfonso Reyes* . . . , 49–61.

WILLIAM HENRY RHODES

"The Case of Summerfield"
Panshin, Alexel, and Cory Panshin. *The World Beyond* . . . , 71–72.

JEAN RHYS [ELLA GWENDOLEN REES WILLIAMS]

"Goodbye Marcus, Goodbye Rose"
Morrell, A. C. "The World of Jean Rhys's Short Stories," in Frickey, Pierrette M., Ed. *Critical Perspectives* . . . , 96–98.

"I Used to Live Here Once"
Morrell, A. C. "The World . . . ," 100–101.

"In a Café"
Morrell, A. C. "The World . . . ," 95–96.

"Kikimora"
Angier, Carole. *Jean Rhys* . . . , 367–368.

"Let Them Call It Jazz"
Carrera Suárez, Isabel, and Esther Álvarez López. "Social and Personal Selves: Race, Gender, and Otherness in Rhys's 'Let Them Call It Jazz' and *Wide Sargasso Sea*," *Dutch Q R*, 20, ii (1990), 154–162.

"Susan and Suzanne"
Angier, Carole. *Jean Rhys* . . . , 166–169.

"Till September Petronella"
Angier, Carole. *Jean Rhys* . . . , 89–93.
Morrell, A. C. "The World . . . ," 98–100.

ALIFA RIFAAT

"Bahiyya's Eyes"
Nwachukwu-Agbada, J. O. J. "The Lifted Veil: Protest in Alifa Rifaat's Short Stories," *Int'l Fiction R*, 17 (1990), 108–109.

"Mansoura"
Nwachukwu-Agbada, J. O. J. "The Lifted Veil . . . ," 109.

"My World of the Unknown"
Nwachukwu-Agbada, J. O. J. "The Lifted Veil . . . ," 109.

AIDA RIVERA

"Love Among the Cornhusks"
Bernad, Miguel A. *Bamboo and the Greenwood Tree* . . . , 87–89.

TOMÁS RIVERA

". . . And the Earth Did Not Part"
Rodríguez, Alfonso. "Tomás Rivera: The Creation of the Chicano Experience in Fiction," in Lattin, Vernon R., Rolando Hinojosa, and Gary D. Keller, Eds. *Tomás Rivera, 1936–1984* . . . , 77–82.

"First Holy Communion"
Daydí-Tolson, Santiago. "Ritual and Religion in Tomás Rivera's Work," in Lattin, Vernon R., Rolando Hinojosa, and Gary D. Keller, Eds. *Tomás Rivera, 1936–1984* . . . , 146–147.
Rodríguez, Teresa B. "Nociones sobre el arte narrativo en '. . . *y no se lo trago la tierra'* de Tomás Rivera," in Lattin, Vernon R., Rolando Hinojosa, and Gary D. Keller, Eds. *Tomás Rivera, 1936–1984* . . . , 132–133.

"It Was a Silvery Night"
Saldívar, Ramón. *Chicano Narrative* . . . , 79–81.

"The Lost Year"
Daydí-Tolson, Santiago. "Ritual and Religion . . . ," 144.

"The Night of the Blackout"
Rodríguez, Teresa B. "Nociones . . . ," 133.

"The Salamanders"
Vallejos, Thomas. "The Beetfield as Battlefield: Ritual Process and Realization in Tomás Rivera's 'Las salamandras,' " *Americas R*, 17, ii (1989), 100–109.

"Under the House"
Daydí-Tolson, Santiago. "Ritual and Religion . . . ," 138.
Saldívar, Ramón. *Chicano Narrative* . . . , 88–90.

"When We Arrive"
Saldívar, Ramón. *Chicano Narrative* . . . , 86–88.

AUGUSTO ROA BASTOS

"Borrador de un informe"
Burgos, Fernando. " 'Borrador de un informe': Duplicidades de la escritura," *Anthropos*, 115 (1990), 51–54.

"Contar un cuento"
Horl, Sabine. "La forma como portador de significado: Acera de 'Contar un cuento,' " *Cuadernos Americanos*, 3 (1990), 77–85.

"Moriencia"
Barrientos, Juan José. "Un tema de Mauricio Magdaleno y Roa Bastos y un figura del relatos," in Neumeister, Sebastián, Ed. *Actas del IX Congreso* . . . , II, 457–461.

"The Sleepwalker"
Rama, Angel. "Más allá de *Yo el Supremo*: El escritor latinoamericano como traidor," *Escritura*, 12, xxiii–xxiv (1987), 249–262.

KEITH ROBERTS

"Brother John"
Ruddick, Nicholas. "Flaws in the Timestream: Unity and Disunity in Keith Roberts's Story-Cycles," *Foundation*, 45 (Spring, 1989), 43–44.

"Corfe Gate"
Ruddick, Nicholas. "Flaws in the Timestream . . . ," 45–46.

"The Lady Margaret"
Ruddick, Nicholas. "Flaws in the Timestream . . . ," 42–43.

"Lords and Ladies"
Ruddick, Nicholas. "Flaws in the Timestream . . . ," 44.

"The Signaller"
Ruddick, Nicholas. "Flaws in the Timestream . . . ," 43.

"The White Boat"
Ruddick, Nicholas. "Flaws in the Timestream . . . ," 44–45.

ALBERT ROBIDA

"War in the Twentieth Century"
Pierce, John J. *Foundations of Science Fiction* . . . , 53.

ALEJANDRO R. ROCES

"Of Cocks and Barratry"
Bernad, Miguel A. *Bamboo and the Greenwood Tree* . . . , 27–28.

"Of Cocks and Hens" [originally "My Brother's Peculiar Chicken"]
Bernad, Miguel A. *Bamboo and the Greenwood Tree* . . . , 26–27.

"We Filipinos Are Mild Drinkers"
Bernad, Miguel A. *Bamboo and the Greenwood Tree* . . . , 25–26.

ARGENIS RODRÍGUEZ

"Afuera el resplandor"
Ramos, Elías A. *El cuento venezolano* . . . , 93–94.

"El aire salvaje"
Ramos, Elías A. *El cuento venezolano . . .*, 91–92.

"Aquí-aquí, entre las breñas"
Ramos, Elías A. *El cuento venezolano . . .*, 92–93.

"Así fue como salimos de Mario"
Ramos, Elías A. *El cuento venezolano . . .*, 94–95.

"Con la mirada puesta"
Ramos, Elías A. *El cuento venezolano . . .*, 93.

"El derrumbe-historia de una caída"
Ramos, Elías A. *El cuento venezolano . . .*, 95.

JOSEFIN RODRÍGUEZ

"Transbordo en Sol"
Jordan, Barry. *Writing and Politics . . .*, 75.

"Voces Amigas"
Jordan, Barry. *Writing and Politics . . .*, 74–75.

IGNACIO RODRÍGUEZ GALVÁN

"La hija del oidor"
Pavón, Alfredo. "De la violencia en los modernistas," in Pavón, Alfredo, Ed. *Paquette: Cuento . . .*, 55–56.

"Manolito el pisaverda"
Pavón, Alfredo. "De la violencia . . .," 56–57.

LEON ROOKE

"The Birth Control King of the Upper Volta"
Spriet, Pierre. "La Construction de l'indécidable dans une nouvelle de Leon Rooke," *Recherches Anglaises et Nord-Américaines*, 20 (1987), 137–146.

"The Blue Baby"
Kaltembach, Michèle. "A Man Locked Up in a Freezer: A Reading of Leon Rooke's Story 'The Blue Baby,' " *Commonwealth Essays & Studs*, 12, i (1989), 54–59.

"Dirty Heels of the Fine Young Children"
Pitavy-Souques, Danièle. "Tissu de Rêve/Tissé de Rêves: *A Bolt of White Cloth*," *Recherches Anglaises et Nord-Américaines*, 20 (1987), 132–133.

"Saks Fifth Avenue"
Pitavy-Souques, Danièle. "Tissu de Rêve/Tissé de Rêves . . .," 130–131.

"Why the Heathens Are No More"
Pitavy-Souques, Danièle. "Tissu de Rêve/Tissé de Rêves . . . , 129–130.

JOÃO GUIMARÃES ROSA

"The Third Bank of the River"
Banãles, Victoria. "Diversidad y congruencia: Los ríos de Rulfo, Benét, Guimarães Rosa y Hesse," *Romance Lang Annual*, 1 (1989), 376–377.

JULIO H. ROSALES

"Iban tres rapaces por el sendero"
Ratcliff, Dillwyn F. *Venezuelan Prose Fiction*, 112–113.

ANNE F. ROSNER

"Prize Tomatoes"
Yahnke, Robert E., and Richard M. Eastman. *Aging in Literature* . . . , 60.

SARAH ROSSITER

"Civil War"
Yahnke, Robert E., and Richard M. Eastman. *Aging in Literature* . . . , 60–61.

"Star Light, Star Bright"
Yahnke, Robert E., and Richard M. Eastman. *Aging in Literature* . . . , 61.

PHILIP ROTH

"The Conversion of the Jews"
Baumgarten, Murray, and Barbara Gottfried. *Understanding Philip Roth*, 42–47.

"Defender of the Faith"
Baumgarten, Murray, and Barbara Gottfried. *Understanding Philip Roth*, 48–51.

"Eli the Fanatic"
Baumgarten, Murray, and Barbara Gottfried. *Understanding Philip Roth*, 54–58.
Gittleman, Sol. "The Pecks of Woodenton, Long Island, Thirty Years Later: Another Look at 'Eli the Fanatic,' " *Stud Am Jewish Lit*, 8, ii (1989), 138–142.

"Goodbye, Columbus"
Baumgarten, Murray, and Barbara Gottfried. *Understanding Philip Roth*, 21–42.

"The Prague Orgy"
Baumgarten, Murray, and Barbara Gottfried. *Understanding Philip Roth*, 192–200.

ARTURO BELLEZA ROTOR

"At Last This Fragrance"
Cruz, Isagani R. "Illusion and the Inner Cell: A Critical Analysis of the Later Stories of Arturo B. Rotor," *Philippine Stud*, 18 (1970), 758–761.

"Because I Did Not Ask"
CoSeteng, Alice M. L. "A. B. Rotor and His Place in Philippine Literature," *Diliman R*, 6 (1958), 285–286.
Cruz, Isagani R. "Illusion and the Inner Cell . . . ," 765–767.

"Convict's Twilight"
CoSeteng, Alice M. L. "A. B. Rotor and His Place . . . ," 282–283.
Cruz, Isagani R. "Illusion and the Inner Cell . . . ," 763–765.
Grow, L. M. "Distillation and Essence: The Coherent Universe of Arturo B. Rotor," *Pilipinas*, 13 (Fall, 1989), 14–15.
Cruz, Isagani R. "Illusion and the Inner Cell . . . ," 757–758.

"Dahong-Palay"
CoSeteng, Alice M. L. "A. B. Rotor and His Place . . . ," 283–284.

"Dance Music"
CoSeteng, Alice M. L. "A. B. Rotor and His Place . . . ," 289–290.
Grow, L. M. "Distillation . . . ," 8–9.

"Deny the Mockery"
CoSeteng, Alice M. L. "A. B. Rotor and His Place . . . ," 280–282.
Cruz, Isagani R. "Illusion and the Inner Cell . . . ," 761–763.
Grow, L. M. "Distillation . . . ," 12–13.

"Flower Shop"
CoSeteng, Alice M. L. "A. B. Rotor and His Place . . . ," 284–285.
Grow, L. M. "Distillation . . . ," 9–10.

"How They Transferred the Convicts to Davao"
CoSeteng, Alice M. L. "A. B. Rotor and His Place . . . ," 278–280.
Cruz, Isagani R. "Illusion and the Inner Cell . . . ," 756–757.
Grow, L. M. "Distillation . . . ," 11–12.

"Kingdom by the Sea"
Grow, L. M. "Distillation . . . ," 5–7.

"Zita"
CoSeteng, Alice M. L. "A. B. Rotor and His Place . . . ," 287–289.
Grow, L. M. "Distillation . . . ," 4–5.

ROU SHI

"The Story of 'Man-Devil' and His Wife"
Bordahl, Vibeke. "Rou Shi," in Slupski, Zbigniew, Ed. *A Selective Guide* . . . , II, 150–151.

RU ZHIJUAN [JU CHIH-CHÜAN]

"Lilies"
Hegel, Robert E. "Political Integration in Ru Zhijuan's 'Lilies,' " in Huters, Theodore, Ed. . . . *Modern Chinese Short Story*, 92–104.

JUAN RULFO

"Anacleto Morones"
Jiménez de Báez, Yvette. "Destrucción de los mitos—posibilidad de la Historia?—*El llano en llamas* de Juan Rulfo," in Neumeister, Sebastián, Ed. *Actas del IX Congreso* . . . , II, 584.

"The Burning Plain"
Jiménez de Báez, Yvette. "Destrucción de los mitos . . . ," 577–581.

"The Hill of the *Comadres*"
Acker, Bertie. *El cuento mexicano contemporaneo* . . . , 18–19.

"Luvina"
Jiménez de Báez, Yvette. "Destrucción de los mitos . . . ," 583.

"Macario"
Jiménez de Báez, Yvette. "Destrucción de los mitos . . . ," 580–581.
Szanto, George. "Mediation by Place: Juan Rulfo's 'Macario' and Hugh Garner's 'The Yellow Sweater,' " in Bauer, Roger, et al. [10], Eds. *Proceedings of the XIIth Congress* . . . , II, 71–76.
Vidal Ortiz, Guillermo. "El punto de vista en dos cuentos de Juan Rulfo," *Universidad*, 232 [n.d.], 179–183.

"No Dogs Bark"
Jiménez de Báez, Yvette. "Destrucción de los mitos . . . ," 583–584.
Katra, William H. " 'No oyes ladrar los perros': La excepcionalidad y el fracaso," *Revista Iberoamericana*, 56 (1990), 181–191.
Lasarte, Pedro. " 'No oyes ladrar los perros' de Juan Rulfo: Peregrinaje hacia el origen," *Inti*, 29–30 (Spring-Fall, 1989), 101–118.
Vidal Ortiz, Guillermo. "El punto de vista . . . ," 179–183.

"Talpa"
Acker, Bertie. *El cuento mexicano contemporaneo* . . . , 21–22.

"They Gave Us the Land"
Jiménez de Báez, Yvette. "Destrucción de los mitos . . . ," 581.

"We Are Very Poor"
Banãles, Victoria. "Diversidad y congruencia: Los ríos de Rulfo, Benét, Guimarães Rosa y Hesse," *Romance Lang Annual*, 1 (1989), 373–374.

JOANNA RUSS

"The Adventuress"
Spencer, Kathleen L. "Rescuing the Female Child: The Fiction of Joanna Russ," *Sci-Fiction Stud*, 17 (1990), 168–169.

"The Autobiography of My Mother"
Spencer, Kathleen L. "Rescuing the Female Child . . . ," 176–177.

"The Little Dirty Girl"
Spencer, Kathleen L. "Rescuing the Female Child . . . ," 180–182.

"The Second Inquisition"
Spencer, Kathleen L. "Rescuing the Female Child . . . ," 171–172.

"When It Changed"
Allman, John. "Motherless Creation: Motifs in Science Fiction," *No Dakota Q*, 58, ii (1990), 131.

SAKI [HECTOR HUGH MUNRO]

"Esmé"
Salemi, Joseph S. "An Asp Lurking in an Apple-Charlotte: Animal Violence in Saki's *The Chronicles of Clovis*," *Stud Short Fiction*, 26 (1989), 425–426.

"Ministers of Grace"
Salemi, Joseph S. "An Asp Lurking . . . ," 429.

"The Music on the Hill"
Salemi, Joseph S. "An Asp Lurking . . . ," 427–428.

"Sredni Vashtar"
Salemi, Joseph S. "An Asp Lurking . . . ," 426–427.

"Tobermory"
Salemi, Joseph S. "An Asp Lurking . . . ," 426.

J. D. SALINGER

"Franny"
Seed, David. "Keeping It in the Family: The Novellas of J. D. Salinger," in Lee, A. Robert, Ed. *The Modern American Novella*, 142–149.

"Hapworth 16, 1924"
Seed, David. "Keeping It in the Family . . . ," 158–159.

"Pretty Mouth and Green My Eyes"
Happe, François. "Signe et production du sens dans 'Pretty Mouth and Green My Eyes' de J. D. Salinger," *Revue Française d'Études Américaines*, 13, xxxvii (July, 1988), 227–234.

"Raise High the Roofbeam, Carpenters"
Seed, David. "Keeping It in the Family . . . ," 154–156.

"Seymour: An Introduction"
Seed, David. "Keeping It in the Family . . . ," 157–158.

"Zooey"
Seed, David. "Keeping It in the Family . . . ," 149–153.

ANDREW SALKEY

"The Rains Will Come"
Cobham, Rhonda. "The *Caribbean Voice* Programme and the Development of West Indian Short Fiction: 1945–1958," in Stummer, Peter O., Ed. *The Story Must Be Told* . . . , 152.

VICKI SALLOUM

"Sitty Victoria"
Yahnke, Robert E., and Richard M. Eastman. *Aging in Literature* . . . , 61–62.

ISHAK SAMOKOVLIJA

"The Sarajevo Megilla"
Bertram, Carèl. "*Kafana Konak Čaršija Ćuprija* (Perception of Place in Ottoman Bosnia): Literary Narrative as an Art-Historical Resource," *Turkish Stud Assoc Bull*, 14 (1990), 171–172.

ELENA SANTIAGO

"Cada invierno"
Cortés, Eladio. "Los cuentos de Elena Santiago: temática y técnica," in Fernández Jiménez, Juan, José J. Labrador Herraiz, and L. Teresa Valdivieso, Eds. *Estudios en homenaje* . . . , 110–111.

"Un cuento pequeño hábito de penumbra"
Cortés, Eladio. "Los centos de Elena Santiago . . . ," 112–113.

"Hacia un camino"
Cortés, Eladio. "Los cuentos de Elena Santiago . . . ," 111–112.

"Una mujer vulgar de insomnios amarillos"
Cortés, Eladio. "Los cuentos de Elena Santiago . . . ," 113–114.

"Una noche llena de agujeros"
Cortés, Eladio. "Los cuentos de Elena Santiago . . . ," 107–108.

"La última puerta"
Cortés, Eladio. "Los cuentos de Elena Santiago . . . ," 109–110.

FERNÁNDEZ SANTOS

"Cabeza Rapada"
Jordan, Barry. *Writing and Politics* . . . , 72–73.

"Hombres"
Jordan, Barry. *Writing and Politics* . . . , 73.

"El Sargento"
Jordan, Barry. *Writing and Politics* . . . , 73.

VILAS SARANG

"Bajarang the Great Indian Bustard"
Badve, V. V. "Vilas Sarang as Short Story Writer: An Assessment," *Quest*, 84 (1990), 342.

"The Departure"
Badve, V. V. "Vilas Sarang . . . ," 341.

"An Excursion"
Badve, V. V. "Vilas Sarang . . . ," 339–340.

"Flies"
Badve, V. V. "Vilas Sarang . . . ," 340–341.

"History Is on Our Side"
Badve, V. V. "Vilas Sarang . . . ," 339.

"An Interview with M. Chakko"
Badve, V. V. "Vilas Sarang . . . ," 346–347.

"Letters from Nikhil"
Badve, V. V. "Vilas Sarang . . . ," 345.

"The Life and Death of Manu"
Badve, V. V. "Vilas Sarang . . . ," 345.

"On the Stone Steps"
Badve, V. V. "Vilas Sarang . . . ," 341–342.

"The Phonemate"
Badve, V. V. "Vilas Sarang . . . ," 342–343.

"A Revolt of the Gods"
Badve, V. V. "Vilas Sarang . . . ," 345–346.

"The Tree of Death"
Badve, V. V. "Vilas Sarang . . . ," 343–344.

FRANK SARGESON

"The Hole That Jack Dug"
Jensen, Kai. "Holes, Wholeness and Holiness in Frank Sargeson's Writing," *Landfall*, 44, i (1990), 32–44.

JOSÉ SARNEY

"Beatinho do Mãe de Deus"
Silverman, Malcolm. "Satire in the Regionalist Stories of José Sarney," *Romance Q*, 36 (1989), 94.

"História de Dona Cota"
Silverman, Malcolm. "Satire . . . ," 88–89.
"Joaquim, José, Margarido, filhos do relho Antão"
Silverman, Malcolm. "Satire . . . ," 92–93.
"Merícia do riacho bem-querer"
Silverman, Malcolm. "Satire . . . ," 90.

JEAN-PAUL SARTRE

"The Childhood of a Leader"
Leak, Andrew N. *The Perverted Consciousness* . . . , 80–81, 117, 119.
"Erostratus"
Bellemin-Noël, Jean. "Le Diamant noir: Echographie d' 'Erostrate,' " *Littérature*, 64 (December, 1986), 71–89.
"Intimacy"
Leak, Andrew N. *The Perverted Consciousness* . . . , 31–32.
"The Room"
Bellemin-Noël, Jean. "Derrière 'La Chambre' dans la fabrique d'un délice," *Temps Modernes*, 46 (1990), 665–683.
"The Wall"
Argyros, Alexander J. "The Sense of an Ending: Sartre's 'The Wall,' " *Mod Lang Stud*, 18, iii (1988), 46–52.

REG SAUNDERS

"Parabah the Shark"
Bosse-Bearlin, Jenny. "Black-White Relations in the Contemporary Black and White Short Story in Australia," in Stummer, Peter O., Ed. *The Story Must Be Told* . . . , 166.
"Tragedy at the Ridge"
Bosse-Bearlin, Jenny. "Black-White Relations . . . ," 166.

RIMANTAS ŠAVELIS

"The Heart of Spangis"
Silbajoris, Rimvydas. "Socialist Realism and Fantastic Reality in Recent Soviet Lithuanian Prose," in Mandelker, Amy, and Robert Reeder, Eds. *The Supernatural* . . . , 305–307.
"The Ladder"
Silbajoris, Rimvydas. "Socialist Realism . . . ," 307–308.

DOROTHY L. SAYERS

"The House of the Poplars"
Christopher, Joe R. "Three 'Unknown' Stories—Two of Them Unpublished—by Dorothy Sayers," *Mystery Fancier*, 11, i (1989), 17–18.

"The Incredible Elopement of Lord Peter Wimsey"
Leonardi, Susan J. *Dangerous by Degrees* . . . , 101–106.

"The Leopard Lady"
Christopher, Joe R. "Three 'Unknown' Stories . . . ," 17.

"The Travelling Rug"
Christopher, Joe R. "Three 'Unknown' Stories . . . ," 18–19.

JOHN SAYLES

"At the Anarchists' Convention"
Yahnke, Robert E., and Richard M. Eastman. *Aging in Literature* . . . , 62–63.

ARTHUR SCHNITZLER

"Doktor Gräsler, Badearzt"
Thompson, Bruce. *Schnitzler's Vienna* . . . , 78–79.

"Flight into Darkness"
Thompson, Bruce. *Schnitzler's Vienna* . . . , 40–43.

"Frau Beate and Her Son"
Thompson, Bruce. *Schnitzler's Vienna* . . . , 46–48.

"Frau Berta Garland"
Thompson, Bruce. *Schnitzler's Vienna* . . . , 71–75.

"Fräulein Else"
Segal, Naomi. " 'Style indirect libre' to Stream-of-Consciousness: Flaubert, Joyce, Schnitzler," in Collier, Peter, and Judy Davies, Eds. *Modernism* . . . , 103–105.
Thompson, Bruce. *Schnitzler's Vienna* . . . , 43–46.

"Die Fremde"
Thompson, Bruce. *Schnitzler's Vienna* . . . , 33–35.

"Lieutenant Gustl"
Donahue, William C. "The Role of the *Oratorium* in Schnitzler's 'Leutnant Gustl': Divine and Decadent," *New Germ R*, 5–6 (1989–1990), 29–42.
Segal, Naomi. " 'Style indirect libre' . . . ," 103–105.
Thompson, Bruce. *Schnitzler's Vienna* . . . , 137–141.

"Rhapsody"
Thompson, Bruce. *Schnitzler's Vienna* . . . , 48–52.

"The Second"
Martens, Lorna. "A Dream Narrative: Schnitzler's 'Der Sekundant,' " *Mod Austrian Lit*, 23, i (1990), 1–17.
Thompson, Bruce. *Schnitzler's Vienna* . . . , 119–121.

OLIVE SCHREINER

"The Buddhist Priest's Wife"
Showalter, Elaine. *Sexual Anarchy* . . . , 57–58.

"Dream Life and Real Life"
Berkman, Joyce A. *The Healing Imagination* . . . , 216–217.

"A Dream of Wild Bees"
Christman, Laura. "Allegory, Feminist Thought and the *Dreams* of Olive Schreiner," in Brown, Tony, Ed. . . . *Late Victorian Realism*, 145–146.

"The Great Heart of England"
Berkman, Joyce A. *The Healing Imagination* . . . , 215–216.

"In a Ruined Chapel"
Christman, Laura. "Allegory . . . ," 143–145.

"The Sunlight Lay Across My Bed"
Christman, Laura. "Allegory . . . ," 146–148.

"Three Dreams in a Desert"
Christman, Laura. "Allegory . . . ," 141–143.

"Who Knocks at the Door?"
Berkman, Joyce A. *The Healing Imagination* . . . , 216.

HELGA SCHUBERT

"Das verbotene Zimmer"
Reid, J. H. *Writing Without Taboos* . . . , 20–21.

ADAM SCHWARTZ

"The Grammar of Love"
Larriere, Claire. " 'The Grammar of Love': In Search of New Rules," *J Short Story Engl*, 13 (Autumn, 1989), 67–75.

SANDRA SCOFIELD

"Loving Leo"
Yahnke, Robert E., and Richard M. Eastman. *Aging in Literature* . . . , 63.

WALTER SCOTT

"The Highland Widow"
Riese, Teut A. "Sir Walter Scott as a Master of the Short Tale," in Bauer, Gero, Franz K. Stanzel, and Franz Zaic, Eds. *Festschrift: Prof. Dr. Herbert Koziol* . . . , 259–261.

"The Two Drovers"
Riese, Teut A. "Sir Walter Scott . . . ," 262–264.

SHA DING [same as SHA TING or YANG TONGFAN or YANG CHENFANG]

"Deputy Magistrate of the County"
Anderson, Marston. *The Limits . . .*, 191–192.

"In the Aromara Teahouse"
Wong Kam-ming. "Animals in a Teahouse: The Art of Sha Ting," *La Littérature chinoise . . .*, 249–254.
———. "Sha Ding," in Slupski, Zbigniew, Ed. *A Selective Guide . . .*, II, 152–153.

"In the Family Temple"
Wong Kam-ming. "Animals in a Teahouse . . . ," 249.
———. "Sha Ding," 156.

"Magnet"
Anderson, Marston. *The Limits . . .*, 192–193.

"Scenes from Kanchajia"
Wong Kam-ming. "Sha Ding," 158.

"Spring Dawn"
Wong Kam-ming. "Sha Ding," 158–159.

"Voyage Beyond Law"
Wong Kam-ming. "Animals in a Teahouse . . . ," 246–249.

"The Way of the Beast"
Wong, Kam-ming. "Animals in a Teahouse . . . ," 249–254.
———. "Sha Ding," 155–156.

BOB SHACOCHIS

"Where Pelham Fell"
Yahnke, Robert E., and Richard M. Eastman. *Aging in Literature . . .*, 64.

NATHAN SHAHAM

"The Seven"
Ramras-Rauch, Gila. *The Arab . . .*, 106–108.

YITZHAK SHAMI

"Jum'ah the Fool"
Ramras-Rauch, Gila. *The Arab . . .*, 29–30.

"The Vengeance of the Fathers"
Ramras-Rauch, Gila. *The Arab* . . . , 31–33.

SHAO QUANLIN

"The Hero"
Wedell-Wedellsborg, Anne. "Shao Quanlin," in Slupski, Zbigniew, Ed. *A Selective Guide* . . . , II, 160–161.

LAMED SHAPIRO

"White *Challah*"
Roskies, David G. "The Self Under Siege," in Roskies, David G., Ed. *The Literature of Destruction* . . . , 246.

VERA SHASHI

"The Unrepentant"
Riemenschneider, Dieter. "Indian Women Writing in English: The Short Story," in Stummer, Peter O., Ed. *The Story Must Be Told* . . . , 175–176.

ROBIN SHEINER

"The Call of the Magpie"
Bosse-Bearlin, Jenny. "Black-White Relations in the Contemporary Black and White Short Story in Australia," in Stummer, Peter O., Ed. *The Story Must Be Told* . . . , 167–169.

MARY WOLLSTONECRAFT SHELLEY

"The Evil Eye"
Roberts, Marie. *Gothic Immortality* . . . , 95.

"The Mortal Immortal"
Roberts, Marie. *Gothic Immortality* . . . , 87–92.

"Roger Dodsworth"
Roberts, Marie. *Gothic Immortality* . . . , 92–94.

"Transformation"
Roberts, Marie. *Gothic Immortality* . . . , 94–95.

"Valerius: The Reanimated Roman"
Roberts, Marie. *Gothic Immortality* . . . , 92.

SHEN CONGWEN [SHEN TS'UNG-WEN]

"After Entering the Ranks"
Kinkley, Jeffrey. "Shen Congwen," in Slupski, Zbigniew, Ed. *A Selective Guide . . .*, II, 163–164.

"Camp Messenger"
Kinkley, Jeffrey. "Shen Congwen," 164.

"The Guileless One"
Kinkley, Jeffrey. "Shen Congwen," 168.

"Long Zhu"
Kinkley, Jeffrey. "Shen Congwen," 174.

"My Education"
Martin, Helmut. "Shen Congwen," in Slupski, Zbigniew, Ed. *A Selective Guide . . .*, II, 169–170.

"Portrait of Eight Steeds"
Kinkley, Jeffrey. "Shen Congwen," 173–174.

"Spring"
Kinkley, Jeffrey. "Shen Congwen," 172–173.

SHEN RONG

"An Abnormal Woman"
Larson, Wendy. "Women, Writers, Social Reform: Issues in Shen Rong's Fiction," in Duke, Michael S., Ed. *Modern Chinese Women Writers . . .*, 176–177.

"At Middle Age"
Larson, Wendy. "Women, Writers . . . ," 182–184.

"The Moonlight of Wanwan"
Larson, Wendy. "Women, Writers . . . ," 176.

"A Rose-Colored Dinner"
Larson, Wendy. "Women, Writers . . . ," 177–178.

"Scattered People"
Larson, Wendy. "Women, Writers . . . ," 178–179, 185.

"Spring Forever"
Larson, Wendy. "Women, Writers . . . ," 180–182.

"A Troublesome Sunday"
Larson, Wendy. "Women, Writers . . . ," 179.

"True True, False False"
Larson, Wendy. "Women, Writers . . . ," 184–185.

"Wide-Screen Technicolor"
Larson, Wendy. "Women, Writers . . . ," 185–186.

"Yang Yueyue and the Study of Sartre"
Larson, Wendy. "Women, Writers . . . ," 186–190.

ISAAC SHENBERG

"The Seven Who Left"
Wallenrod, Reuben. . . . *Modern Israel*, 220–221.

YITZHAK SHENHAR

"The Tamarisk"
Ramras-Rauch, Gila. *The Arab* . . . , 47–49.

LUCIUS SHEPHARD

"Delta Sly Honey"
Franklin, H. Bruce. "The Vietnam War as American Science Fiction and Fantasy," *Sci-Fiction Stud*, 17 (1990), 350.

"Mengele"
Franklin, H. Bruce. "The Vietnam War . . . ," 353.

SHI TUO [same as LU FEN or WANG CHANGJIAN]

"Baishun Street"
Ma Sen. "Shi Tuo," in Slupski, Zbigniew, Ed. *A Selective Guide* . . , II, 180.

"The Head"
Slupski, Zbigniew. "Shi Tuo," in Slupski, Zbigniew, Ed. *A Selective Guide* . . . , II, 175–176.

"A Kiss"
Huters, Theodore. "The Telling of Shi Tuo's 'A Kiss': Few Words and Several Voices," in Huters, Theodore, Ed. . . . *Modern Chinese Short Story*, 74–91.

"The Sufferer"
Ma Sen. "Shi Tuo," 179–180.

"The Underdog"
Slupski, Zbigniew. "Shi Tuo," 177–178.

"The Valley"
Slupski, Zbigniew. "Shi Tuo," 176–177.

SHI ZHICUN [QING PING]

"The Family Tomb"
Gálik, Marián. "On the Social and Literary Context in Modern Chinese Literature of the 1920's and 1930's," in Malmqvist, Göran, Ed. *Modern Chinese Literature* . . . , 29–32.

CAROL SHIELDS

"Mrs. Turner Cutting the Grass"
Vauthier, Simone. "On Carol Shields's 'Mrs. Turner Cutting the Grass,' " *Commonwealth Essays & Studs*, 11, ii (1989), 63–74.

SHIH T'O

"Song of the Forward March"
Hsia, C. T. "Residual Femininity: Women in Chinese Communist Fiction," in Birch, Cyril, Ed. *Chinese Communist Literature*, 165.
Wilhelm, Hellmut. "The Image of Youth and Age in Chinese Communist Literature," in Birch, Cyril, Ed. *Chinese Communist Literature*, 196–197.

LEWIS SHINER

"The War at Home"
Franklin, H. Bruce. "The Vietnam War as American Science Fiction and Fantasy," *Sci-Fiction Stud*, 17 (1990), 353.

SHIRA MASAYUKI

"The Experiment of Mr. Jamaica"
Matthew, Robert. *Japanese Science Fiction* . . . , 28.

HENRYK SIENKIEWICZ

"Be Blessed"
Eber, Irene. *Voices from Afar* . . . , 53.

"Sachem"
Eber, Irene. *Voices from Afar* . . . , 55–56.

LESLIE MARMON SILKO

"Lullaby"
Roberts, Edgar V., and Henry E. Jacobs. *Instructor's Manual* . . . , 2nd ed., 87–88.

ALAN SILLITOE

"The Good Woman"
Hitchcock, Peter. *Working-Class Fiction* . . . , 45–55.

"The Loneliness of the Long-Distance Runner"
Hitchcock, Peter. *Working-Class Fiction* . . . , 102–103.

CLIFFORD D. SIMAK

"Desertion"
Lomax, William. "The 'Invisible Alien' in the Science Fiction of Clifford Simak," *Extrapolation*, 30 (1989), 133.
Panshin, Alexel, and Cory Panshin. *The World Beyond* . . . , 620–622.

"Shadow Show"
Lomax, William. "The 'Invisible Alien' . . . ," 140–143.

CLIVE SINCLAIR

"The Creature of My Book"
Sicher, Efraim. "The Burden of Remembrance: Second Generation Literature," *Jewish Book Forum*, 45 (1990), 35–36.

ISAAC BASHEVIS SINGER

"Altele"
Alexander, Edward. *Isaac Bashevis Singer* . . . , 59–60.
"The Beggar Said So"
Alexander, Edward. *Isaac Bashevis Singer* . . . , 49–50.
"The Black Wedding"
Alexander, Edward. *Isaac Bashevis Singer* . . . , 18–19.
"The Blasphemer"
Alexander, Edward. *Isaac Bashevis Singer* . . . , 47–48.
"Blood"
Alexander, Edward. *Isaac Bashevis Singer* . . . , 60–62.
"The Cafeteria"
Alexander, Edward. *Isaac Bashevis Singer* . . . , 73–74.
Kremer, S. Lillian. *Witness Through Imagination* . . . , 203–204.
"Caricature"
Alexander, Edward. *Isaac Bashevis Singer* . . . , 58–59.
"Cockadoodledoo"
Alexander, Edward. *Isaac Bashevis Singer* . . . , 68–69.
"The Colony"
Alexander, Edward. *Isaac Bashevis Singer* . . . , 12–13.
"The Destruction of Kreshev"
Alexander, Edward. *Isaac Bashevis Singer* . . . , 38–39.
"The Gentleman from Cracow"
Alexander, Edward. *Isaac Bashevis Singer* . . . , 36–38.
"Gimpel the Fool"
Alexander, Edward. *Isaac Bashevis Singer* . . . , 50–52.
"Hanka"
Kremer, S. Lillian. *Witness Through Imagination* . . . , 203.

"Henne Fire"
Alexander. Edward. *Isaac Bashevis Singer* . . . , 24–25.

"Jachid and Jechidah"
Alexander, Edward. *Isaac Bashevis Singer* . . . , 14–15.

"Joy"
Alexander, Edward. *Isaac Bashevis Singer* . . . , 44–45.

"The Last Demon"
Alexander, Edward. *Isaac Bashevis Singer* . . . , 11–13.
Roskies, David F. "Broken Tablets," in Roskies, David G., Ed. *The Literature of Destruction* . . . , 567–568.

"The Lecture"
Alexander, Edward. *Isaac Bashevis Singer* . . . , 71–73.

"The Letter Writer"
Alexander, Edward. *Isaac Bashevis Singer* . . . , 73.

"The Little Shoemaker"
Alexander, Edward. *Isaac Bashevis Singer* . . . , 31–34.

"The Mentor"
Kremer, S. Lillian. *Witness Through Imagination* . . . , 202–203.

"The New Year Party"
Alexander, Edward. *Isaac Bashevis Singer* . . . , 9–10.

"Old Love"
Yahnke, Robert E., and Richard M. Eastman. *Aging in Literature* . . . , 64–65.

"The Old Man"
Alexander, Edward. *Isaac Bashevis Singer* . . . , 29–30.

"Passion"
Alexander, Edward. *Isaac Bashevis Singer* . . . , 21–23.

"A Piece of Advice"
Alexander, Edward. *Isaac Bashevis Singer* . . . , 26–27.

"The Plagiarist"
Alexander, Edward. *Isaac Bashevis Singer* . . . , 25–26.

"The Primper"
Alexander, Edward. *Isaac Bashevis Singer* . . . , 23–24.

"Property"
Alexander, Edward. *Isaac Bashevis Singer* . . . , 41–42.

"The Riddle"
Alexander, Edward. *Isaac Bashevis Singer* . . . , 59.

"Sabbath in Portugal"
Alexander, Edward. *Isaac Bashevis Singer* . . . , 43–44.

"The Shadow of a Crib"
Alexander, Edward. *Isaac Bashevis Singer* . . . , 28–29, 56–57.

"Shiddah and Kuzibah"
Alexander, Edward. *Isaac Bashevis Singer* . . . , 16–17.

"Short Friday"
Alexander, Edward. *Isaac Bashevis Singer* . . . , 54–55.
Eppich, Linda N. "Isaac Bashevis Singer's 'Short Friday': Parallelism and Chiasmus in Happily-Ever-Aftering," *Stud Short Fiction*, 27 (1990), 357–363.

"The Slaughterer"
Alexander, Edward. *Isaac Bashevis Singer* . . . , 66–68.

"Something Is There"
Alexander, Edward. *Isaac Bashevis Singer* . . . , 45–47.

"The Son"
Alexander, Edward. *Isaac Bashevis Singer* . . . , 40–41, 70–71.

"The Spinoza of Market Street"
Alexander, Edward. *Isaac Bashevis Singer* . . . , 55–56.

"Three Encounters"
Alexander, Edward. *Isaac Bashevis Singer* . . . , 7–8.

"Two Markets"
Alexander, Edward. *Isaac Bashevis Singer* . . . , 30–31.

"The Unseen"
Alexander, Edward. *Isaac Bashevis Singer* . . . , 57–58.

"The Warehouse"
Alexander, Edward. *Isaac Bashevis Singer* . . . , 15–16.

"A Wedding in Brownsville"
Alexander, Edward. *Isaac Bashevis Singer* . . . , 75.
Kremer, S. Lillian. *Witness Through Imagination* . . . , 204–205.

"Yentl the Yeshiva Boy"
Alexander, Edward. *Isaac Bashevis Singer* . . . , 62–64.

"Zeidlus the Pope"
Alexander, Edward. *Isaac Bashevis Singer* . . . , 48–49.

BARTHO SMIT

"I Reclaim My Country"
Trump, Martin. "Afrikaner Literature and the South African Liberation Struggle," *J Commonwealth Lit*, 25, i (1990), 50–51.

CORDWAINER SMITH [PAUL MYRON ANTHONY LINEBARGER]

"Dead Lady of Clown Town"
Roberts, Thomas J. *An Aesthetics* . . . , 136–139.

"Scanners Live in Vain"
Huntington, John. *Rationalizing Genius* . . . , 85–88.

PAULINE SMITH

"The Doctor"
Driver, Dorothy. "God, Fathers, and White South Africans: The World of Pauline Smith," in Clayton, Cherry, Ed. *Women and Writing* . . . , 89–90.

"The Schoolmaster"
Driver, Dorothy. "God, Fathers . . . ," 90–91.

OREST MIKHAILOVICH SOMOV

"A Command from the Other World"
Mersereau, John. *Orest Somov* . . . , 120–126.

"An Epigraph Instead of a Title"
Mersereau, John. *Orest Somov* . . . , 106–113.

"The Evil Eye"
Mersereau, John. *Orest Somov* . . . , 84–86.

"The Frightening Guest"
Mersereau, John. *Orest Somov* . . . , 131–135.

"The Holy Fool: A True Ukrainian Tale"
Mersereau, John. *Orest Somov* . . . , 120–126.

"In the Field, Birth Doesn't Count"
Mersereau, John. *Orest Somov* . . . , 78.

"Kievan Witches"
Mersereau, John. *Orest Somov* . . . , 82–84.

"Kupala Eve"
Mersereau, John. *Orest Somov* . . . , 79–80.

"The Legend of the Brave Knight, Ukrom Tabunshchik"
Mersereau, John. *Orest Somov* . . . , 77–78.

"Mary, or the Tavern Servant"
Mersereau, John. *Orest Somov* . . . , 147–148.

"Matchmaking"
Mersereau, John. *Orest Somov* . . . , 95–98.

"Mommy and Sonny-Boy"
Mersereau, John. *Orest Somov* . . . , 113–118.

"Monster"
Mersereau, John. *Orest Somov* . . . , 91–93.

"A Novel in Two Letters"
Mersereau, John. *Orest Somov* . . . , 98–106.

"The Post Station in Chateau Thierry"
Mersereau, John. *Orest Somov* . . . , 148–151.

"The Signboard"
Mersereau, John. *Orest Somov* . . . , 145–147.

"The Suicide"
Mersereau, John. *Orest Somov* . . . , 135–142.

"The Tale About Bone-Breaking Bear and Ivan the Merchant"
Mersereau, John. *Orest Somov* . . . , 76–77.

"The Tale of Nikita the Widow's Son"
Mersereau, John. *Orest Somov* . . . , 80–81.

"Tales of Buried Treasure"
Mersereau, John. *Orest Somov* . . . , 93–95.

"A Vision While Awake"
Mersereau, John. *Orest Somov* . . . , 142–143.

FERNANDO SORRENTINO

"The Fetid Tale of Antulín"
Meehan, Thomas C., Ed. "Introduction," *"Sanitary Centennial"* . . . [by Fernando Sorrentino], xxi–xxiii.

ENRIQUE SOUBLETTE

"La fajina"
Ratcliff, Dillwyn F. *Venezuelan Prose Fiction*, 115.

"El pocito en el monte"
Ratcliff, Dillwyn F. *Venezuelan Prose Fiction*, 114.

WOLE SOYINKA

"Johnny Just Come"
Gibbs, James. " 'A Storyteller on the *Gbohun-Gbohun*': An Analysis of Wole Soyinka's Three Johnny Stories," *Research African Lit*, 20, i (1989), 56.

"Johnny versus the Post Office"
Gibbs, James. ". . . Johnny Stories," 57–58.

"The Trial of Bowler"
Gibbs, James. ". . . Johnny Stories," 56–57.

MURIEL SPARK

"Miss Pinkerton's Apocalypse"
Black, Elizabeth. "The Nature of Fictional Discourse: A Case Study," *Applied Linguistics*, 10, iii (1989), 281–293.

NORMAN SPINRAD

"The Big Flash"
Franklin, H. Bruce. "The Vietnam War as American Science Fiction and Fantasy," *Sci-Fiction Stud*, 17 (1990), 346–347.

HARRIET PRESCOTT SPOFFORD

"The Amber Gods"
Bendixen, Alfred, Ed. "Introduction," *"The Amber Gods"* . . . [by Harriet Prescott Spofford], xxiii–xxiv.

"The Black Bess"
Bendixen, Alfred, Ed. "Introduction," xxx–xxxi.

"Circumstances"
Bendixen, Alfred, Ed. "Introduction," xxiv–xxix.

"The Godmothers"
Bendixen, Alfred, Ed. "Introduction," xxxiii–xxxiv.

"Her Story"
Bendixen, Alfred, Ed. "Introduction," xxxi–xxxii.

"In a Cellar"
Bendixen, Alfred, Ed. "Introduction," xxii–xxiii.

"The Moonstone Mass"
Bendixen, Alfred, Ed. "Introduction," xxix–xxx.

"Old Madame"
Bendixen, Alfred, Ed. "Introduction," xxxii–xxxiii.

JEAN STAFFORD

"And Lots of Solid Color"
Goodman, Charlotte M. *Jean Stafford* . . . , 74–75.

"Beatrice Trueblood's Story"
Goodman, Charlotte M. *Jean Stafford* . . . , 213–214.

"Between the Porch and the Altar"
Goodman, Charlotte M. *Jean Stafford* . . . , 137–138.

"The Bleeding Heart"
Goodman, Charlotte M. *Jean Stafford* . . . , 89–90.

"Children Are Bored on Sunday"
Goodman, Charlotte M. *Jean Stafford* . . . , 186–187.

"The Children's Game"
Goodman, Charlotte M. *Jean Stafford* . . . , 263–264.

"Going West"
Goodman, Charlotte M. *Jean Stafford* . . . , 16–17.

"The Home Front"
Goodman, Charlotte M. *Jean Stafford* . . . , 138–139.

"In the Zoo"
Goodman, Charlotte M. *Jean Stafford* . . . , 240–242.

"An Influx of Poets"
Goodman, Charlotte M. *Jean Stafford* . . . , 119–120.

"The Interior Castle"
Goodman, Charlotte M. *Jean Stafford* . . . , 94–95.

"Old Flaming Youth"
Goodman, Charlotte M. *Jean Stafford* . . . , 209–210.

"Polite Conversation"
Goodman, Charlotte M. *Jean Stafford* . . . , 153–154.

"A Slight Maneuver"
Goodman, Charlotte M. *Jean Stafford* . . . , 177–178.

"The Tea Time of the Stouthearted Ladies"
Goodman, Charlotte M. *Jean Stafford* . . . , 30–31.

"The Violet Rock"
Goodman, Charlotte M. *Jean Stafford* . . . , 239–240.

OLAF STAPLEDON

"A Modern Magician"
Herr, Cheryl. "Convention and Spirit in Olaf Stapledon's Fiction," in McCarthy, Patrick A., Charles Elkins, and Martin H. Greenberg, Eds. *The Legacy* . . . , 23–24.

CHRISTINA STEAD

"The Dianas"
Brydon, Diana. *Christina Stead*, 120–121.

"The Girl from the Beach"
Brydon, Diana. *Christina Stead*, 121–123.

"A Household"
Garner, Helen. "Christina Stead's Magic Stories," *Scripsi*, 4, i (1986), 193.

"My Friend, Lafe Tilly"
Garner, Helen. ". . . Magic Stories," 193–194.

"The Old School"
Garner, Helen. ". . . Magic Stories," 192–193.

"The Puzzleheaded Girl"
Brydon, Diana. *Christina Stead*, 116–120.

"The Right-Angled Creek"
Brydon, Diana. *Christina Stead*, 123–126.

FLORA ANNIE STEEL

"Mussumat Kirpo's Doll"
Hennessy, Rosemary, and Rajeswari Mohan. "The Construction of Woman in Three Popular Texts of Empire: Towards a Critique of Materialist Feminism," *Textual Practice*, 3 (1989), 337–347.

GERTRUDE STEIN

"Fernhurst"
Knapp, Bettina L. *Gertrude Stein*, 27–28.

"Melanctha"
Knapp, Bettina L. *Gertrude Stein*, 86–89.
Ruddick, Lisa. *Reading Gertrude Stein* . . . , 12–54.

"Miss Furr and Miss Skeene"
Knapp, Bettina L. *Gertrude Stein*, 93–94.

"*Q. E. D.*"
Knapp, Bettina L. *Gertrude Stein*, 79–82.

JOHN STEINBECK

"Adventures in Arcademy"
Timmerman, John H. *The Dramatic Landscape* . . . , 16–19.

"The Affair at 7, Rue de M---"
Hughes, Robert S. "Steinbeck's Uncollected Stories," *Steinbeck Q*, 18 (1985), 86–87; rpt. in his *Beyond the Red Pony* . . . , 118–120; and his *John Steinbeck* . . . , 82–84.
Timmerman, John H. *The Dramatic Landscape* . . . , 271–274.

"The Battle Farm" [same as "The Munroes"]
Timmerman, John H. *The Dramatic Landscape* . . . , 59–70.

"Breakfast"
Hughes, R. S. *John Steinbeck* . . . , 48–49.
Timmerman, John H. *The Dramatic Landscape* . . . , 205–207.

"Case History"
Timmerman, John H. *The Dramatic Landscape* . . . , 215–221.

"The Case of the Hotel Ghost . . ." [same as "A Reunion at the Quiet Hotel"]
Hughes, Robert S. ". . . Uncollected Stories," 90–91; rpt. in his *Beyond the Red Pony* . . , 124–125; and his *John Steinbeck* . . . , 88–90.
Timmerman, John H. *The Dramatic Landscape* . . . , 253–254.

"Christmas Story"
Timmerman, John H. *The Dramatic Landscape* . . . , 24–25.

"The Chrysanthemums"
Higdon, David L. "Dionysian Madness in Steinbeck's 'The Chrysanthemums,' " *Classical & Mod Lit*, 11, i (1990), 59–65.
Hughes, R. S. *John Steinbeck* . . . , 21–27.
Pellow, C. Kenneth. " 'The Chrysanthemums' Revisited," *Steinbeck Q*, 22, i (1989), 8–16.
Timmerman, John H. *The Dramatic Landscape* . . . , 169–177.

"The Cottage That Wasn't There"
Hughes, R. S. *Beyond the Red Pony* . . . , 110–111; rpt. in his *John Steinbeck* . . . , 74–75.

"Craps"
Hughes, R. S. *Beyond the Red Pony* . . . , 111; rpt. in his *John Steinbeck* . . . , 75.

"The Crapshooter"
Timmerman, John H. *The Dramatic Landscape* . . . , 252–253.

"The Days of Long March"
Timmerman, John H. *The Dramatic Landscape* . . . , 25–26.

"The Elf of Algiers" [same as "The Story of an Elf"]
Hughes, R. S. *Beyond the Red Pony* . . . , 110; rpt. in his *John Steinbeck* . . . , 74.

"Fingers of Cloud"
Timmerman, John H. *The Dramatic Landscape* . . . , 10–15.

"Flight"
Hughes, R. S. *John Steinbeck* . . . , 32–37.
Timmerman, John H. *The Dramatic Landscape* . . . , 189–198.

"The Gift"
Hughes, R. S. *John Steinbeck* . . . , 59–61.
+Levant, Howard. "John Steinbeck's *The Red Pony*: A Study in Narrative Technique," in Benson, Jackson J., Ed. *The Short Novels* . . . , 85–89.
Tammaro, Thomas M. "Erik Erikson Meets John Steinbeck: Psychological Development in 'The Gift,' " in Hayashi, Tetsumaro, and Thomas J. Moore, Eds. *Steinbeck's "The Red Pony"* . . . , 1–9.
Timmerman, John H. *The Dramatic Landscape* . . . , 117–139.

"The Gifts of Iban"
Timmerman, John H. *The Dramatic Landscape* . . . , 27–30.

"The Great Mountains"
Hughes, R. S. *John Steinbeck* . . . , 61–63.
+Levant, Howard. ". . . Narrative Technique," 89–91.
Timmerman, John H. *The Dramatic Landscape* . . . , 117–139.

"The Harness"
Hughes, R. S. *John Steinbeck* . . . , 29–32.
Timmerman, John H. *The Dramatic Landscape* . . . , 184–189.

"Helen Van Deventer"
Hughes, R. S. *John Steinbeck* . . . , 101–103.
Timmerman, John H. *The Dramatic Landscape* . . . , 107–112.

"His Father"
Hughes, Robert S. ". . . Uncollected Stories," 85; rpt. in his *Beyond the Red Pony* . . . , 117; and his *John Steinbeck* . . . , 81.
Timmerman, John H. *The Dramatic Landscape* . . . , 261–265.

"How Edith McGillcuddy Met R. L. Stevenson"
Hughes, Robert S. ". . . Uncollected Stories," 80–82; rpt. in his *Beyond the Red Pony* . . . , 106–108; and his *John Steinbeck* . . . , 70–72.
Timmerman, John H. *The Dramatic Landscape* . . . , 149–159.

"How Mr. Hogan Robbed a Bank"
Hughes, Robert S. ". . . Uncollected Stories," 89–90; rpt. in his *Beyond the Red Pony* . . . , 122–124; and his *John Steinbeck* . . . , 86–88.
Timmerman, John H. *The Dramatic Landscape* . . . , 274–277.

"Johnny Bear"
Hughes, R. S. *John Steinbeck* . . . , 49–53.
Timmerman, John H. *The Dramatic Landscape* . . . , 234–244.

"Junius Maltby"
Hughes, R. S. *John Steinbeck* . . . , 103–106.
Timmerman, John H. *The Dramatic Landscape* . . . , 73–77.

"The Leader of the People"
Glatstein, Mimi R. " 'The Leader of the People': A Boy Becomes a 'Mench,' " in Hayashi, Tetsumaro, and Thomas J. Moore, Eds. *Steinbeck's "The Red Pony"* . . . , 27–37.
Hughes, R. S. *John Steinbeck* . . . , 65–68.
Timmerman, John H. *The Dramatic Landscape* . . . , 117–139.
Yahnke, Robert E., and Richard M. Eastman. *Aging in Literature* . . . , 65–66.

"The Lopez Sisters"
Hughes, R. S. *John Steinbeck* . . . , 106–108.
Timmerman, John H. *The Dramatic Landscape* . . . , 77–82.

"The Miracle of Tepayac"
Hughes, Robert S. ". . . Uncollected Stories," 83–84; rpt. in his *Beyond the Red Pony* . . . , 115–116; and his *John Steinbeck* . . . , 79–80.
Timmerman, John H. *The Dramatic Landscape* . . . , 258–261.

"Molly Morgan"
Hughes, R. S. *John Steinbeck* . . . , 109–111.
Timmerman, John H. *The Dramatic Landscape* . . . , 82–89.

"The Murder"
Ditsky, John. "Steinbeck's 'Slav Girl' and the Role of Narrator in 'The Murder,' " *Steinbeck Q*, 22 (1989), 68–76.
Hadella, Charlotte. "Point of View in John Steinbeck's 'The Murder,' " *Steinbeck Q*, 22 (1989), 77–83.
Hughes, R. S. *John Steinbeck* . . . , 55–56.
Timmerman, John H. *The Dramatic Landscape* . . . , 159–166.

"Nothing So Monstrous"
Timmerman, John H. *The Dramatic Landscape* . . . , 76–77.

"Pat Humbert"
Hughes, R. S. *John Steinbeck* . . . , 113–115.
Timmerman, John H. *The Dramatic Landscape* . . . , 112–116.

"The Promise"
Hughes, Robert S. "The Black Cypress and the Green Tub: Death and Procreation in Steinbeck's 'The Promise,' " in Hayashi, Tetsumaro, and Thomas J. Moore, Eds. *Steinbeck's "The Red Pony"* . . . , 9–16.

———. *John Steinbeck* . . . , 63–65.
+Levant, Howard. "... Narrative Technique," 91–94.
Timmerman, John H. *The Dramatic Landscape* . . . , 117–139.

"The Raid"
Hughes, R. S. *John Steinbeck* . . . , 41–44.
Timmerman, John H. *The Dramatic Landscape* . . . , 224–234.

"Raymond Banks"
Hughes, R. S. *John Steinbeck* . . . , 111–113.
Timmerman, John H. *The Dramatic Landscape* . . . , 102–107.

"Saint Katy the Virgin"
Hughes, R. S. *John Steinbeck* . . . , 56–58.
Timmerman, John H. *The Dramatic Landscape* . . . , 142–149.

"The Short-Short Story of Mankind" [same as "We're Holding Our Own"]
Hughes, Robert S. "... Uncollected Stories," 88–89; rpt. in his *Beyond the Red Pony* . . . , 121–122; and his *John Steinbeck* . . . , 85–86.
Timmerman, John H. *The Dramatic Landscape* . . . , 276–280.

"The Snake"
Hughes, R. S. *John Steinbeck* . . . , 38–41.
Timmerman, John H. *The Dramatic Landscape* . . . , 198–205.
Weston, Cheryl, and John V. Knapp. "Profiles in Scientific Personality: John Steinbeck's 'The Snake,' " *Mosaic*, 22, i (1989), 87–100.

"The Summer Before"
Hughes, Robert S. "... Uncollected Stories," 87–88; rpt. in his *Beyond the Red Pony* . . . , 120–121; and his *John Steinbeck* . . . , 84–85.
Timmerman, John H. *The Dramatic Landscape* . . . , 265–269.

"The Time the Wolves Ate the Vice-Principal"
Hughes, Robert S. "... Uncollected Stories," 82–83; rpt. in his *Beyond the Red Pony* . . . , 112–113; and his *John Steinbeck* . . . , 76–77.
Timmerman, John H. *The Dramatic Landscape* . . . , 250.

"Tularecito"
Hughes, R. S. *John Steinbeck* . . . , 99–101.
Timmerman, John H. *The Dramatic Landscape* . . . , 70–72.

"The Vigilante"
Hughes, R. S. *John Steinbeck* . . . , 45–48.
Timmerman, John H. *The Dramatic Landscape* . . . , 207–224.

"The White Quail"
Hughes, R. S. *John Steinbeck* . . . , 27–29.
Timmerman, John H. *The Dramatic Landscape* . . . , 177–184.

"The Whiteside Family" [same as "The Whitesides"]
Hughes, R. S. *John Steinbeck* . . . , 115–117.
Timmerman, John H. *The Dramatic Landscape* . . . , 59–70.

"The Wicks Family" [same as "Shark Wicks"]
Hughes, R. S. *John Steinbeck* . . . , 94–98.
Timmerman, John H. *The Dramatic Landscape* . . . , 96–107.

"The Wizard of Maine"
Timmerman, John H. *The Dramatic Landscape* . . . , 305–306.

GEORGE STEINER

"Cake"
Kremer, S. Lillian. *Witness Through Imagination* . . . , 329–332.

"Return No More"
Kremer, S. Lillian. *Witness Through Imagination* . . . , 327–329.

ANTONIA STEMPEL PARÍS

"Las manos atadas"
Ramos, Elías A. *El cuento venezolano* . . . , 84–85.

RICHARD STERN

"Dr. Cahn's Visit"
Yahnke, Robert E., and Richard M. Eastman. *Aging in Literature* . . . , 66–67.

ROBERT LOUIS STEVENSON

"The Adventure of Prince Florizel and the Detective"
Menikoff, Barry M. "*New Arabian Nights*: Stevenson's Experiment in Fiction," *Nineteenth-Century Lit*, 45 (1990), 355–356.

"The Beach of Falesá"
Linehan, Katherine B. "Taking up with Kanakas: Stevenson's Complex Social Criticism in 'The Beach of Falesá,' " *Engl Lit Transition*, 33 (1990), 407–422.

"The Misadventures of John Nicholson"
Gelder, Kenneth. "R. L. Stevenson's Scottish Christmas Story: 'The Misadventures of John Nicholson,' the Free Church, and the Prodigal Son," *Stud Scottish Lit*, 23 (1988), 123–135.

"Olalla"
Naugrette, Jean-Pierre. "Décor, désir, espace: Une Lecture de Stevenson," *Littérature*, 61 (1986), 49–64.

"Story of the Young Man with the Cream Tart"
Mallardi, Rosella. "La commedia dell'onore: Un racconto 'arabo' di R. L. Stevenson," *Lingua e Stile*, 24 (1989), 265–293.

"The Strange Case of Dr. Jekyll and Mr. Hyde"
Doane, Janice, and Devon Hodges. "Demonic Disturbances of Sexual Identity: The Strange Case of Dr. Jekyll and Mr/s. Hyde," *Novel*, 23 (1989), 63–74.
Koestenbaum, Wayne. "The Shadow on the Bed: Dr. Jekyll, Mr. Hyde, and the Labouchère Amendment," *Critical Matrix*, 1 (Spring, 1988), 31–55.
Thomas, Ronald R. *Dreams of Authority* . . . , 237–253.
Tropp, Martin. *Images of Fear* . . . , 119–134.

"Will o' the Mill"
Menikoff, Barry M. "*New Arabian Nights* . . . ," 354–355.

ADALBERT STIFTER

"Abdias"
Pettersson, Torsten. " 'Eine Welt aus Sehen und Blindheit': Consciousness and World in Stifter's 'Abdias,' " *Germanisch-Romanische Monatsschrift*, 40 (1990), 41–53.

GLORIA STOLK

"Dinero"
Ramos, Elías A. *El cuento venezolano* . . . , 25–26.

THEODOR STORM

"Am Kamin"
Freund, Winfried. "Der Bürger und das Grauen: Theodor Storms Erzählung 'Am Kamin' und die phantastische Literatur im 19. Jahrhundert," in Coghlan, Brian, and Karl E. Laage, Eds. *Theodor Storm und das 19. Jahrhundert* . . . , 108–114.

"A Doppelgänger"
Webber, Andrew. "The Uncanny Rides Again: Theodor Storm's Double Vision," *Mod Lang R*, 84 (1989), 863–865.

"In St. Jürgen"
Webber, Andrew. "The Uncanny . . . ," 866–868.

"Ein Malerarbeit"
Webber, Andrew. "The Uncanny . . . ," 868–869.

"The Rider of the White Horse"
Webber, Andrew. "The Uncanny . . . ," 871–872.

"Der Spiegel des Cyprianus"
Webber, Andrew. "The Uncanny . . . ," 870.

RUTH McENERY STUART

"Blink"
Taylor, Helen. *Gender, Race, and Region* . . . , 114–116.

"Caesar"
Taylor, Helen. *Gender, Race, and Region* . . . , 112–114.

"Queen O'Sheba's Triumph"
Taylor, Helen. *Gender, Race, and Region* . . . , 126–127.

"The Unlived Life of Little Mary Ellen"
Taylor, Helen. *Gender, Race, and Region* . . . , 124–126.

"Weeds"
Taylor, Helen. *Gender, Race, and Region* . . . , 122.

"The Woman's Exchange of Simkinsville"
Taylor, Helen. *Gender, Race, and Region* . . . , 122–124.

THEODORE STURGEON

"Microcosmic God"
Huntington, John. *Rationalizing Genius* . . . , 53–59.

WILLIAM STYRON

"The Long March"
Messent, Peter. "Continuity and Change in the Southern Novella," in Lee, A. Robert, Ed. *The Modern American Novella*, 119–120.

SU MANSHU [PEV MANDJU or SU JIAN]

"The Tale of a Broken Hairpin"
Fong, Gilbert C. F. "Su Manshu," in Slupski, Zbigniew, Ed. *A Selective Guide* . . . , II, 183.
Liu, Wu-chi. *Su Man-shu*, 116–119.

"A Tale of Crimson Silk"
Fong, Gilbert C. F. "Su Manshu," 182.
Liu, Wu-chi. *Su Man-shu*, 111–113.

"A Tale of the Burning of the Sword"
Fong, Gilbert C. F. "Su Manshu," 182–183.
Liu, Wu-chi. *Su Man-shu*, 113–115.

"The Tale That Was Not a Dream"
Fong, Gilbert C. F. "Su Manshu," 183–184.
Liu, Wu-chi. *Su Man-shu*, 119.

SUI SIN FAR [EDITH EATON]

"The Heart's Desire"
Ling, Amy. *Between Worlds* . . . , 47.

"Mrs. Spring Fragrance"
Ling, Amy. *Between Worlds* . . . , 42–43.

"Pat and Pan"
Ling, Amy. *Between Worlds* . . . , 45–46.

"The Wisdom of the New"
Ling, Amy. *Between Worlds* . . . , 44–45.

RONALD SUKENICK

"What's Your Story?"
Saltzman, Arthur M. *Design of Darkness* . . . , 105–106.

ITALO SVEVO [ETTORE SCHMITZ]

"Lo specifico del Dottor Menghi"
Weiss, Beno. "Italo Svevo's 'Lo specifico del Dottor Menghi': Science Fiction?" in López Criado, Fidel, Ed. *Studies in Modern and Classical Languages* . . . , 163–169.

GLENDON SWARTHOUT

"The Ball Really Carries in the Cactus League Because the Air Is So Dry"
Vanderwerken, David L. "Of Steak, Compliments, and Death in Glendon Swarthout's Cactus League," *Stud Am Humor*, 5, ii–iii (1986), 99–105.

TAKAHASHI YAZUKUNI

"Cosmic Dust"
Matthew, Robert. *Japanese Science Fiction* . . . , 138.

BENJAMIN TAMMUZ

"The Swimming Race"
Ramras-Rauch, Gila. *The Arab* . . . , 168–170.

TANIZAKI JUN'ICHIRŌ

"The Bridge of Dreams"
DeZure, Deborah. "Tanizaki's 'The Bridge of Dreams' from the Perspective of *Amae* Psychology," *Lit & Psych*, 35, i–ii (1989), 46–65.

AHMET HAMDI TANPINAR

"Adam and Eve"
Oğuzertem, Süha. "Fiction of Narcissism: Metaphysical and Psychosexual Conflicts in the Stories of Ahmet Hamdi Tanpinar," *Turkish Stud Assoc Bull*, 14 (1990), 228–229.

PETER TAYLOR

"The Gift of the Prodigal"
York, Lamar. "Peter Taylor's Version of Initiation," *Mississippi Q*, 40, iii (1987), 315–317.

"Guests"
Shear, Walter. "Peter Taylor's Fiction: The Encounter with the Other," *Southern Lit J*, 22, iii (1989), 56–57.

"In the Miro District"
York, Lamar. ". . . Version of Initiation," 318–319.

"Je Suis Perdu"
Shear, Walter. "Peter Taylor's Fiction . . . ," 55.

"A Long Fourth"
Sullivan, Walter. *"In Praise of Bloody Sports"* . . . , 18–19.

"Miss Lenora When Last Seen"
Shear, Walter. "Peter Taylor's Fiction . . . ," 52–53.

"The Old Forest"
Robinson, David M. "Engaging the Past: Peter Taylor's 'The Old Forest,' " *Southern Lit J*, 22, ii (1990), 63–77.
Shear, Walter. "Peter Taylor's Fiction . . . ," 60–61.

"Porte Cochère"
Vauthier, Simone. "Peter Taylor's 'Porte Cochère': The Geometry of Generation," in Humphries, Jefferson, Ed. *Southern Literature* . . . , 318–338.
Yahnke, Robert E., and Richard M. Eastman. *Aging in Literature* . . . , 68.

"Promise of Rain"
York, Lamar. ". . . Version of Initiation," 310–312.

"The Scoutmaster"
York, Lamar. ". . . Version of Initiation," 312–315.

"A Spinster's Tale"
Shear, Walter. "Peter Taylor's Fiction . . . ," 58.

"Two Ladies in Retirement"
Shear, Walter. "Peter Taylor's Fiction . . . ," 59–60.

"Venus, Cupid, Folly and Time"
Shear, Walter. "Peter Taylor's Fiction . . . ," 61–62.

VLADIMIR FËDOROVICH TENDRIAKOV

"Atonement"
Shneidman, N. N. *Soviet Literature* . . . , 88–89.

"The Day That Dislodged a Life"
Shneidman, N. N. *Soviet Literature* . . . , 120–121.

"The Night after Graduation"
Shneidman, N. N. *Soviet Literature* . . . , 86–88.

"The Seventh Day"
Shneidman, N. N. *Soviet Literature* . . . , 121–122.

"Sixty Candles"
Shneidman, N. N. *Soviet Literature* . . . , 89–91.

ANNABEL THOMAS

"Ashur and Evir"
Yahnke, Robert E., and Richard M. Eastman. *Aging in Literature* . . . , 68–69.

AUDREY THOMAS

"Natural History"
Howells, Coral A. "Inheritance and Instability: Audrey Thomas's 'Real Mothers,' " *Recherches Anglaises et Nord-Américaines*, 20 (1987), 157–162.

DYLAN THOMAS

"An Adventure from a Work in Progress"
Rowe, Margaret M. "Living 'under the shadow of the bowler': *Portrait of the Artist as a Young Dog*," in Bold, Alan, Ed. *Dylan Thomas* . . . , 57–58.

"Just Like Little Dogs"
Rowe, Margaret M. "Living 'under the shadow of the bowler' . . . ," 126–127.

"Old Garbo"
Rowe, Margaret M. "Living 'under the shadow of the bowler' . . . ," 132–133.

"One Warm Saturday"
Rowe, Margaret M. "Living 'under the shadow of the bowler' . . . ," 133–136.

"Patricia, Edith and Arnold"
Rowe, Margaret M. "Living 'under the shadow of the bowler' . . . ," 131–132.

"The Peaches"
Rowe, Margaret M. "Living 'under the shadow of the bowler' . . . ," 129–131.

"Where the Tawe Flows"
Rowe, Margaret M. "Living 'under the shadow of the bowler' . . . ," 127–128.

EDITH THOMAS

"F. T. P."
Atack, Margaret. *Literature and the French Resistance* . . . , 142–145.

"The Mussels and the Teacher"
Atack, Margaret. *Literature and the French Resistance* . . . , 90–93.

"La Relève"
Atack, Margaret. *Literature and the French Resistance* . . . , 111–113.

THOMAS BANGS THORPE

"The Big Bear of Arkansas"
Fisher, Benjamin F. "Devils and Devilishness in Comic Yarns of the Old Southwest," *ESQ: J Am Renaissance*, 36 (1990), 53–56.

JAMES THURBER

"The Secret Life of Walter Mitty"
Cheatham, George. "The Secret Sin of Walter Mitty?" *Stud Short Fiction*, 27 (1990), 608–610.

JOHANN LUDWIG TIECK

"Die Gemälde"
Ziolkowski, Theodore. *German Romanticism* . . . , 369–372.

"Des Lebens Überfluss"
Gould, Robert. "Tieck's 'Des Lebens Überfluss' as a Self-Conscious Text," *Seminar*, 26 (1990), 237–255.

"Der Runenberg"
Ziolkowski, Theodore. *German Romanticism* . . . , 51–53.

EDITH TIEMPO

"The Dam"
Lumbera, Bienbenido. "Philippine Literature and the Filipino Personality," in Manuud, Antonio G., Ed. *Brown Heritage* . . . , 8–11.

LYNNE TILLMAN

"Absence Makes the Heart"
Siegle, Robert. *Suburban Ambush* . . . , 175–176.

"Dead Talk"
Siegle, Robert. *Suburban Ambush* . . . , 177–178.

"Diary of a Masochist"
Siegle, Robert. *Suburban Ambush* . . . , 176–177.

"Hung Up"
Siegle, Robert. *Suburban Ambush* . . . , 173–174.

"The Interpretation of Facts"
Siegle, Robert. *Suburban Ambush* . . . , 170–171.

JAMES TIPTREE, JR. [ALICE HASTINGS SHELDON]

"Backward, Turn Backward"
Steffen-Fluhr, Nancy. "The Case of the Haploid Heart: Psychological Patterns in the Science Fiction of Alice Sheldon ("James Tiptree, Jr."), *Sci-Fiction Stud*, 17 (1990), 210–212.

"The Girl Who Was Plugged In"
Steffen-Fluhr, Nancy. "The Case of the Haploid Heart . . . ," 202–203.

"Houston, Houston, Do You Read?"
Allman, John. "Motherless Creation: Motifs in Science Fiction," *No Dakota Q*, 58, ii (1990), 130–131.
Hollinger, Veronica. " 'The Most Grisly Truth': Responses to the Human Condition in the Works of James Tiptree, Jr.," *Extrapolation*, 30 (1989), 122.
Seal, Julia L. "James Tiptree, Jr.: Fostering the Future, Not Condemning It," *Extrapolation*, 31, i (1990), 76–78.
Steffen-Fluhr, Nancy. "The Case of the Haploid Heart . . . ," 205–208.

"Love Is the Plan, the Plan Is Death"
Steffen-Fluhr, Nancy. "The Case of the Haploid Heart . . . ," 199–202.

"The Milk of Paradise"
Seal, Julia L. "James Tiptree, Jr. . . . ," 79–82.

"Mother in the Sky with Diamonds"
Steffen-Fluhr, Nancy. "The Case of the Haploid Heart . . . ," 196–199.

"The Only Neat Thing"
Steffen-Fluhr, Nancy. "The Case of the Haploid Heart . . . ," 209–210.

"The Screwfly Solution" [also sometimes listed under Raccoona Sheldon, another of Sheldon's pseudonyms]
Hollinger, Veronica. " 'The Most Grisly Truth' . . . ," 123.
Pierce, John J. *Great Themes of Science Fiction* . . . , 122–123.

"The Women Men Don't See"
Hollinger, Veronica. " 'The Most Grisly Truth' . . . ," 125–126.
Seal, Julia L. "James Tiptree, Jr. . . . ," 74–76.

"Your Face, O My Sister! Your Face Filled of Light!"
Hollinger, Veronica. " 'The Most Grisly Truth' . . . ," 122–123.

"Your Haploid Heart"
Steffen-Fluhr, Nancy. "The Case of the Haploid Heart . . . ," 204–205.

SALLIE TISDALE

"Dancing in the Wind"
Yahnke, Robert E., and Richard M. Eastman. *Aging in Literature* . . . , 69.

LEO TOLSTOY

"The Death of Ivan Ilych"
Banks, Joanne T. "Death Labors," *Lit & Med*, 9 (1990), 162–171.
Connelly, Julia E. "The Whole Story," *Lit & Med*, 9 (1990), 150–161.
Connolly, Julian. "The Nineteenth Century: Between Realism and Modernism, 1880–85," in Moser, Charles H., Ed. . . . *Russian Literature*, 341–342.
Engelberg, Edward. *Elegiac Fictions* . . . , 87–96.
Fleishman, Avrom. "Three Ways of Thinking about Fiction and Society," in Belknap, Robert L., Ed. *Russianness* . . . , 185–195.
Harder, Worth T. "Granny and Ivan: Katherine Anne Porter's Mirror for Tolstoy," *Renascence*, 42 (1990), 149–156.
Jahn, Gary R. "A Note on Miracle Motifs in Later Works of Lev Tolstoj," in Mandelker, Amy, and Robert Reeder, Eds. *The Supernatural* . . . , 196–198.
Miller, Jerome A. "Vertigo and Genuflection: A Philosophical Meditation," *Mod Age*, 31 (1987), 369–377.
Sharma, R. S. " 'The Death of Ivan Ilyich': A Study in Point of View," in Sharma, T. R., Ed. *Essays on Leo Tolstoy*, 219–233.
Yahnke, Robert E., and Richard M. Eastman. *Aging in Literature* . . . , 70.

"The Devil"
Kopper, John M. "Tolstoy and the Narrative of Sex: A Reading of 'Father Sergius,' 'The Devil,' and 'The Kreutzer Sonata,' " in McLean, Hugh, Ed. *In the Shade* . . . , 164–168, 170–176.

"Father Sergius"
Kopper, John M. "Tolstoy and the Narrative of Sex . . . ," 171–180.

"Hadji Murat"
Orwin, Donna T. "Nature and the Narrator in 'Chadži-Murat,'' *Russian, Croatian*, 28, i (July 1, 1990), 125–144.

"The Kreutzer Sonata"
Rischin, Ruth. "*Allegro Tumultuosissimamente*: Beethoven in Tolstoy's Fiction," in McLean, Hugh, Ed. *In the Shade* . . . , 43–48.

"Master and Man"
Jahn, Gary R. "A Note on Miracle Motifs . . . ," 194–196.

JEAN TOOMER

"Break"
Jones, Robert B. "Jean Toomer's *Lost and Dominant*: Landscape of the Modern Wasteland," *Stud Am Fiction*, 18 (1990), 79–80.
"Easter"
Jones, Robert B. "Jean Toomer's *Lost and Dominant* . . . ," 80–81.
"Front"
Jones, Robert B. "Jean Toomer's *Lost and Dominant* . . . ," 82.
"Love on a Train"
Jones, Robert B. "Jean Toomer's *Lost and Dominant* . . . ," 78–79.
"Mr. Costyve Duditch"
Jones, Robert B. "Jean Toomer's *Lost and Dominant* . . . ," 78.
"Winter on Earth"
Jones, Robert B. "Jean Toomer's *Lost and Dominant* . . . ," 82–84.

SÁNDOR SOMOGYI TOTH

"How Do We Stand, Young Man?"
Cushing, George F. "Social Criticism in Hungarian Literature Since 1956," in Hoskins, Geoffrey, and George F. Cushing, Eds. *Perspectives on Literature* . . . , 111–112.

AILEEN LA TOURETTE

"Passing"
Palmer, Paulina. *Contemporary Women's Fiction* . . . , 57–59.

OSWALDO TREJO

"Las islas"
Ramos, Elías A. *El cuento venezolano* . . . , 120.
"Victoria"
Ramos, Elías A. *El cuento venezolano* . . . , 121.

DALTON TREVISAN

"Pedrinko"
Ledford-Miller, Linda. "Shoes for Little Peter: Narrative Technique in Trevisan's Not-At-All Exemplary Novella," *Brasil/Brazil*, 3, iv (1990), 37–50.

WILLIAM TREVOR [TREVOR COX]

"Access to the Children"
Schirmer, Gregory A. *William Trevor* . . . , 96–99.

"Angels at the Ritz"
Schirmer, Gregory A. *William Trevor* . . . , 102–104.

"Another Christmas"
Schirmer, Gregory A. *William Trevor* . . . , 139–140.

"Attracta"
Yahnke, Robert E., and Richard M. Eastman. *Aging in Literature* . . . , 71–72.

"The Ballroom of Romance"
Schirmer, Gregory A. *William Trevor* . . . , 129–130.

"Beyond the Pale"
Schirmer, Gregory A. *William Trevor* . . . , 142–145.

"The Blue Dress"
Schirmer, Gregory A. *William Trevor* . . . , 117–119.

"Broken Homes"
Schirmer, Gergory A. *William Trevor* . . . , 108–110.
Yahnke, Robert E., and Richard M. Eastman. *Aging in Literature* . . . , 71.

"A Complicated Nature"
Schirmer, Gregory A. *William Trevor* . . . , 106–108.

"The Day We Got Drunk on Cake"
Schirmer, Gregory A. *William Trevor* . . . , 92–95.

"The Distant Past"
Schirmer, Gregory A. *William Trevor* . . . , 138–139.

"The Drawing-Room"
Schirmer, Gregory A. *William Trevor* . . . , 113–115.

"An Evening with John Joe Dempsey"
Schirmer, Gregory A. *William Trevor* . . . , 125–126.

"Events at Drimghleen"
Rhodes, Robert E. " 'The Rest Is Silence': Secrets in Some William Trevor Stories," in Brophy, James D., and Eamon Grennan, Eds. *New Irish Writing* . . . , 42–48.

"The General's Day"
Schirmer, Gregory A. *William Trevor* . . . , 90–92.

"The Grass Widows"
Schirmer, Gregory A. *William Trevor* . . . , 99–102.

"Lovers of Their Time"
Schirmer, Gregory A. *William Trevor* . . . , 115–117.

"Lunch in Winter"
Schirmer, Gregory A. *William Trevor* . . . , 119–121.

"Matilda's England"
Schirmer, Gregory A. *William Trevor* . . . , 110–115.

"Mr. McNamara"
Schirmer, Gregory A. *William Trevor* . . . , 132–134.

"Mrs. Silly"
Schirmer, Gregory A. *William Trevor* . . . , 104–106.

"Music"
Schirmer, Gregory A. *William Trevor* . . . , 136–137.

"News"
Rhodes, Robert E. " 'The Rest Is Silence' . . . ," 39–42.

"The News from Ireland"
Schirmer, Gregory A. *William Trevor* . . . , 145–147.

"The Paradise Lounge"
Schirmer, Gregory A. *William Trevor* . . . , 130–131.

"Raymond Bamber and Mrs. Fitch"
Schirmer, Gregory A. *William Trevor* . . . , 94–96.

"The Summer-House"
Schirmer, Gregory A. *William Trevor* . . . , 112–113.

"The Table"
Schirmer, Gregory A. *William Trevor* . . . , 89–90.

"The Tennis Court"
Schirmer, Gregory A. *William Trevor* . . . , 110–112.

"Teresa's Wedding"
Schirmer, Gregory A. *William Trevor* . . . , 127–130.

"The Wedding in the Garden"
Schirmer, Gregory A. *William Trevor* . . . , 133–134.

IURII TRIFONOV

"The End of the Season"
Chapple, Richard. "Moral Dilemmas in the Work of Yury Trifonov," *Stud Twentieth-Century Lit*, 13 (1989), 287–288.

"The Last Hunt"
Chapple, Richard. "Moral Dilemmas . . . ," 288–289.

MANUEL TRUJILLO

"Mira la puerta y dice"
Ramos, Elías A. *El cuento venezolano* . . . , 64–65.

TSUKUSHI MICHIO

"The Image-Freezing Business"
Matthew, Robert. *Japanese Science Fiction* . . . , 53–54.

TSUTSUI YASUTAKA

"The African Bomb"
Matthew, Robert. *Japanese Science Fiction* . . . , 52–53.

IVAN SERGEEVICH TURGENEV

ANNE TURYN

MARK TWAIN [SAMUEL L. CLEMENS]

"The Story of Mamie Grant, the Child Missionary"
Marotti, Maria O. *The Duplicating Imagination* . . . , 38–39.

"The Story of the Old Ram"
Busskohl, James L. " 'The Story of the Old Ram' and the Tenderfoot Writer," *Stud Am Fiction*, 18 (1990), 183–192.

"Three Thousand Years Among the Microbes"
Gillman, Susan. *Dark Twins* . . . , 172–176.

"Which Was It?"
Gillman, Susan. *Dark Twins* . . . , 173–174.

ANNE TYLER

"The Common Courtesies"
Voelker, Joseph C. *Art and the Accidental* . . . , 110–111.

"The Geologist's Maid"
Shafer, Aileen C. "Anne Tyler's 'The Geologist's Maid': 'Till Human Voices Wake Us and We Drown,' " *Stud Short Fiction*, 27 (1990), 65–71.

"Half-Truths and Semi-Miracles"
Voelker, Joseph C. *Art and the Accidental* . . . , 55–56.

"I'm Not Going to Ask You Again"
Voelker, Joseph C. *Art and the Accidental* . . . , 108–110.

"A Misstep of the Mind"
Voelker, Joseph C. *Art and the Accidental* . . . , 53–55.

MIGUEL DE UNAMUNO

"Abel Sánchez"
Jurkevich, Gayana. "Archetypal Motifs of the Double in Unamuno's 'Abel Sánchez,' " *Hispania*, 73, ii (1990), 345–352.

"Aunt Tula"
Turner, Harriet S. "Distortiones teresianas de 'La tía Tula,' " in Crispin, John, Enrique Pupo-Walker, and Luis Lorenzo-Rivero, Eds. *Los hallazgos de la lectura* . . . , 131–151.

"Saint Manuel the Good, Martyr"
Garret, Brad. "The Dual Structures Within the Characters in the Literary Works of Miguel de Unamuno," in Menchacatorre, Félix, Ed. *Ensayos de literatura* . . . , 188–189.
Jiménez-Vera, Arturo. "San Manuel Bueno y su filosofía del vivir," in Menchacatorre, Félix, Ed. *Ensayos de literatura* . . . , 241–245.

UNNO JUZA

"The Demon of Vibration"
Matthew, Robert. *Japanese Science Fiction* . . . , 22–23.

"The Music Bath at 1800 Hours"
Matthew, Robert. *Japanese Science Fiction . . .*, 23–25.

"The Patented Formula for a Multi-Armed Man"
Matthew, Robert. *Japanese Science Fiction . . .*, 25–26.

DAVID UPDIKE

"Indian Summer"
Yahnke, Robert E., and Richard M. Eastman. *Aging in Literature . . .*, 72–73.

JOHN UPDIKE

"A & P"
Hurley, C. Harold. "Updike's 'A & P': An 'Initial' Response," *Notes Contemp Lit*, 20, iii (1990), 12.

"A Sense of Shelter"
Hait, Elizabeth A. "John Updike's 'A Sense of Shelter,' " *Stud Short Fiction*, 26 (1989), 555–557.

LUIS MANUEL URBANEJA ACHELPOHL

"La campana"
Ratcliff, Dillwyn F. *Venezuelan Prose Fiction*, 108–109.

"Don Mauro"
Ratcliff, Dillwyn F. *Venezuelan Prose Fiction*, 106–107.

"En la Fundación"
Ratcliff, Dillwyn F. *Venezuelan Prose Fiction*, 107–108.

"Flor de las selvas"
Ratcliff, Dillwyn F. *Venezuelan Prose Fiction*, 99–100.

"Las hazañas de Chango Carpio y Sietecueros"
Ratcliff, Dillwyn F. *Venezuelan Prose Fiction*, 109.

"Mechita la linda"
Ratcliff, Dillwyn F. *Venezuelan Prose Fiction*, 101.

"Ovejón"
Ratcliff, Dillwyn F. *Venezuelan Prose Fiction*, 102.

"La parejona"
Ratcliff, Dillwyn F. *Venezuelan Prose Fiction*, 101.

"Tierra del sol"
Ratcliff, Dillwyn F. *Venezuelan Prose Fiction*, 97–98.

ARTURO USLAR PIETRI

"Un mundo de humo"
Ramos, Elías A. *El cuento venezolano . . .*, 123–124.

NIKOLAI USPENSKY

"A Good Life"
Offord, Derek. "Literature and Ideas in Russia after the Crimean War: The 'Plebian' Writers," in Freeborn, Richard, and Jane Grayson, Eds. *Ideology* . . . , 53.

"The Old Woman"
Offord, Derek. "Literature and Ideas . . . ," 52.

"The Piglet"
Offord, Derek. "Literature and Ideas . . . ," 52–53.

EDMUNDO VALADÉS

"Los dos"
Patan, Federico. "La narrativo de Edmundo Valadés," in Pavón, Alfredo, Ed. *Paquette: Cuento* . . . , 139–140.

LUISA VALENZUELA

"Hijo de Kermaria"
Addis, Mary K. "Fictions of Motherhood: Three Short Stories by Luisa Valenzuela," *Romance Lang Annual,* 1 (1989), 355–356.

"Los Menestreles"
Addis, Mary K. "Fictions of Motherhood . . . ," 358–359.

"La profesora"
Addis, Mary K. "Fictions of Motherhood . . . ," 357–358.

RAMÓN DEL VALLE-INCLÁN

"My Sister Antonia"
Gonzalez del Valle, Luis T. " 'Mi hermana Antonia' y la estetica del enigma inenigmato," in Loureiro, Angel G., Ed. *Estelas, laberintos* . . . , 171–190.

CÉSAR VALLEJO

"Los caynas"
von Buelow, Christiane. "César Vallejo and the Stones of Darwinian Risk," *Stud Twentieth-Century Lit,* 14, i (1990), 9–19.

A. E. VAN VOGT

"Asylum"
Panshin, Alexel, and Cory Panshin. *The World Beyond* . . . , 514–519.

MARIO VARGAS LLOSA

"A Visitor"
Williams, Raymond L. *Mario Vargas Llosa*, 23–24.

"A Younger Brother"
Williams, Raymond L. *Mario Vargas Llosa*, 26–27.

JOHN VARLEY

"Persistence of Vision"
Roberts, Thomas J. *An Aesthetics . . .*, 17–18.

GIOVANNI VERGA

"Rosso Malpelo"
Toscano, Antonio. "Verga: Una rilettura di 'Malpelo,' " *Gradiva*, 4, ii (1988), 70–75.

JULES VERNE

"A Balloon Journey"
Panshin, Alexel, and Cory Panshin. *The World Beyond . . .*, 40–41.

"L'Eternel Adam"
Butcher, William. *Verne's Journey . . .*, 88–91.

"Maître Zacharius"
Butcher, William. *Verne's Journey . . .*, 85–87.

MEYER VILKANSKI

"Bahar"
Wallenrod, Reuben. . . . *Modern Israel*, 19–20.

HELENA MARÍA VIRAMONTES

"Growing"
Alarcón, Norma. "Making *Familia* from Scratch: Split Subjectivities in the Work of Helena María Viramontes and Cherríe Moraga," in Herrera-Sobek, María, and Helena María Viramontes, Eds. *Chicano Creativity* . . . , 148–150.

"Snapshots"
Alarcón, Norma. "Making *Familia* . . . , 150–154.

ARTURO VIVANTE

"The Soft Core"
Yahnke, Robert E., and Richard M. Eastman. *Aging in Literature* . . . , 73.

KURT VONNEGUT

"Tomorrow and Tomorrow and Tomorrow"
Yahnke, Robert E., and Richard M. Eastman. *Aging in Literature* . . . , 74.

VLADIMIR VOYNOVICH

"By Means of Mutual Correspondence"
Porter, Robert. *Four Contemporary Russian Writers*, 102.

"I Want to Be Honest"
Porter, Robert. *Four Contemporary Russian Writers*, 89–90.

"In a Circle of Friends"
Porter, Robert. *Four Contemporary Russian Writers*, 100–102.

MIRIAM WADDINGTON

"A Summer at Lonely Beach"
LeClaire, Jacques. "La Quête de l'identité dans 'A Summer at Lonely Beach' de Miriam Waddington," *Recherches Anglaises et Nord-Américaines*, 20 (1987), 61–69.

ALICE WALKER

"Advancing Luna and Ida B. Wells"
Byerman, Keith. "Desire and Alice Walker: The Quest for a Womanist Narrative," *Callaloo*, 12 (1989), 327–331.
Jarrett, Mary. "The Idea of Audience in the Short Stories of Zora Neale Hurston and Alice Walker," *J Short Story Engl*, 12 (Spring, 1989), 38.

"Coming Apart"
Byerman, Keith. "Desire and Alice Walker . . . ," 322–325.

"Everyday Use"
Hirsch, Marianne. *The Mother/Daughter Plot* . . . , 189–191.
Jarrett, Mary. "The Idea of Audience . . . ," 39–40.

"Laurel"
Petry, Alice H. "Alice Walker: The Achievement of the Short Fiction," *Mod Lang Stud*, 19, i (1989), 15–16.

"The Lover"
Petry, Alice H. "Alice Walker . . . ," 16.

"Nineteen Fifty-Five"
Jarrett, Mary. "The Idea of Audience . . . ," 40–42.

"Porn"
Byerman, Keith. "Desire and Alice Walker . . . ," 325–327.

"The Revenge of Hannah Kemhuff"
Braxton, Joanne M. "Ancestral Presence: The Outraged Mother Figure in Contemporary Afro-American Writing," in Braxton, Joanne M., and Andrée N. McLaughlin, Eds. *Wild Women* . . . , 310-313.

"A Sudden Trip Home in the Spring"
Jarrett, Mary. "The Idea of Audience . . . ," 38.

"To Hell with Dying"
Hollister, Michael. "Tradition in Alice Walker's 'To Hell with Dying,' " *Stud Short Fiction*, 26 (1989), 90–94.
Jarrett, Mary. "The Idea of Audience . . . ," 37–38.
Yahnke, Robert E., and Richard M. Eastman. *Aging in Literature* . . . , 74–75.

HORACE BINNEY WALLACE

"Victims of Passion"
Hatvary, George E. *Horace Binney Wallace*, 58–59.

MARTIN WALSER

"Ein fliehendes Pferd"
Wain, Anthony. "Martin Walser," in Bullivant, Keith, Ed. *After the "Death of Literature"* . . . , 352–354.

"Der Umzug"
Pickar, Gertrud B. " 'Kalte Grotesken': Walser, Aichinger, and Dürrenmatt and the Kafka Legacy," in Haymes, Edward R., Ed. *Crossings-Kreuzungen* . . . , 122–123.

"Was wären wir ohne Belmonte"
Pickar, Gertrud B. " 'Kalte Grotesken' . . . ," 120–121.

ROBERT WALSER

"The Honeymoon"
Whalen, Tom. "Between Heaven and Earth: Robert Walser's 'Die Hochzeitsreise,' " *Stud Short Fiction*, 27 (1990), 191–196.

WANG LUYAN [WANG HENG]

"Mouse Teeth"
Ma Sen. "Wang Luyan," in Slupski, Zbigniew, Ed. *A Selective Guide* . . . , II, 192.

"Under the Roof"
Ma Sen. "Wang Luyan," 191–192.

WANG MENG

"The Dappled Horse"
Wong, Kam-ming, trans. Bettina Vogel. "Reise zum Selbst: Unterwegs auf einem alter Gaul—zu Wang Mengs Erzählung 'Der Schecke,' " *Horen*, 34, iii (1989), 244–261.

WANG TONGZHAO [JIANSAN]

"Frost Scars"
Liu, Baisha. "Wang Tongzhao," in Slupski, Zbigniew, Ed. *A Selective Guide* . . . , II, 196.

"One Rank of the Living and Dead"
Liu, Baisha. "Wang Tongzhao," 196–197.

"The Smile"
Liu, Baisha. "Wang Tongzhao," 194.

MRS. HUMPHRY WARD [MARY ARNOLD]

"A Gay Life"
Sutherland, John. *Mrs. Humphry Ward* . . . , 38.

"A Tale of the Moors"
Sutherland, John. *Mrs. Humphry Ward* . . . , 19–21.

OYZER WARSHAWSKI

"Smugglers"
Roskies, David G. "The Rape of the Shtetl," in Roskies, David G., Ed. *The Literature of Destruction* . . . , 279–280.

WATANABE ATSUSHI

"A Soldier's Death"
Matthew, Robert. *Japanese Science Fiction* . . . , 21–22.

EVELYN WAUGH

"The Balance"
Carpenter, Humphry. *The Brideshead Generation* . . . , 142–143.

"Charles Ryder's Schooldays"
Davis, Robert M. *Evelyn Waugh* . . . , 183–188.

"The Ordeal of Gilbert Pinfold"
Hadas, Pamela W. "Madness and Medicine," *Lit & Med*, 9 (1990), 181–193.
Post, Stephen L. "His and Hers: Mental Breakdown as Depicted by Evelyn Waugh and Charlotte Perkins Gilman," *Lit & Med*, 9 (1990), 172–180.

STANLEY G. WEINBAUM

"The Lotus Eaters"
Panshin, Alexel, and Cory Panshin. *The World Beyond* . . . , 244–245.

"A Martian Odyssey"
Panshin, Alexel, and Cory Panshin. *The World Beyond* . . . , 237–242.

H. G. WELLS

"The Country of the Blind"
Pissarello, Giulia. "Un apologo darwiniano: 'The Country of the Blind' di H. G. Wells," *Rivista di Letterature*, 43 (1990), 399–409.
Roberts, Thomas J. *An Aesthetics* . . . , 17–18.

"The Croquet Player"
Murray, Brian. *H. G. Wells*, 142–144.

"In the Abyss"
Scheick, William J. *Fictional Structure and Ethics* . . . , 40–46.

"The Time Machine"
Gustafsson, Lars. "The Present as the Museum of the Future," in Berghahn, Klaus L., Reinhold Grimm, and Helmut Kreuzer, Eds. *Utopian Vision* . . . , 105–110.
Hume, Kathryn. "Eat or Be Eaten: H. G. Wells's 'Time Machine,' " *Philol Q*, 69 (1990), 233–251.
Manlove, Colin. "Dualism in Wells's 'The Time Machine' and *The War of the Worlds*," *Riverside Q*, 8, iii (1990), 173–181.
Murray, Brian. *H. G. Wells*, 87–90.

EUDORA WELTY

"Asphodel"
Westling, Louise. *Eudora Welty*, 76–78.

"At the Landing"
Pollack, Harriet. "On Welty's Use of Allusion: Expectations and Their Revisions in 'The Wide Net,' *The Robber Bridegroom*, and 'At the Landing,' " *Southern Q*, 29, i (1990), 22–29.
+Warren, Robert P. "The Love and the Separateness of Miss Welty," in Turner, W. Craig, and Lee E. Harding, Eds. *Critical Essays* . . . , 48–49.
Westling, Louise. *Eudora Welty*, 80–84.

"The Bride of Innisfallen"
+Jones, Alun R. "A Frail Travelling Coincidence: Three Later Stories of Eudora Welty," in Turner, W. Craig, and Lee E. Harding, Eds. *Critical Essays* . . . , 187–189.
Pitavy-Souques, Danièle. "Of Suffering and Joy: Aspects of Storytelling in Welty's Short Fiction," in Trouard, Dawn, Ed. *Eudora Welty* . . . , 145–146, 147–148.
+Rubin, Louis D. "Two Ladies of the South," in Turner, W. Craig, and Lee E. Harding, Eds. *Critical Essays* . . . , 180.

"The Burning"
Howell, Elmo. "Eudora Welty and the City of Man," *Georgia R*, 33 (1979), 776–777; rpt. Turner, W. Craig, and Lee E. Harding, Eds. *Critical Essays* . . . , 273–274.

"Circe"
Romines, Ann. "How Not to Tell a Story: Eudora Welty's First-Person Tales," in Trouard, Dawn, Ed. *Eudora Welty* . . . , 100–104.

"Clytie"
Westling, Louise. *Eudora Welty*, 68–69.

"A Curtain of Green"
Westling, Louise. *Eudora Welty*, 67–68.

"Death of a Traveling Salesman"
+Kreyling, Michael. "Modernism in Welty's *A Curtain of Green and Other Stories*," in Turner, W. Craig, and Lee E. Harding, Eds. *Critical Essays* . . . , 22–24.
Piwinsky, David J. "The Mule in the Window: The Theme of Sterility in Eudora Welty's 'Death of a Traveling Salesman,' " *Notes Mississippi Writers*, 22 (1990), 65–67.
Westling, Louise. *Eudora Welty*, 72–73.

"The Delta Cousins"
Westling, Louise. *Eudora Welty*, 85.

"The Demonstrators"
Ferguson, Suzanne. "The 'Assault of Hope': Style's Substance in Welty's 'The Demonstrators,' " in Trouard, Dawn, Ed. *Eudora Welty* . . . , 44–54.

"Flowers for Marjorie"
Westling, Louise. *Eudora Welty*, 72.

"Going to Naples"
+Jones, Alun R. "A Frail . . . Coincidence . . . ," 189–190.
Polk, Noel. "Going to Naples and Other Places in Eudora Welty's Fiction," in Trouard, Dawn, Ed. *Eudora Welty* . . . , 159–162.

"The Hitch-Hikers"
+Hicks, Granville. "Eudora Welty," in Turner, W. Craig, and Lee E. Harding, Eds. *Critical Essays* . . . , 261.
+Kreyling, Michael. "Modernism . . . ," 21–22.

"June Recital"
+Bryant, J. A. "Seeing Double in *The Golden Apples*," in Turner, W. Craig, and Lee E. Harding, Eds. *Critical Essays* . . . , 142–153.
Howell, Elmo. "Eudora Welty . . . ," 772–774; rpt. Turner, W. Craig, and Lee E. Harding, Eds. *Critical Essays* . . . , 269–272.
+McHaney, Thomas L. "Eudora Welty and the Multitudinous Golden Apples," in Turner, W. Craig, and Lee E. Harding, Eds. *Critical Essays* . . . , 117–124.
Wall, Cary. " 'June Recital': Virgie Rainey Saved," in Trouard, Dawn, Ed. *Eudora Welty* . . . , 14–31.
Westling, Louise. *Eudora Welty*, 133–141.

"Keela, the Outcast Indian Maiden"
Hussein, Ayman. "A Freudian Reading of Eudora Welty's 'Keela, the Outcast Indian Maiden,' " *Midwest Q*, 31, iv (1990), 523–536.
Westling, Louise. *Eudora Welty*, 60–62.

"The Key"
+Kreyling, Michael. "Modernism . . . ," 25–27.

"Kin"
+Rubin, Louis D. "Two Ladies . . . ," 175–179.
Vande Kieft, Ruth M. " 'Where Is the Voice Coming From?': Teaching Eudora Welty," in Trouard, Dawn, Ed. *Eudora Welty* . . . , 198–200.

"Lily Daw and the Three Ladies"
Weston, Ruth D. "American Folk Art, Fine Art, and Eudora Welty: Aesthetic Precedents for 'Lily Daw and the Three Ladies,' " in Trouard, Dawn, Ed. *Eudora Welty . . .*, 8–13.

"Livvie"
+Warren, Robert P. "The Love . . . ," 48.
Westling, Louise. *Eudora Welty*, 78–80.

"A Memory"
Burgess, Cheryll. "From Metaphor to Manifestation: The Artist in Eudora Welty's *A Curtain of Green*," in Trouard, Dawn, Ed. *Eudora Welty . . .*, 134–136.
+Warren, Robert P. "The Love . . . ," 46–47.
Westling, Louise. *Eudora Welty*, 65–66.

"Moon Lake"
Caldwell, Price. "Sexual Politics in Welty's 'Moon Lake' and 'Petrified Man,' " *Stud Am Fiction*, 18 (1990), 171–175.
+McHaney, Thomas L. "Eudora Welty . . . ," 124–126.

"Music from Spain"
+McHaney, Thomas L. "Eudora Welty . . . ," 128–132.
Westling, Louise. *Eudora Welty*, 19.

"No Place for You, My Love"
+Jones, Alun R. "A Frail . . . Coincidence . . . ," 185–187.

"Petrified Man"
Berlant, Lauren. "Re-Writing the Medusa: Welty's 'Petrified Man,' " *Stud Short Fiction*, 26 (1989), 59–70.
Caldwell, Price. "Sexual Politics . . . ," 175–179.
Schmidt, Peter. "Sibyls in Eudora Welty's Stories," in Trouard, Dawn, Ed. *Eudora Welty . . .*, 82–86.
Westling, Louise. *Eudora Welty*, 69–72.

"Powerhouse"
+Kreyling, Michael. "Modernism . . . ," 24–25.
Pitavy-Souques, Danièle. "Of Suffering and Joy . . . ," 143–144.
Schmidt, Peter. "Sibyls in Eudora Welty's Stories," 80–81.

"Shower of Gold"
+McHaney, Thomas L. "Eudora Welty . . . ," 115–117.
Westling, Louise. *Eudora Welty*, 130–131.

"Sir Rabbit"
Kendig, Daun. "Realities in 'Sir Rabbit': A Frame Analysis," in Trouard, Dawn, Ed. *Eudora Welty . . .*, 122–132.
+McHaney, Thomas L. "Eudora Welty . . . ," 124.
Westling, Louise. *Eudora Welty*, 131–132.

"A Still Moment"
McHaney, Pearl A. "Historical Perspectives in 'A Still Moment,' " in Turner, W. Craig, and Lee E. Harding, Eds. *Critical Essays . . .*, 52–69.
+Warren, Robert P. "The Love . . . ," 45–46.

"A Visit of Charity"
Westling, Louise. *Eudora Welty*, 64–65.
Yahnke, Robert E., and Richard M. Eastman. *Aging in Literature* . . . , 75–76.

"The Wanderers"
Westling, Louise. *Eudora Welty*, 149–154.

"The Whistle"
Westling, Louise. *Eudora Welty*, 63–64.

"The Whole World Knows"
+McHaney, Thomas L. "Eudora Welty . . . ," 126–128.

"Why I Live at the P.O."
Romines, Ann. "How Not to Tell a Story . . . ," 94–100.

"The Wide Net"
Pollack, Harriet. "On Welty's Use of Allusion . . . ," 7–12.
+Warren, Robert P. "The Love . . . ," 47–48.

"A Worn Path"
Butterworth, Nancy K. "From Civil War to Civil Rights: Race Relations in Welty's 'A Worn Path,' " in Trouard, Dawn, Ed. *Eudora Welty* . . . , 165–172.
Westling, Louise. *Eudora Welty*, 62–63.
Yahnke, Robert E., and Richard M. Eastman. *Aging in Literature* . . . , 76.

NATHANAEL WEST

"The Adventurer"
Wisker, Alistair. *The Writing* . . . , 144–145.

"A Cool Million"
McElroy, Bernard. . . . *Modern Grotesque*, 132–133.
Schulz, Dieter. "Nathanael West's 'A Cool Million' and the Myth of Success," in Diedrich, Maria, and Christoph Schöneich, Eds. *Studien zur Englischen und Amerikanischen Prosa* . . . , 164–175.
Simonson, Harold P. *Beyond the Frontier* . . . , 115–118.
Wisker, Alistair. *The Writing* . . . , 83–95.

"The Dream Life of Balso Snell"
McElroy, Bernard. . . . *Modern Grotesque*, 137–138.
Simonson, Harold P. *Beyond the Frontier* . . . , 107–111.
Wisker, Alistair. *The Writing* . . . , 36–57.

"The Impostor" [same as "The False" or "L'Affaire Beano"]
Wisker, Alistair. *The Writing* . . . , 149–151.

"Miss Lonelyhearts"
Beaver, Harold. "Nathanael West's 'Chamber of American Horror,'" in Lee, A. Robert, Ed. *The Modern American Novella*, 89–92.
Jones, Beverly. "Shrike as the Modernist Anti-Hero in Nathanael West's 'Miss Lonelyhearts,' " *Mod Fiction Stud*, 36 (1990), 218–224.

McElroy, Bernard. . . . *Modern Grotesque*, 138–139.
Simonson, Harold P. *Beyond the Frontier* . . . , 111–115.
Wisker, Alistair. *The Writing* . . . , 58–82.

"Mr. Potts of Pottstown"
Wisker, Alistair. *The Writing* . . . , 148–149.

"Western Union"
Wisker, Alistair. *The Writing* . . . , 145–146.

PAUL WEST

"The Glass Bottom Boat"
Pope, Dan. "A Different Kind of Post-Modernism," *Gettysburg R*, 3 (1990), 668.

CHRISTINE WESTON

"The Devil Has the Moon"
Cowasjee, Saros. "The Sahibs and the Natives: Short Fiction of the Raj, 1857–1947," *World Lit Written Engl*, 27, ii (1989), 67–68.

EDITH WHARTON

"Afterward"
Carroll, Noël. *The Philosophy of Horror*, 112–113.

"The Angel at the Grave"
Donovan, Josephine. *After the Fall* . . . , 53–54.

"Beatrice Palmato"
Papke, Mary E. *Verging on the Abyss* . . . , 172–173.

"The Descent of Man"
Donovan, Josephine. *After the Fall* . . . , 56–57.

"Friends"
Papke, Mary E. *Verging on the Abyss* . . . , 108–109.

"The Fullness of Life"
Papke, Mary E. *Verging on the Abyss* . . . , 106–107.

"The Hermit and the Wild Woman"
Donovan, Josephine. *After the Fall* . . . , 61–62.

"The House of the Dead Hand"
Donovan, Josephine. *After the Fall* . . . , 57–58.

"The Introduction"
Papke, Mary E. *Verging on the Abyss* . . . , 142.

"Kerfol"
Donovan, Josephine. *After the Fall* . . . , 72–73.

"The Lady's Maid's Bell"
Stengel, Ellen P. "Edith Wharton Rings 'The Lady's Maid's Bell,' " *Edith Wharton R*, 7, i (1990), 3–9.

"The Lamp of Psyche"
Papke, Mary E. *Verging on the Abyss* . . . , 107–108.

"Miss Mary Pask"
Papke, Mary E. *Verging on the Abyss* . . . , 177–178.

"The Mission of Jane"
Donovan, Josephine. *After the Fall* . . . , 57.

"Mrs. Manstey's View"
Papke, Mary E. *Verging on the Abyss* . . . , 124–125.

"The Muse's Tragedy"
Papke, Mary E. *Verging on the Abyss* . . . , 111–112.

"The Other Two"
Papke, Mary E. *Verging on the Abyss* . . . , 116–117.

"Pomegranate Seed"
Murray, Margaret P. "The Gothic Arsenal of Edith Wharton," *J Evolutionary Psych*, 10, iii–iv (1989), 315–321.

"Roman Fever"
Donovan, Josephine. *After the Fall* . . . , 82–83.

"Souls Belated"
Papke, Mary E. *Verging on the Abyss* . . . , 114–115.

JORDAN WHEELER

"Hearse in Snow"
Petrone, Penny. *Native Literature* . . . , 147–148.

"Red Wave"
Petrone, Penny. *Native Literature* . . . , 148.

JOHN EDGAR WIDEMAN

"Across the Wide Missouri"
Coleman, James W. *Blackness and Modernism* . . . , 88–91.

"The Beginning of Homewood"
Coleman, James W. *Blackness and Modernism* . . . , 93–95.

"The Chinaman"
Coleman, James W. *Blackness and Modernism* . . . , 86–87.

"The Courting of Lucy Tate"
Coleman, James W. *Blackness and Modernism* . . . , 105–112.

"Daddy Garbage"
Coleman, James W. *Blackness and Modernism* . . . , 85–86.

"Hazel"
Coleman, James W. *Blackness and Modernism* . . . , 82–83.

"In Heaven with Brother Tate"
Coleman, James W. *Blackness and Modernism* . . . , 100.

"Lizabeth: The Caterpillar Story"
Coleman, James W. *Blackness and Modernism* . . . , 82.

"Rashad"
Coleman, James W. *Blackness and Modernism* . . . , 83–84.

"The Return of Albert Wilkes"
Coleman, James W. *Blackness and Modernism* . . . , 100–105.

"Solitary"
Coleman, James W. *Blackness and Modernism* . . . , 84–85.

"Tommy"
Coleman, James W. *Blackness and Modernism* . . . , 91–93.

"The Watermelon Story"
Coleman, James W. *Blackness and Modernism* . . . , 87–88.

RUDY WIEBE

"The Naming of Albert Johnson"
Robb, Kenneth A. "Getting Lost in Rudy Wiebe's 'The Naming of Albert Johnson,' " *Notes Contemp Lit*, 20, v (1990), 7–9.

RICHARD WILBUR

"A Game of Catch"
Coulthard, A. R. "Poetic Justice in Wilbur's 'A Game of Catch,' " *Notes Contemp Lit*, 19, v (1989), 5.

OSCAR WILDE

"The Canterville Ghost"
Kohl, Norbert. *Oscar Wilde* . . . , 64–65.

"The Fisherman and His Soul"
Kohl, Norbert. *Oscar Wilde* . . . , 58–60.

"Lord Arthur Savile's Crime"
Kohl, Norbert. *Oscar Wilde* . . . , 61–64.

"The Portrait of Mr. W. H."
Kohl, Norbert. *Oscar Wilde* . . . , 112–115.
Summers, Claude J. *Gay Fictions* . . . , 34–42.

MICHAEL WILDING

"What It Was Like, Sometimes"
Vauthier, Simone. "Lost and Found: The Narrative and the Descriptive Modes in Michael Wilding's 'What It Was Like, Sometimes,' " *J Short Story Engl*, 12 (Spring, 1989), 63–76.

JOAN WILLIAMS

"Rain Later"
Wittenberg, Judith B. "Joan Williams: The Rebellious Heart," in Inge, Tonette B., Ed. *Southern Women Writers* . . . , 98–99.

REESE WILLIAMS

"Common Origin"
Siegle, Robert. *Suburban Ambush* . . . , 205–206.

"Gift Waves"
Siegle, Robert. *Suburban Ambush* . . . , 218–219.

TENNESSEE WILLIAMS [THOMAS LANIER WILLIAMS]

"Desire and the Black Masseur"
Summers, Claude J. *Gay Fictions* . . . , 137–140.

"Hard Candy"
Summers, Claude J. *Gay Fictions* . . . , 147–150.

"Mysteries of the Joy Rio"
Summers, Claude J. *Gay Fictions* . . . , 145–147.

"The Night of the Iguana"
Summers, Claude J. *Gay Fictions* . . . , 141–144.

"One Arm"
Summers, Claude J. *Gay Fictions* . . . , 134–137.

"Two on a Party"
Summers, Claude J. *Gay Fictions* . . . , 150–154.

WILLIAM CARLOS WILLIAMS

"Above the River"
Gish, Robert F. *William Carlos Williams* . . . , 89–90.

"The Accident"
Gish, Robert F. *William Carlos Williams* . . . , 77–78.
+Perloff, Marjorie. "The Man Who Loved Women: The Medical Fictions of William Carlos Williams," in Gish, Robert F., Ed. *William Carlos Williams* . . . , 191–192.

"The Buffalos"
Gish, Robert F. *William Carlos Williams* . . . , 60–62.

"Comedy Entombed: 1930"
Monteiro, George. "A Note on William Carlos Williams' 'Comedy Entombed: 1930,' " *William Carlos Williams R*, 15, ii (1989), 49–50.

"Danse Pseudomacabre"
Gish, Robert F. *William Carlos Williams* . . . , 76–77.

"The Dawn of Another Day"
Gish, Robert F. *William Carlos Williams . . .*, 88–89.

"A Face of Stone"
Gish, Robert F. *William Carlos Williams . . .*, 72–74.

"The Farmers' Daughters" [originally "Relique of the Farm"]
Gish, Robert F. *William Carlos Williams . . .*, 91–95.
+Perloff, Marjorie. "The Man Who Loved Women . . . ," 192–195.

"Four Bottles of Beer"
Gish, Robert F. *William Carlos Williams . . .*, 75–76.

"The Girl with the Pimply Face"
Gish, Robert F. *William Carlos Williams . . .*, 69–71.
+Perloff, Marjorie. "The Man Who Loved Women . . . ," 186–188.

"Hands Across the Sea"
Gish, Robert F. *William Carlos Williams . . .*, 44–48.

"The Insane"
Gish, Robert F. *William Carlos Williams . . .*, 90–91.

"Jean Beicke"
Gish, Robert F. *William Carlos Williams . . .*, 74–75.
+Monteiro, George. "The Doctor's Black Bag: William Carlos Williams' Passaic River Stories," in Gish, Robert F., Ed. *William Carlos Williams . . .*, 169–171.

"The Knife of the Times"
Gish, Robert F. *William Carlos Williams . . .*, 65–66.

"Life Along the Passaic River"
Gish, Robert F. *William Carlos Williams . . .*, 67–69.

"Mind and Body"
Gish, Robert F. *William Carlos Williams . . .*, 47–50.

"A Night in June"
Gish, Robert F. *William Carlos Williams . . .*, 86–88.
+Monteiro, George. "The Doctor's Black Bag . . . ," 171–174.
+Perloff, Marjorie. "The Man Who Loved Women . . . ," 188–190.

"Old Doc Rivers"
Gish, Robert F. *William Carlos Williams . . .*, 54–59.

"An Old Time Raid"
Gish, Robert F. *William Carlos Williams . . .*, 63–64.

"Pink and Blue"
Gish, Robert F. *William Carlos Williams . . .*, 60.

"The Use of Force"
Gish, Robert F. *William Carlos Williams . . .*, 71–72.
Peschel, Richard E., and Enid Rhodes Peschel. "When a Doctor Hates a Patient: Case History, Literary Histories," *Michigan Q R*, 21 (1984), 405–407; rpt. Gish, Robert F. *William Carlos Williams . . .*, 155–157.
+Slate, J. E. "William Carlos Williams and the Modern Short Story," in Gish, Robert F. *William Carlos Williams . . .*, 160–169.

"The Venus"
Gish, Robert F. *William Carlos Williams* . . . , 31–35.
+Perloff, Marjorie. "The Man Who Loved Women . . . ," 190–191.

"A Visit to the Fair"
Gish, Robert F. *William Carlos Williams* . . . , 59–60.

JACK WILLIAMSON

"After World's End"
Panshin, Alexel, and Cory Panshin. *The World Beyond* . . . , 523–527.

"Born of the Sun"
Panshin, Alexel, and Cory Panshin. *The World Beyond* . . . , 235–236.

"Breakdown"
Panshin, Alexel, and Cory Panshin. *The World Beyond* . . . , 541–542.

ETHEL WILSON

"Lilly's Story"
Smyth, Donna E. "Strong Women in the Web: Women's Work and Community in Ethel Wilson's Fiction," in McMullen, Lorraine, Ed. *The Ethel Wilson Symposium*, 89–90.
Sonthoff, Helen. "Companion in a Different Country," in McMullen, Lorraine, Ed. *The Ethel Wilson Symposium*, 101–108.

WILLIAM WISER

"The Man Who Wrote Letters to Presidents"
Yahnke, Robert E., and Richard M. Eastman. *Aging in Literature* . . . , 76–77.

CHRISTA WOLF

"An Afternoon in June"
Fehervary, Helen. "Christa Wolf's Prose: *A Landscape of Masks*," in Fries, Marilyn S., Ed. *Responses to Christa Wolf* . . . , 179–182.
Reid, J. H. *Writing Without Taboos* . . . , 62–65.

"Self-Experiment"
Werner, Hans-George. "*Unter den Linden:* Three Improbable Stories," in Fries, Marilyn S., Ed. *Responses to Christa Wolf* . . . , 292–294.

"A Step Toward Gomorrah"
Werner, Hans-George. ". . . Three Improbable Stories," 294–297.

"Unter den Linden"
Peucker, Brigitte. "Dream, Fairy Tale, and the Literary Subtexts of 'Unter den Linden,' " in Fries, Marilyn S., Ed. *Responses to Christa Wolf* . . . , 303–311.
Werner, Hans-George. ". . . Three Improbable Stories," 280–292.

GENE WOLFE

"The Horars [sic] of War"
Spark, Alasdair. "Vietnam: The War in Science Fiction," in Davies, Philip J., Ed. *Science Fiction* . . . , 121–122.

THOMAS WOLFE

"The Good Child's River"
Stutman, Suzanne. "Reconsideration: Mediation, Aline Bernstein, and Thomas Wolfe's 'The Good Child's River,' " *MELUS*, 14, ii (1987), 95–101.

"I Have a Thing to Tell You"
Gillin, Edward. " 'Julia' and Julia's Son," *Mod Lang Stud*, 19, ii (1989), 3–11.

VIRGINIA WOOLF

"Ancestors"
Baldwin, Dean R. *Virginia Woolf* . . . , 38–39.

"The Duchess and the Jeweller"
Baldwin, Dean R. *Virginia Woolf* . . . , 61–62.

"The Evening Party"
Baldwin, Dean R. *Virginia Woolf* . . . , 18.

"The Fascination of the Pool"
Dick, Susan. " 'I Am Not Trying to Tell a Story': Three Short Fictions by Virginia Woolf," *Engl Stud Canada*, 15, ii (1989), 170–172.

"Gipsy, the Mongrel"
Baldwin, Dean R. *Virginia Woolf* . . . , 68–70.

"Happiness"
Baldwin, Dean R. *Virginia Woolf* . . . , 38.

"A Haunted House"
+Araujo, Victor de. " 'A Haunted House'—The Shattered Glass," in Baldwin, Dean R., *Virginia Woolf* . . . , 121–129.
Reynier-Girardin, Christine. " 'A Haunted House' or the Genesis of *To the Lighthouse*," *J Short Story Engl*, 14 (Spring, 1990), 63–78.
Steele, Elizabeth. " 'A Haunted House': Virginia Woolf's *Noh* Story," *Stud Short Fiction*, 26 (1989), 151–161.

"In the Orchard"
Baldwin, Dean R. *Virginia Woolf* . . . , 26–27.

"The Introduction"
Baldwin, Dean R. *Virginia Woolf* . . . , 39–41.

"The Journal of Mistress Joan Martyn"
Baldwin, Dean R. *Virginia Woolf* . . . , 8–9.
DeSalvo, Louise. *Virginia Woolf* . . . , 265–272.
Dick, Susan. *Virginia Woolf*, 3–4.

"Kew Gardens"
Baldwin, Dean R. *Virginia Woolf* . . . , 15–19.
+Bishop, Edward L. "Pursuing 'It' Through 'Kew Gardens,' " in Baldwin, Dean R. *Virginia Woolf* . . . , 109–117.
Dick, Susan. *Virginia Woolf*, 21–22.
Jackson, Gertrude. "Virginia Woolf's *A Haunted House*: Reality and 'Moment of Being' in Her 'Kew Gardens,' " in Bauer, Gero, Franz K. Stanzel, and Franz Zaic, Eds. *Festschrift: Prof. Dr. Herbert Koziol* . . . , 259–261.

"The Lady in the Looking Glass"
Baldwin, Dean R. *Virginia Woolf* . . . , 55–57.
Barzilai, Shuli. "Virginia Woolf's Pursuit of Truth: 'Monday or Tuesday,' 'Moments of Being,' and 'The Lady in the Looking Glass,' " *J Narrative Technique*, 18 (1988), 205–208.
Chapman, Robert T. " 'The Lady in the Looking Glass': Modes of Perception in a Short Story by Virginia Woolf," *Mod Fiction Stud*, 18 (1972), 331–337.
Dick, Susan. " 'I Am Not Trying . . . ,' " 166–170.
Herrmann, Anne. *The Dialogic* . . . , 81–85.

"Lappin and Lapinova"
Baldwin, Dean R. *Virginia Woolf* . . . , 64–67.

"The Legacy"
Baldwin, Dean R. *Virginia Woolf* . . . , 70–71.

"The Man Who Loved His Kind"
Baldwin, Dean R. *Virginia Woolf* . . . , 43–45.
Worrell, Elizabeth. "The Unspoken Word," in Doyle, Esther M., and Victoria H. Floyd, Eds. *Studies in Interpretation*, 195–198.

"The Mark on the Wall"
Baldwin, Dean R. *Virginia Woolf* . . . , 13–15.
Dick, Susan. *Virginia Woolf*, 18–21.
Lumpkin, Janet. "Woolf's 'Mark on the Wall,' " *Conference Coll Teachers Engl Stud*, 54 (September, 1989), 28–33.

"Memoirs of a Novelist"
Baldwin, Dean R. *Virginia Woolf* . . . , 10–11.
Dick, Susan. *Virginia Woolf*, 4–5.

"Miss Pryme"
Baldwin, Dean R. *Virginia Woolf* . . . , 58–59.

"Moments of Being"
Baldwin, Dean R. *Virginia Woolf* . . . , 52–55.
Barzilai, Shuli. "Virginia Woolf's Pursuit of Truth . . . ," 203–205.
+Hafley, James. "On One of Virginia Woolf's Short Stories," in Baldwin, Dean R. *Virginia Woolf* . . . , 139–144.

"Monday or Tuesday"
Baldwin, Dean R. *Virginia Woolf* . . . , 25–26.
Barzilai, Shuli. "Virginia Woolf's Pursuit of Truth . . . ," 201–203.

"The Mysterious Case of Miss V."
Baldwin, Dean R. *Virginia Woolf* . . . , 8.
Dick, Susan. *Virginia Woolf*, 2–3.

"The New Dress"
Baldwin, Dean R. *Virginia Woolf* . . . , 36–37.
Worrell, Elizabeth. "The Unspoken Word," 193–195.

"Nurse Lugton's Curtain"
Baldwin, Dean R. *Virginia Woolf* . . . , 50–51.

"Phyllis and Rosamond"
Baldwin, Dean R. *Virginia Woolf* . . . , 7–8.

"Portraits"
Baldwin, Dean R. *Virginia Woolf* . . . , 59–60.

"The Searchlight"
Baldwin, Dean R. *Virginia Woolf* . . . , 67–68.

"The Shooting Party"
Baldwin, Dean R. *Virginia Woolf* . . . , 62–64.

"A Simple Melody"
Baldwin, Dean R. *Virginia Woolf* . . . , 45–48.

"A Society"
Baldwin, Dean R. *Virginia Woolf* . . . , 27–29.

"Solid Objects"
Baldwin, Dean R. *Virginia Woolf* . . . , 19–20.

"String Quartet"
Baldwin, Dean R. *Virginia Woolf* . . . , 29–31.

"A Summing Up"
Baldwin, Dean R. *Virginia Woolf* . . . , 48–50.
Worrell, Elizabeth. "The Unspoken Word," 200–202.

"The Symbol"
Baldwin, Dean R. *Virginia Woolf* . . . , 71.
Dick, Susan. " 'The Writing "I" Has Vanished': Virginia Woolf's Last Short Stories," in Dick, Susan, Declan Kiberd, Dougald McMillan, and Joseph Ronsley, Eds. *Essays for Richard Ellmann* . . . , 138–140.

"Sympathy"
Baldwin, Dean R. *Virginia Woolf* . . . , 20–21.

"Three Pictures"
Baldwin, Dean R. *Virginia Woolf* . . . , 57–59.
Dick, Susan. " 'I Am Not Trying . . . ,' " 172–174.

"Together and Apart"
Baldwin, Dean R. *Virginia Woolf* . . . , 41–43.
Worrell, Elizabeth. "The Unspoken Word," 198–200.

"An Unwritten Novel"
Baldwin, Dean R. *Virginia Woolf* . . . , 21–23.
Dick, Susan. *Virginia Woolf*, 20–21.

"The Watering Place"
Baldwin, Dean R. *Virginia Woolf* . . . , 71–72.

"The Widow and the Parrot"
Baldwin, Dean R. *Virginia Woolf* . . . , 51–52.

CORNELL WOOLRICH [CORNELL GEORGE HOPLEY-WOOLRICH]

"Baal's Daughter"
Lachman, Marvin. "Religious Cults and Mystery," in Breen, Jon L., and Martin Greenberg, Eds. *Synod of Sleuths* . . . , 87–88.

"Graves for the Living"
Lachman, Marvin. "Religious Cults . . . ," 88.

CONSTANCE FENIMORE WOOLSON

"At the Château of Corinne"
Torsney, Cheryl B. *The Grief of Artistry*, 88–107.

"Felipa"
Torsney, Cheryl B. *The Grief of Artistry*, 62–69.

"The Front Yard"
Torsney, Cheryl B. *The Grief of Artistry*, 148–150.

"In Sloane Street"
Torsney, Cheryl B. *The Grief of Artistry*, 150–153.

"Miss Elisabetha"
Torsney, Cheryl B. *The Grief of Artistry*, 54–61.

"Miss Grief"
Torsney, Cheryl B. *The Grief of Artistry*, 72–86.

"The Street of the Hyacinth"
Torsney, Cheryl B. *The Grief of Artistry*, 108–126.

RICHARD WRIGHT

"Big Boy Leaves Home"
Blythe, Hal, and Charlie Sweet. " 'Yo Mama Don Wear No Drawers': Suspended Sexuality in 'Big Boy Leaves Home,' " *Notes Mississippi Writers*, 21, i (1989), 31–36.

"The Man Who Lived Underground"
Lynch, Michael F. *Creative Revolt* . . . , 161–166.
Mayberry, Susan N. "Symbols in the Sewer: A Symbolic Renunciation of Symbols in Richard Wright's 'The Man Who Lived Underground,' " *So Atlantic R*, 54, i (1989), 71–83.
Watkins, Patricia D. "The Paradoxical Structure of Richard Wright's 'The Man Who Lived Underground,' " *Black Am Lit Forum*, 22 (1989), 767–783.

"The Man Who Was Almost a Man" [originally "Almos' a Man"]
Bredella, Lothar. "Das Verstechen literarischer Texte im Fremdsprachenunterricht," *Die Neueren Sprachen*, 86, vi (1990), 562–583.

WU ZUXIANG [WU TSU-HSIANG]

"Eighteen Hundred Piculs of Rice"
Klöpsch, Volker. "Wu Zuxiang," in Slupski, Zbigniew, Ed. *A Selective Guide* . . . , II, 201.

"Fan Family Village"
Anderson, Marston. *The Limits* . . . , 197–198.

"Great Peace in the Empire"
Klöpsch, Volker. "Wu Zuxiang," 201–202.

"Guanguan's Tonic"
Klöpsch, Volker. "Wu Zuxiang," 200–201.

XI XI

"Spring View"
Chung, Ling. "Perspective and Spatiality in the Fiction of Three Hong Kong Women Writers," in Duke, Michael S., Ed. *Modern Chinese Women Writers* . . . , 222–223.

XIAO JUN [same as LIU JUN, TIAN JUN, HSIAO CHÜN or SAN LANG]

"Goats"
Anderson, Marston. "The Barred View: On the Enigmatic Narrator in Xiao Jun's 'Goats,' " in Huters, Theodore, Ed. . . . *Modern Chinese Short Story*, 37–50.
Ptak, Roderich. "Xiao Jun," in Slupski, Zbigniew, Ed. *A Selective Guide* . . . , II, 208–209.

XIAO QIAN

"At the Side of the Road"
McDougall, Bonnie S. "Xiao Qian," in Slupski, Zbigniew, Ed. *A Selective Guide* . . . , II, 212.

"Chestnuts"
McDougall, Bonnie S. "Xiao Qian," 215–216.

"Dawn Flower"
McDougall, Bonnie S. "Xiao Qian," 216.

"The Rickshaw Leaser's Fate"
McDougall, Bonnie S. "Xiao Qian," 212–213.

"The Roc's Flight"
McDougall, Bonnie S. "Xiao Qian," 216.

"Shandong Deng"
McDougall, Bonnie S. "Xiao Qian," 211.

"Under the Fence"
McDougall, Bonnie S. "Xiao Qian," 211.

"When Your Eaves Are Low"
Sanders, Tao Liu. "Xiao Qian," in Slupski, Zbigniew, Ed. *A Selective Guide* . . . , II, 219.

XIE BINGYING [XIE MINGWANG]

"Settling Accounts"
Lundberg, Lennart. "Xie Bingying," in Slupski, Zbigniew, Ed. *A Selective Guide* . . . , II, 221.

XU DISHAN [HSÜ TI-SHAN or LUO HUASHENG]

"Chuntao"
Ng, Mau-sang. "Xu Dishan," in Slupski, Zbigniew, Ed. *A Selective Guide* . . . , II, 224–226.

"A Merchant's Wife"
Ng, Mau-sang. "Xu Dishan," 222–223.

"Yu-kuan"
Robinson, Lewis S. " 'Yu-Kuan': The Spiritual Testament of Hsü Ti-shan," *Tamkang R*, 8, ii (1977), 147–169.

XU QINWEN [same as QINWEN or SHU BIN]

"By the Lake Shore"
Pollard, David. "Xu Qinwen," in Slupski, Zbigniew, Ed. *A Selective Guide* . . . , II, 228–229.

HISAYE YAMAMOTO

"Seventeen Syllables"
Mistri, Zenobia B. " 'Seventeen Syllables': A Symbolic Haiku," *Stud Short Fiction*, 27 (1990), 197–202.
Yogi, Stan. "Legacies Revealed: Uncovering Buried Plots in the Stories of Hisaye Yamamoto," *Stud Am Fiction*, 17 (1989), 170–174.

"Yoneko's Earthquake"
Yogi, Stan. "Legacies Revealed . . . ," 174–178.

YANO TETSU

"The Origins of Mt. Miminari"
Matthew, Robert. *Japanese Science Fiction* . . . , 160–161.

YAO XUEYIN [YAO XUEHEN]

"Half a Load Short"
Denton, Kirk. "Yao Xueyin," in Slupski, Zbigniew, Ed. *A Selective Guide* . . . , II, 230.

YE ZI [YU HELIN]

"Abundant Harvest"
Schäfer, Ingo. "Ye Zi," in Slupski, Zbigniew, Ed. *A Selective Guide* . . . , II, 252–253.

"Fire"
Schäfer, Ingo. "Ye Zi," 253.

"Grandpa Yang's New Year"
Schäfer, Ingo. "Ye Zi," 254–255.

"The Night Sentinel"
Schäfer, Ingo. "Ye Zi," 255–256.

"Outside the Electric Fence"
Schäfer, Ingo. "Ye Zi," 253–254.

YEH SHAO-CHÜN [same as YE SHAOJUN or YE SHENGTAO]

"Bitter Greens"
Anderson, Marston. *The Limits* . . . , 98–99.

"Conflagration"
Anderson, Marston. *The Limits* . . . , 100–102.

"The Glory of Spring Is Not for Her"
Průšek, Jaroslav. *The Lyrical* . . . , 190.

"A Heavy Load of Grief"
Průšek, Jaroslav. *The Lyrical* . . . , 184–185.

"Horsebell Melons"
Holoch, Donald. "Ye Shaojun," in Slupski, Zbigniew, Ed. *A Selective Guide* . . . , II, 241.

"In the City"
Holoch, Donald. "Ye Shaojun," 244–245.

"A Life"
Anderson, Marston. *The Limits* . . . , 97–98.
Holoch, Donald. "Ye Shaojun," 233–236.
Průšek, Jaroslav. *The Lyrical* . . . , 182–183.

"Lonely" [same as "Deserted"]
Průšek, Jaroslav. *The Lyrical* . . . , 190–191.

"Lute on a Chill Dawn"
Holoch, Donald. "Ye Shaojun," 239–240.

"Mr. Pan in Distress"
Anderson, Marston. *The Limits* . . . , 107–108.

"Nebulae"
Anderson, Marston. *The Limits* . . . , 102–104.

"On the Bridge"
Anderson, Marston. *The Limits* . . . , 108.
Holoch, Donald. "Ye Shaojun," 239–240.

"The Package"
Anderson, Marston. *The Limits* . . . , 108–109.

"Rice"
Průšek, Jaroslav. *The Lyrical* . . . , 189.

"Travel Companions"
Průšek, Jaroslav. *The Lyrical* . . . , 185–186.

ABRAHAM B. YEHOSHUA

"The Death of an Old Man"
Cohen, Joseph. *Voices of Israel* . . . , 46.

"Early in the Summer of 1970"
Cohen, Joseph. *Voices of Israel* . . . , 54–56.

"Facing the Forest"
Alter, Robert, Ed. *Modern Hebrew Literature*, 353–356.
Cohen, Joseph. *Voices of Israel* . . . , 46–51.
Ramras-Rauch, Gila. *The Arab* . . . , 129–140.

"A Long Hot Day, His Despair, His Wife and His Daughter"
Cohen, Joseph. *Voices of Israel*, 52–54.

S. YIZHAR [YIZHAR SMILANSKY]

"Before Zero Hour"
Ramras-Rauch, Gila. *The Arab* . . . , 59–60.

"Ephraim Returns"
Wallenrod, Reuben. . . . *Modern Israel*, 218.

"The Hill in the Woods"
Wallenrod, Reuben. . . . *Modern Israel*, 218–219.

"Hirbet Hizah"
Ramras-Rauch, Gila. *The Arab* . . . , 71–74.

"Midnight Convoy"
Ramras-Rauch, Gila. *The Arab . . .*, 60–61.

"The Prisoner"
Alter, Robert, Ed. *Modern Hebrew Literature*, 291–293.
Ramras-Rauch, Gila. *The Arab . . .*, 62–64.

"A Story That Did Not Begin"
Ramras-Rauch, Gila. *The Arab . . .*, 79–80.

YOKOMITSU RIICHI

"The Machine"
Matthew, Robert. *Japanese Science Fiction . . .*, 152–153.

"Silent Ranks"
Matthew, Robert. *Japanese Science Fiction . . .*, 153–154.

YOKOMIZO SEISHI

"After Twenty-Five Million Years"
Matthew, Robert. *Japanese Science Fiction . . .*, 35–37.

YU DAFU [YÜ TA-FU or CHAO LIEN]

"Bayberry Wine"
Zhang Xiaoling. "Yu Dafu," in Slupski, Zbigniew, Ed. *A Selective Guide . . .*, II, 263–264.

"Deep Night"
Prušek, Jaroslav. *The Lyrical . . .*, 149–150.

"Drowning"
Prušek, Jaroslav. *The Lyrical . . .*, 146–147.

"Escape"
Zhang Xiaoling. "Yu Dafu," 265.

"A Humble Sacrifice"
Doležalová, Anna. *Yü Ta-fu . . .*, 40–42.
———. "Yu Dafu," in Slupski, Zbigniew, Ed. *A Selective Guide . . .*, II, 260.
Prušek, Jaroslav. *The Lyrical . . .*, 156–158.

"In the Cold Wind"
Zhang Xiaoling. "Yu Dafu," 264.

"In the Middle of the Road"
Doležalová, Anna. *Yü Ta-fu . . .*, 22–23.

"Intoxicating Spring Night"
Doležalová, Anna. *Yü Ta-fu . . .*, 37–40.
———. "Yu Dafu," 259–260.
Prušek, Jaroslav. *The Lyrical . . .*, 154–155.

"Late-Blooming Cassia"
Doležalová, Anna. *Yü Ta-fu* . . . , 58–60.

"A Lonely Man on a Journey"
Doležalová, Anna. *Yü Ta-fu* . . . , 48–50.
Prušek, Jaroslav. *The Lyrical* . . . , 152–153, 160–161.

"Marital Episode"
Doležalová, Anna. *Yü Ta-fu* . . . , 25–27.

"Moving South"
Doležalová, Anna. *Yü Ta-fu* . . . , 13–14.

"The Night of the Moth's Funeral"
Doležalová, Anna. *Yü Ta-fu* . . . , 68–69.
Zhang Xiaoling. "Yu Dafu," 264–265.

"The Past"
Doležalová, Anna. *Yü Ta-fu* . . . , 52–53.

"The Shadow of Smoke"
Doležalová, Anna. *Yü Ta-fu* . . . , 65–69.
Prušek, Jaroslav. *The Lyrical* . . . , 162–165.

"Silver-Grey Death"
Doležalová, Anna. *Yü Ta-fu* . . . , 13, 17–18.

"Sinking"
Doležalová, Anna. *Yü Ta-fu* . . . , 12–13, 16–17.
Ng, Mao-sang. *The Russian Hero* . . . , 89–90.

"Snowy Morning"
Doležalová, Anna. *Yü Ta-fu* . . . , 60–65.

"A Sorrowful Journey"
Zhang Xiaoling. "Yu Dafu," 263.

"A Start"
Doležalová, Anna. *Yü Ta-fu* . . . , 74.

"Stray Sheep"
Doležalová, Anna. *Yü Ta-fu* . . . , 53–56.

"A Superfluous Man"
Doležalová, Anna. *Yü Ta-fu* . . . , 23–25.

"The Third Day of the Eleventh Month"
Doležalová, Anna. *Yü Ta-fu* . . . , 45–48.
———. "Yu Dafu," 260.
Prušek, Jaroslav. *The Lyrical* . . . , 145–146, 150–151.

"Thirteen Nights"
Zhang Xiaoling. "Yu Dafu," 265.

"Wasp's Sting"
Doležalová, Anna. *Yü Ta-fu* . . . , 69–72.

YUMENO KYUSAKU

"The Scarabaeus"
Matthew, Robert. *Japanese Science Fiction* . . . , 26–27.

SOL YURICK

"The Siege"
Yahnke, Robert E., and Richard M. Eastman. *Aging in Literature* . . . , 77–78.

EVGENII ZAMYATIN [ZAMIATIN, ZAMJATIN]

"The Flood"
Heldt, Barbara. "Men Who Give Birth: A Feminist Perspective on Russian Literature," in Kelly, Catriona, Michael Makin, and Donald Shepherd, Eds. *Discontinuous Discourses* . . . , 163–164.

ISRAEL ZANGWILL

"Bethulah"
Upelson, Joseph H. *Dreamer of the Ghetto* . . . , 115–116.

"Incurable"
Upelson, Joseph H. *Dreamer of the Ghetto* . . . , 113–114.

"The Jewish Trinity"
Upelson, Joseph H. *Dreamer of the Ghetto* . . . , 120–121.

"The Model of Sorrows"
Upelson, Joseph H. *Dreamer of the Ghetto* . . . , 118–120.

"Noah's Ark"
Upelson, Joseph H. *Dreamer of the Ghetto* . . . , 114–115.

"Samooborona"
Upelson, Joseph H. *Dreamer of the Ghetto* . . . , 121–122.

"To Die in Jerusalem"
Upelson, Joseph H. *Dreamer of the Ghetto* . . . , 117.

ROGER ZELAZNY

"The Doors of His Face, the Lamps of His Mouth"
Krulik, Theodore. *Roger Zelazny*, 15–20.

"The Engine at Heartspring's Center"
Krulik, Theodore. *Roger Zelazny*, 128–129.

"The Eve of RUMOKO"
Krulik, Theodore. *Roger Zelazny*, 24–27.

"Home Is the Hangman"
Krulik, Theodore. *Roger Zelazny*, 124–125.

"A Rose for Ecclesiastes"
Huntington, John. *Rationalizing Genius* . . . , 107–110.
Krulik, Theodore. *Roger Zelazny*, 13–15, 19–23.

"This Moment of the Storm"
Krulik, Theodore. *Roger Zelazny*, 28–29.

STEFAN ZEREMSKI

"The Stronger Sex"
Eber, Irene. *Voices from Afar* . . . , 72–73.

ZHANG HENSHUI [ZHANG XINYUAN]

"Extra! Extra!"
Fong, Gilbert C. F. "Zhang Henshui," in Slupski, Zbigniew, Ed. *A Selective Guide* . . . , II, 272.

"The Honest Elements"
Fong, Gilbert C. F. "Zhang Henshui," 272.

"I Am the Monkey King"
Fong, Gilbert C. F. "Zhang Henshui," 273–274.

"A Trip to Heaven"
Fong, Gilbert C. F. "Zhang Henshui," 273.

ZHANG JIE

"The Ark"
Bailey, Alison. "Travelling Together: Narrative Technique in Zhang Jie's 'The Ark,' " in Duke, Michael S., Ed. *Modern Chinese Women Writers* . . . , 96–111.

ZHANG KANGKANG

"Northern Lights"
Bryant, Daniel. "Making It Happen: Aspects of Narrative Method in Zhang Kangkang's 'Northern Lights,' " in Duke, Michael S., Ed. *Modern Chinese Women Writers* . . . , 112–134.
Leung, Lai-fong. "In Search of Love and Self: The Image of Young Female Intellectuals in Post-Mao Women's Fiction," in Duke, Michael S., Ed. *Modern Chinese Women Writers* . . . , 144–145.

"Summer"
Leung, Lai-fong. "In Search of Love and Self . . . ," 139–140.

ZHANG TIANYI

"The Bulwark"
Anderson, Marston. *The Limits* . . . , 164–165.

"Enmity"
Anderson, Marston. *The Limits* . . . , 186–187.

"Honeymoon Life"
Pollard, David. "Zhang Tianyi," in Slupski, Zbigniew, Ed. *A Selective Guide* . . . , II, 280–281.

"A Hyphenated Story"
  Anderson, Marston. *The Limits . . .*, 172–173.

"The Inspector General"
  Tsau Shu-ying. "Zhang Tianyi's Satirical Wartime Stories," in *La Littérature chinoise . . .*, 184.

"Invitation to Dinner"
  Pollard, David. "Zhang Tianyi," 280.

"Little Peter"
  Bedford, Nigel. "Zhang Tianyi," in Slupski, Zbigniew, Ed. *A Selective Guide . . .*, II, 276–277.

"Mr. Hua Wei"
  Klöpsch, Volker. "Zhang Tianyi," in Slupski, Zbigniew, Ed. *A Selective Guide . . .*, II, 282.
  Tsau Shu-ying. ". . . Wartime Stories," 178–179, 185.

"Mr. Jing Ye"
  Anderson, Marston. *The Limits . . .*, 157–158.

"Mr. Tanjiu's Work"
  Tsau Shu-jing. ". . . Wartime Stories," 179–180.

"New Life"
  Klöpsch, Volker. "Zhang Tianyi," 282–283.
  Tsau Shu-jing. ". . . Wartime Stories," 180–181.

"Revenge"
  Anderson, Marston. *The Limits . . .*, 171.

"Smile"
  Anderson, Marston. *The Limits . . .*, 171–172.

"Spring Breeze"
  Tsau Shu-jing. ". . . Wartime Stories," 181–182.

"A Subject Matter"
  Anderson, Marston. *The Limits . . .*, 175–177.

"A Summer Night's Dream"
  Anderson, Marston. *The Limits . . .*, 174–175.

"A Three-and-a-Half-Days' Dream"
  Anderson, Marston. *The Limits . . .*, 153–155.

"Tips"
  Pollard, David. "Zhang Tianyi," 279–280.

"A Trifling Love Story"
  Bedford, Nigel. "Zhang Tianyi," 277–278.

ZHANG XINXIN

"The Dream of Our Generation"
  Wakeman, Carolyn, and Yue Daiyun. "Fiction's End: Zhang Xinxin's New Approaches to Creativity," in Duke, Michael S., Ed. *Modern Chinese Women Writers . . .*, 203–204.

"On the Same Horizon"
Wakeman, Carolyn, and Yue Daiyun. "Fiction's End . . . ," 201–202.

"Orchid Madness"
Wakeman, Carolyn, and Yue Daiyun. "Fiction's End . . . ," 205–206.

"A Quiet Evening"
Wakeman, Carolyn, and Yue Daiyun. "Fiction's End . . . ," 199–200.

"Theatrical Effects"
Wakeman, Carolyn, and Yue Daiyun. "Fiction's End . . . ," 204–205.

"Where Did I Miss You?"
Leung, Lai-fong. "In Search of Love and Self: The Image of Young Female Intellectuals in Post-Mao Women's Fiction," in Duke, Michael S., Ed. *Modern Chinese Women Writers* . . . , 137–139.
Wakeman, Carolyn, and Yue Daiyun. "Fiction's End . . . ," 200–201.

ZHANG ZIPING

"Spring in Mei Mountain"
Pollard, David. "Zhang Ziping," in Slupski, Zbigniew, Ed. *A Selective Guide* . . . , II, 285–286.

ZHAO SHULI

"Land"
Wivell, Charles. "Zhao Shuli," in Slupski, Zbigniew, Ed. *A Selective Guide* . . . , II, 288.

"The Marriage of Young Blacky"
Wivell, Charles. "Zhao Shuli," 287–288.

ZHENG ZHENDUO

"Fifty Grand Uncle"
Ng, Mau-sang. "Zheng Zhenduo," in Slupski, Zbigniew, Ed. *A Selective Guide* . . . , II, 292.

"Red Packet"
Ng, Mau-sang. "Zheng Zhenduo," 291.

"Wang Wu"
Ng, Mau-sang. "Zheng Zhenduo," 292.

ZHONG XIAOYANG

"The Two-Stringed Erhu"
Chung, Ling. "Perspective and Spatiality in the Fiction of Three Hong Kong Women Writers," in Duke, Michael S., Ed. *Modern Chinese Women Writers* . . . , 220.

ZHU LIN

"Eyes"
King, Richard. "Images of Sexual Oppression in Zhu Lin's *Snake's Pillow Collection*," in Duke, Michael S., Ed. *Modern Chinese Women Writers* . . . , 160–163.

"Pear Blossoms Lighten a Poplar-Lined Road"
King, Richard. "Images of Sexual Oppression . . . ," 163–165.

"Snake's Pillow"
King, Richard. "Images of Sexual Oppression . . . ," 154–160.

"The Web"
King, Richard. "Images of Sexual Oppression . . . ," 166–167.

ZHU XINING

"Daybreak"
Birch, Cyril. "The Function of Intertextual Reference in Zhu Xining's 'Daybreak,' " in Huters, Theodore, Ed. . . . *Modern Chinese Short Story*, 105–118.

ÉMILE ÉDOUARD CHARLES ANTOINE ZOLA

"L'attaque du moulin"
Baguley, David B. *Naturalist Fiction* . . . , 146–147.

MIKHAIL MIKHAĬLOVICH ZOSHCHENKO

"The Christmas Tree"
Hanson, Krista. "*Kto vinovat*? Guilt and Rebellion in Zoščenko's Accounts of Childhood," in Rancour-Laferriere, Daniel, Ed. *Russian Literature* . . . , 295–296.

"Galoshes and Ice Cream"
Hanson, Krista. ". . . Accounts of Childhood," 296–297.

"I Am Not to Blame"
Hanson, Krista. ". . . Accounts of Childhood," 293–294.

JUAN EDUARDO ZÚÑIGA

"Nubes de polvo y humo"
Percival, Anthony. "The Spanish Civil War Story: From Neo-Realism to Postmodernism," in Bevan, David, Ed. *Literature and War*, 89–91.

"Presagios de noche"
Percival, Anthony. "The Spanish Civil War Story . . . ," 92–93.

A Checklist of Books Used

Aberbach, David. *Surviving Trauma: Loss, Literature and Psychoanalysis*. New Haven: Yale Univ. Press, 1989.
Abramson, Glenda. *The Writing of Yehuda Amichai: A Thematic Approach*. Albany: State Univ. of New York Press, 1989.
Acker, Bertie. *El cuento mexicano contemporaneo: Rulfo, Arreola y Fuentes*. Madrid: Editorial Playor, 1984.
Actas de las I jornadas de lengua y literatura inglesa y norteamericana. Logroño: Univ. de Logroño, 1990.
Actas del Tercer Congreso Internacional de Estudios Galdosianos, II. Las Palmas, Canary Islands: Excmo. Cabildo Insular de Gran Canaria, 1990.
Aderman, Ralph M., Ed. *Critical Essays on Washington Irving*. Boston: Hall, 1990.
Ahern, Maureen, and Mary S. Vásquez, Eds. *Homenaje a Rosario Castellanos*. Valencia: Albatros, 1980.
Aiken, Susan H. *Isak Dinesen and the Engendering of Narrative*. Chicago: Univ. of Chicago Press, 1990.
Alexander, Edward. *Isaac Bashevis Singer: A Study of the Short Fiction*. Boston: Twayne, 1990.
Allen, Michael, and Angela Wilcox, Eds. *Critical Approaches to Anglo-Irish Literature*. Gerrards Cross: Smythe, 1989; Am. ed. Totowa, N.J.: Barnes & Noble, 1989.
Alter, Robert. *After the Tradition: Essays on Modern Jewish Writing*. New York: Dutton, 1969.
———, Ed. *Modern Hebrew Literature*. New York: Behrman, 1975.
Amoia, Alba. *Albert Camus*. New York: Continuum, 1989.
Amrine, Frederick, Ed. *Literature and Science as Modes of Expression*. Dordrecht: Kluwer Academic Publications, 1989.
Anderson, Douglas. *A House Undivided: Domesticity and Community in American Literature*. Cambridge: Cambridge Univ. Press, 1990.
Anderson, Mark, Ed. *Reading Kafka: Prague, Politics and the "Fin de Siècle."* New York: Schocken, 1989.
Anderson, Marston. *The Limits of Realism: Chinese Fiction in the Revolutionary Period*. Berkeley: Univ. of California Press, 1990.
Angier, Carole. *Jean Rhys: Life and Work*. Boston: Little, Brown, 1990.
Apter, Emily S. *André Gide and the Codes of Homotextuality*. Saratoga, Calif.: Anma Libri, 1987.
Asedio a Alfonso Reyes: 1889–1989. Mexico City: IMSS/UAM-A, 1989.
Astro, Alan. *Understanding Samuel Beckett*. Columbia: Univ. of South Carolina Press, 1990.
Atack, Margaret. *Literature and the French Resistance: Cultural Politics and Narrative Form, 1940–1950*. Manchester: Manchester Univ. Press, 1989.
Auerbach, Jonathan. *The Romance of Failure: First-Person Fictions of Poe, Hawthorne, and James*. New York: Oxford Univ. Press, 1989.
Auslander, Adrienne. *Andromeda's Chains: Gender and Interpretation in Victorian Literature*. New York: Columbia Univ. Press, 1989.
Avni, Ora. *The Resistance of Reference: Linguistics, Philosophy, and the Literary Text*. Baltimore: Johns Hopkins Univ. Press, 1990.

Baguley, David B. *Naturalist Fiction: The Entropic Vision*. Cambridge: Cambridge Univ. Press, 1990.
Balbert, Peter. *D. H. Lawrence and the Phallic Imagination*. New York: St. Martin's Press, 1989.
Baldwin, Dean R. *Virginia Woolf: A Study of the Short Fiction*. Boston: Twayne, 1989.
Barnes, Christopher. *Boris Pasternak: A Literary Biography*, I. Cambridge: Cambridge Univ. Press, 1989.
Barratt, Andrew, and A. D. P. Briggs. *A Wicked Irony: The Rhetoric of Lermontov's "A Hero of Our Time."* Bristol: Bristol Classical Press, 1989.
Barreca, Regina, Ed. *Sex and Death in Victorian Literature*. Bloomington: Indiana Univ. Press, 1990.
Bassett, John E. *Visions and Revisions: Essays on Faulkner*. West Cornwall, Conn.: Locust Hill Press, 1989.
Bassnett, Susan, Ed. *Knives and Angels: Women Writers in Latin America*. London: Zed, 1990.
Bauer, Gero, Franz K. Stanzel, and Franz Zaic, Eds. *Festschrift: Prof. Dr. Herbert Koziol zum Siebzigsten Geburtstag*. Vienna: Braumüller, 1973.
Bauer, Roger, Douwe Fokkema, Michael de Graat, John Boening, Gerald Gillespie, Maria Moog-Grünewald, Virgil Nemoianu, Joseph Ricapito, Manfred Schmeling, Joachim von der Thüsen, and Claus Uhlig, Eds. *Proceedings of the XIIth Congress of the International Comparative Literature Association*, II. Munich: Iudicium, 1990.
———, and Douwe Fokkema, Eds. *Proceedings of the XIIth Congress of the International Comparative Literature Association*, III. Munich: Iudicium, 1990.
Baumgarten, Murray, and Barbara Gottfried. *Understanding Philip Roth*. Columbia: Univ. of South Carolina Press, 1990.
Beegel, Susan F., Ed. *Hemingway's Neglected Short Fiction: New Perspectives*. Ann Arbor: UMI Research Press, 1989.
Beidler, Peter G. *Ghosts, Demons, and Henry James: "The Turn of the Screw" and the Turn of the Century*. Columbia: Univ. of Missouri Press, 1989.
Beizer, Janet L. *Family Plots: Balzac's Narrative Generation*. New Haven: Yale Univ. Press, 1986.
Belknap, Robert L., Ed. *Russianness: An Examination of Russia and the West—In Memory of Rufus W. Mathewson*. Ann Arbor: Ardis, 1990.
Bell, Michael. *The Sentiment of Reality: Truth of Feeling in the European Novel*. London: Allen & Unwin, 1983.
Bellis, Peter J. *No Mysteries Out of Ourselves: Identity and Textual Form in the Novels of Herman Melville*. Philadelphia: Univ. of Pennsylvania Press, 1990.
Bell-Villada, Gene H. *García Márquez: The Man and His Work*. Chapel Hill: Univ. of North Carolina Press, 1990.
Benedetti, Mario. *Crítica cómplice*. Madrid: Alianza Editorial, 1988.
Ben-Merre, Diana A., and Maureen Murphy, Eds. *James Joyce and His Contemporaries*. Westport: Greenwood, 1989.
Bennett, Tony, Ed. *Popular Fiction: Technology, Ideology, Production, Reading*. London: Routledge, 1990.
Benson, Jackson J., Ed. *The Short Novels of John Steinbeck*. Durham: Duke Univ. Press, 1990.
———. *New Critical Approaches to the Short Stories of Ernest Hemingway*. Durham: Duke Univ. Press, 1990.
Berghahn, Klaus L., Reinhold Grimm, and Helmut Kreuzer, Eds. *Utopian Vision, Technological Innovation, and Poetic Imagination*. Heidelberg: Winter, 1990.
Berkman, Joyce A. *The Healing Imagination of Olive Schreiner: Beyond South African Colonialism*. Amherst: Univ. of Massachusetts Press, 1989.
Bernad, Miguel A. *Bamboo and the Greenwood Tree: Essays in Filipino Literature in English*. Manila: Bookmark, 1961.

Bernheimer, Charles. *Figures of Ill Repute: Representing Prostitution in Nineteenth-Century France*. Cambridge: Harvard Univ. Press, 1989.
Bersani, Leo. *The Culture of Redemption*. Cambridge: Harvard Univ. Press, 1990.
Bevan, David, Ed. *Literature and War*. Amsterdam: Rodopi, 1990.
Birch, Cyril, Ed. *Chinese Communist Literature*. New York: Praeger, 1963.
Bleznick, Donald, Ed. *Variaciones interpretativas en torno a la nueva narrativa hispanoamericana*. Santiago de Chile: Editorial Universitaria, 1972.
Bloom, Clive, Ed. *Twentieth-Century Suspense: The Thriller Comes of Age*. New York: St. Martin's Press, 1990.
———, Brian Docherty, Jane Gibb, and Keith Shand, Eds. *Nineteenth-Century Suspense: From Poe to Conan Doyle*. New York: St. Martin's Press, 1988.
Bloom, Harold, Ed. *Modern Latin American Fiction*. New York: Chelsea House, 1990.
Bock, Martin. *Crossing the Shadow-Line: The Literature of Estrangement*. Columbus: Ohio State Univ. Press, 1989.
Bogue, Ronald. *Deleuze and Guattari*. London: Routledge, 1989.
Bold, Alan, Ed. *Dylan Thomas: Craft or Sullen Art*. London: Vision, 1990; Am. ed. New York: St. Martin's Press, 1990.
Bouson, J. Brooks. *The Empathic Reader: A Study of the Narcissistic Character and the Drama of the Self*. Amherst: Univ. of Massachusetts Press, 1989.
Boyd, Brian. *Vladimir Nabokov: The Russian Years*. Princeton: Princeton Univ. Press, 1990.
Bradbury, Malcolm. *The Modern World: Ten Great Writers*. New York: Viking, 1989.
Bramsbäck, Birgit, Ed. *Homage to Ireland: Aspects of Culture, Literature, and Language*. Uppsala: Univ. of Uppsala, 1990.
Brandford, Richard. *Kingsley Amis*. London: Arnold, 1989.
Braxton, Joanne M., and Andrée N. McLaughlin, Eds. *Wild Women in the Whirlwind: Afra [sic]-American Culture and the Contemporary Literary Renaissance*. New Brunswick: Rutgers Univ. Press, 1989.
Bredahl, A. Carl. *New Ground: Western American Narrative and the Literary Canon*. Kent: Kent State Univ. Press, 1989.
Breen, Jon L., and Martin Greenberg, Eds. *Synod of Sleuths: Essays on Judeo-Christian Detective Fiction*. Metuchen, N.J.: Scarecrow, 1990.
Breger, Louis. *Dostoevsky: The Author as Psychoanalyst*. New York: New York Univ. Press, 1989.
Brinkmeyer, Robert H. *The Art & Vision of Flannery O'Connor*. Baton Rouge: Louisiana State Univ. Press, 1989.
Broe, Mary L., and Angela Ingram, Eds. *Women's Writing in Exile*. Chapel Hill: Univ. of North Carolina Press, 1989.
Brophy, James D., and Eamon Grennan, Eds. *New Irish Writing: Essays in Memory of Raymond J. Porter*. Boston: Twayne [for Iona College Press], 1989.
Brown, Dennis. *The Modernist Self in Twentieth-Century English Literature: A Study in Self-Fragmentation*. New York: St. Martin's Press, 1989.
Brown, Frieda S., Malcolm A. Compiletto, Victor M. Howard, and Robert A. Martin, Eds. *Rewriting the Good Fight: Critical Essays on the Literature of the Spanish Civil War*. East Lansing: Michigan State Univ. Press, 1989.
Brown, Tony, Ed. *Edward Carpenter and Late Victorian Realism*. London: Cass, 1990.
Brown, William E. *A History of Russian Literature of the Romantic Period*, III. Ann Arbor: Ardis, 1986.
———. *A History of Russian Literature of the Romantic Period*, IV. Ann Arbor: Ardis, 1986.
Browning, Gary. *Boris Pilniak: Scythian at a Typewriter*. Ann Arbor: Ardis, 1985.
Brydon, Diana. *Christina Stead*. Totowa, N.J.: Barnes & Noble, 1987.
Budick, Emily. *Fiction and Historical Consciousness: The American Romance Tradition*. New Haven: Yale Univ. Press, 1989.

Bullivant, Keith, Ed. *After the "Death of Literature": West German Writing of the 1970s*. Oxford: Berg, 1989.
Burleson, Donald R. *Lovecraft: Disturbing the Universe*. Lexington: Univ. Press of Kentucky, 1990.
Butcher, William. *Verne's Journey to the Centre of the Self: Space and Time in the "Voyages extraordinaires."* New York: St. Martin's Press, 1990.
Cady, Edwin H., and Louis J. Budd, Eds. *On Hawthorne: The Best from "American Literature."* Durham: Duke Univ. Press, 1990.
Cameron, Sharon. *Thinking in Henry James*. Chicago: Univ. of Chicago Press, 1989.
Cannon, JoAnn. *Postmodern Italian Fiction: The Crisis of Reason in Calvino, Eco, Sciascia, Malerba*. Cranbury, N.J.: Assoc. Univ. Presses [for Fairleigh Dickinson Univ. Press], 1989.
Carpenter, Humphry. *The Brideshead Generation: Evelyn Waugh and His Friends*. Boston: Houghton Mifflin, 1990.
Carr, Virginia S. *Understanding Carson McCullers*. Columbia: Univ. of South Carolina Press, 1990.
Carrillo, Germán D. *La narrativa de Gabriel García Márquez (Ensayos de interpretatión)*. Madrid: Editorial Castalia, 1975.
Carrington, Ildikó de Papp. *Controlling the Uncontrollable: The Fiction of Alice Munro*. DeKalb: Northern Illinois Univ. Press, 1989.
Carroll, Noël. *The Philosophy of Horror*. New York: Routledge, 1990.
Chances, Ellen B. *Conformity's Children: An Approach to the Superfluous Man in Russian Literature*. Columbus: Slavica, 1978.
Chang Jun-mei. *Ting Ling: Her Life and Her Work*. Taipei, Taiwan: Institute of International Relations, 1978.
Chapman, Sara S. *Henry James's Portrait of the Writer as Hero*. New York: St. Martin's Press, 1989.
Clarke, Graham, Ed. *The New American Writing: Essays on American Literature Since 1970*. London: Vision, 1990; Am. ed. New York: St. Martin's Press, 1990.
Clayton, Cherry, Ed. *Women and Writing in South Africa: A Critical Anthology*. Marshalltown: Heinemann, 1989.
Clayton, J. Douglas, Ed. *Issues in Russian Literature Before 1917*. Columbus: Slavica, 1989.
———, and Gunter Schaarschmidt, Eds. *Poetica Slavica: Studies in Honour of Zbigniew Folejewski*. Ottawa: Univ. of Ottawa Press, 1981.
Coghlan, Brian, and Karl E. Laage, Eds. *Theodor Storm und das 19. Jahrhundert: Vorträge und Berichte des Internationalen Storm-Symposions aus Anlass des 100. Todestages Theodor Storms*. Berlin: Schmidt, 1989.
Cohen, Joseph. *Voices of Israel: Yehuda Amicai, A. B. Yehoshua, T. Carmi, Aheron Appelfeld, and Amos Oz*. Albany: State Univ. of New York Press, 1990.
Coleman, James W. *Blackness and Modernism: The Literary Career of John Edgar Wideman*. Jackson: Univ. Press of Mississippi, 1989.
Collier, Peter, and Judy Davies, Eds. *Modernism and the European Unconscious*. New York: St. Martin's Press, 1990.
Collings, Michael R. *In the Image of God: Theme, Characterization, and Landscape in the Fiction of Orson Scott Card*. Westport: Greenwood, 1990.
Conway, James C. *D. H. Lawrence and the Trembling Balance*. University Park: Pennsylvania State Univ. Press, 1990.
Costlow, Jane T. *Worlds Within Worlds: The Novels of Ivan Turgenev*. Princeton: Princeton Univ. Press, 1990.
Crick, Bernard. *Essays on Politics and Literature*. Edinburgh: Edinburgh Univ. Press, 1989.
Crispin, John, Enrique Pupo-Walker, and Luis Lorenzo-Rivero, Eds. *Los hallazgos de la lectura: Estudios dedicato a Miguel Enguídanos*. Madrid: Porrúa Turanzas, 1989.

Cronin, Gloria L., and L. H. Goldman, Eds. *Saul Bellow in the 1980s: A Collection of Critical Essays*. East Lansing: Michigan State Univ. Press, 1989.
Crook, Nora. *Kipling's Myth of Love and Death*. New York: St. Martin's Press, 1989.
Crowley, John W. *The Mask of Fiction: Essays on W. D. Howells*. Amherst: Univ. of Massachusetts Press, 1989.
———, Ed. *New Essays on "Winesburg, Ohio."* Cambridge: Cambridge Univ. Press, 1990.
Cummins, Elizabeth. *Understanding Ursula K. Le Guin*. Columbia: Univ. of South Carolina Press, 1990.
Dargan, Edwin P. *Anatole France*. New York: Oxford Univ. Press, 1937.
Davies, Philip J., Ed. *Science Fiction, Social Conflict and War*. Manchester: Manchester Univ. Press, 1990.
Davis, Robert M. *Evelyn Waugh and the Forms of His Time*. Washington: Catholic Univ. of America, 1989.
Deats, Sara M., and Lagretta T. Lenker, Eds. *Youth Suicide Prevention: Lessons from Literature*. New York: Plenum, 1989.
Deely, John, and Jonathan Evans, Eds. *Semiotics 1986*. Lanaham, Md.: Univ. Press of America, 1987.
Dellamora, Richard. *Masculine Desire: The Sexual Politics of Victorian Aestheticism*. Chapel Hill: Univ. of North Carolina Press, 1990.
Dembo, L. S. *Detotalized Totalities: Synthesis and Disintegration in Naturalist, Existential, and Socialist Fiction*. Madison: Univ. of Wisconsin Press, 1989.
Dennis, Philip, and Wendell Aycock, Eds. *Literature and Anthropology*. Lubbock: Texas Tech Univ. Press, 1989.
DeSalvo, Louise. *Virginia Woolf: The Impact of Childhood Sexual Abuse on Her Life and Work*. Boston: Beacon, 1989.
Detweiler, Robert. *Breaking the Fall: Religious Readings of Contemporary Fiction*. San Francisco: Harper & Row, 1989.
———, and Willard G. Doty, Eds. *The Daemonic Imagination: Biblical Text and Secular Story*. Atlanta: Scholars, 1990.
D'haen, Theo, and Hans Bertens, Eds. *History and Post-war Writing*. Amsterdam: Rodopi, 1990.
DiAntonio, Robert E. *Brazilian Fiction: Aspects and Evolution of Contemporary Narrative*. Fayetteville: Univ. of Arkansas Press, 1989.
Dick, Susan. *Virginia Woolf*. London: Arnold, 1989.
———, Declan Kiberd, Douglas McMillan, and Joseph Ronsley, Eds. *Essays for Richard Ellmann: Omnium Gatherum*. Kingston, Ont.: McGill-Queen's Univ. Press, 1989; Brt. ed. Gerrards Cross: Smythe, 1989.
Diedrich, Maria, and Christoph Schöneich, Eds. *Studien zur Englischen und Amerikanischen Prosa nach dem Ersten Weltkrieg: Festschrift für Kurt Otten zum 60. Geburtstag*. Darmstadt: Wissenschaftliche Buchgesellschaft, 1986.
———, and Dorothy F. Hornung, Eds. *Women and War: The Changing Status of American Women from the 1930s to the 1950s*. New York: Berg, 1990.
Di Fazio, Margharita, Ed. *Narrare: Percorsi possibili*. Ravenna: Longo, 1989.
Dillard, Annie. *Living by Fiction*. New York: Harper & Row, 1982.
Dobrinsky, Joseph. *The Artist in Conrad's Fiction: A Psychocritical Study*. Ann Arbor: UMI Research Press, 1989.
Doležalová, Anna. *Yü Ta-fu: Specific Traits of His Literary Creation*. Bratislava: Slovak Academy of Sciences, 1971; Am ed. New York: Paragon, 1971.
Donovan, Josephine. *After the Fall: The Demeter-Persephone Myth in Wharton, Cather, and Glasgow*. University Park: Pennsylvania State Univ. Press, 1989.
Dougherty, David C. *Stanley Elkin*. Boston: Twayne, 1990.
Doyle, Esther M., and Victoria H. Floyd, Eds. *Studies in Interpretation*. Amsterdam: Rodopi, 1972.

Drew, Bettina. *Nelson Algren: A Life on the Wild Side*. New York: Putnam, 1989.
Dugdale, John. *Thomas Pynchon: Allusive Parables of Power*. New York: St. Martin's Press, 1990.
Duke, Michael S., Ed. *Modern Chinese Women Writers: Critical Appraisals*. Armonk, N.Y.: Sharpe, 1989.
Dunham, Lowell, and Ivar Ivask, Eds. *The Cardinal Points of Borges*. Norman: Univ. of Oklahoma Press, 1971; Spanish ed. *Asedio a Jorge Luis Borges*, ed. Joaquín Marco. Barcelona: Ultramar, 1982.
Eber, Irene. *Voices from Afar: Modern Chinese Writers on Oppressed Peoples and Their Literature*. Ann Arbor: Univ. of Michigan, 1980.
Eckstein, Barbara J. *The Language of Fiction in a World of Pain: Reading Politics as Paradox*. Philadelphia: Univ. of Pennsylvania Press, 1990.
Eekman, Thomas A., Ed. *Critical Essays on Anton Chekhov*. Boston: Hall, 1989.
Elfenbein, Anna S. *Women on the Color Line: Evolving Stereotypes and the Writings of George Washington Cable, Grace King, and Kate Chopin*. Charlottesville: Univ. Press of Virginia, 1989.
Ellison, David R. *Understanding Albert Camus*. Columbia: Univ. of South Carolina Press, 1990.
Engelberg, Edward. *Elegiac Fictions: The Motif of the Unlived Life*. University Park: Pennsylvania State Univ. Press, 1989.
Enninger, Werner, Joachim Raith, and Karl-Heinz Wandt, Eds. *Internal and External Perspectives on Amish and Mennonite Life*, II. Essen: Unipress, 1986.
Fanning, Charles. *The Irish Voice in America: Irish-American Fiction from the 1790s to the 1980s*. Lexington: Univ. Press of Kentucky, 1990.
Feldstein, Richard, and Judith Roof, Eds. *Feminism and Psychoanalysis*. Ithaca: Cornell Univ. Press, 1989.
Fernández Jiménez, Juan, José J. Labrador Herraiz, and L. Teresa Valdivieso, Eds. *Estudios en homenaje a Enrique Ruiz-Fornells*. Erie, Pa.: Asociación de Licenciados & Doctores Españoles en Estados Unidos, 1990.
Fisher, Benjamin F., Ed. *Poe and His Times: The Artist and His Milieu*. Baltimore: Edgar Allan Poe Society, 1990.
Flora, Joseph M. *Ernest Hemingway: A Study of the Short Fiction*. Boston: Twayne, 1989.
Flower, John E., and Bernard C. Smith, Eds. *François Mauriac: Visions and Reappraisals*. Oxford: Berg, 1989.
Fogel, Daniel M. *"Daisy Miller": A Dark Comedy of Manners*. Boston: Twayne, 1990.
Fogel, Stan, and Gordon Slethaug. *Understanding John Barth*. Columbia: Univ. of South Carolina Press, 1990.
Fonquerne, Yves-René, and Aurora Egido, Eds. *Formas breves del relato*. Madrid: Univ. of Zaragoza, 1986.
Fothergill, Anthony. *Heart of Darkness*. Stony Stratford, England: Open Univ. Press, 1989; Am. ed. Philadelphia: Milton Keynes, 1989.
Fowler, Doreen, and Ann J. Abadie, Eds. *Faulkner and the Craft of Fiction: Faulkner and Yoknapatawpha, 1987*. Jackson: Univ. Press of Mississippi, 1989.
Fraser, Robert, Ed. *Sir James Frazer and the Literary Imagination: Essays in Affinity and Influence*. New York: St. Martin's Press, 1990.
Freeborn, Richard. *The Rise of the Russian Novel*. Cambridge: Cambridge Univ. Press, 1973.
———, R. R. Milner-Gulland, and Charles A. Ward, Eds. *Russian and Slavic Literature*. Cambridge, Mass.: Slavica, 1976.
———, and Jane Grayson, Eds. *Ideology in Russian Literature*. New York: St. Martin's Press, 1990.
Freese, Peter, Ed. *Germany and German Thought in American Literature and Cultural Criticism*. Essen: Blaue Eule, 1990.

Frickey, Pierrette M., Ed. *Critical Perspectives on Jean Rhys*. Washington: Three Continents, 1990.

Friedman, Ellen G., and Miriam Fuchs, Eds. *Breaking the Sequence: Women's Experimental Fiction*. Princeton: Princeton Univ. Press, 1989.

Fries, Marilyn S., Ed. *Responses to Christa Wolf: Critical Essays*. Detroit: Wayne State Univ. Press, 1989.

Fussell, Edwin S. *The French Side of Henry James*. New York: Columbia Univ. Press, 1990.

Gallagher, Susan V., and Roger Lundin. *Literature Through the Eyes of Faith*. New York: Harper & Row, 1989.

Garnett, Rhys, and R. J. Ellis, Eds. *Science Fiction Roots and Branches: Contemporary Critical Approaches*. New York: St. Martin's Press, 1990.

Gaskell, Elizabeth. *"Cousin Phillis" and Other Tales*, ed. Angus Easson. Oxford: Oxford Univ. Press, 1981.

———. *"My Lady Ludlow" and Other Stories*, ed. Edgar Wright. Oxford: Oxford Univ. Press, 1989.

Giannone, Richard. *Flannery O'Connor and the Mystery of Love*. Urbana: Univ. of Illinois Press, 1989.

Gibson, Colin, Ed. *Art and Society in the Victorian Novel*. New York: St. Martin's Press, 1989.

Gillespie, Michael P. *Reading the Book of Himself*. Columbus: Ohio State Univ. Press, 1989.

Gillman, Susan. *Dark Twins: Imposture and Identity in Mark Twain's America*. Chicago: Univ. of Chicago Press, 1989.

Gilman, Stephen. *Galdós and the Art of the European Novel: 1867–1887*. Princeton: Princeton Univ. Press, 1981.

Girgus, Sam B. *Desire and the Political Unconscious in American Literature*. London: Macmillan, 1989; Am. ed. New York: St. Martin's Press, 1990.

Gish, Robert F. *William Carlos Williams: A Study of the Short Fiction*. Boston: Twayne, 1989.

Godden, Richard. *Fiction of Capital: The American Novel from James to Mailer*. Cambridge: Cambridge Univ. Press, 1990.

Goodman, Charlotte M. *Jean Stafford: The Savage Heart*. Austin: Univ. of Texas Press, 1990.

Goonetilleke, D. C. R. A. *Joseph Conrad: Beyond Culture and Background*. New York: St. Martin's Press, 1990.

Graham, Kenneth W., Ed. *Gothic Fictions: Prohibition/Transgression*. New York: AMS, 1989.

Grayson, Jane, and Faith Wigzell. *Nikolay Gogol: Text and Context*. New York: St. Martin's Press, 1989.

Greenstein, Michael. *Third Solitudes: Tradition and Discontinuity in Jewish-Canadian Literature*. Kingston, Ont.: McGill-Queen's Univ. Press, 1989.

Grenberg, Bruce L. *Some Other World to Find: Quest and Negotiation in the Works of Herman Melville*. Urbana: Univ. of Illinois Press, 1989.

Gross, Ruth V., Ed. *Critical Essays on Franz Kafka*. Boston: Hall, 1990.

Gunn, Judith. *Dostoyevsky: Dreamer and Prophet*. Oxford: Lion, 1990.

Guthrie, John. *Annette von Droste-Hülshoff: A German Poet Between Romanticism and Realism*. Oxford: Berg, 1989.

Haggerty, George E. *Gothic Fiction/Gothic Form*. University Park: Pennsylvania State Univ. Press, 1989.

Halliburton, David. *The Color of the Sky: A Study of Stephen Crane*. Cambridge: Cambridge Univ. Press, 1989.

Hanson, Clare, Ed. *Re-reading the Short Story*. New York: St. Martin's Press, 1989.

Harris, Trevor A. Le V. *Maupassant in the Hall of Mirrors: Ironies of Repetition in the Work of Guy de Maupassant*. New York: St. Martin's Press, 1990.

Hart, Gail K. *Readers and Their Fictions in the Novels and Novellas of Gottfried Keller*. Chapel Hill: Univ. of North Carolina Press, 1989.
Hatvary, George E. *Horace Binney Wallace*. Boston: Twayne, 1977.
Hawthorn, Jeremy. *Joseph Conrad: Narrative Technique and Ideological Commitment*. London: Arnold, 1990.
Hayashi, Tetsumaro, and Thomas J. Moore, Eds. *Steinbeck's "The Red Pony": Essays in Criticism*. Muncie, Ind.: Steinbeck Research Institute, Ball State Univ., 1988.
Haymes, Edward R., Ed. *Crossings-Kreuzungen: A Festschrift for Helmut Kreuzer*. Columbia, S.C.: Camden House, 1990.
Hays, Peter L. *Ernest Hemingway*. New York: Continuum, 1990.
Heller, Terry. *"The Turn of the Screw": Bewildered Vision*. Boston: Twayne, 1989.
Henke, Suzette A. *James Joyce and the Politics of Desire*. London: Routledge, 1990.
Herget, Winfried, Klaus P. Jochum, and Ingeborg Weber, Eds. *Theorie und Praxis im Erzählen des 19. und 20. Jahrhunderts: Studien zur englischen und amerikanischen Literatur zu Ehren von Willi Erzgräber*. Tübingen: Narr, 1986.
Hernández, Felisberto. *Obras completas de Felisberto Hernández*, IV. Montevideo: Arca, 1967.
Hernández de López, Ana María, Ed. *La obra de Carlos Fuentes: Una visión múltiple*. Madrid: Pliegos, 1988.
Herrera-Sobek, María, and Helena María Viramontes, Eds. *Chicano Creativity and Criticism: Charting New Frontiers in American Literature*. Houston: Arte Publico, 1988.
Herrmann, Anne. *The Dialogic Difference: "An/Other Woman" in Virginia Woolf and Christa Wolf*. New York: Columbia Univ. Press, 1989.
Hildebidle, John. *Five Irish Writers: The Errand of Keeping Alive*. Cambridge: Harvard Univ. Press, 1989.
Hirsch, Marianne. *The Mother/Daughter Plot: Narrative, Psychoanalysis, Feminism*. Bloomington: Indiana Univ. Press, 1989.
Hitchcock, Peter. *Working-Class Fiction in Theory and Practice: A Reading of Alan Sillitoe*. Ann Arbor: UMI Research Press, 1989.
Hocks, Richard A. *Henry James: A Study of the Short Fiction*. Boston: Twayne, 1990.
Hoffman, Daniel. *Faulkner's Country Matters: Folklore and Folklife in Yoknapatawpha*. Baton Rouge: Louisiana State Univ. Press, 1989.
Hönnighausen, Lothar, Ed. *Faulkner's Discourse: An International Symposium*. Tübingen: Niemeyer, 1989.
Hoskins, Geoffrey, and George F. Cushing, Eds. *Perspectives on Literature and Society in Eastern and Western Europe*. New York: St. Martin's Press, 1989.
Hughes, R. S. *Beyond the Red Pony: A Reader's Companion to Steinbeck's Complete Short Stories*. Metuchen, N.J.: Scarecrow, 1987.
———. *John Steinbeck: A Study of the Short Fiction*. Boston: Twayne, 1989.
Humphries, Jefferson, Ed. *Southern Literature and Literary Theory*. Athens: Univ. of Georgia Press, 1990.
Huntington, John. *Rationalizing Genius: Ideological Strategies in the Classic American Science Fiction Short Story*. New Brunswick: Rutgers Univ. Press, 1989.
Hurst, Mary J. *The Voice of the Child in American Literature: Linguistic Approaches to Fictional Child Language*. Lexington: Univ. Press of Kentucky, 1990.
Hutcheon, Linda. *The Politics of Postmodernism*. London: Routledge, 1989.
Hutchings, Stephen. *A Semiotic Analysis of The Short Stories of Leonid Andreev, 1900–1909*. London: Modern Humanities Research Association, 1990.
Huters, Theodore, Ed. *Reading the Modern Chinese Short Story*. Armonk, N.Y.: Sharpe, 1990.
Huyssen, Andreas, and David Bathrick, Eds. *Modernity and the Text: Revisions of German Modernism*. New York: Columbia Univ. Press, 1989.

Hwang Sun-won. *The Book of Masks: Stories by Hwang Sun-won*, ed. Martin Holman. London: Readers International, 1989.
Imhof, Rüdiger. *John Banville: A Critical Introduction*. Dublin: Wolfhound, 1989.
Inge, Tonette B., Ed. *Southern Women Writers: The New Generation*. Tuscaloosa: Univ. of Alabama Press, 1990.
Innes, C. L. *Chinua Achebe*. Cambridge: Cambridge Univ. Press, 1990.
Irizarry, Estelle. *Francisco Ayala*. Boston: Twayne, 1977.
Isaacs, Neil D. *Grace Paley: A Study of the Short Fiction*. Boston: Twayne, 1990.
Jacobs, Carl. *Uncontainable Romanticism: Shelley, Brontë, Kleist*. Baltimore: Johns Hopkins Univ. Press, 1989.
Jay, Gregory S. *America the Scrivener: Deconstruction and the Subject of Literary History*. Ithaca: Cornell Univ. Press, 1990.
Johnson, Barbara. *The Critical Difference: Essays in the Contemporary Rhetoric of Reading*. Baltimore: Johns Hopkins Univ. Press, 1980.
Jordan, Barry. *Writing and Politics in Franco's Spain*. London: Routledge, 1990.
Jordan, Cynthia S. *Second Stories: The Politics of Language, Form, and Gender in Early American Fiction*. Chapel Hill: Univ. of North Carolina Press, 1989.
Joshi, S. T. *John Dickson Carr: A Critical Study*. Bowling Green: Bowling Green State Univ. Popular Press, 1990.
———. *The Weird Tale*. Austin: Univ. of Texas Press, 1990.
Kakouriotis, A., and R. Parkin-Gounelas, Eds. *Working Papers in Linguistics and Literature*. Thessaloniki: Aristotle Univ., 1989.
Katz-Roy, Ginette, Ed. *Études lawrenciennes*. Paris: Univ. de Paris, 1988.
Keefer, Janice K. *Reading Mavis Gallant*. Toronto: Oxford Univ. Press, 1989.
Kelly, Catriona, Michael Makin, and Donald Shepherd, Eds. *Discontinuous Discourses in Modern Russian Literature*. New York: St. Martin's Press, 1989.
Kelly, Dorothy. *Fictional Genders: Role and Representation in Nineteenth-Century French Narrative*. Lincoln: Univ. of Nebraska Press, 1989.
Kelly, Richard. *V. S. Naipaul*. New York: Continuum, 1989.
Kerr, R. A. *Mario Vargas Llosa: Critical Essays on Characterization*. Potomac, Md.: Scripta Humanistica, 1990.
Kershner, R. B. *Joyce, Bakhtin, and Popular Literature: Chronicles of Disorder*. Chapel Hill: Univ. of North Carolina Press, 1989.
Kielsky, Vera E. *Inevitable Exiles: Cynthia Ozick's View of the Precariousness of Jewish Existence in a Gentile Society*. New York: Lang, 1989.
Kiernan, Robert F. *Saul Bellow*. New York: Continuum, 1989.
King, Adele. *French Women Novelists: Defining Female Style*. New York: St. Martin's Press, 1989.
Kinney, Arthur F., Ed. *Critical Essays on William Faulkner: The McCaslin Family*. Boston: Hall, 1990.
Kipling, Rudyard. *Picking Up Gold and Silver: Stories by Rudyard Kipling*, ed. M. M. Kaye. New York: St. Martin's Press, 1989.
Kirchhoff, Frederick. *William Morris: The Construction of a Male Self, 1856–1872*. Athens: Ohio Univ. Press, 1990.
Knapp, Bettina L. *Machine, Metaphor, and the Writer: A Jungian View*. University Park: Pennsylvania State Univ. Press, 1989.
———. *Gertrude Stein*. New York: Ungar, 1990.
Koelb, Clayton. *Kafka's Rhetoric: The Passion of Reading*. Ithaca: Cornell Univ. Press, 1989.
Kohl, Norbert. *Oscar Wilde: The Works of a Conformist Rebel*, trans. David H. Wilson. 1980; Cambridge: Cambridge Univ. Press, 1989.
Komesu, Okifumi, and Masaru Sekine, Eds. *Irish Writers and Politics*. Savage, Md.: Barnes & Noble, 1990.
Kremer, S. Lillian. *Witness Through Imagination: Jewish American Holocaust Literature*. Detroit: Wayne State Univ. Press, 1989.

Krulik, Theodore. *Roger Zelazny*. New York: Ungar, 1986.
Kuehl, John. *Alternate Worlds: A Study of Postmodern Antirealistic American Fiction*. New York: New York Univ. Press, 1989.
La Bossière, Camille R. *The Victorian "Fol Sage": Comparative Readings on Carlyle, Emerson, Melville and Conrad*. Cranbury, N.J.: Associated Univ. Presses [for Bucknell Univ. Press], 1989.
Land, Stephen K. *Challenge and Conventionality in the Fiction of E. M. Forster*. New York: AMS Press, 1990.
Lane, Ann J. *To "Herland" and Beyond: The Life and Work of Charlotte Perkins Gilman*. New York: Pantheon, 1990.
Lang, Olga. *Pa Chin and His Writings: Chinese Youth Between the Two Revolutions*. Cambridge: Harvard Univ. Press, 1967.
Lattin, Vernon R., Rolando Hinojosa, and Gary D. Keller, Eds. *Tomás Rivera, 1936–1984: The Man and His Work*. Tempe: Bilingual Press, 1988.
Leak, Andrew N. *The Perverted Consciousness: Sexuality and Sartre*. New York: St. Martin's Press, 1989.
Lee, A. Robert, Ed. *The Modern American Novella*. London: Vision, 1989; Am. ed. New York: St. Martin's Press, 1989.
———. *Scott Fitzgerald: The Promise of Life*. London: Vision, 1989; Am. ed. New York: St. Martin's Press, 1989.
Lee, Hermione. *Willa Cather: Double Lives*. New York: Pantheon, 1989.
Lee, Yee, Ed. *The New Realism: Writings from China after the Cultural Revolution*. New York: Hippocrene, 1983.
Leonardi, Susan J. *Dangerous by Degrees: Women at Oxford and the Somerville College Novelists*. New Brunswick: Rutgers Univ. Press, 1989.
Lerner, Lia S., and Isaís Lerner, Eds. *Homenaje a Ana María Barrenchea*. Madrid: Castalia, 1984.
Lesér, Esther H. *Thomas Mann's Short Fiction: An Intellectual Biography*. Cranbury, N.J.: Associated Univ. Presses [for Fairleigh Dickinson Univ. Press], 1989.
Leverenz, David. *Manhood and the American Renaissance*. Ithaca: Cornell Univ. Press, 1989.
Levine, Robert. *Conspiracy and Romance: Studies in Brockden Brown, Cooper, Hawthorne, and Melville*. Cambridge: Cambridge Univ. Press, 1989.
Lewis, Paul. *Comic Effects: Interdisciplinary Approaches to Humor in Literature*. Albany: State Univ. of New York Press, 1989.
Lewis, Robert W., Ed. *"Hemingway in Italy" and Other Essays*. New York: Praeger, 1990.
Limon, John. *The Place of Fiction in the Time of Science: A Disciplinary History of American Writing*. Cambridge: Cambridge Univ. Press, 1990.
Lindstrom, Naomi. *Literary Expressionism in Argentina: The Presentation of Incoherence*. Tempe: Arizona State Univ., 1977.
Ling, Amy. *Between Worlds: Women Writers of Chinese Ancestry*. New York: Pergamon, 1990.
La Littérature chinoise au temps de la guerre de résistance contre le Japon (de 1937 à 1945). Paris: Singer-Polignac Foundation, 1982.
Liu, Wu-chi. *Su Man-shu*. New York: Twayne, 1972.
Lohafer, Susan, and Jo Ellyn Clarey, Eds. *Short Story Theory at a Crossroads*. Baton Rouge: Louisiana State Univ. Press, 1989.
López Criado, Fidel, Ed. *Studies in Modern and Classical Languages and Literatures*, I. Madrid: Orígenes, 1988.
López González, Aralia, Amelia Malagamba, and Elena Urrutia, Eds. *Mujer y literatura mexicana y chicana: Culturas en contacto*. Mexico City: El Colegio de México, 1990.
Loureiro, Angel G., Ed. *Estelas, laberintos, nuevas sendas: Unamuno, Valle-Inclán, García Lorca, la Guerra Civil*. Barcelona: Anthropos, 1988.

Lowe, David A., Ed. *Critical Essays on Ivan Turgenev*. Boston: Hall, 1989.
Lu Xün. *"Diary of a Madman" and Other Stories*, ed. & trans. William A. Lyell. Honolulu: Univ. of Hawaii Press, 1990.
Luedtke, Luther. *Nathaniel Hawthorne and the Romance of the Orient*. Bloomington: Indiana Univ. Press, 1989.
Lynch, Michael F. *Creative Revolt: A Study of Wright, Ellison, and Dostoevsky*. New York: Lang, 1990.
Lynn, David H. *The Hero's Tale: Narrators in the Early Modern Novel*. New York: St. Martin's Press, 1989.
McCall, Dan. *The Silence of Bartleby*. Ithaca: Cornell Univ. Press, 1989.
McCann, Graham. *Woody Allen, New Yorker*. Cambridge, England: Polity, 1990.
McCarthy, Patrick A., Charles Elkins, and Martin H. Greenberg, Eds. *The Legacy of Olaf Stapledon*. Westport: Greenwood, 1989.
McCarthy, Paul. *"The Twisted Mind": Madness in Herman Melville's Fiction*. Iowa City: Univ. of Iowa Press, 1990.
McDermott, John. *Kingsley Amis: English Moralist*. New York: St. Martin's Press, 1989.
Macdonald, Michael H., and Andrew A. Tadie, Eds. *G. K. Chesterton and C. S. Lewis: The Riddle of Joy*. Grand Rapids: Eerdmans, 1989.
McDowell, Nicholas: *Hemingway*. Vero Beach, Fla.: Rourke, 1989.
McElroy, Bernard. *Fiction of the Modern Grotesque*. New York: St. Martin's Press, 1989.
Machado de Assis, Joaquim M. *Cuentos*, ed. Alfredo Bosi. Caracas: Biblioteca Ayacucho, 1978.
McLean, Hugh, Ed. *In the Shade of the Giant: Essays in Tolstoy*. Berkeley: Univ. of California Press, 1989.
McMullen, Lorraine, Ed. *The Ethel Wilson Symposium*. Ottawa: Univ. of Ottawa Press, 1982.
McNerney, Kathleen. *Understanding Gabriel García Márquez*. Columbia: Univ. of South Carolina Press, 1989.
Maida, Patricia D. *Mother of Detective Fiction: The Life and Works of Anna Katharine Green*. Bowling Green: Bowling Green Univ. Popular Press, 1989.
Mailloux, Peter. *A Hesitation before Birth: The Life of Franz Kafka*. Cranbury, N.J.: Associated Univ. Presses [for Univ. of Delaware Press], 1989.
Majewski, Henry. *Paradigm & Parody: Images of Creativity in French Romanticism—Vigny, Hugo, Balzac, Gautier, Musset*. Charlottesville: Univ. Press of Virginia, 1989.
Makowsky, Veronica A. *Caroline Gordon: A Biography*. New York: Oxford Univ. Press, 1989.
Mallett, Phillip, Ed. *Kipling Considered*. New York: St. Martin's Press, 1989.
Malmqvist, Göran, Ed. *Modern Chinese Literature and Its Social Context*. Stockholm: Nobel Foundation, 1975.
Mancini, Albert N., Paolo A. Giordano, and Anthony J. Tamburri, Eds. *Italiana 1988*. River Forest, Ill.: Rosary College, 1990.
Mandelker, Amy, and Robert Reeder, Eds. *The Supernatural in Slavic and Baltic Literature: Essays in Honor of Victor Terras*. Columbus: Slavica, 1988.
Manning, Susan. *The Puritan-Provincial Vision: Scottish and American Literature of the Nineteenth Century*. Cambridge: Cambridge Univ. Press, 1990.
Manuud, Antonio G., Ed. *Brown Heritage: Essays on Philippine Cultural Tradition and Literature*. Quezon City: Manila Univ. Press, 1967.
Marco, Joaquín, Ed. *Asedio a Jorge Luis Borges*. Madrid: Ultramar, 1981.
Marotti, Maria O. *The Duplicating Imagination: Twain and the Twain Papers*. University Park: Pennsylvania State Univ. Press, 1990.
Massa, Ann, Ed. *American Declarations of Love*. New York: St. Martin's Press, 1990.

Matthew, Robert. *Japanese Science Fiction: A View of a Changing Society*. London: Routledge, 1989.
Melada, Ivan. *Sheridan Le Fanu*. Boston: Twayne, 1987.
Menchacatorre, Félix, Ed. *Ensayos de literatura europea e hispanoamericana*. San Sebastián: Univ. de País Vasco, 1990.
Mersereau, John. *Mikhail Lermontov*. Carbondale: Southern Illinois Univ. Press, 1962.
———. *Russian Romantic Fiction*. Ann Arbor: Ardis, 1983.
———. *Orest Somov: Russian Fiction Between Romanticism and Realism*. Ann Arbor: Ardis, 1989.
Meyer, Jeffrey, Ed. *Graham Greene: A Revaluation*. New York: St. Martin's Press, 1990.
Meyering, Sheryl L., Ed. *Charlotte Perkins Gilman: The Woman and Her Works*. Ann Arbor: UMI Research Press, 1989.
Milder, Robert, Ed. *Critical Essays on Melville's "Billy Budd, Sailor."* Boston: Hall, 1989.
Mileck, Joseph. *Hermann Hesse: Life, Work, and Criticism*. Fredericton, N.B.: York, 1984.
Miller, David. *W. H. Hudson and the Elusive Paradise*. New York: St. Martin's Press, 1990.
Miller, J. Hillis. *Versions of Pygmalion*. Cambridge: Harvard Univ. Press, 1990.
Miller, Karl. *Authors*. Oxford: Oxford Univ. Press, 1989.
Miller, R. Baxter. *The Art and Imagination of Langston Hughes*. Lexington: Univ. Press of Kentucky, 1989.
Miller, R. H. *Understanding Graham Greene*. Columbia: Univ. of South Carolina Press, 1990.
Milne, Lesley. *Mikhail Bulgakov: A Critical Biography*. Cambridge: Cambridge Univ. Press, 1990.
Moates, Marianne M. *A Bridge of Childhood: Truman Capote's Southern Years*. New York: Holt, 1989.
Mogen, David, Mark Busby, and Paul Bryant, Eds. *The Frontier Experience and the American Dream*. College Station: Texas A&M Univ. Press, 1989.
Moi, Toril. *Feminist Theory & Simone de Beauvoir*. Oxford: Blackwell, 1990.
Monday, Henrietta, Ed. *The Waking Sphinx: South African Essays on Russian Culture*. Johannesburg: Univ. of Witwatersrand, 1989.
Morris, Virginia B. *Double Jeopardy: Women Who Kill in Victorian Fiction*. Lexington: Univ. Press of Kentucky, 1990.
Mose, Kenrick. *Defamiliarization in the Work of Gabriel García Márquez from 1947–1967*. Lewiston, N.Y.: Mellen, 1989.
Moser, Charles H., Ed. *The Cambridge History of Russian Literature*. Cambridge: Cambridge Univ. Press, 1989.
Mukerji, Vanita S. *Ivo Andrić: A Critical Biography*. Jefferson, N.C.: McFarland, 1990.
Murfin, Ross C., Ed. *Conrad Revisited: Essays for the Eighties*. University: Univ. of Alabama Press, 1985.
———. *Joseph Conrad—"Heart of Darkness": A Case Study in Contemporary Criticism*. New York: St. Martin's Press, 1989.
Murphy, John J., Linda H. Adams, and Paul Rawlins, Eds. *Willa Cather: Family, Community, and History*. Provo: Brigham Young Univ., 1990.
Murphy, P. J. *Reconstructing Beckett: Language for Being in Samuel Beckett's Fiction*. Toronto: Univ. of Toronto Press, 1990.
Murray, Brian. *H. G. Wells*. New York: Continuum, 1990.
Nelson, Roy J. *Causality and Narrative in French Fiction from Zola to Robbe-Grillet*. Columbus: Ohio State Univ. Press, 1990.
Neumeister, Sebastián, Ed. *Actas del IX Congreso de la Asociación International de Hispanistas*, II. Frankfurt: Vervuert, 1989.

Newcomb, Mildred. *The Imagined World of Charles Dickens*. Columbus: Ohio State Univ. Press, 1989.

Ng, Mao-sang. *The Russian Hero in Modern Chinese Fiction*. Hong Kong: Chinese Univ. Press, 1988; Am. ed. Albany: State Univ. of New York Press, 1988.

Nicholson, Colin, Ed. *Critical Approaches to the Fiction of Margaret Laurence*. Vancouver: Univ. of British Columbia Press, 1990.

Nischik, Reingard M., and Barbara Korte, Eds. *Modes of Narrative: Approaches to American, Canadian and British Fiction—Presented to Helmut Bonheim*. Würzburg: Königshausen & Neumann, 1990.

Ochshorn, Kathleen G. *The Heart's Essential Landscape: Bernard Malamud's Hero*. New York: Lang, 1990.

O'Hara, James E. *John Cheever: A Study of the Short Fiction*. Boston: Twayne, 1989.

O'Healy, Áine. *Cesare Pavese*. Boston: Twayne, 1988.

Olsen, Lance. *Circus of the Mind in Motion: Postmodernism and the Comic Vision*. Detroit: Wayne State Univ. Press, 1990.

Olster, Stacey. *Reminiscence and Re-Creation in Contemporary American Fiction*. Cambridge: Cambridge Univ. Press, 1989.

Ostwalt, Conrad E. *After Eden: The Secularization of American Space in the Fiction of Willa Cather and Theodore Dreiser*. Cranbury. N.J.: Associated Univ. Presses [for Bucknell Univ. Press], 1990.

Padhi, Bibhu. *D. H. Lawrence: Modes of Fictional Style*. Troy, N.Y.: Whitston, 1989.

Paffard, Mark. *Kipling's Indian Fiction*. New York: St. Martin's Press, 1989.

Paglia, Camille. *Sexual Personae: Art and Decadence from Nefertite to Emily Dickinson*. New Haven: Yale Univ. Press, 1990.

Pahl, Dennis. *Architects of the Abyss: The Indeterminate Fictions of Poe, Hawthorne, and Melville*. Columbia: Univ. of Missouri Press, 1989.

Palmer, Paulina. *Contemporary Women's Fiction: Narrative Practice and Feminist Theory*. Jackson: Univ. Press of Mississippi, 1989.

Panshin, Alexel, and Cory Panshin. *The World Beyond the Hill: Science Fiction and the Quest for Transcendence*. Los Angeles: Tarcher, 1989.

Paolini, Gilbert, Ed. *La Chispa '89: Selected Proceedings*. New Orleans: Tulane Univ., 1989.

Papke, Mary E. *Verging on the Abyss: The Social Fiction of Kate Chopin and Edith Wharton*. Westport: Greenwood, 1990.

Parker, Hershel. *Reading "Billy Budd."* Evanston: Northwestern Univ. Press, 1990.

Patterson, Yolanda. *Simone de Beauvoir and the Demystification of Motherhood*. Ann Arbor: UMI Research Press, 1989.

Pavón, Alfredo, Ed. *Paquette: Cuento—La ficción en México*. Tlaxcala: Univ. Autónoma de Tlaxcala, 1990.

Pearlman, Mickey, Ed. *American Women Writing Fiction: Memory, Identity, Family, Space*. Lexington: Univ. Press of Kentucky, 1989.

———. *Mother Puzzles: Daughters and Mothers in Contemporary American Literature*. Westport: Greenwood, 1989.

Pecora, Vincent P. *Self and Form in Modern Narrative*. Baltimore: Johns Hopkins Univ. Press, 1989.

Peppard, Victor. *The Poetics of Yury Olesha*. Gainesville: Univ. of Florida Press, 1989.

Pérez Firmat, Gustavo, Ed. *Do the Americas Have a Common Literature?* Durham: Duke Univ. Press, 1990.

Petrone, Penny. *Native Literature in Canada: From the Oral Tradition to the Present*. Toronto: Oxford Univ. Press, 1990.

Petry, Alice H. *Fitzgerald's Craft of Short Fiction: The Collected Stories, 1920–1935*. Ann Arbor: UMI Research Press, 1989.

Phelan, James, Ed. *Reading Narrative: Form, Ethics, Ideology*. Columbus: Ohio State Univ. Press, 1989.

Phillips, K. J. *Dying Gods in Twentieth-Century Fiction*. Cranbury, N.J.: Associated Univ. Presses [for Bucknell Univ. Press], 1990.
Pierce, John J. *Foundations of Science Fiction: A Study in Imagination and Evolution*. Westport: Greenwood, 1987.
———. *Great Themes of Science Fiction: A Study in Imagination and Evolution*. Westport: Greenwood, 1987.
Polowy, Teresa. *The Novellas of Valentin Rasputin: Genre, Language and Style*. New York: Lang, 1989.
Porter, Robert. *Four Contemporary Russian Writers*. Oxford: Berg, 1989.
Preston, Peter, and Peter Hoare, Eds. *D. H. Lawrence in the Modern World*. New York: Cambridge Univ. Press, 1989.
Priebe, Richard K., Ed. *Ghanaian Literatures*. Westport: Greenwood, 1988.
Prušek, Jaroslav. *The Lyrical and the Epic: Studies in Modern Chinese Literature*. Bloomington: Indiana Univ. Press, 1980.
———, Ed. *Studies in Modern Chinese Literature*. Berlin: Akademie-Verlag, 1964.
Punter, David. *The Romantic Unconscious: A Study in Narcissism and Patriarchy*. New York: New York Univ. Press, 1989.
Purdy, John L. *Word Ways: The Novels of D'Arcy McNickle*. Tucson: Univ. of Arizona Press, 1990.
Ragen, Brian A. *A Wreck on the Road to Damascus: Innocence, Guilt, and Conversion in Flannery O'Connor*. Chicago: Loyola Univ. Press, 1989.
Ramírez Mattei, Aida Elsa. *La Narrativa de Carlos Fuentes*. Río Piedras: Univ. of Puerto Rico, 1983.
Ramos, Elías A. *El cuento venezolano: 1950–1970*. Madrid: Editorial Playor, 1979.
Ramras-Rauch, Gila. *The Arab in Israeli Literature*. Bloomington: Indiana Univ. Press, 1989; Brt. ed. London: Taurus, 1989.
Rancour-Laferriere, Daniel, Ed. *Russian Literature and Psychoanalysis*. Amsterdam: Benjamins, 1989.
Rasporich, Beverly J. *Dance of the Sexes: Art and Gender in the Fiction of Alice Munro*. Edmonton: Univ. of Alberta Press, 1990.
Ratcliff, Dillwyn F. *Venezuelan Prose Fiction*. New York: Instituto de las Españas, 1933.
Re, Lucia. *Calvino and the Age of Neorealism: Fables of Estrangement*. Stanford: Stanford Univ. Press, 1990.
Reed, W. L. *Meditations on the Hero: A Study of the Romantic Hero in Nineteenth-Century Fiction*. New Haven: Yale Univ. Press, 1974.
Reh, Albert M. *Literatur und Psychologie*. Bern: Lang, 1986.
Reid, J. H. *Writing Without Taboos: The New East German Literature*. Oxford: Berg, 1990.
Restuccia, Frances L. *Joyce and the Law of the Father*. New Haven: Yale Univ. Press, 1989.
Ricci, Franco. *Difficult Games: A Reading of "I racconti" by Italo Calvino*. Waterloo, Ont.: Wilfrid Laurier Univ. Press, 1990.
Riemer, James D. *From Satire to Subversion: The Fantasies of James Branch Cabell*. Westport: Greenwood, 1989.
Rising, Catharine. *Darkness at Heart: Fathers and Sons in Conrad*. Westport: Greenwood, 1990.
Roberts, Edgar V., and Henry E. Jacobs. *Instructor's Manual [for] "Fiction: An Introduction to Reading and Writing, Second Edition."* Englewood Cliffs: Prentice-Hall, 1989.
Roberts, Marie. *Gothic Immortality: The Brotherhood of the Rosy Cross*. London: Routledge, 1990.
Roberts, Thomas J. *An Aesthetics of Junk Fiction*. Athens: Univ. of Georgia Press, 1990.
Roe, David. *Gustave Flaubert*. New York: St. Martin's Press, 1989.

Roman, Judith A. *Annie Adams Fields: The Spirit of Charles Street*. Bloomington: Indiana Univ. Press, 1990.
Rooke, Constance. *Fear of the Open Heart: Essays on Contemporary Canadian Writing*. Toronto: Coach House, 1989.
Roskies, David G., Ed. *The Literature of Destruction: Jewish Responses to Catastrophe*. Philadelphia: Jewish Publication Society, 1989.
Rosowski, Susan J., Ed. *Cather Studies*, I. Lincoln: Univ. of Nebraska Press, 1990.
Ross, Stephen M. *Fiction's Inexhaustible Voice: Speech and Writing in Faulkner*. Athens: Univ. of Georgia Press, 1989.
Rubin, Louis D., Ed. *The Comic Imagination in American Literature*. New Brunswick: Rutgers Univ. Press, 1973.
Ruddick, Lisa. *Reading Gertrude Stein: Body, Text, Gnosis*. Ithaca: Cornell Univ. Press, 1990.
Ruffin, Paul, and Stuart Wright, Eds. *To Come Up Grinning: A Tribute to George Garrett*. Huntsville: The Texas Review Press, 1989.
Ruffinelli, Jorge. *El otro México: México en la obra de B. Traven, D. H. Lawrence y Malcolm Lowry*. Mexico City: Nueva Imagen, 1978.
Sachs, Viola. *The Myth of America: Essays in the Structures of Literary Imagination*. The Hague: Mouton, 1973.
Saciuk, Olena H., Ed. *The Shape of the Fantastic: Selected Essays from the Seventh International Conference on the Fantastic in the Arts*. Westport: Greenwood, 1990.
Saldívar, Ramón. *Chicano Narrative: The Dialectics of Difference*. Madison: Univ. of Wisconsin Press, 1990.
Saltzman, Arthur M. *Design of Darkness in Contemporary American Fiction*. Philadelphia: Univ. of Pennsylvania Press, 1990.
Samson, John. *White Lies: Melville's Narratives of Facts*. Ithaca: Cornell Univ. Press, 1989.
Sandbank, Shimon. *After Kafka: The Influence of Kafka's Fiction*. Athens: Univ. of Georgia Press, 1989.
Sander, Reinhard W. *The Trinidad Awakening: West Indian Literature of the Nineteen-Thirties*. Westport: Greenwood, 1988.
Sanders, David. *John Hersey*. New York: Twayne, 1967.
———. *John Hersey Revisited*. Boston: Twayne, 1990.
Scheick, William J. *Fictional Structure and Ethics: The Turn-of-the-Century English Novel*. Athens: Univ. of Georgia Press, 1990.
Schirmeister, Pamela. *The Consolations of Space: The Place of Romance in Hawthorne, Melville, and James*. Stanford: Stanford Univ. Press, 1990.
Schirmer, Gregory A. *William Trevor: A Study of His Fiction*. London: Routledge, 1990.
Schmid, Wolf, Ed. *Mythos in der Slawischen Moderne*. Vienna: Gesellschaft zür Förderung Slawistischer, 1987.
Scholes, Robert. *Semiotics and Interpretation*. New Haven: Yale Univ. Press, 1982.
Schulz, Max F. *The Muses of John Barth*. Baltimore: Johns Hopkins Univ. Press, 1990.
Schulz, Volker. *Das kurzepische Werk Graham Greenes: Gesamtdarstellung und Einzelinterpretationen*. Trier: Wissenschaftlicher, 1987.
Schwerdt, Lisa M. *Isherwood's Fiction: The Self and Technique*. New York: St. Martin's Press, 1989.
Scott, Malcolm. *The Struggle for the Soul of the French Novel: French Catholic and Realist Novelists, 1850–1970*. Washington: Catholic Univ. of America Press, 1990.
Seed, David. *The Fiction of Joseph Heller: Against the Grain*. New York: St. Martin's Press, 1989.
Segal, Naomi. *Narcissus and Echo: Women in the French "Recit."* Manchester: Manchester Univ. Press, 1988.

Seymour-Smith, Martin. *Rudyard Kipling*. New York: St. Martin's Press, 1989.
Sharma, T. R., Ed. *Essays on Leo Tolstoy*. Meerut: Shalabh Prakashan, 1989.
Shaw, W. David. *Victorians and Mystery: Crises of Representation*. Ithaca: Cornell Univ. Press, 1990.
Sherman, Sarah W. *Sarah Orne Jewett, An American Persephone*. Hanover, N.H.: Univ. Press of New England [for Univ. of New Hampshire Press], 1989.
Shneidman, N. N. *Soviet Literature in the 1980s: Decade of Transition*. Toronto: Univ. of Toronto Press, 1989.
Showalter, Elaine. *Sexual Anarchy: Gender and Culture at the Fin de Siècle*. New York: Viking, 1990.
———, Ed. *Speaking of Gender*. New York: Routledge, 1989.
Showalter, English. *"The Stranger": Humanity and the Absurd*. Boston: Twayne, 1989.
Siegel, Ben, Ed. *The American Writer and the University*. Cranbury, N.J.: Associated Univ. Presses [for Univ. of Delaware Press], 1989.
Siegle, Robert. *Suburban Ambush: Downtown Writing and the Fiction of Insurgency*. Baltimore: Johns Hopkins Univ. Press, 1989.
Simonson, Harold P. *Beyond the Frontier: Writers, Western Regionalism, and a Sense of Place*. Fort Worth: Texas Christian Univ. Press, 1989.
Simpson, Amelia S. *Detective Fiction from Latin America*. Cranbury, N.J.: Associated Univ. Presses [for Fairleigh Dickinson Univ. Press], 1990.
Singh, Amritjit, and K. Ayyappa Paniker, Eds. *The Magic Circle of Henry James: Essays in Honour of Darshan Singh Maini*. New York: Envoy, 1989.
Slade, Joseph W. *Thomas Pynchon*. New York: Lang, 1990.
———, and Judith Y. Lee, Eds. *Beyond the Two Cultures: Essays on Science, Technology, and Literature*. Ames: Iowa State Univ. Press, 1990.
Slupski, Zbigniew, Ed. *A Selective Guide to Chinese Literature 1900–1949*, II. Leiden: Brill, 1988.
Solotaroff, Robert. *Bernard Malamud: A Study of the Short Fiction*. Boston: Twayne, 1989.
Sorkin, Adam J., Ed. *Politics and the Muse: Studies in the Politics of Recent American Literature*. Bowling Green: Bowling Green State Univ. Popular Press, 1989.
Sorrentino, Fernando. *"Sanitary Centennial" and Selected Short Stories*, ed. Thomas C. Meehan. Austin: Univ. of Texas Press, 1988.
Spivey, Ted R., and Arthur Waterman, Eds. *Conrad Aiken: A Priest of Consciousness*. New York: AMS Press, 1989.
Spofford, Harriet Prescott. *"The Amber Gods" and Other Stories*, ed. Alfred Bendixen. New Brunswick: Rutgers Univ. Press, 1989.
Spolsky, Ellen, Ed. *The Uses of Adversity: Failure and Accommodation in Reader Response*. Cranbury, N.J.: Associated Univ. Presses [for Bucknell Univ. Press], 1990.
Sprague, Claire, Ed. *In Pursuit of Doris Lessing: Nine Nations Reading*. New York: St. Martin's Press, 1990.
Squires, Michael, and Keith Cushman, Eds. *The Challenge of D. H. Lawrence*. Madison: Univ. of Wisconsin Press, 1990.
Staines, David, Ed. *Stephen Leacock: A Reappraisal*. Ottawa: Univ. of Ottawa Press, 1986.
Stanton, Edward F. *Hemingway and Spain: A Pursuit*. Seattle: Univ. of Washington Press, 1989.
Stelzig, Eugene L. *Hermann Hesse's Fiction of the Self: Autobiography and the Confessional Imagination*. Princeton: Princeton Univ. Press, 1988.
Stevenson, Anne. *Bitter Fame: A Life of Sylvia Plath*. Boston: Houghton Mifflin, 1989.
Stich, K. R., Ed. *Reflections: Autobiography and Canadian Literature*. Ottawa: Univ. of Ottawa Press, 1988.

Stock, R. D. *The Flutes of Dionysus: Daemonic Enthrallment in Literature*. Lincoln: Univ. of Nebraska Press, 1989.
Stoll, Anita K., Ed. *A Different Reality: Studies in Elena Garro*. Cranbury, N.J.: Associated Univ. Presses [for Bucknell Univ. Press], 1990.
Stover, Leon. *Harry Harrison*. Boston: Twayne, 1990.
Stummer, Peter O., Ed. *The Story Must Be Told: Short Narrative Prose in the New English Literature*. Würzburg: Königshausen and Neumann, 1986.
Sucher, Laurie. *The Fiction of Ruth Prawer Jhabvala: The Politics of Passion*. New York: St. Martin's Press, 1989.
Sullivan, Walter. *"In Praise of Bloody Sports" and Other Essays*. Baton Rouge: Louisiana State Univ. Press, 1990.
Summers, Claude J. *Gay Fictions: Wilde to Stonewall*. New York: Continuum, 1990.
Sundquist, Eric J., Ed. *Frederick Douglass: New Literary and Historical Essays*. Cambridge: Cambridge Univ. Press, 1990.
Sussman, Henry. *Afterimages of Modernity: Structure and Indifference in Twentieth-Century Literature*. Baltimore: Johns Hopkins Univ. Press, 1990.
Sutherland, John. *Mrs. Humphry Ward: Eminent Victorian, Pre-eminent Edwardian*. Oxford: Oxford Univ. Press, 1990.
Swain, James O. *Juan Marin—Chilean: The Man and His Writings*. Cleveland, Tenn.: Pathway Press, 1971.
Swanson, Philip, Ed. *Landmarks in Modern Latin American Fiction*. London: Routledge, 1990.
Taylor, Helen. *Gender, Race, and Region in the Writing of Grace King, Ruth McEnery Stuart, and Kate Chopin*. Baton Rouge: Louisiana State Univ. Press, 1989.
Taylor, Irene. *Holy Ghosts: The Male Muses of Emily and Charlotte Brontë*. New York: Columbia Univ. Press, 1990.
Taylor, Jacqueline. *Grace Paley: Illuminating the Dark Lives*. Austin: Univ. of Texas Press, 1990.
Terras, Victor, Ed. *American Contributions to the Seventh International Congress of Slavists, Warsaw, August 21–27, 1973*, II. The Hague: Mouton, 1973.
Thacker, Robert. *The Great Prairie Fact and Literary Imagination*. Albuquerque: Univ. of New Mexico Press, 1989.
Thody, Philip. *Albert Camus*. New York: St. Martin's Press, 1989.
Thomas, Ronald R. *Dreams of Authority: Freud and the Fictions of the Unconscious*. Ithaca: Cornell Univ. Press, 1990.
Thompson, Bruce. *Schnitzler's Vienna: Image of a Society*. London: Routledge, 1990.
Thompson, Richard J. *Everlasting Voices: Aspects of the Modern Irish Short Story*. Troy, N.Y.: Whitston, 1989.
Thurin, Erik I. *The Humanization of Willa Cather: Classicism in an American Classic*. Lund: Lund Univ. Press, 1990.
Timmerman, John H. *The Dramatic Landscape of Steinbeck's Short Stories*. Norman: Univ. of Oklahoma Press, 1990.
Toker, Leona. *Nabokov: The Mystery of Literary Structures*. Ithaca: Cornell Univ. Press, 1989.
Torres, Carmen L. *La cuentística de Virgilio Piñera: Estrategias humorísticas*. Madrid: Pliegos, 1989.
Torsney, Cheryl B. *The Grief of Artistry*. Athens: Univ. of Georgia Press, 1989.
Trachtenberg, Stanley. *Understanding Donald Barthelme*. Columbia: Univ. of South Carolina Press, 1990.
Trodd, Anthea. *Domestic Crimes in the Victorian Novel*. New York: St. Martin's Press, 1989.
Tropp, Martin. *Images of Fear: How Horror Stories Helped Shape Modern Culture, 1818–1918*. Jefferson, N.C.: McFarland, 1990.

Trouard, Dawn, Ed. *Eudora Welty: Eye of the Storyteller*. Kent: Kent State Univ. Press, 1989.
Turner, C. J. G. *Pechorin: An Essay on Lermontov's "A Hero of Our Time."* Birmingham: Univ. of Birmingham, 1978.
Turner, Frederick. *Spirit of Place: The Making of an American Literary Landscape*. San Francisco: Sierra Club, 1989.
Turner, W. Craig, and Lee E. Harding, Eds. *Critical Essays on Eudora Welty*. Boston: Hall, 1989.
Upelson, Joseph H. *Dreamer of the Ghetto: The Life and Works of Israel Zangwill*. Tuscaloosa: Univ. of Alabama Press, 1990.
Valis, Noël, Ed. *"Malevolent Insemination" and Other Essays on Clarín*. Ann Arbor: Univ. of Michigan, 1990.
———, and Carol Maiser, Eds. *In the Feminine Mode: Essays on Hispanic Women Writers*. Cranbury, N.J.: Associated Univ. Presses [for Bucknell Univ. Press], 1990.
Villacorta, Wilfrido V., Isagani R. Cruz, and Ma. Lourdes Brillantes, Eds. *Manila: History, People, and Culture*. Manila: De La Salle Univ. Press, 1989.
Voelker, Joseph C. *Art and the Accidental in Anne Tyler*. Columbia: Univ. of Missouri Press, 1989.
Vohra, Ranbir. *Lao She and the Chinese Revolution*. Cambridge, Mass.: East Asian Research Center, 1974.
Waldron, Ann. *Close Connections: Caroline Gordon and the Southern Renaissance*. Knoxville: Univ. of Tennessee Press, 1989.
Walker, David H. *André Gide*. New York: St. Martin's Press, 1990.
Walker, Ronald G., and June M. Frazer, Eds. *The Cunning Craft: Original Essays on Detective Fiction and Contemporary Literary Theory*. Macomb: Western Illinois Univ. Press, 1990.
Wallenrod, Reuben. *The Literature of Modern Israel*. New York: Abelard-Schuman, 1956.
Warner, Keith Q., Ed. *Critical Perspectives on Léon-Gontran Damas*. Washington: Three Continents, 1988.
Watkins, G. K. *God and Circumstance: A Study of Intent in Edgar Allan Poe's "The Narrative of Arthur Gordon Pym" and Mark Twain's "The Great Dark."* New York: Lang, 1989.
Waxman, Barbara F. *From the Hearth to the Open Road: A Feminist Study of Aging in Contemporary Literature*. Westport: Greenwood, 1990.
Welch, Robert, and Suheil Badi Bushrui, Eds. *Literature and the Art of Criticism*. Gerrards Cross, Buckinghamshire: Smythe, 1988; Am. ed. Totowa, N.J.: Barnes & Noble, 1988.
Westling, Louise. *Eudora Welty*. Totowa, N.J.: Barnes & Noble, 1989.
White, Ray L. *"Winesburg, Ohio": An Exploration*. Boston: Twayne, 1990.
Whitton, Kenneth S. *Dürrenmatt: Reinterpretation in Retrospect*. New York: Berg, 1990.
Wilde, Alan. *Horizons of Assent: Modernism, Postmodernism, and the Ironic Imagination*. Baltimore: Johns Hopkins Univ. Press, 1981.
Williams, Raymond L. *Mario Vargas Llosa*. New York: Ungar, 1986.
Wilt, Judith. *Abortion, Choice, and Contemporary Fiction: The Armageddon of the Maternal Instinct*. Chicago: Univ. of Chicago Press, 1990.
Wisker, Alistair. *The Writing of Nathanael West*. New York: St. Martin's Press, 1990.
Wolfe, Alan. *Suicidal Narrative in Japanese: The Case of Dazai Osamu*. Princeton: Princeton Univ. Press, 1990.
Wolfe, Peter. *Yukio Mishima*. New York: Continuum, 1989.
Wolford, Chester L. *Stephen Crane: A Study of the Short Fiction*. Boston: Twayne, 1989.

Wollaeger, Mark A. *Joseph Conrad and the Fictions of Skepticism*. Stanford: Stanford Univ. Press, 1990.
Woodring, Carl. *Nature into Art: Cultural Transformations in Nineteenth-Century Britain*. Cambridge: Harvard Univ. Press, 1989.
Woodward, James B. *Leonid Andreyev: A Study*. Oxford: Oxford Univ. Press, 1969.
Worton, Michael, and Judith Still, Eds. *Intertextuality: Theories and Practice*. Manchester: Manchester Univ. Press, 1990.
Wright, A. Colin. *Mikhail Bulgakov: Life and Interpretations*. Toronto: Univ. of Toronto Press, 1978.
Wright, T. R. *Hardy and the Erotic*. New York: St. Martin's Press, 1989.
Yaeger, Patricia, and Beth Kowaleski-Wallace, Eds. *Refiguring the Father: New Feminist Readings of Patriarchy*. Carbondale: Southern Illinois Univ. Press, 1989.
Yahnke, Robert E., and Richard M. Eastman. *Aging in Literature: A Reader's Guide*. Chicago: American Library Association, 1990.
Yudkin, Leon I., Ed. *Agnon: Text and Context in English Translation*. New York: Wiener, 1988.
Zamora, Lois P. *Writing the Apocalypse: Historical Vision in Contemporary U. S. and Latin American Fiction*. Cambridge: Cambridge Univ. Press, 1989.
Ziegler, Heide, Ed. *Facing Texts: Encounters Between Contemporary Writers and Critics*. Durham: Duke Univ. Press, 1988.
Ziolkowski, Theodore. *German Romanticism and Its Institutions*. Princeton: Princeton Univ. Press, 1990.
Zuckert, Catherine H. *Natural Right and the American Imagination: Political Philosophy in Novel Form*. Savage, Md.: Rowman & Littlefield, 1990.

A Checklist of Journals Used

Acta Germanica	*Acta Germanica: Jahrbuch des Südafrikanischen Germanistenverbandes*
	Alba de América
Aligarh Crit Misc	*The Aligarh Critical Miscellany*
Am Imago	*American Imago: A Psychoanalytic Journal for Culture, Science, and the Arts*
Am Lit	*American Literature: A Journal of Literary History, Criticism, and Bibliography*
Am Lit Hist	*American Literary History*
Am Lit Realism	*American Literary Realism, 1870–1910*
Am Notes & Queries	*American Notes and Queries*
Am Q	*American Quarterly*
Am Stud Scandinavia	*American Studies in Scandinavia*
Am Transcendental Q	*American Transcendental Quarterly*
Americas R	*The Americas Review: A Review of Hispanic Literature and Art of the USA*
Anales de la Literatura Española	*Anales de la Literatura Española Contemporánea*
	L'Année Balzacienne
Anthropos	*Anthropos: International Review of Ethnology and Linguistics*
Antigonish R	*The Antigonish Review*
Appalachian J	*Appalachian Journal: A Regional Studies Review*
	Applied Linguistics
Archiv	*Archiv für das Studium der Neueren Sprachen und Literaturen*
Ariel	*Ariel: A Review of International English Literature*

Ariel I	*Ariel: A Review of Arts & Letters in Israel*
Arizona Q	*Arizona Quarterly*
Australian Lit Stud	*Australian Literary Studies*
Baker Street J	*The Baker Street Journal: An Irregular Quarterly of Sherlockiana*
Black Am Lit Forum	*Black American Literature Forum* [formerly *Negro American Literature Forum*]
Books Abroad	*Books Abroad* [retitled *World Literature Today: A Literary Quarterly of the University of Oklahoma*]
Brasil/Brazil	*Brasil/Brazil: Revista de Literatura Brasileira/A Journal of Brazilian Literature*
Bucknell R	*Bucknell Review: A Scholarly Journal of Letters, Arts and Sciences*
Bull de la Soc Théophile Gautier	*Bulletin de la Société Théophile Gautier*
Bull des Amis	*Bulletin des Amis d'André Gide*
Bull Hispanic Stud	*Bulletin of Hispanic Studies*
Cadernos de Lingüística	*Cadernos de Lingüística e Teoria da Literatura*
Callaloo	*Callaloo: An Afro-American and African Journal of Arts and Letters*
Canadian J Irish Stud	*Canadian Journal of Irish Studies*
Canadian Lit	*Canadian Literature*
CEA Critic	*College English Association Critic*
Celfan R	*Revue Celfan/Celfan Review*
Cenobio	*Cenobio: Revista Trimestrale di Cultura*
Chasqui	*Chasqui: Revista de Literatura Latinoamericana*
Chicago R	*Chicago Review*
Chinese Lit	*Chinese Literature*
Christianity & Lit	*Christianity and Literature*
Chu-Shikoku Stud Am Lit	*Chu-Shikoku Studies in American Literature*
Cincinnati Romance R	*Cincinnati Romance Review*

Círculo	*Círculo: Revista de Cultura Panamericana*
Cithara	*Cithara: Essays in the Judaeo-Christian Tradition*
Classical & Mod Lit	*Classical and Modern Literature: A Quarterly*
Claudel Stud	*Claudel Studies*
Clergy R	*Clergy Review*
Clio	*Clio: A Journal of Literature, History, and the Philosophy of History*
Clues	*Clues: A Journal of Detection*
Colby Q [formerly *Colby Lib Q*]	*Colby Quarterly* [formerly *Colby Library Quarterly*]
Coll Lang Assoc J	*College Language Association Journal*
Coll Lit	*College Literature*
Colloquia Germanica	*Colloquia Germanica, Internationale Zeitschrift für Germanische Sprach- und Literaturwissenschaft*
Commonwealth Essays & Studs	*Commonwealth Essays and Studies*
Comparatist	*The Comparatist: Journal of the Southern Comparative Literature Association*
Conference Coll Teachers Engl Stud	*Conference of College Teachers of English Studies* [formerly *Conference of College Teachers of English of Texas*]
Conradian	*The Conradian: Journal of the Joseph Conrad Society* [U.K.]
Conradiana	*Conradiana: A Journal of Joseph Conrad Studies*
Cristallo	*Cristallo: Rassegna di Varia Umanità*
	Crítica Hispánica
	Critical Inquiry
Critical Matrix	*Critical Matrix: Princeton Working Papers in Women's Studies*
Critical Q	*Critical Quarterly*
Criticism	*Criticism: A Quarterly for Literature and the Arts*
Critique S	*Critique: Studies in Contemporary Fiction*

Cross Currents	*Cross Currents: A Yearbook of Central European Culture*
	Cuadernos Americanos
Cuadernos Hispanoamericanos	*Cuadernos Hispanoamericanos: Revista Mensual de Cultura Hispanica*
	Cycnos
D. H. Lawrence R	*The D. H. Lawrence Review*
	Dactylus
Dalhousie R	*Dalhousie Review*
Degré Second	*Degré Second: Studies in French Literature*
Delta	*Delta: Revue du Centre d'Études et de Recherche sur les Écrivains du Sud aux États-Unis*
Diálogos Hispánicos	*Diálogos Hispánicos de Amsterdam*
Dickensian	*The Dickensian*
Diliman R	*Diliman Review*
Discurso literario	*Discurso literario: Revista de estudios iberoamericanos*
Dutch Q R	*Dutch Quarterly Review of Anglo-American Letters*
	Enclitic
Engl Lang Notes	*English Language Notes*
Engl Lit Transition	*English Literature in Transition*
Engl Stud Africa	*English Studies in Africa: A Journal of the Humanities*
Engl Stud Canada	*English Studies in Canada*
Epos	*Epos: Revista de Filología*
Escritura	*Escritura: Revista de Teoría y Crítica Literaria*
	L'Esprit Créateur
ESQ: J Am Renaissance	*Emerson Society Quarterly: Journal of the American Renaissance*
Essays Lit	*Essays in Literature* (Western Illinois)

Essays Poetics	*Essays in Poetics*
	Estudios Anglo-Americanos
	Études Germaniques
Euphorion	*Euphorion: Zeitschrift für Literaturgeschichte*
	Explicación de Textos Literarios
	Explicator
	Extrapolation
Faulkner J	*Faulkner Journal*
Feminist Stud	*Feminist Studies*
Flannery O'Connor Bull	*Flannery O'Connor Bulletin*
Focus on Robert Graves	*Focus on Robert Graves and His Contemporaries*
Forum Homo	*Forum Homosexualität und Literatur*
Forum Mod Lang Stud	*Forum for Modern Language Studies*
Foundation	*Foundation: Review of Science Fiction*
Francofonia	*Francofonia: Studi e Ricerche Sulle Letterature di Lingua Francese*
	Französisch Heute
	French Forum
French R	*French Review: Journal of the American Association of Teachers of French*
Fu Jen Stud	*Fu Jen Studies: Literature & Linguistics* (Taipei)
Germ Life & Letters	*German Life and Letters*
Germ Notes	*Germanic Notes*
Germ Q	*German Quarterly*
Germ R	*Germanic Review*
Germanisch-Romanische Monatsschrift	*Germanisch-Romanische Monatsschrift*, Neue Folge
Germanistische Mitteilungen	*Germanistische Mitteilungen: Zeitschrift für deutsche Sprache, Literatur und Kultur in Wissenschaft und Praxis*

Germano-Slavica	*Germano-Slavica: A Canadian Journal of Germanic and Slavic Comparative Studies*
Gettysburg R	*Gettysburg Review*
Gradiva	*Gradiva: International Journal of Italian Literature*
Hemingway R	*Hemingway Review* [formerly *Hemingway Notes*]
Henry James R	*Henry James Review*
Hispania	*Hispania: A Journal Devoted to the Interests of the Teaching of Spanish and Portuguese*
Hispanic J	*Hispanic Journal*
Hispanic R	*Hispanic Review*
Hispano	*Hispanófila*
	Hollins Critic
Horen	*Die Horen: Zeitschrift für Literatur, Kunst und Kritik*
Humanities Assoc R	*Humanities Association Review*
Ideologies and Literature	*Ideologies and Literature: A Journal of Hispanic and Luso-Brazilian Studies*
Int'l Fiction R	*International Fiction Review*
Inti	*Inti: Revista de literatura Hispánica*
	Iris
Italian Q	*Italian Quarterly*
	Jack London Newsletter
	Jahrbuch für Internationale Germanistik
James Joyce Q	*James Joyce Quarterly*
	Jewish Book Annual
J Am Stud	*Journal of American Studies*
J Commonwealth Lit	*The Journal of Commonwealth Literature*
J Evolutionary Psych	*Journal of Evolutionary Psychology*
J Kafka Soc Am	*Journal of the Kafka Society of America*

J Mod Lit	*Journal of Modern Literature*
J Narrative Technique	*Journal of Narrative Technique*
J Short Story Engl	*Journal of the Short Story in English*
J William Morris Soc	*Journal of the William Morris Society*
Kipling J	*The Kipling Journal*
	Kleist-Jahrbuch
	Kultur og Klasse
Kyushu Am Lit	*Kyushu American Literature*
Lamar J Hum	*Lamar Journal of the Humanities*
Landfall	*Landfall: A New Zealand Quarterly*
Latin Am Lit R	*Latin American Literary Review*
Legacy	*Legacy: A Journal of Nineteenth-Century American Women Writers*
Letras	*Letras* (Univ. Católica Argentina)
	Letras Femeninas
	Letras Peninsulares
Lingua e Stile	*Lingua e Stile: Trimestrale di Linguistica e Critica Letteraria*
Linguistics & Lit	*Linguistics and Literature* (Ben Gurion Univ.)
Lit & Med	*Literature and Medicine*
Lit & Psych	*Literature and Psychology*
Lit Apprentice	*The Literary Apprentice*
Lit Criterion	*Literary Criterion*
Lit Endeavour	*The Literary Endeavour: A Quarterly Journal Devoted to English Studies*
Lit/Film Q	*Literature/Film Quarterly*
Lit Performance	*Literature in Performance: A Journal of Literary and Performing Art*
Lit Theory Classroom	*Literary Theory in the Classroom*
Literaturwissenschaftliches Jahrbuch	*Literaturwissenschaftliches Jahrbuch im Auftrage der Görresgesellschaft*

Littérature	*Littérature* (Paris)
Lost Generation J	*Lost Generation Journal*
Lovecraft Stud	*Lovecraft Studies*
Luso-Brazilian R	*Luso-Brazilian Review*
MELUS	*The Journal of the Society for the Study of the Multi-Ethnic Literature of the United States*
Melville Soc Extracts	*Melville Society Extracts* [supersedes *Extracts: An Occasional Newsletter*]
	Mester
Michigan Q R	*Michigan Quarterly Review*
Mid-American R	*Mid-American Review*
Mid-Hudson Lang Stud	*Mid-Hudson Language Studies* (Bulletin of the Mid-Hudson Modern Language Association)
Midwest Q	*Midwest Quarterly: A Journal of Contemporary Thought*
Mississippi Q	*Mississippi Quarterly: The Journal of Southern Culture*
Mod Age	*Modern Age: A Quarterly Review*
Mod Austrian Lit	*Modern Austrian Literature: Journal of the International Arthur Schnitzler Research Association*
Mod China	*Modern China*
Mod Chinese Lit	*Modern Chinese Literature*
Mod Fiction Stud	*Modern Fiction Studies*
Mod Lang Notes	*MLN: Modern Language Notes*
Mod Lang Q	*Modern Language Quarterly*
Mod Lang R	*Modern Language Review*
Mod Lang Stud	*Modern Language Studies*
Mod Langs	*Modern Languages: Journal of the Modern Language Association* (London)
Monatshefte	*Monatshefte: Für Deutschen Unterricht, Deutsche Sprache und Literatur*

Mosaic	*Mosaic: A Journal for the Comparative Study of Literature and Ideas for the Interdisciplinary Study of Literature*
Mount Olive R	*Mount Olive Review*
Mystery Fancier	*The Mystery Fancier*
Mythlore	*Mythlore: A Journal of J. R. R. Tolkien, C. S. Lewis, Charles Williams, General Fantasy and Mythic Studies*
	Neophilologus
	Die Neueren Sprachen
New Comparison	*New Comparison: A Journal of Comparative and General Literature*
New Germ R	*New German Review: A Journal of Germanic Studies*
New Hungarian Q	*New Hungarian Quarterly*
New Lit Hist	*New Literary History*
New Orleans R	*New Orleans Review*
New Welsh R	*New Welsh Review*
	Nineteenth-Century Contexts
Nineteenth-Century French Stud	*Nineteenth-Century French Studies*
Nineteenth-Century Lit	*Nineteenth-Century Literature* [formerly *Nineteenth-Century Fiction*]
No Dakota Q	*North Dakota Quarterly*
Notes Contemp Lit	*Notes on Contemporary Literature*
Notes Mississippi Writers	*Notes on Mississippi Writers*
Notes Mod Irish Lit	*Notes on Modern Irish Literature*
Nottingham French Stud	*Nottingham French Studies*
Novel	*Novel: A Forum on Fiction*
	Nuevo Texto Crítico
Ometeca	*Ometeca: Ciancia & Literatura*
Orbis Litterarum	*Orbis Litterarum: International Review of Literary Studies*

La Palabra	*La Palabra: Revista de Literatura Chicana* (Tempe, Ariz.)
Papers Lang & Lit	*Papers on Language and Literature: A Journal for Scholars and Critics of Language and Literature*
Paragraph	*Paragraph: The Journal of the Modern Critical Theory Group*
Philippine Stud	*Philippine Studies* (Manila)
Philol Q	*Philological Quarterly*
Pilipinas	*Pilipinas: Journal of Philippine Studies*
Plural	*Plural: Revista Cultural de Excelsior*
PMLA	*PMLA: Publications of the Modern Language Association of America*
Poe Stud	*Poe Studies*
Poetica	*Poetica: Zeitschrift für Sprach- und Literaturwissenschaft*
Postscript	*Postscript: Publication of the Philological Association of the Carolinas*
Pubs Arkansas Philol Assoc	*Publications of the Arkansas Philological Association*
Quest	*Quest: New Quest* (Pune, India)
	Recherches Anglaises et Nord-Américaines
	Recherches Germaniques
Religion & Lit	*Religion and Literature*
Renascence	*Renascence: Essays on Value in Literature*
Research African Lit	*Research in African Literature*
Researcher	*Researcher: An Interdisciplinary Journal*
R	*Review: Latin American Literature and Arts*
R Contemp Fiction	*Review of Contemporary Fiction*
Revista Canadiense	*Revista Canadiense de Estudios Hispánicos*
	Revista Chilena de Literatura

Revista de Crítica	*Revista de Crítica Literaria Latinoamericana*
	Revista de Estudios Hispánicos (Poughkeepsie)
	Revista de Occidente
	Revista Iberoamericana
Revista Interamericana	*Revista Interamericana de Bibliografía/Inter-American Review of Bibliography*
	Revista Letras
La Revue des Lettres Modernes	*La Revue des Lettres Modernes: Histoire des Idées et des Littératures*
	Revue des Sciences Humaines
Río de la Plata	*Río de la Plata: Culturas*
Riverside Q	*Riverside Quarterly*
Rivista di Letterature	*Rivista di Letterature Moderne e Comparate*
Romance Lang Annual	*RLA: Romance Languages Annual*
	Romance Notes
Romance Q	*Romance Quarterly* [formerly *Kentucky Romance Quarterly*]
Romanic R	*Romanic Review*
	Romanistisches Jahrbuch
Russian, Croatian	*Russian, Croatian and Serbian, Czech and Slovak, Polish Literature*
Russian Lang J	*Russian Language Journal*
Russian R	*Russian Review: An American Quarterly Devoted to Russia Past and Present*
Saul Bellow J	*Saul Bellow Journal* [formerly *Saul Bellow Newsletter*]
Scandinavian Stud	*Scandinavian Studies*
Scandinavica	*Scandinavica: An International Journal of Scandinavian Studies*
Sci-Fiction Stud	*Science-Fiction Studies*
	Scripsi

Seminar	*Seminar: A Journal of Germanic Studies*
	Shenandoah
Slavic & East European J	*Slavic and East European Journal*
Slavic R	*Slavic Review: American Quarterly of Soviet and East European Studies*
Slavonic & East European R	*Slavonic & East European Review*
So Asian R	*South Asian Review*
So Atlantic Q	*South Atlantic Quarterly*
So Atlantic R	*South Atlantic Review*
So Central R	*South Central Review*
Southern Hum R	*Southern Humanities Review*
Southern Lit J	*Southern Literary Journal*
Southern Q	*The Southern Quarterly: A Journal of the Arts in the South*
Southwest R	*Southwest Review*
Soviet Stud	*Soviet Studies*
Soviet Stud Lit	*Soviet Studies in Literature*
Stanford French R	*Stanford French Review*
Steinbeck Q	*Steinbeck Quarterly*
Strumenti Critici	*Strumenti Critici: Rivista Quadrimestrale di Cultura e Critica Letteraria*
Stud Am Fiction	*Studies in American Fiction*
Stud Am Humor	*Studies in American Humor*
Stud Am Jewish Lit	*Studies in American Jewish Literature*
Stud Canadian Lit	*Studies in Canadian Literature*
Stud Hogg	*Studies in Hogg and His World*
Stud Hum	*Studies in the Humanities*
Stud Novel	*Studies in the Novel*
Stud Scottish Lit	*Studies in Scottish Literature*

Stud Short Fiction	*Studies in Short Fiction*
Stud Twentieth-Century Lit	*Studies in Twentieth-Century Literature*
Stud Weird Fiction	*Studies in Weird Fiction*
	Style
SubStance	*SubStance: A Review of Theory and Literary Criticism*
Symposium	*Symposium: A Quarterly Journal of Modern Literatures*
Tamkang R	*Tamkang Review*
	Temps Modernes
Tennessee Philol Bull	*Tennessee Philological Bulletin*
Texas Stud Lit & Lang	*Texas Studies in Literature and Language: A Journal of the Humanities*
	Texto Crítico
	Textual Practice
Thalia	*Thalia: Studies in Literary Humor*
	Thomas Mann Jahrbuch
Thomas Wolfe R	*The Thomas Wolfe Review*
	TriQuarterly
	Turn-of-the-Century Women
Twentieth Century Lit	*Twentieth Century Literature: A Scholarly and Critical Journal*
Universidad	*Universidad de La Habana*
Univ Dayton R	*University of Dayton Review*
Ventanal	*Ventanal: Revista de Creación y Critica*
Victorian Institute J	*Victorian Institute Journal*
Virginia Q R	*Virginia Quarterly Review: A National Journal of Literature and Discussion*
Weber Stud	*Weber Studies: An Interdisciplinary Humanities Journal*
West Virginia Univ Philol Papers	*West Virginia University Philological Papers*

Western Am Lit	*Western American Literature*
	Wiener Slawistischer Almanach
William Carlos Williams R	*William Carlos Williams Review*
Wirkendes Wort	*Wirkendes Wort: Deutsche Sprache in Forschung und Lehre*
	Wissenschaftliche Zeitschrift der Ernst Moritz Arndt-Universität Greifswald
Works & Days	*Works & Days: Essays in the Socio-Historical Dimensions of Literature and the Arts*
World Lit Today	*World Literature Today: A Literary Quarterly of the University of Oklahoma*
Yale J Criticism	*Yale Journal of Criticism*
	Zeitschrift für Deutsche Philologie

Index of Short Story Writers